A Life Awheel

The 'auto' biography of W de Forte

Wilberforce de Forte

Edited by Richard Skelton

Illustrated by Peter Entwistle

VELOCE

A selection of books from Veloce:

Hubble Hattie
www.hubbleandhattie.com

For post publication news, updates and amendments relating to this book please visit www.veloce.co.uk/books/V4844

www.veloce.co.uk

First published in April 2016 by Veloce Publishing Limited, Veloce House, Parkway Farm Business Park, Middle Farm Way, Poundbury, Dorchester DT1 3AR, England. Fax 01305 268864 / e-mail info@veloce.co.uk / web www.veloce.co.uk or www.velocebooks.com.
ISBN: 978-1-845848-44-6; UPC: 6-36847-04844-0.

A Life Awheel

The 'auto' biography of W de Forte

VELOCE PUBLISHING

THE PUBLISHER OF FINE AUTOMOTIVE BOOKS

Contents

Acknowledgements

MY THANKS ARE DUE to the owners of the magazine titles, from which I have purloined a number of examples of my past work for inclusion in this book, namely *The Auto*, *Classic Auto* and *Motorcycle Review*. Thanks are also due to the publishers of *The Chap*, where some of these have been reproduced. I am indebted to Richard Skelton for sub-editing, and also to Rod Ker for his general assistance and sage advice. I must also acknowledge Peter Entwistle for his splendid cover illustration and other drawings in the book.

W de Forte, Bales, Shropshire

Publisher's Note

In a weaving together of fact and fiction, certain disclaimers and clarifications are deemed necessary.

W de Forte is a fictional character, as are all members of his family, his best friend, Algy, and many other personages in the book. Any resemblance between the fictional characters portrayed in this publication and real individuals, living or dead, is purely coincidental. The village of Bales is also an artificial creation, as are Beedle Market, and Greenfirth in Yorkshire. Famous motor industry figures of the past are portrayed in order to come across as true to their real personalities, so far as this can be ascertained, but of course their interaction with the book's narrator is entirely fanciful. Having said that, the author has striven for technical and historical accuracy in all matters motoring and motorcycling, and also with regard to social history. Further, the wider geography of the British Isles and beyond is generally portrayed as accurately as possible.

John Betjeman excerpts from his *Collected Poems*, used with permission from John Murray Press, a division of Hodder & Stoughton.

Introduction

OH CALAMITY! QUITE WHY Aldwych stalwart Robertson Hare's catchphrase should have come to mind as I flew through the gelid air on that damp and misty March morning at Chimay in southern Belgium I know not. But it did. Seconds earlier the old Rudge and I were cracking on as well as ever. In fact we had just passed that tiresome old walloon Rik van Erik on his hotted up Flying Squirrel and I was feeling rather pleased with myself (somewhat hubristically as it turned out!), having caught a glimpse of his empurpled countenance as I tucked myself into the smallest possible compass, yanked hard on the bravery cable, and rocketed down the new start/finish straight towards Virage Frère. Then it all went badly wrong.

The roaring Rudge Ulster is a full-blooded speed iron, and, when operating near its limits, a pilot's full concentration is required. But with my chin bouncing on the petrol tank as we rapidly developed flying speed, I am ashamed to admit I was rather enjoying the warm huff of oil-scented breath from the engine, and I had allowed myself to drift away from the present moment and bask in the crazed and deluded fantasy that at the impossibly ancient age of 90, I might soon be revelling in the achievement of having set the fastest lap of the session. How ineffably foolish.

It was a sombre, battleship-grey morning and the air was moist and chill. Mist carpeted the fields but not the roads, and the grass alongside the track was wet with morning dew and thick as a sponge. The cold rain which had been off since scrutineering was now back on again, and no doubt contributed to the events that were about to unfold.

When I spotted two brown hares by the track up ahead I took no more than a bemused and detached interest, but when the speedy herbivores stretched their long legs and took to the tarmacadam right in front of Jean-Paul Hisson's misfiring Manx Norton just as he reached the Virage Frère right-hander at the end of the straight, I belatedly snapped out of my vainglorious reverie.

Realising too late and with utter horror that the snail-like Froggie was cutting across my path to avoid the hares, and that furthermore, due to my daydreaming I had completely missed my braking marker for the fast approaching right-angled corner, all I could do was sit up and stamp hard on the brake pedal to engender a full-blooded broadside.

I would estimate I was travelling at over 100mph. My front wheel narrowly missed his rear, but my back wheel slithered onto the wet grass, spinning the bus right round, before rejoining the hard stuff, whereupon its racing Avon hoop gripped firmly and fiercely, sitting the Rudge momentarily and very violently upright. This is what pitched me into spectacular and high orbit.

After taking in a rather interesting aerial view of proceedings, which included open-mouthed marshals (crammed with a soft cheese baguette in one case, I recall), a blissfully unaware Frenchman departing on a sick Norton and two terrified skedaddling hares, I was unceremoniously slammed down hard onto the very hard stuff.

And then, as I slid towards the straw bales on my ear, and then on my aged and bony posterior, and then on my other ear, the Rudge cartwheeled past alongside me, and as it did I recorded the damage in real time. Tank. Ouch! That'll be expensive. Bugger, there goes an exhaust pipe. Cripes, that's the other one as well. Strange how the mind works.

A Scott shrieked past like a shell (drat!), and then a mighty Egli Vincent smashed by just inches from my noggin (yikes!). I wasn't in pain at that point, nor was I when everything came to a gentle stop a few seconds later. That was when everything fell to near silence, or so it appeared, the audio seemingly sucked out of the world, leaving me in a peculiar vacuum.

I was aware of marshals running and waving flags, and a kindly gallic man with crumbs in his beard was speaking to me, but I could not hear or comprehend what he was saying. Next to me the Rudge was looking very sorry for itself, lying on its side in a steadily enlarging pool of oil. I sensed the soft hiss of tyres close by on the wetted surface as more machines passed, then I detected rain spotting on the upturned side of my helmet. Senses returning. All was going to be well, I thought. But then I tried to stand up. I couldn't. A stab of excruciating pain. A rivulet of water ran down the cracked lens of my goggles. Trails of vapour streamed away to the trees. The sky darkened.

I awoke in near blackness feeling tired, achey and somewhat trussed up. From the few twinkly lights by my bed which flashed to the accompaniment of beeps reminiscent of checkout barcode readers (globalisation, eh?), I soon became aware I was in a hospital bed. And from the gentle squeaky footfalls and occasional soft murmur of voices nearby, it was clear I was in some sort of room 'off'. Hah! Not dead yet then. I tried to sit up. Not a good idea. Oh Calamity!

It was indeed all rather farcical. High-sided from a racing motorcycle, an exceedingly rich American collector's very rare and expensive racing motorcycle at that, is not the best thing to do at any time of life, let alone at my advanced state of decrepitude. What had I been thinking?

I was in Belgium to test classic racing bikes for *Moto Classique*. It had all begun several weeks before when the telephone bell rang in my study in Bales, just as I was putting the finishing touches to a classic road test of a Lotus Cortina, of which more anon. 'De Forte old boy,' said a familiar voice, 'this is Leslie speaking. Will you take Waverley's Ulster for a canter at Chimay next month? We'd prefer Cathcart to ride it but he's already signed up.'

'Do you know how old I am?' I replied. ''Good grief yes, we know you're positively ancient, and you've absolutely no chance of winning on the thing,' he said, somewhat unnecessarily I thought, 'but Waverley paid for the entry and the transportation weeks ago, and since then I've asked absolutely everybody we can think of but everyone's already booked. Even Otto von Schoffl has got a ride.' Hmm, von Schoffl eh? I thought uncharitably, well at least I won't be last.

'I'll do it,' I heard myself say. 'Excellent!' said Leslie. 'We'll fix up a licence and cover all your expenses. Just pobble round at the back, get some good foties and knock out a few eulogistic pars on the Rudge for *Classic Cycle*. Waverley wants to raise its profile in the States before flogging it to some pal of his next year.' And with that Les Flewelling, American billionaire Waverley Scrunge Jr's English Mr Fixit, laughed and ended the call.

After some swift telephoning I replaced the receiver once more tingling with well being, having fixed up not only to file copy on the Rudge for *Classic Cycle* in New York, but to write extensive features on it for *Classic Motorcycling* and *Moto Classique*, and to give one or two other choice classic thoroughbreds a gallop up the road for yet further financial reward. A trip to the continent with all expenses paid by the odious Mr Scrunge, and lots more work on the back of it. A most providential arrangement indeed.

But as I lay in a Belgian hospital bed, the victim of my own stupidity, vanity, greed, and quite unconscionable ego, I got to thinking. I've always said freelancers don't know they've retired until a year after it happens. Well, in my case the phone was still ringing occasionally, but enough, I now decided, was enough.

A fortnight later, back in Blighty, propped up in my own bed looking out over Bales and the barley fields beyond on a sunny Shropshire afternoon, I took a deep and painful breath and got Veloce Publishing boss Rod Grainger on the blower. Do you still want my life story old chap? If so, send me a contract. Now is the time. The next morning Martha brought the post up with the toast and Frank Cooper's, and it became abundantly clear Mr Grainger is nothing if not a man of action. There among the bills was lucrative contract from Veloce accompanied by a most encouraging note. 'Deliver on time de Forte, and don't overwrite!' This book, dear readers, not too many years later, is the result of my decidedly crummy efforts to comply with that command.

Chapter One

Toad went up to town by an early train this morning. And he has ordered a large and very expensive motor-car.

The Wind in the Willows – Kenneth Grahame

HAPPY DAYS

IT PLEASES ME THAT being born after War One qualifies me as vintage, not veteran. I was born into a motoring family in 1920, and my earliest automotive memory is of standing on a beechwood armchair in the drawing room watching the gigantic dancing shadows cast by the huge headlamps of my father's Rolls-Royce motor car, as he arrived home for dinner on a wild and windy winter's night.

With Mater holding back the curtain swags, I watch on tip-toe as he picks his way carefully up the potholed track to the house. Then he leaves the mighty Royce Six ticking over while he swings open and chocks the huge doors of the top barn. This he achieves with some difficulty, as he is obliged to hold his Homburg fast upon his head against the squally wind. Then he lets the reverse in, and the long and magnificent machine glides slowly backwards into the barn. There is a heavy metallic crashing sound. Evidently Bert had left the wheelbarrow out again.

Even now I can see the splendid lines of the forest-green four-light saloon body by Gurney Nutting of Chelsea, set off by gold pinstripes and its chromium-plated fittings. I recall a glimpse of the engine-turned pattern on the instrument board with dials backlit in mauve – surely the very pinnacle of sophistication – and I picture the swinging trees held in the lancing headlight beams, illuminated as if by powerful industrial arc lights, and their dancing shadows on the back lawn as Pater and his Phantom make their silent approach.

Other early recollections are of Aunt Araminta's summer visits in her 'Silent Knight' Daimler landaulette, a vehicle of Edwardian design, but very much a 19th century coach. We choked in its deadly smoke waving her goodbye, and it took half an hour to regain visibility on the road out of Bales after her departing chauffeur had churned up the white dust that rose in suffocating clouds. On one occasion the old dowager was pursued by a hooting crowd of urchins, one of whom threw a large stone which knocked her hat box clean off the trunk.

My pater, Basil, was rare among Royce owners in being an owner-driver, and there were very few motor vehicles of any description in our Shropshire village back in the roaring 20s. He eschewed motor servants, and to a degree he even carried out his own maintenance. My paternal grandfather, Cecil, also drove. A pioneering enthusiast, he carried the distinction of having owned the first car in the county, an 1896 Coventry Daimler (a devilishly dangerous device that could barely achieve 20mph!), and went on to compete in the Gordon Bennett Cup. Even my dear mother, Constantia, got in on the act. Mama would regularly be seen behind the wheel of her beloved baby Austin, batting off to Beedle Market and beyond on an almost daily basis.

The only other 'enthusiast' motorists in Bales in the 1920s were my best pal Algernon Tomlinson's parents, Hugo and Marjorie. Algy's father was an American who did something up in the city until it all went terribly wrong for them in the crash of 1929. In the subsequent depression years they were obliged to scrape by, but until then the Tomlinsons lived a life of luxury at Hornbeam Hall, a 35 room mansion on the edge of the village.

I cherish vivid memories of Christmas parties at the Tomlinsons' as a small child. After walking up through the substantial grounds and arriving at the medieval-style oak front door, we would admire the several motor cars gathered there, and Pater and Grandpapa would chat amiably to the chauffeurs for as long as Mama would allow. Then I would be lifted up to operate the push-pull doorknob, and, upon entry, we would be ushered into a large hall where numerous tusked and antlered things glowered down on proceedings. At floor level a florid pianist played Christmas carols and a cellist scraped and groaned away miserably in accompaniment, while around 50 beautiful people yakkity-yakked and sipped New York cocktails, filling the tall space as they did so with a bee-like hum of happiness.

Christmas tree candles were lit for an hour, and as they burned perilously, footmen attended with sponges. In later years the party took place in a veritable crystal palace of a conservatory, where an even larger tree would be erected and wired for electric light. We children were always handed particularly handsome presents, and on one occasion I recall us staying later than usual and seeing the staff standing in line at the end of the night being given their seasonal gifts. Happy days, but alas it would all come to an abrupt end as the '20s turned into the '30s.

Hah! You will have noted that I am prone to digression. I apologise, but while this is primarily a book of nostalgic reminiscences about motor cars and, of course, motorcycles, as it covers such an extensive period it is also bound, I feel, to some extent at least, to be something of a work of social history, albeit as seen through the particular prism of a motoring life.

And to digress once more, is that not a perfectly valid viewpoint from which to observe trends and developments in our society? After all, the motor car has radically changed the world at least as much as art and literature, and at various times particular cars have represented different things to owners from different social classes. To provide some obvious post-war examples, the Rover was once the choice of the doctor, headmaster, or gentleman farmer, while the Jag was popular with the self-made man, and the Morris Minor was transport for everyman.

Hugo Tomlinson drove American cars and the first I can recall was a bright red 1925 Chrysler 70 which joined his chauffeur's 40-50hp in the Hall's motor house (a mock Tudor building screened by trees in the grounds which boasted a chauffeur's dressing room, and a lathe and other equipment in an adjoining workshop). Walter P Chrysler was a senior manager at General Motors who left to set up on his own, employing Willys-Overland engineers Carl Breer, Owen Skelton and Fred Zeder to design his first car. The result was the B-70, an advanced machine with a smooth six cylinder engine and hydraulic brakes on all its wheels. It was fast too, and not least through good results at Le Mans, it gained something of a reputation in Britain as a poor man's Bentley. Pater drove the red tourer and declared himself impressed.

After moving up to an able, but ultimately forgettable, Lincoln L-Series for a couple of years (Lincolns were luxury Fords from 1922 onwards), the Tomlinsons decided to splash out, and in September 1929 they ordered and reportedly paid up front for a new Cadillac 452 (why buy rather than sell, sell, sell? Clearly they knew not what was coming).

When the gargantuan and gorgeous gloss-black Fisher-bodied machine was delivered in February 1930, complete with American whitewall tyres, it was the only one in the country, but by that time the hapless couple had been ruined on Wall Street. To keep it out of the hands of the repo men (large and frightening characters with crowbars had begun skulking by the padlocked Hall gates), the beast was secreted in the bottom barn here on the farm, and eventually an arrangement was made whereby Mater bought it from the Tomlinsons for a fair price, and Mrs T took over the ageing de Forte Austin Seven.

An overhead valve V16, it in fact cost as much as 20 new Austin Sevens, made 165bhp, and sucked a gallon of Pratt's every ten miles through its twin carburettors. It featured servo brakes and a three speed synchro box (like most Americans, Mr T did not care for changing gear and, had he kept the car, no doubt it would have travelled everywhere in top!), and its appointments included a radio aerial (extraordinary!), a goddess mascot and an ersatz family crest emblazoned upon the carriage door.

It was a quality motor car and Mater loved it. For the most part she drove quite decorously, but despite its great size and weight (148″ wheelbase, 5,850lb), it would whistle up to 90mph on Conrod Straight (much to Pater's chagrin one day, as Algy and I waved to him from its rear-facing opera seats while he strained to keep up in his Phantom!), and the roadster version with a high ratio gearbox would reportedly top the ton.

We kept the Cadillac until shortly before the war, whereupon it was sold via a middleman to a notorious Liverpool gangster who reputedly modelled himself on George Raft. It then disappeared, presumed lost, until five years ago when I came across it in the auction results in *Hemmings Motor News*. Despite having being assigned a totally erroneous and fanciful early history, and acquiring a garish banana-yellow paint job, it had been bought by a Chinese collector for a cool $1 million.

GORDON BENNETT!
(First published *Classic Auto* – September 2006)

My paternal grandfather was a true motoring pioneer. His first car was an 1896 Coventry Daimler, essentially a copy of the French Panhard-Levassor, and quite probably the first motor car in the county. He took delivery in time to take part in the London to Brighton emancipation run of that year, celebrating the raising of the national speed limit to a giddy 14mph.

Grandpapa would come to own several more British Daimlers in his lifetime, but when, at the beginning of the new century, he decided to replace his tiller-steered Victorian dog cart for something a little more modern, the firm was in a deep financial crisis brought about by the absurd over-ambition of its megalomaniac founder, Harry J Lawson.

Daimler would regroup under new stewardship and come back to supply cars to royalty and dominate the dowager trade, but in 1901 their cars were behind the times and Grandpapa purchased a magnificent 70hp Mors (which both he and Pater raced in France with some success) and, in late 1903, a rather special Mercedes joined it in the de Forte motor house.

The Mercedes marque came into existence in 1900 after the brusque Jewish entrepreneur Emil Jellinek commissioned Daimler Motoren Gesellschaft of Germany to build a series of sports cars named after his young daughter. He told chief designer Wilhelm Maybach: 'I don't want a car for today or tomorrow, I need a car for the day after tomorrow.'

The new cars were quite outstanding goers. They set records, won races and transformed DMG's fortunes. Jellinek set up Mercedes agencies all over Europe and appended his own name, becoming Jellinek-Mercedes. And the Stuttgart firm eventually adopted the name as its sole automotive trademark.

Exceptionally well made, the Jellinek-funded Mercedes were ahead of the competition in many respects. Their low, pressed steel chassis aided road-holding, and they were safer at speed than the teetering top-heavy cars prevalent at the time. They also boasted a gated gear change, efficient cooling, dependable electrics and superb brakes. Furthermore, a then new-fangled carburettor and throttle arrangement made fine control of engine speed possible over a wide range. All this made them strong, reliable, and relatively simple to drive at breakneck speeds.

A policy of continued improvements and race successes all over Europe persuaded Grandpapa to buy one of these Teutonic marvels for his boy, and in June 1903 the pair travelled to Stuttgart to collect their spanking new machine. But they had driven it less than 400 miles when an urgent telegram reached the de Fortes at their Paris hotel. Dearest Cecil and Bazil (sic). Factory destroyed in huge fire. Please turn back. Car needed for Gordon Bennett. Substantial reward. Wilhelm, DMG. A remarkable document I still keep in my desk drawer in Bales.

Following an embarrassing end to his engagement to a New York socialite, stupendously wealthy American newspaper publisher James Gordon Bennett Junior lived mainly in Europe, running the New York Herald group of newspapers by telegraph from Paris or from his ocean-going yacht, Lysistrata. A talented journalist, he was also a hedonistic playboy who spent much of his family fortune on the lavish patronage of ballooning and air and road racing.

Famously excessive, outrageous, boorish and newsworthy, his name became an eponymous expletive associated with scandalous behaviour and is still in use today. Bennett sent Stanley to find Livingstone (he wasn't even lost!), fought an illegal duel, drove a four horse carriage naked through New York for a bet, drove a car so fast round a corner, Jennie Jerome, Winston Churchill's mother, fell out, and kept a cow on his yacht to ensure a supply of fresh cream.

The embarrassing incident? Arriving late at a New Year party being held at his fiancee's family home, Bennett was so drunk he urinated in the fireplace in front of his bride-to-be, future in-laws and assembled New York high society. He was subsequently flogged by the young lady's brother.

Before my future father and his paternal parent had time to digest the news from Stuttgart, a message arrived requesting they meet Bennett himself at his favourite restaurant. After dispersing surrounding diners by whipping the loaded tablecloths from their tables and showering them with money by way of compensation, the moustachioed American settled down with my antecedents for a private chinwag.

Race cars being prepared for the German entry in the following month's Gordon Bennett Cup car race in Ireland had been destroyed in the blaze, explained the outrageous tycoon, and Maybach needed three 60hp road cars to convert to 90hp race specification. New York millionaire Clarence Gray Dinsmore had already pledged his car to the cause and other enthusiast owners had been contacted. Could the de Fortes do their bit for Britain?

Heroic drinking ensued, during which arrangements were somehow made for the car to be collected by Jellinek's Paris dealership and returned to its city of origin for modification to 90hp specification. Presuming it survived the race, the Mercedes would then be restored to de Forte colours (having been painted German racing white before transportation to Ireland) and delivered to the farm in full Gordon Bennett race trim.

Held in France in 1900, the first Gordon Bennett Cup race was chaotic. Drivers got lost, sheep got on the road and inaugural winner Fernand Charron had to stop to extricate an unfortunate St Bernard dog from under his Panhard. Slippery car salesman, Selwyn Edge won the 1902 race in his Napier (almost everyone else having broken down), scoring Britain's first international motor racing success in the process.

As a result, the next event had to be held on British soil, but horseless carriages were deeply unpopular in England at the time, and motor racing was totally banned. Parliament would not be persuaded to close the roads for competition so a highly effective campaign was mounted to hold the races in Ireland. After months of intensive lobbying, the Light Locomotives (Ireland) Bill was passed in March 1903.

Thousands of race-starved English motorists travelled to the Emerald Isle for the event in July. Grandpapa made the trip in Pater's canary-yellow Rochet Voiturette, taking the night boat to Dublin and driving to County Kildare in the early hours of race day morning. Proffering his VIP badge at the Ballyshannon Crossroads start-point at 6am, he was informed he had arrived only just in time. Indeed, all the side roads were in the process of being roped off and blocked by farmers' carts and wagons, buglers were taking up position at strategic points and hordes of spectators were already lining the course.

The Mercedes team was headed by florid Belgian eccentric, Camille Jenatzy. Nicknamed 'Le Diable Rouge' because of his red beard and volcanic temperament, the 35-year-old daredevil was a speed record specialist, famous for his wild and dramatic driving style. Similarly bohemian and boasting an even bigger beard, was cognac quaffing Frenchman Chevalier Rene de Knyff. The French aristocrat defied national stereotyping, enjoying an international reputation for impeccable sportsmanship and fair play.

Britain entered a pair of racing cyclists turned motor dealers, the risk-taking Charles Jarrott and the cooler, steadier, Selwyn Edge. Both drove Napiers. Other competitors included French entries Fernand Gabriel in his Paris-Madrid winning Mors (a race stopped at Bordeaux due to the multiple deaths of both drivers and spectators) and future aeroplane designer Henry Farman in a Panhard. The Mercedes team was completed by American playboy Foxhall Parker-Keene and blue-blooded Belgian, Baron Pierre de Caters.

After meeting these extraordinary characters and their courageous riding mechanics, and taking the opportunity to make a close study of their wonderful racing machines, Grandpapa was deep in discussion with a car-mad priest from Skellig, when he was greeted heartily by representatives of the GMB factory and the pair were ushered to the refreshment tent for an early morning livener.

Sadly, my grandfather's memory of the rest of the day was always somewhat disjointed, although I will forever cherish the vivid if fragmented and abstract images of derring do he conveyed to me in his later years. Whether in expansive mood, flourishing a Remy Martin Louis XIII while sitting on a dusty old relic in the motor house after a dinner party, or reminiscing wistfully, rheumy-eyed and Rowley Birkin-like, over a few bottles of the black stuff at the fireside in the Rose & Crown in Bales, he could always bring the day to life in spectacular fashion.

But while the act of driving a fire-breathing Edwardian racing car at speeds over 70mph on the rutted tracks which served as roads in those far off days (actually barely more treacherous than today's potholed English byways!) was an heroic and terrifying feat in itself, it must be said the unfolding story of the 1903 race is actually fairly unremarkable, and a chronological account of what was, in effect, a 327 mile time trial, would serve only to bore the reader and can have no place on these pages.

The record books show the race was won by the excitable Belgian Camille Jenatzy who made his rivals eat dust in the most successful race of his career. Was he driving the de Forte car? There is no way of knowing. Grandpapa certainly did not seek to disprove the claim by Clarence Gray Dinsmore that it was his 90hp that won the race. Neither of the other Mercedes completed the course.

Napier driver Charles Jarrott, who survived being thrown from his machine in a monumental end-over-end crash, later wrote of Jenatzy: 'Some of his skids on the corners were hair-raising, and he missed several stone walls only by a fraction, judging by his wheel marks. I did not think it possible that he could continue to take such risks and survive. But his brilliance was not to be denied and he came through in magnificent style.'

I cannot resist adding this postscript. While the 1903 runner-up Rene de Knyff would live to be 90, dying in 1954, Jenatzy would not see the start of the Kaiser's War. On a shooting holiday with wealthy friends, the silly bugger hid behind some bushes and made grunting noises pretending to be a wild boar. Unfortunately he fooled one of his chums so completely the chap discharged his shotgun into the undergrowth. Despite having half his side blown away by the blast, the mad Belgian did not die straight away, and ironically, in bleeding to death while being rushed to hospital, he fulfilled his own prophecy that he would meet his death in a Mercedes.

EARLY DAYS

Motor cars were still a rare sight in Bales in the early 1920s. The days of steam and gaslight were not yet done, and in rural Shropshire the hippo-mobile was still central to everyday life. The horse lobby, which had so vigorously resisted the automobile's advance, still had its highly vocal adherents on our patch, and while Hugo Tomlinson's habit of driving his own motors was considered an amusing eccentricity, our rich American resident being generally relied upon to provide gossip and local colour, the de Fortes, on the other hand, were looked at askance by most of the local population. We were regarded as a family of dangerous lunatics which scandalised the neighbourhood. Even in the third decade of the twentieth century a motor bicycle or car provoked lively feelings of fear and hatred, as well as respect and awe. Stones and insults were still thrown at motorists in the 1920s.

The 1896 Emancipation Act, which famously dispensed with the obligation for a man to walk in front of all mechanically propelled road vehicles carrying a red flag, and simultaneously tripled the British speed limit from 4mph to a heady 12mph, had come as a surprise in rural England. There were more than three million horses in Britain at the end of the nineteenth century, and their use was deeply set in British culture. Britain was a horse-riding nation and its narrow, dusty roads were the trading and fighting routes of its ancestors. The country's magistrates and MPs were horsemen and traditionalists. Motor vehicles were not popular in the corridors of power and this put the pace of British motorisation in the slow lane. But there were signs the tide would eventually turn. *Truth* magazine in 1899 made the point: any scoundrel is at liberty to drive, without any test whatsoever, a strange animal with its own will and no brakes. The horse! Remarkably, that is still the case in the 21st century.

The first motor vehicles were merely amusing technical toys for wealthy amateurs. According to Pater's dear friend and fellow pioneer motorcyclist Basil Davies (that incomparable preacher, Ixion), the new-fangled cars and motor bicycles were monstrosities that offended both the establishment and hoi polloi. They demanded the same road rights as the horse and the pedestrian. They smelt. They were incredibly noisy. They dripped oil. They stirred up the dust. Even pedal cyclists were 'cads on castors' who were stalked, trapped and fined for speeding.

In late Victorian England railways had been King, although there were none within 15 miles of Bales (and thanks to Doctor Beeching that is again the case), and the adaptation of steam power for use on the roads was much constrained by the Locomotives on Highways Act 1865. Not that they were eminently suitable anyway.

Chas O'Rourke's father's Yorkshire Steam Wagon could only manage 0-20 in 37 minutes from a standing start (35 of them to get its steam up!). Furthermore, obtaining, taking on and carrying sufficient water was a constant problem, and, although I was always grateful to the burly O'Rourkes for an occasional impromptu lift home for school, I was never entirely comfortable sitting atop an ebullient boiler working at 200psi. I feigned excitement as 'Yorkie' trembled and juddered away, and as we rumbled along venting violent jets of scalding steam upon passers-by, and vomiting fire and black smoke to an accompaniment of weird groans, ominous gurgles and sepulchral clankings, but all the while I was secretly terrified it was about to burst like an inferior pistol, sending us all to kingdom come.

At the time of my birth some nearby roads were merely rough dirt tracks – rutted and dusty in the summer months, treacherously muddy in winter. Engines ingested abrasive grit and wore themselves out while showering it over passers-by. The century's second decade had seen the tarring of many roads, but poor and ignorant workmanship, manifested not least in an almost total lack of proper preparation, led rapidly to corrugation, crumbling, and the appearance of perilous and quite frightful potholes.

Heated tar had been used as a binder in British road construction instead of soil and water since we stole the idea from the Froggies in 1905, and in 1909 future wartime Prime Minister David Lloyd George hit upon the ruse of creating a 'Road Fund'. Money was raised from duty on petrol and a new horsepower tax, and a new Roads Board took control of the country's 2,000 separate road authorities and began issuing grants for road repairs. The Fund supposedly existed exclusively to 'safeguard and improve the national roadways', but dear old Ixion got it absolutely right when he said it would be 'callously milked by a succession of chancellors'.

Getting back to motor cars powered by internal combustion engines, it has been said, and I do not disagree, that the years 1885 to 1900 were spent getting the infernal things to work at all, the period from 1900 to 1910 was devoted to making them tolerably reliable, and the pre-war era from 1910 to 1914 saw the addition of some degree of refinement. After that, of course, the necessities of War One brought about more rapid progress in all respects.

Yet post-war automobiles remained tall, heavy, short of wheelbase and high of centre of gravity, and in overall terms hugely inefficient. The 'Systeme Panhard' was beginning to dominate (engine in front, gearbox amidships transmitting drive to the rear), which was a jolly good thing as cars with other layouts were usually little more than motorised buggies or dog carts, but overall the move away from the horse model was far from complete. Solid tyres remained common, you had to light their acetylene headlamps with a match, and they still belched, spluttered and shook.

They were also still difficult to start, hard to control, and a bind to maintain. The last of these was a particularly major deterrent. Pater deplored the idea of motor servants, but most could not afford them in any event, and hammer-wielding blacksmiths far and wide began adapting their rudimentary skills and setting themselves up as motor mechanics. The scrofulous Harry Haynes in Bales was one such. Really no more than an ambitious cycle repairer, he learned his trade on his customers' cars, but then the same was happening in every village blacksmith's shop for 50 miles around.

When I first arrived on the scene the country had just undergone a bout of high inflation. Motor cars were expensive and there were very few non-de Forte motor vehicles in the district. War One hero and local MP Colonel Fortescue Green had retained his 16hp Sunbeam staff car in which he was driven around by his wartime batman Eddie Potter. But because this personage of distinction spent so much time in smoke-filled rooms down in the smoke, the impressive Wolverhampton-built tourer was more often to be seen languishing outside the Rose & Crown in Bales than at action stations outside Beedle Manor.

There were other motoring toffs. The boorish and imperturbably terrifying Sir Guy Blood kept a beetroot-coloured Vauxhall to match his puffy aspect, while the aptly named Sir Thomas Sly had the good taste to buy Rovers. Among the lower orders the enterprising Kays in the village had a hard-working Model T.

Other than that I can only recall a Garrett traction engine or two, a decrepit Maudslay lorry, and the coal merchant's three ton Albion which had served behind the lines in Flanders. The Albion had solid wheels and periodically it would be brought to Haynes' to be 're-tyred'. Its driver, I recall with a shudder, was a tall, toothsome individual known to all as Spindleshanks, an unpleasant character who possessed a moronic level of intelligence, smoked vigorously and rapped out the most horrible oaths at any watching children lest we attempt to steal any of his load while he waited impatiently for Harry to finish his bi-annual task.

In order to complete his deliveries in the shortest possible time, wherever and whenever the topography allowed, this ineffably foolish fellow would endeavour to achieve great speed by freewheeling downhill with the Albion's clutch pedal hard on the floor. Carrying such massive weight, at such great velocity, in so primitive a vehicle with metal tyres, with no brakes at all on its front wheels and binders at the rear of only lilliputian efficiency, was clearly a dashed dangerous practice if not a downright suicidal one.

Leaving Beedle early one Autumn morning the inevitable happened. Fully laden, gunning it, flying down Magpie Dip, standing up and shouting Charge! he found the road unexpectedly occupied by a Burrell showman's locomotive from Shrewsbury called Lucky Lady. In attempting to steer around this formidable and colourful obstacle, he lost control on wet leaves engendering a diabolical skid. The poor Albion then smashed sideways into the ten foot wall of the sewage works, laying it flat along half its length while a sweeping cannonade of coal sprayed skywards, bombarding all around and landing in gardens and on roofs up to half a mile away.

The truck, which had been compressed instanter into a mangled mess of scrap iron, perished vermilionly in the rubble. 'Sure as the Sunrise' had been the phrase proudly embossed on its radiator, but alas the noble war veteran would see no more of these. It was utterly destroyed. As for the wretched Spindleshanks, his beanpole body was never found. The last anyone saw of him were the soles of his feet flying over the collapsing corporation wall to the sludge vats beyond.

Although only ten years old the Albion was already a rare relic. With the 1920s came the widespread adoption of the pneumatic tyre and shaft drive (no more boiling chains!), the adoption of the monobloc, and of mechanically activated inlet valves enabling engine speed control over a wider rev band; and a degree of reliability was brought to electric ignition and gear selection.

But in my infancy I was not yet aware of most of this, and frankly I'm glad it passed me by. By the time I started taking an active interest in driving motor cars, motoring as a whole had become altogether more civilised and agreeable, and no less exciting because of it.

HALCYON DAYS

Bales was a quite marvellous place to begin my days, and without wishing to be maudlin, it will be a quite satisfactory place to end them.

I have lived in Bales all my life, and much has remained constant or in continuity. As I write this one early August morning, the milk is being delivered to the doorstep (when I was a boy the milk was delivered by the same family firm, but by pony cart, and ladled into measuring jugs), and the Rose & Crown's landlord has just stumbled by on tip-toes, inclined forwards at a 45 degree angle, with arms outstretched before him, as he is towed around the village by his over eager saffron and white hound. The victualler in question, one Vernon Mallard, is the third generation from a family of long-lived licensees to keep our village pub.

Bales is a perpetual still point in the gyre of history, and in my childhood in the 1920s it was a kind of rural idyll. I recall perfect scorching summers, the bleached out fields rowing away to distant horizons, while at night, as the village nestled in its privileged position in the gentle rolls of the Shropshire countryside, I would lie awake in my bedroom, curtains open and billowing gently, tracking the argent moon's slow progress across a heavenful of glittering stars. And if Bales was a kind of heaven on earth, part of the reason for that was motorcycling.

Motorcycling was my first love, and I fell under its charm while still in infancy. The spice of danger is attractive to the young and the motorbike is a machine full of lethal possibilities, and while I may have missed the worst hardships and horrors of pioneer motoring, I discovered retrospectively, and at first hand, the perils and pitfalls of riding and owning early motorcycles.

I was indoctrinated from a young age. Pater was a pioneer motor-bicyclist and he had competed in motor trials and a few sprints, although with limited success in the latter, and before the Kaiser War, my beloved Uncle Bof had raced at the TT. He would bounce me on his knee, and tell me stories about dicing with a young Edgar Jessop – that legendary TT rider – before he made his name, and of coming a purler at Creg Willys, but sadly, the poor old duffer was too shot up by the Boche to pick up where he left off when racing got under way again in 1920.

It was soon after that date when Pater first persuaded the Tomlinsons to allow the Beedle Wheelers to hold some sprint meetings at Hornbeam Hall. He also had the ear of Colonel Fortescue Green MP, and circuit races once took place on the rides and link roads in the grounds of Beedle Manor. The massed starts were electrifying, the frenzied rush of the early laps quite breathtaking, and the bumping and boring was nobody's business. The Italian ace Achille Varzi was there on a Sunbeam. Handsome, stylish, and immaculately attired, the ladies swooned and the gentlemen kept a stiff upper lip. There is a photo of him here on the sideboard in the dining room. Looking impossibly dapper, he wears the victor's garlands, a cigarette dangles from his lips, and he has an arm around my mother.

But I am getting ahead of myself. My first ever race meeting was a sprint at Hornbeam Hall. In the 1920s motorcycle sprints were frightening affairs – 100mph dashes up private drives – and at Hornbeam Hall the course ran up the main approach to the house between spectacular sweeps of rhododendron bushes, and through groves of slender ash trees.

I sniffed the heady scent of dope and Castrol R, and marvelled at magnificent Broughs, raucous Scotts, 'specials' drilled like sieves with tiny sprint fuel tanks and no oil tanks at all, and a glorious sounding vee-type Harley from Milwaukee. But the day would be dominated by black and gold Sunbeams ridden by a team of stars headed by the young yet avuncular Graham Walker. Already a war veteran and a TT-winner, 'Uncle' Graham would in the future become editor of the Green 'Un (*The Motor Cycle*, published by Iliffe) and a well-known radio and television commentator. He was there with his young son, an amiable and inquisitive toddler who was the subject of much tiresome cooing from the women present. Of course this feted child was none other than Murray Walker, who went on to become even more famous than his father.

Sunbeams really were the most beautifully-made machines in the history of motorcycles, at least until the firm was bought up by Associated Motorcycles (AMC) in 1937. The concern also made bicycles, and the Golden Sunbeam of 1913 is arguably the most splendid factory-produced push-cycle ever built.

The parent company, John Marston Ltd, was originally a japanning concern in Bilston, but two-wheeler output was from a tall brick-built Wolverhampton manufactory called Sunbeamland (a proud building which still stands). Production remained there when Sunbeam became part of the ICI group in the 1920s, but was moved to London after the AMC sale. The cockernee Collier brothers (of Matchless fame, and the owners of AMC) took pains to look after the Sunbeam pedigree and reputation, but this was less the case when the marque later returned to the Midlands, having been flogged to Birmingham giant BSA in 1943. Consequently, the lumbering, BMW-inspired post-War Two Sunbeams designed by Erling Poppe, son of Rover engineer Peter, are an altogether different kettle of fish.

Inter-war Sunbeams had an inherent and virtuous goodness about them. Even as a small boy that day at Hornbeam Hall I could well appreciate their beautifully enamelled frames and petrol tanks (the latter hand-lined in gold), the quality black japanning of the oil tanks, the understated beauty of their unpolished aluminium matt casings, and the high-calibre nickel plate that featured everywhere. And as well as being superbly finished with no expense spared, they were superbly engineered with careful attention to detail in their design, and meticulously put together.

The Sunbeam team consisted of big Graham Walker, the slightly puffed up Tommy de la Hay, quiet man George Dance, and chief engineer John Greenwood, a wiry, bespectacled and pugnacious northerner. Fast Tees-sider Freddie Dixon was there on a Douglas, and Londoner Bert le Vack came up from the capital with a big booming JAP. Fine development engineers both, those two. There were also one or two top continentals, but to the great disappointment of the ladies present, the name Varzi was not on the card.

While Pater chatted to John Greenwood, an acquaintance of many years, I noticed a non-trade man, Shrewsbury rider Robbie Blackledge, arrive late on his Norton 18, and I proceeded to watch, fascinated, although only dimly comprehending, as in short order he removed the headlamp, changed the final drive sprocket, adjusted chain length to suit, took off the silencer, fitted an extension exhaust pipe, put special dope internals in the carb, changed the sparking plug, and donned his racing bib ready to go.

Most of the bikes taking part featured the extreme hillclimb handlebars of the day, drooping and long with grips almost level with the front wheel spindle;

and one or two modern models on show even boasted the then new-fangled saddle tank. But no part of a sprinter exists for appearance or affectation. Sprint machines are full blooded speed irons, spare, lean and displaying utter honesty of purpose. And there is nothing quite like an iron engine running on dope! As the machinery was warmed up in the paddock that morning, I was transfixed by cherry-red exhaust pipes; pushrods like stair rods; and lashing, exposed rocker gear with glinting, blurred rocker arms punching away tirelessly at similarly shimmering valve-springs.

The riders were called to action, and one by one they came to the line, thumbed their throttles, smoked their rudimentary clutches and roared away from the start. Careering up the drive, they fought for control all the while as if riding wild broncos, and as they went bombing through on the footrest ends, the bark from the bikes' open exhausts bounced off the trees in a veritable triumph of acoustics. Then, after streaking over the line and shutting off, a glorious salvo of misfires saluted the achievement.

De la Hay was imperious, Bert le Vack was noticeably smooth, Freddie Dixon tigered spectacularly, and the determined but untidy Greenwood, who was aboard an overhead cam experimental job which made an undignified clattery racket, drew gasps when he disappeared at speed into the rhododendrons (the flag marshals found him eventually!), but the fastest time of the day was set by George Dance.

Tough, strong and brave, Dance was a fabulous sprinter, tuner, test rider, and engineer who was known in motorcycling circles well beyond the Sunbeam factory for his hatred of paperwork. 'Go or Bust' was his motto, and that was how he rode. His handlebars were particularly wide, the better, he felt, for grappling while battling over the bumps, and his petrol tanks were fitted with special knee grips of his own specification, better by design for gripping tightly and a vital aid to steering. He scorched up the hill half a second quicker than his fellows, and also put up the quickest time in the sidecar class.

Dance had a reputation for grumpiness, but he was kind to me that afternoon, and a white-knuckle blast back down to the paddock in the chair of his racing outfit at day's end is a vivid memory to this day. Yes, George Dance became my hero and favourite, and to motorcycling I was hooked. I maintain to this day you can't spend a day at a motorcycle race meeting and go home a normal man.

MODEL T FORD

The entrepreneurial Kay family, headed by perpetually pomaded and perennially shirt-sleeved patriarch Reg, ran a shop from the front room of their house in Bales, selling newspapers, sweets, bottles of pop, jars of jam and packets of tea etc. Later this enterprise was transferred to a lean-to wooden shed in the garden.

Sometime in 1923, Reg bought a driving licence from the council offices in Beedle Market (that's what one did in those days), and clasping a cash inheritance from his Auntie Agnes, made his way to the Ford factory at Trafford Park in Manchester where he bought a brand new Model T (in black, of course, and one of 150,000 made there that year) and then jerked and bounced his way home again in true Laurel and Hardy style.

He soon learned to drive it properly, and the hard-working T spent the next 16 years plying backwards and forwards to Beedle on a daily basis fetching newspapers, goods and provisions, as well as making many much longer trips to big smoky townships such as Stafford and Stoke-on-Trent. It also carried the extended Kay clan to many happy seaside holidays on the Welsh coast, and all without breakdown or great incident.

Reg made a good choice. Despite lightness and a cheap price, the Model T was made of fine materials, and that made it tougher than many more expensive machines. It was utilitarian by design; the positioning of its rear seats reputedly determined by the size of American milk churns so farmers could stand them on the floor in the back. Furthermore, an ordinary man could keep it going with pliers, an adjustable spanner and a screwdriver. Our village mechanic Harry Haynes never got his hands on Reg's black Ford.

At the time of its launch in 1908 the Model T had offered highly innovative and a quite brilliant solutions to problems that were taxing the minds of automobile makers and engineers around the globe, not least gear-changing. Everybody was struggling with it. Just three years earlier CS Rolls had broken his Rolls-Royce gearbox during the Isle of Man Tourist Trophy Races for automobiles, but Ford's unconventional apparatus enabled the man in the street to manage a motor car with variable gears.

American farmers loved the Model T. Its height and suspension coped well with rough tracks and it opened up possibilities for trade and travel. Henry Ford was a farm boy himself and that was his idea. In 1909 he said: 'I'm going to democratise the automobile. When I'm through, everybody will be able to afford one, and nearly everybody will have one.' That year was a big one for Ford. Mining millionaire Robert Guggenheim sponsored a motor race across the States from New York to Seattle and the only cars that made it were two Model Ts. 'I believe Mr. Ford has the solution of the popular automobile,' said Guggenheim.

Ford made much use of chrome vanadium steel, which had much greater tensile strength than the steels other manufacturers were using at the time. According to legend, an exotic French racing car with an engine block made of the stuff, blew itself to smithereens in a race on Daytona Beach. Ford picked up a fragment from the sands and popped it in his pocket for his engineers to analyse. Poppycock! According to his grandson Henry Ford II, whom I would meet at an American stock car race in 1955, Henry took advice from an English metallurgist called J Kent Smith.

The Model T Ford used a 2.9 litre, 22hp, four cylinder engine with a detachable head, the magneto sat in the flywheel (an idea purloined from Lanchester) and the engine, planetary transmission, flywheel, and universal joint all ran in a common oil bath. One top up did the lot! Its narrow chassis featured traverse springs fore and aft and rolled on cartwheels, and the sun and planet steering boasted phenomenal lock giving great manoeuvrability.

Interestingly, the T was the first Ford to have a steering wheel on the left. Although America became a right-side driving country more than 100 years before, at least in part to divest itself of a visible British influence, many US manufacturers seated the driver on the right. The sales success of the Ford brought about standardisation.

It must be said the T was not a great looker. American scribe and cartoonist Ralph Stein described it as '...about as beautiful as a kitchen coal store precariously balanced on the cat's cradle of springs and rods above four impossibly skinny wheels, with a huge top ballooned aloft over the passengers'.

Truck versions and different bodies became available in later years, and over time it gained lights, electric starting, detachable wire wheels with modern tyres, and even a few additions to its meagre interior appointments, but it remained the same primitive mechanical device, and it changed little in appearance throughout a 19 year production run which ended in 1927. For ten years from 1917, half of all the cars made in America were Ford Model Ts, and an astonishing 15.5 million were built.

Henry Ford was a man of good ideas and sound common sense (as well as ill-judgement, extreme stubbornness, and bigotry), and he achieved success by simplifying seemingly complex problems. He is acknowledged for being the first industrialist to use timed conveyor belts on a large scale to aid mass production, although the method had long been deployed in the clock and watch industry in Connecticut, and Ford got the idea from the use of overhead trolleys in a Chicago meat packing plant.

In 1909 his workers turned out 100 cars a day and the T sold in America for $850, but following a self-funded move to a new factory (Ford always held massive cash reserves), output rose and prices fell. In 1912 the T cost $600, by 1918 it had fallen to $450, and by 1924 it had plunged to an incredible $290. Production times dropped too. In 1913 the factory was producing 400 Ts a day and it took two and a half man hours to build each chassis, but by January 1914 it was taking just one hour and 33 minutes. Subsequently, they were turned out even more quickly, but Ford started keeping the information close to his chest.

By the way, Henry never said you can have any colour you like as long as it's black. The early tourers were, in fact, Brewster green, and some early Ts were red. It was all about efficiency with the coming of automation, and it was only later that black became the norm. Black enamel paint dried quicker than other colours you see, and was therefore better suited to the pace of the conveyor belts.

But while Henry and his customers were happy, his production workers, many of them immigrants, were becoming seriously cheesed off. Having been much simplified, most factory tasks became tedious and repetitive and called for no great cerebration or skill, and therefore spending nine hours a day at the bench or belt became intolerable for all but the dullest of dullards.

High staff turnover became a serious problem as workers left in droves, and the company had to spend fortunes on rudimentary training programmes just to keep the production line rolling. Despite introducing bonuses and benefits, the problem persisted, and as other manufacturers imitated Ford's production methods, the American car industry as a whole began to factor the ongoing cost of recruitment and training into the prices of their cars. Henry, however, came up with a bold solution.

In January 1914 he announced higher wages, reduced hours, and a profit-sharing plan. The hard of thinking hailed Ford as a madman and, far worse, a socialist. What was he thinking? The company would be ruined.

But the myopic gloom-mongers were wrong, and the far-sighted farm lad from Michigan was on the money. Retaining his employees lowered the firm's costs dramatically, and a happy workforce led to ever greater productivity. So while Europe was bogged down in war, Ford's profits jumped from $30 million to $60 million, and Ford claimed paying his workers more for less was '…one of the finest cost-cutting moves we ever made', and added: 'when you pay men well you can talk to 'em.'

His workers also bought the cars they made, speeding the democratisation process Ford had envisaged when the T was born. So you see, Henry Ford was a genius. But the silly bugger could also be an obtuse and short-sighted nitwit.

As the years rolled on the T changed little and the opposition steadily caught up and overtook it, but Henry absolutely refused even to even consider replacing his creation, and would fly into fits of rage if an underling even suggested it. His son Edsel tried hardest to persuade him, but the stubborn old goat would not shift his position one jot. In fact, after a blazing row, the lad was forbidden ever to speak of the matter again, and the disagreement hung about the factory and their relationship like a bad smell.

The invigorating wind of competition blew ever colder. Chevrolet in particular took Ford customers in droves, and by 1926, sales of the T fell to such a low Henry was finally forced to accept reality. He took drastic and brutal action. The following year the factory closed for six months and the workers were laid off. It was a disaster, but it could have been even worse. The boy Edsel had the enterprise to have been working in secret with some of the firm's designers on a new model. A good job or it might have spelled the end for the Ford Motor Company. The factory was retooled and the utterly conventional Model A was launched in December 1927. Fortunately for Ford it was a big success.

Lest I am accused of over-romanticising about Henry Ford, let me put on the record he could be a nasty and narrow-minded so-and-so. He spied on his workers, attempted to control how they spent their money, and he bought a newspaper specifically to spread his distasteful anti-semitic views. Hitler was an admirer, and the American industrialist is even mentioned in glowing terms in *Mein Kampf.*

Henry Ford died in 1947, aged 83. Yes, he was a complete fruitcake and had dreadful failings, but there is no doubt the eccentric motor car he invented is an all-time classic. In 1939, when Reg Kay put his Model T into storage for the duration and 12 years after the last one was built, an estimated two million Model Ts were still active in the USA alone.

The Model T Ford is a noble instrument of considerable historical importance. There is something somehow right about it. Its looks can now be considered sweet and charming, it is full of personality, it is well made and a considerable performer in its own way, but much more significantly than all of that, the Model T Ford was the car that changed the world.

AN INFURIATING INSTRUMENT

Piloting a Model T is no easy matter, especially for an accomplished older driver, and I can vouch for this from humiliating personal experience. Astonishingly, I did not properly get to grips with one until a press day at Beaulieu in 2010, and I am moved to say I found it an odd contraption beyond my immediate and instinctive understanding. An habitué can drive a Model T smoothly, as was ably demonstrated that day by Baron Edward, but not a novice. It takes time to become familiar with its unique rhythms, and until then driving one can be something of an adventure. Certainly, entirely new techniques have to be learned.

To accelerate, one moves a lever on steering column where a spark advance/retard control lever is mounted also. There is no hand gear shift. Instead, two forward speeds and reverse are controlled by foot pedals. A further pedal tightens brake bands inside the gearbox, while a dual-purpose hand lever operates tiny brakes inboard of the rear wheels as well as allowing the selection of gears to take place.

Starting was by hand-crank only until 1919, and one must retard the ignition, or the engine might run backwards or backfire and break your wrist, and, unless the car's various levers and pedals are set correctly one can get run over by one's own vehicle (thankfully the test car, like Reg's, was a 1923 model with an electric starter, so I was spared these risks).

Once running, adjust the timing to get her ticking smoothly, then to move off, hold the car with the right foot brake, release the hand brake lever and put the left pedal fully down to engage low gear. Then release the foot brake gently while moving the throttle lever upwards and, all being well, she should be off and running in low gear.

At 10mph or so, ease the throttle slightly and take one's foot off the left pedal. As it rises there will likely be a violent jerk and a howl of protest from the transmission as the car moves into top. With practice, I am assured complete smoothness can eventually be achieved.

The brake pedal engages bands in the transmission. These bands run in oil, so it pays to restrict use of this brake to short bursts to avoid scorching and allow cooling, and because the wheels are not affected directly, the differential can allow one driving wheel to spin forwards and the other backwards. Lurid skids can result from over-zealous use of the footbrake in slippery conditions. In the wet, I found to my embarrassment, it can be safer to use the emergency hand-brake.

Lurid skids can result from over-zealous use of the footbrake in slippery conditions.

To stop with grace and aplomb, close the hand throttle and hold the gear pedal halfway down to put the gears in neutral (although pushing the left pedal down into low gives engine braking, and one can ease it back into neutral as she comes to a stop), then move the right foot across to brake pedal. Confusingly, the hand lever can also be used to put the car in neutral as well as a brake, and this lever must be in a forward position to facilitate driving. I was also informed reverse can be engaged while moving forwards to provide extra braking effort, and as a way of saving band wear. Confused? There's more.

To reverse the car, come to a complete stop, put the left pedal halfway down into neutral and then tread gently on the middle pedal, although one can ping backwards and forwards Laurel and Hardy style by pressing the reverse pedal while going forwards, and the gear pedal while travelling backwards.

On level going, on a good day, a Model T will puff its way to 40mph and sail along happily, although the direct steering is mighty twitchy. The trick, as ever, is to hold the wheel loose in the hands and let it get on with it. The car can climb steep hills without strain and come back down them on tick-over without any need for brakes, but a T with badly worn transmission bands can be incapable of climbing even the most modest gradient. Except, that is, in reverse, and that, I realised 80 years later, is probably why I would sometimes see Reg Kay tackling Attorney's Rump and other local mounds in backwards fashion, although it could also have been because he was low on fuel. The T's petrol tank is located under the front seats and the carburettor is gravity-fed. Going up hills backwards serves to raise the fuel supply above the atomising instrument.

While I found the Beaulieu Model T Ford something of a pig to drive that rainy day in Hampshire, I came away not at all hostile to the breed. I readily concede that my lumpish reflexes, dulled senses and clumsy hands were at the heart of the problem. Alas it was me, not the T, that was the most antiquated old crock in action that morning.

RELIABILITY TRIAL

Harry Haynes was not a motorcyclist, and far less a socialist, so it was a surprise in spring 1927 when he took on a dealership for Lichfield Lion machines, smart Villiers-engined lightweights made by a failed workers' co-operative from that Cathedral city; a brave but ultimately doomed venture originally bankrolled by the well known and progressive Somerset philanthropist Sir G Godfrey Pullen.

It turned out an eponymous firm of cycle engineers, Smale Brothers of Brummagem, had acquired the co-op's bankrupt stock for an undisclosed sum, and the red and chromium-plated Lions that appeared for sale outside Haynes' former blacksmith's shop in Bales, by now sporting a large painted sign declaring itself to be 'Haynes Garage – Repairers of Motors of all Types', had purportedly been 'significantly re-engineered' by the hitherto little known pair. To generate publicity for his new venture, Haynes thought he'd have a go at organising a Reliability Trial.

Reliability Trials peaked in popularity before War One, when road surfaces were either dusty, rutted and rocky, or slithery, slippery and boggy, and when climbing even minor hills required lashings of lpa (light pedal assistance – a misnomer if ever there was one). By all accounts it was an altogether exhausting business. Belts slipped and snapped, engines expired, there was much falling off, and a great deal of puffing and pushing.

As a small boy I sat rapt as Pater and his pals talked at length of being reduced to quivering wrecks by having hauled their spindly mounts up Sutton Bank and over similarly vile and vertiginous escarpments as far afield as Scotland, Devon and the Emerald Isle. They told of a wonderful spectacle, of great gatherings of motorcycles, of herculean human effort, and of life affirming fellowship and camaraderie.

But by the outbreak of War One, in fact by around 1911, improvements in metallurgy, the widespread adoption of the variable gear, the invention of reliable electrical systems, and the laying of better road surfaces made reliability trials either too easy, or else restricted entirely to the most freakish routes and obstacles. Pater and his chums dropped out of the game.

Undeterred, Haynes took out an advert in *Motor Cycling* and had 25 gold medals struck at no little expense. Hoping to sell Lions by attracting motorcyclists from miles around to his garage, he had devised a trial of the hub and spoke variety. A route was charted in a star pattern with Bales at its centre; thus the competitors would return to the village after each leg, whereupon they would be obliged to purchase petrol from him, and possibly spare parts, and maybe take advantage of tyre changing facilities and other services all supplied by himself, and where his impressive new machines would be prominently displayed.

All trials organisers attempted to include at least one engine-breaker of a climb, and Haynes knew there was none such within his ambit, but he reckoned Harbinger's Lump, a small but steep mound ten miles west of Bales, would be his trump card. Harbinger's achieves no great altitude, but at the time it had a loose stony road running over it of the worst colonial type. Haynes scheduled his riders to ride up and over this scraggy pile, then immediately turn about and negotiate it again in reverse. Furthermore, on its eastern approach, a fast-running and deceptively deep stream ran over slimy and slithery rocks straight across the trail: a treacherous water-splash feature if taken at speed, or a dispiritingly wet and perilous push should a rider choose to dismount before crossing.

A wholly unrealistic time was set for the completion of this, the penultimate leg of the trial, and Haynes no doubt rubbed his hoary hands with glee, confident none but the very hardiest types on the most exceptional machinery would earn one of his expensive gold medals.

A date was set on a May Sunday, and an attractive enrolment fee drew an entry of nearly 200 riders, pillionists and sidecar passengers from far and wide, many of whom stayed at the Wellington on Beedle High Street. While not a swagger hotel, this respected establishment on the town's main thoroughfare had just been refurbished at no little expense to celebrate its centenary. As well as being given elaborate new fixtures and fittings, Waterloo scenes and portraits of the great man had been sought out, secured and hung, and, perhaps unwisely, Arthur Wellesley's motto 'Never Apologise, Never Explain' was sign-written in flowing gold script above the porter's hatch in the entrance hallway.

Now motorcyclists are not the cleanest travellers, nor, when in a group, are they generally the meekest of characters, and on that Saturday night the incoming horde deposited dirt and grime on the fresh carpets and newly reupholstered seats, drank the Duke bar dry in rowdy fashion (to the great chagrin of the locals), and then in reckless high spirits wrecked the serving counter and some Lincrusta panelling in the new Tudor grill room. By all accounts the hotel did not fall quiet until 3am, and following further chaotic scenes at breakfast, the Wellington's indignant owner and manager, Mr Matthew Paynter, sat down, fuming, and schemed a letter to Tibballs and Holmes, solicitors of Beedle, requesting they pursue damages and reparation from one Henry Horace Haynes, Blacksmith of Bales.

Haynes in blissful ignorance, proudly wheeled demonstration machines out for display, set up his tyre changing facilities, laid out his spares, lined up his cans of Pratt's, and discreetly jingled the change in his leather money pouch. Meanwhile, the Smale brothers arrived with a newly-painted sandwich board announcing 'Haynes of Bales, Lichfield Lions County Agents'.

The village was abuzz as upwards of 150 machines rolled into the village on that Sunday morning. We, of course, had been up with the lark for what promised to be the most exciting day of the year. Exhausts smoked the air, bunting flicked and flapped outside the garage, dogs and children ran excitedly hither and thither, Grandpapa waved his stick aloft in salute to each new arrival, and I held Pater's hand tightly while he pointed out Matadors, Bradburys, New Gerrards, and Coventry Eagles.

Our vicar, the Rev Jeremiah McShane, was not impressed. Scowling as he made his way to church on foot, having wisely left his pony and trap in the barn (the lazy article only had to walk 50 yards!), he then scolded Alf and Rose Marshall's young granddaughter Martha who had set up a trestle table outside St Bede's to sell ginger beer and pilchard and cucumber sandwiches (dear old Alf was the gardener and underemployed chauffeur at Hornbeam Hall).

Having swept inside St Bede's the crabby clergyman quite deliberately left the main doors open before encouraging the God-fearing burgesses within to extra vigorous renditions of that morning's hymns. But the piping organ and hearty strains of *Onward Christian Soldiers* and *Jerusalem*, commingling with the crack, boom and pop-pop-pop of the two-wheeled congregation outside only combined to create a most memorable soundscape that has stamped itself indelibly on my memory. Quite marvellous!

I would add at this point the de Fortes were not entirely non-believing, but the Rev McShane's thundering sermons against the motor car had long since driven our brood to St Jude's in Beedle, where the vicar, the Rev Barnabus Wilmott, or Barnie as he preferred to be called, welcomed us in with open arms. Simultaneously wise and practical, and kind and gentle, Rev Barnie was everything a man of the cloth should be. Furthermore, when his sister Nettie was in the parish, they would call across to see us in her Morgan three-wheeler, and Rev Barnie would always arrive glowing.

A team of youngsters had been sent out on push-cycles at the crack of dawn to mark the route with confetti strewn at the corners. Haynes' young son Colin returned abruptly. Travelling like a shell from a gun, he burst into the village parting the crowds. His face was puce and streaked with grey, and his pedals revolved in an invisible blur. After skidding to a stop at the garage, the lad threw down his velocipede with a crash and ran panting to his father as if he personally was carrying the good news from Ghent to Aix.

But the news was bad. Unknown to the hapless Haynes, just two days earlier the council had arrived at Harbinger's Lump with their red flags, stonecarts and tar engines, and a smooth and carpet-like surface now awaited the participants on both sides of the mound. Worse, the treacherous stream had been diverted to run quite harmlessly through a Yorkshire clay conduit deep under the road's new crust.

Wee Colin had arrived too late. Route cards had been issued and the first contestants were already being flagged away by the chief timekeeper, none other than the formidable Arthur Bourne, a vibrant young Auto Cycle Union official and cub reporter who would become Torrens of *The Motor Cycle*. Although chiefly stationed in Bales that day, Torrens would also don his riding beret, clamp his pipe tightly in his teeth and zoom off on his Ariel, coat-tails streaming, to settle disputes and keep an eye on proceedings.

The weather was ideal that Sunday in May. The sun was soft and warm, flower-heads swayed in a gentle breeze, and bees worked the meadows, while overhead skylarks pierced the scented air with their speedy song. In the village centre there were frequent shouts of bravo and small spatters of spontaneous applause as riders came and went on schedule, and by mid afternoon it was becoming plain almost all the contestants were looking likely to finish on good time. All that is except for the three unfortunate fellows competing on Lions.

In two cases the Lichfield cats had sat down on their rears at very brief notice, their underspecified back wheels having become ovoid following the departure of a number of spokes which had fallen tinkling to the ground; and in the third the clutch in the rear hub had seized solid, bringing about a dramatic lock-up, the immediate ripping out of all wheel spokes at once, and a subsequent skid and collapse. In the first two cases the riders had to carry their bicycles several miles back to Bales, or else guide them nose down in wheelbarrow-fashion, while the third unfortunate fellow was rushed painfully by bumpy horse and cart to the cottage hospital in Beedle where the terrifying matron Nurse Carter administered stinging ointment to his grazed derriere.

When reports reached Haynes the leaders had cleared Harbinger's without incident he could see he'd dropped a mighty clanger. Realising his plight, the scabby fellow removed his fuel cans and equipment and hid with them inside inside his garage so nobody could buy juice for the final leg. One by one the riders returned in search of propellant to complete the course. There was much banging on the door, and soon a noisy scrum ensued, with two hot and angry Lion buyers waving handfuls of spokes and egg-shaped rims – the most vociferous complainants of all.

Finally, following a megaphone tirade by Torrens, the beleaguered and shame-faced proprietor appeared blinking into the open, sheepishly claiming he'd got sunstroke and fallen asleep or somesuch bunk. The trial was declared null and void, refunds were administered, the exiguous supply of medals was given out at Torrens' discretion, and all fuel tanks were filled free of charge. All that is, except for those of the poor little Lions. The Smale brothers, by the way, had long since departed the scene on a BSA.

The crowd dispersed, riders either making their weary way home, or repairing to the Rose & Crown where much drinking ensued, the reverie continuing long into the night as I can readily testify having lain awake listening to much bibulous laughter, and occasional forlorn and wretched vomiting, while reliving the events of the day, as well as attempting to differentiate the pretty acoustics of departing Broughs, Triumphs and Ricardos.

Early the next morning Algy and I spotted a Lichfield Lion strung up high in the great chestnut tree in the village. Haynes was nowhere to be seen (remonstrating with the Smales in Brum?), so with the assistance of the perpetually sozzled but surprisingly athletic Dougie Rudd (an extraordinary man who would turn water into wine using any plant or fruit), it was carefully lowered, and we hauled it back to the farm. Its tiddly two-stroke mill proved a surprisingly willing goer and its frame and front fork formed the basis of a lightweight special that completed many flying laps of the Far Field.

Chapter Two

PRE-WAR ERA

IN MAY 1929 A Labour government was formed under Ramsay MacDonald, a Scottish farm labourer's son and Britain's first socialist prime minister. MacDonald had led the country once before, of course, in 1924, albeit only for ten months before a strong Conservative general election victory in October that year. The 1929 election was also significant for the 'flapper vote', so called because, to the great consternation of old buffers everywhere, women under 30 were for the very first time deemed eligible to vote. Less significant flapper freedoms won in the 1920s included the social acceptance of women drinking, smoking and wearing trousers, although not necessarily all at the same time!

The MacDonald Government was quick to pass motoring legislation. Third Party insurance was made compulsory in 1930, and the Road Traffic Act of the same year raised the minimum motorcycling age to 16, and abolished all speed restrictions, because the existing limits were so universally disobeyed it was decided they brought the law into contempt. This decision was reversed in 1934 when Conservative Minister of Transport Leslie Hore-Belisha's Road Traffic Act introduced a speed limit of 30mph in built-up areas, and the following year Hore-Belisha introduced compulsory driving tests, to my great chagrin at the time.

At first the new speed restrictions extended well into the countryside, and the Beedle police would set up traps in the lanes to capture persistent miscreants such as my father. In the evenings and summer holidays, Algy and I organised the village kids into signalling parties whenever the police were about their vindictive business. Later, the limits were moved back to sensible boundaries, and in 1938 Pater was tickled pink to have been 'gonged' by a Wolseley 14/60 police car with a loud ringing bell and an illuminated badge on its grille, the late 1930s having seen the start of the marque's long association with the forces of law and order.

In the 1930s motoring became commonplace, and Algy and I graduated from haring around the Far Field on myriad two and four-wheelers, and duly passed our driving tests. We were not alone. The roads gradually filled up with Austin Sevens and other tin boxes, and then came the war, and a realisation a golden era had been lost forever. Pater would bang on tiresomely about it, saying that even as recently as the 1920s no cars would be seen for miles. That there had recently been a time when, having stopped for a rest and a pipe, a man could find perfect solitude save for the ticking of his cooling engine. But that now the long shadow of Messrs Austin and Morris was falling over the countryside. That each weekend brought more and more little painted tin boxes streaming onto the highways and byways of the land. That no longer could you pull into a field entrance and lean on the gate to enjoy a quiet pipe, watching the summer sun setting over peaceful fields of waving barley, and orange-red clouds sailing across a great wide sky, and that if there were not one there already, you were soon joined by an Austin Seven complete with parents and a horde of repulsive children.

My first motor car was a Rover Eight, a toy-like cheapie, half-way between a cycle car and a modern baby. The Eight was designed by future Triumph owner and BSA chairman Jack Sangster, and was manufactured by the thousand, both in Coventry, and under licence in Germany by Peter und Moritz. The tooling cost Rover £400,000, and the car cost £300 in 1921, reducing to half that by 1924, the year mine was made. It had crude disc wheels, brakes of lilliputian efficiency and fitted only at the rear, and primitive rack and pinion steering. An air-cooled flat twin, its pots projected through cut outs in the sides of the bonnet and glowed cherry red in the dark (at least mine did. It was so terribly abused!). My Rover Eight was a rare, duck egg blue, long-chassis four-seater with a fabric body. I bought it for a bargain price from dear old Uncle Bof and I do not wish to appear ungrateful, but good grief, it was an obstreperous and unrepaying contraption! It was not terra incognita for me to have to crank the blasted thing for more than a quarter of an hour before it would condescend to fire (there was no self-starter), and once this finally occurred, the driver and passenger sat numb-bottomed on uncomfortable, thin upholstery, wedged shoulder to shoulder for lack of elbow room.

More stylish, so-called performance cars of the era had long bonnets, supposedly redolent of power (from the steam locomotive), and were, of necessity, absurdly high inside so one could see where one was going, peering from one's rexine seat, above the soft violet glow of the dashboard's instruments. Rear windows meanwhile were kept mean and small for reasons of privacy and cheapness. Almost all cars smoked liberally, and oil leaks remained commonplace from engines, gearboxes, and back axles alike. Synchromesh came in, and one-shot lubrication was all the rage. Henry Royce reportedly distrusted it, and he was proved right.

TWO WHEELS GOOD

Noting my new-found enthusiasm for motor-bicycling, Pater laid out a test track around the perimeter of the Far Field at the farm in Bales, and built me a cut-down special, powered by a little Levis two-stroke (not exactly a sensational mill, but ideal for a novice). From there I progressed to bigger, and sometimes better, home-made and adapted track irons, and in time I came to preside over a sorry collection of early two-wheeled machinery which all but filled the middle shed at Bales.

Pater obtained most of these early motorcycles for me. Bought cheaply or even given free, they were easy to find, for there was an overabundant supply. I thus recruited an invalid battalion of broken-down motorcycles in varying degrees of deterioration and decrepitude, and with Pater and Grandpapa's help I would attempt to repair them or butcher them to make up specials. This was way before Titch Allen and others formed the Vintage Motorcycle Club, prompting folk to begin valuing vintage and veteran machinery as part of our industrial and cultural heritage. Dear, dear Titch, I apologise.

My father's workshop in the middle shed was a magical place, and he let me use it freely to build and repair my machinery. There was a stout joiner-made workbench featuring a substantial vice and with electric light above, fastened to the far wall between a treadle lathe, and an up to the minute electrical drill. Cabinets contained drill bits, clips and fastenings, tap and die sets, and myriad screws, all conveniently categorised and defined by label in slim tins, tall tins, tobacco tins, cigarette tins, black japanned tins, Oxo tins, and half a lifetime's worth of oval Bourneville Cocoa tins (Mater was an addict!). In handy chests of drawers were to be found tyre patches, glue, wire, wet and dry, wire wool, cigar boxed sets of sparking plugs, wads of cork and paper gaskets, and tray after tray of both sorted and assorted washers, nuts and bolts.

A splendid stencilled tool board took up most of the wall behind the bench, although I was expressly forbidden to touch anything on it. My own rudimentary tool kit comprised hand-me-down spares stored in a super-heavyweight chest under the bench, supplemented by a growing collection of quite useless spanners, seemingly stamped out of biscuit tins. These had been given away 'free' with my pioneer motorcycles when they were new, and I found them surprisingly often in tiny leather or rubber wallets suspended by flimsy buckled straps hanging from the rear of their bicycle-type saddles. Sometimes useful cotter pins or spare carburettor needles were discovered in them, preserved carefully in small squares of folded greaseproof paper, or occasionally in a miniature leather purse.

As well as complete and unadulterated, or barbarically reconfigured machines, the shed became stuffed with tea chests and orange boxes full of mechanical parts, and complete engines ready for transplant stood in a line, each in its own gritty puddle of oil. Additionally, shelves overflowed with carburettor and electrical parts, or else groaned under the weight of cranks, pistons, conrods and valve-gear; and I presided over a plethora of pulleys, an unholy host of handlebars, and an ever-expanding and increasingly diverse range of tyres, tubes, chains, and dope-soaked belts, all hung from huge nails hammered into the rafters (the last of these in myriad sub-varieties of bootlace, link and vee types). And while a heap of pedal cranks piled up in one corner, and a stack of wheels reached nearly to the roof in another, to the great dismay of my mother, an untidy stack of frames appeared to be becoming a permanent fixture out in the yard.

Machines from the beginning of the century were primitive, crude, and bicycle based. Most had foreign engines – including those of De Dion, Minerva (whose engines were fitted by Triumph, a British company founded in Coventry by a German), and the Belgian Kelecom and 3.5hp Ormonde. They all had about as much sheer poke as a toy air pistol.

At first all I felt able to do was rub them down with an oily rag (highly recommended for an air pistol, by the way), but by tearing them down, and building them back up, and by amalgamating their components in unexpected combinations to create awkward and inelegant hybrids (rather in the crazed manner of Mary Shelley's Frankenstein at work in his laboratory!), I developed a few basic and rudimentary skills.

I came to understand the workings of crankshafts, and pistons and valves, and the other fundamental components to be found in the internal combustion engine. I gradually became familiar with the function and construction of sparking plugs, of trembler coils, of primitive clutches, and of brakes of various types and degrees of inefficiency. And to all my specials I fitted George Dance kneegrips. This stylish embellishment aside, the touch of an artist remained forever and entirely absent from my work, but my activities in the middle shed proved an altogether excellent form of basic mechanical training. I wanted to become a motorcycle racer, or else a mechanic, and outside school hours I devoted myself unswervingly to these aims.

Early motorcycles were weird and perilous mounts, and most were fitted with oversized pedalling gear which would become bent in crashes. To the field each day I would take a giant spanner for straightening cranks and pedal arms, and a substantial hammer to provide extra persuasion.

Some engines were tickle starters, springing to life at the merest brush of a carpet slipper, while others, equally willing, needed a hearty lunge to get a big flywheel spinning merrily (compression was often of a minus quantity, but some of these big bangers could recoil with a kick like a mule!). But some of those crocks were never going to run properly again. Some probably never had! The standard starting technique for most early machines was to place the bus on its stand, apply feet to pedals, then whirr away, feet a-blur, for as long as it took. Hours, sometimes. Alternatively, for a flying start on a proven machine, one would push away, listening keenly for the elevating chuff-chuff-chuff of success, and then leap aboard, TT-style.

Light pedal assistance, commonly known as lpa (el-pee-ay) was required to get most of these ancient busses up any sort of hill, even when they were new. Now there aren't any gradients to speak of on the farm, but el-pee-ay is in any event a cruel misnomer, and I would suffer daily the great agony of bashed ankle bones and gashed calves as I pedalled hard to assist tired and reluctant engines. With two enormous pedals revolving in an invisible whizz while I wobbled over the lumps and bumps of the Far Field at little more than walking pace, my legs would become leaden, my back would become soaked in perspiration, and rivulets of sweat would slide down my face and trickle, tickling, down my neck. More often than not I would wheeze to an inevitable conk, and collapse breathless, grey and gasping onto the grass. Recovery, when it came, would see me pushing dejectedly back to the shed for adjustments.

But I did eventually learn to cure non-startitis, or, more often, to recognise when it was a terminal condition and give up on an unrepaying machine before strain or self-injury, and I gradually learned about maintenance of tune (re-tuning most engines was a daily occurrence), and learned some tricks relating to the black art of electrics. And with the coming of a semblance of reliability in my mounts, I came to see glimpses of what I later came to know as the magic of motorcycling.

I began to experience the great exhilaration of riding a motorcycle, even a slow and primitive one. I learned to stir a bicycle up a bit, to ride faster than I dared, to both provoke and control slideslip, to fly over bumps, and to corner full chat. I began to appreciate what a Lancastrian called Jeffrey Smith would describe 40 years later as 'the sheer exhilaration of chasing across broken ground on a wild, free, two-wheeled device'. (Smith was world scrambling champion in 1964 and 1965.)

There is an emotional element to motorcycling. An active engagement that intensifies the experience of life, moving the rider out of a mundane, drab, semi-conscious state into the wide awake intensity of a life lived to the full. Engaging in motorcycling energises and intensifies life to a quite extraordinary degree. It is as though one has plugged oneself into a great psychic consciousness expander! A psychic amplifier I first plugged into as a boy in the Far Field in Bales, and which I could still connect with on a racetrack in Belgium 80 years later.

That's not to say it got easy from then on, back in pre-war Bales. My creations would shake themselves to bits – I was forever tightening things – and failure to proceed remained a standard state of affairs. Flimsy contact breakers required adjusting every few laps; sparking plugs cracked, snapped, and delivered dreadful shocks to the inside of my thighs; spewing battery acid ate my trousers and burned my legs; carburettors (often not much more than tin cans with shallow pools of fuel sloshing inside) either fell apart, or else jets (made of putty, presumably) rapidly wore themselves away to nothing; belts broke and slipped; clutches burnt; gear hubs collapsed; pulleys flew off; and engines became incandescent and would violently blow apart or disintegrate internally following steely argument.

Wheels frequently collapsed, and occasionally I would trudge across the fields to get a rim re-spoked by Arthur Amis, ace cycle repairer of Beedle, for just a few pennies. Amis was a dull dog, but a man renowned county-wide for his genius for restoring ellipticity to rotundity. Rim brakes were pathetic and I learned to manage without them. A hobnailed boot applied to the ground or front tyre generally worked far better in any event. Punctures were a blight and a bind. Rubber solution had to be spread over the hole in the tube, and left for an age before a patch could be applied. More than once I carefully propped my cap over the setting goo to protect it from wind-blown grit, returning 15 minutes later to find my headwear dislodged by the breeze and stuck fast to the tube. At least I didn't have to worry about lamps. In fact, I was banned from using them for much of the year, after setting half the field ablaze during a heat-wave one particularly scorching summer.

And then there were the crashes. I bought a lovely box of tacks on many occasions, but I learned to choose the softest spot in the hedge through which to depart the field! Actually, falling off was often the simplest way of stopping, especially when the track was blocked by a fallen rival, usually Algy Tomlinson. Algy and I hit it off from the start (in truth, Mater said I hit him with a half brick the first time we met, aged two), but we didn't see much of each other in term time until we were ten or so. His parents sent him away to a famous crammer for the rich and thick, but after the Tomlinsons went bust, left Hornbeam Hall and rented a cottage from my parents, Algy went to school in Beedle with me, and we became inseparable pals and partners in crime for the next 70 years.

THREE WHEELS NOT BETTER

Motorcycling is a reckless means of transportation, and non-enthusiasts are possibly correct in considering it an absurd and precarious hobby adopted only by lunatics, but a motor bicycle is nowhere near as perilous as the cycle-car, a wretched and dreadful breed that was more or less extinct by 1925.

An Edwardian pea-green Weevil & Blight cycle-car was kept in a corner of the middle shed under a tarpaulin because Pater was fond of it. He had driven it when courting my mother, and it features in the earliest family photographs of them together. Having grown up with it as part of the family in this way, I was itching to jump in and try it, but it was deemed far too dangerous and I was expressly forbidden to even touch it.

Incidentally, the story of my parents' first meeting might be of nugatory interest. Before my father entered her life, my mama was courting a young chap from Edinburgh. An artist and an aesthete, and a bit of a preening popinjay by all accounts, but nonetheless he was an adventurous cove with excellent taste in women.

During a motor touring holiday together in the Highlands, with his waspish and overweening mother sitting between them as chaperone, they stole away without her one day in his Dalgliesh-Gullane (look it up!), only to sustain a puncture and bump to a stop near the summit of Pass Drumochter. Not keen on getting his lily-whites dirty, her beau at the time suggested they deploy the well tried 'girl attracts help while fellow hides' routine, and upon spotting a small and spidery green cycle-car straining up towards them, he dropped out of sight down a heathery bank, calling out 'You know what to do!'

My father chuffed to a halt and assayed the scene, noting her comeliness and a pair of gentleman's driving gauntlets on the bonnet. 'Hop in,' said Pater. She did, and with a toot on the bulb horn he lobbed a spare John Bull tyre repair kit onto the Dalgliesh's seat, clutched up and pootled off into the sunset (actually to Dalwhinnie in the first instance).

Despite this history, when the tragic news reached Mater one day that a Weevil & Blight of identical type, piloted by a pair of reckless young ripstitches from Stoke-on-Trent (the sons of a much-liked business associate), had turned turtle after hitting a rock while climbing Snowdon, and rolled down the mountainside, catching fire and tossing its wretched occupants out to death, Pater's sentimentality was overruled. The next day the W&B disappeared from the shed while I was at school, never to be seen again. I doubt now there are any extant.

INDIGNATION MEETING

By the 1930s my interest in motor cars and the business of motor cars was also developing, and for family reasons I paid particular attention to Rovers. The de Forte connection with the firm goes back a long way: Grandpapa was a shareholder when the company went public back in 1896, and so too a little later, was Pater, although he preferred his Phantoms and Bentley 4½.

Rover was founded by one John Kemp Starley, an east London lad who moved to Coventry to work in his uncle's bicycle factory, and in 1886 invented the so-called safety bicycle, a sensible machine with wheels of equal size, which finished the absurdly tall, direct-drive Penny Farthing overnight. A good thing too. Have you ever tried riding one? A fall from one of those giraffe-like contraptions is at least partly responsible for my having to walk with a stick throughout most of my adult life.

Later Rover Cycle Company innovations included back-pedalling brakes, and a gear driven shaft for their 'ladies' model, and Rover Imperials won every race in the 1908 London Olympic Games. Sadly, Starley did not live to see this, having popped his clogs in 1901, aged just 46, but he did instigate the creation of the first Rover motor car in 1888, an experimental electric contrivance rather like a bath chair with a tiller attached, which did not go into production.

The company made motor-bicycles, and tricycles, but no more cars until in 1903, when Edmund Lewis (whose impressive calling card announced: Telegrams: 'Combustion, Coventry'!) joined the firm from Daimler. He developed the 8hp which appeared in 1905 (a sparse, no frills, but honest little number with all its components in the right places), and two years later chief tester Ernest Courtis won the Tourist Trophy Race in the Isle of Man in a 20hp.

Rover continued to be innovative, inventing the first-ever dipstick in 1912 – quite something if you think about it – and looking into the possibility of using diesel power. History could have been altogether different if Dr Rudolf Diesel himself had not been lost overboard in suspicious circumstances while travelling on an overnight ferry to Britain in late September 1913. Talks between Rover and the distinguished French-born and English-educated doctor had been ongoing, and Pater drove down to Harwich with factory tester and publicity hound Dudley Noble to meet him off the Antwerp ferry and bring him up to the Midlands, but of course there was no sign of the inventor or his plans when the *Dresden* docked that chilly autumnal morning. The sausage-eaters, as is well known, then developed the diesel engine for use in U-boats during the Kaiser War.

During that bloody conflict Rover swelled its bank balance making munitions, and before and after it, the company settled down to making quality cars and bicycles for discerning customers, although the Rover Eight, built between 1920 and 1925 in a separate factory in Birmingham, was a mass-produced cheapie. As I have already mentioned, my very first car was an Eight, a rare 1924 long-chassis four-seater with a fabric body.

The cadaverous Sir Thomas Sly of nearby Bromchurch was driven around in a succession of Rover Twelves, his last, an Oxford blue 1923 model, being the last of the line, its delivery date coinciding with that of the last dividend he and other Rover shareholders received for some time. By then mascots were all the rage, and Rover's full-bodied viking had appeared. Later, the warrior figure was reduced to a helmeted head, and by the end of the decade, while he remained in place, implacable on the radiator cap, an enamel badge featuring a longship at full sail had started adorning Rover radiator grilles.

Rover's Meteor Works in Coventry was an amazing place for a young boy to visit with his father on a Friday afternoon in 1926. I recall filthy floors and blackened wooden work benches. Sparks flew from lathes, and cutters shrieked. Shafts spun in the roof, machinery roared, and belts thrashed, clattered and slapped. There were spinning handles, and much filing and hammering.

It was a place of slide rules, of setting up and of resetting and adjusting, a place of assembly by hand and checking by eye. I recall the steaming copper tea engines, the kindness of the workmen, the niggardliness of the quality control inspectors, the swaggering of the charge hands, and the flinty eyes of the supervisors. There was the calm of the tool room, the heat of the smithy, the red of the forge, and the ring of the anvil. There was the acrid stench of chemical vats, the sudden shock of clutch plates dipped in cyanide, and, nearing knocking off time, machine tools and gauges were carefully cleaned and oiled, and everything was covered with sheets of brown paper just before the roar of the bull sent the men clattering through the doors, and down iron spiral ladders to the time clocks, and away.

The salaried staff included Norwegian designer Peter Poppe, whom I glimpsed hunched over his drawing board, obscured by a cloud of white pipe smoke. He looked sad and old (he was only 56!). His 14/45 range, released the previous year, was heavy, slow, over-complicated, and expensive to produce, and Rover's customers weren't buying. Around that time he would have been busy scheming a racer called Odin that would never win a race (although in fairness, I must add it was a bit of a goer, lapping Brooklands at well over the magic ton).

Around two years later (it must have been 1928) I was up in my room one evening enjoying a Ryvita and cheese supper before turning in. I had just beaten my own record at tiddlywinks (such is the sad and lonely existence of an only child!), and was idly reading that week's *Rainbow* or *Funny Wonder*, when I became aware of men's voices becoming raised downstairs. Pater and his friends sometimes convened in his study of an evening to play war games, and on such occasions I was used to the rattling of the wires threaded along the table edges to simulate gunfire, the urgent shouts and cries of the battle's keen protagonists, and aromatic swirls of smoke from their combusted pipe tobacco which unerringly found its way through closed doors and up two flights of stairs to my nostrils.

But this was different. For a start, the candlestick telephone in the hall had been ringing every five minutes, and although I had been paying little attention, now I came to think about it, a veritable battalion of balloon-tyred behemoths had scrunched and popped their way up the newly gravelled track to the house in the last half an hour or so. What ho! Here came another one.

I peered out of the window as an Hispano-Suiza H6 drew up at the door, stone dust smoking from its tyres. Surely the epitome of vintage style and excellence, its boat-tailed body was beautiful and elegant to behold in plan view, and its smooth in-line six was inaudible despite my bedroom window being propped slightly ajar. The car's chromium plated flying stork mascot, I knew had been derived from the insignia of a squadron of War One French SPAD fighter planes powered by V8 aero engines made by the same firm.

Our gardener, Bert, whose services Pater had presumably retained for the night, appeared from the yellow haze of his oil lamp-lit shed and directed the newcomer to the parking area outside the top barn, and in the Hispano-Suiza's searching headlights I picked out a Rolls-Royce 20/25, a Hillman, several Daimlers, inevitably, and an inordinately large quota of Rovers.

I put Tiger Tim and the Bruin boys aside, and crept through coils of cigar smoke to the half-landing above the hall, from which point I could hear Pater holding forth from his study doorway, and sometimes catch glimpses of some of the dozen or so four, or even five-figure men in attendance, who were discussing with him in grave terms such things as share prices, loan repayments, and adverse trading conditions. Something was afoot in the wind, as Baldrick later (or earlier!) said, and I sat hugging my knees and listening intently. It was some sort of unofficial shareholder's meeting, and fascinating stuff.

Sir Thomas Sly I recognised at once. Sir Alfred Mays-Smith was there (a formidable bowler-hatted gent in a heavy overcoat, the former president of the society of motor traders), and so was a chap I later learned to be Spencer Wilks (calm, dignified and relaxed, I recall he acknowledged me with a friendly wink, but didn't give me away), and board director and War One tank commander Colonel Frank Searle (rather full of himself) had a lot to say.

The firm was in a pickle, and had run up debt Greek-style. Funding was being drip-fed by its bankers to keep the business afloat, and creditors and shareholders wanted solutions. Now. Rover was also directionless, and badly run, and the cars were not as good as they once had been. Loyal, well-heeled customers were turning away, and to stimulate sales of the everyman Eight, its price had been reduced to the point of non-profitability, although, still, few were tempted. Herbert Austin's Seven was simply a much better little car. As the meeting broke up, I remember Wilks saying quietly to Pater as they bade farewell, that he knew absolutely what needed to be done.

The exact sequence of the events that followed has become rather obscure in the cigar smoke wisps of time. Accounts differ in precise date and detail, but the facts are essentially as follows. Mays-Smith promptly joined the board, and with his support Searle was put in overall charge of the company, usurping long-time chairman Colonel William Fitzherbert Wyley (a senior magistrate, and former Deputy Lieutenant and High Sheriff of Warwickshire. Not used to such treatment, he was apparently mighty peeved!). But Searle's tenure was short and he was himself ousted a year or two later, Mays-Smith having waited until his man was in New Zealand on a sales trip before dropping the bombshell in a telegram (the equivalent of being sacked by telephonic text!). By that time Spencer Wilks had joined Rover as works manager and was already beginning to turn the company around from within. He had proved he did indeed know what needed to be done, and before long Wilks became Rover's managing director.

Wilks soon got rid of tired old Peter Poppe, who frankly had had his day. Poppe's cars were still reminiscent of Victorian railway carriages driven by chauffeurs, and the cheap, mass-produced Rover Eight was not worth retaining either. Increasingly, Rover owners now drove themselves, as Pater always had, but they still expected quality, above all in engineering, but also manifested in refinement, dignity, seemliness and a sense of propriety. Wilks 'got it'. He understood Rovers had to represent good taste, good value, and a certain style of life, that they were representative of traditional old world order, and that the firm needed to get back to that tout de suite. He got costs under control, introduced new models more in tune with Rover values, and gradually profitability returned.

Shortly before the Meteor Works was sold in 1938, I went back there to meet Wilks in my capacity as a fledgling motor noter, and it was quickly apparent that as well as getting the company back on its feet financially, he had worked a miracle that went way beyond the balance sheet. A friendly, relaxed atmosphere was abroad; light-hearted but hard-working and respectful, and a family atmosphere engulfed the place from top to bottom. Indeed, at the top it was a family affair.

Spencer Wilks, from Rickmansworth, a former barrister and War One army Captain, was the son-in-law of William Hillman (and, incidentally, brother-in-law to the dictatorial, but well-meaning Captain John Black of the Standard Motor Company, who had married another of Hillman's daughters). Wilks joined Rover from Hillman and would stay at the helm until 1962, retiring to an honorary position thereafter. His younger brother Maurice Wilks joined Rover in 1930 as chief engineer. A talented designer, and a man of infectious enthusiasms, he too had been at Hillman, and for two years in the late 1920s he had gained invaluable experience working for General Motors in the USA. Later their nephews Spencer King and Peter Wilks would join the firm, and both would have important roles to play in the Rover story, and in British automotive history. William Martin-Hurst, Rover's managing director in the 1960s, was related too.

My interview that day went splendidly, and I got to know Spencer Wilks very well over the next 30 years or so. I found him kind, courteous and considerate at all times, and he extended this commendable behaviour quite naturally to his management colleagues and to employees, no matter how lowly, and also to widows and pensioners connected with the firm.

By War Two, under the Wilks brothers' thoughtful stewardship, Rover had been returned to good physical and mental health. The distinctive P2 range had been introduced in 1937 (P1 was a retrospective title, of course!), and the cars epitomised Rover values. The P2 was tall, handsome, semi-formal, stylish, and identifiable, and it smacked of refinement and good taste. It was smooth and quiet, yet its performance was absolutely first-rate, and handling and ride was excellent in its day. In the cabin, the well-equipped instrument board was of varnished wood, and the comfortable seats were upholstered in pleated leather. On top of all this a Rover P2 promised to give long, reliable service, making it a canny choice as well as a classy one.

DRIVING TEST

It may surprise some of you that I have actually taken a driving test! The motoring boom of the 1930s saw a doubling of the number of vehicles on Britain's roads, and then, as now, ineptitude was rife. At best, new drivers were given rudimentary instruction by the supplying dealer and left to get on with things. Accidents and fatalities were commonplace, and Liberal MP Leslie Hore-Belisha was made Transport Minister by Ramsay MacDonald and told to sort the problem out.

An ex-Army man, Hore-Belisha was a good organiser and not short of ideas. Immortalised, of course, by giving his name to the flashing beacons on striped poles still decorating many crossings on British high streets, Belisha also introduced the Highway Code, and in mid 1935 he brought in the driving test. Later in the decade he made himself unpopular with Tory Prime Minister Neville Chamberlain by badgering for increased military spending while insisting Adolf Hitler was not to be trusted. An astute fellow indeed.

More than a little peeved at having to take the new test as I was not yet quite 15 years of age by the cut off date, let alone 17, I am ashamed to say I contrived to create a bureaucratic error whereby I was called to present myself for scrutiny a full 12 months early (and quite illegally), during the year following the test's introduction. After meeting the examiner at the pre-arranged spot opposite the Red Lion in town (most convenient) we tootled around for half an hour or so in Algy Tomlinson's Morris Eight until it was decided I had passed. Having been driving various of Pater and Grandpapa's racing cars on dirt tracks on the farm since I was 12, including a number of hairy pre-war chain-driven fire breathers, quite frankly I would have been somewhat miffed if I had not done so. Good job he didn't see me knock young Bob the new postman off his bicycle as I emerged hurriedly from the farm gates on my way to the test (at least it stopped his damned whistling for a few minutes).

Incidentally, I took the test in Algy's Morris, as my Rover was temporarily sidelined with a con rod through its block (bored out to the nth degree, the old girl had most aptly let go on Conrod Straight while attempting a new record for a flying lap of the Beedle triangle), and mother was in Shrewsbury for the day with Marjorie in her old baby Austin. It was thought turning up in Pater's Phantom might alienate the examiner somewhat, and as Grandpapa had nothing suitable to spare either, I gave Algy a tinkle and borrowed the little brown Morris for the day. A utilitarian bone-shaker of no great urge, the Eight was an ideal car for the purpose.

Algy would take his test in the same car several months later, and managed to pass despite not being able to find it for a while when he emerged from the Red Lion at the allotted time. Then he discovered to his horror he had left the keys in the ignition and somehow locked the driver's door. Ingress was achieved through the boot and the rest of the test passed without incident until the examiner cracked his head on the windscreen during the emergency stop procedure. I should have told Algy I had fettled the brakes for him the last time he left it at the farm.

BY GEORGE
(First published *Motorcycle Review* – February 1990)

Brough Superiors were the great sporting motorcycles of the 1920s and 1930s, and the machines that command the highest prices at classic motorcycle auctions today. They are the most expensive old motorbikes in the world and they were pricey too when they were new. They offered fine roadholding, true. They were fast and they were daring, true too. And that they were stylish and beautiful is undeniable. But although they really were truly bespoke, and they were put together very carefully indeed, and with love, in the final analysis Broughs were only conventional motorcycles assembled by experts from bought-in and copied components.

The secret of their success and fame? Their creator, George Brough, was a marketing genius. And Brough, who died aged nearly 80, at the beginning of 1970, was a brilliant PR man to the last; his riding cap and goggles were always stowed in his Jaguar E-Type, which was registered GB1001, lest he be asked to pose by one of his machines at any time, and he fizzed with enthusiasm for motorcycles even at the very end of his life.

Brough's father William made flat twin 'Brough' motorcycles, and young George took an early inheritance in order to build a factory in Nottingham for his 'Superior' machines. His philosophy was to build prototype bikes for himself, and then, after a period of testing and reviewing, and having made improvements, publicise his work and make replicas for discerning purchasers. Early Brough Superiors were powered by JAPs and later machines mainly by Matchless engines.

Like the Phils, Vincent and Irving (the founders of Vincent-HRD – ed), who followed in his wheel tracks, George Brough was dedicated to perfection, and his Brough Superiors were glamorous and glorious. They became known as the Rolls-Royce of motorcycles, and they were ridden even by royalty. Brough's rakish motorbikes were made to measure after a personal interview (if deemed suitable, the customer would then be measured up, and his preferences accommodated), and between 3,000 and 6,000 left the works (sadly, factory records were lost in War Two). They were hugely expensive but they were the fastest and very best motorcycles on the road.

An interesting story regarding Rolls-Royce. Peeved by the epithet 'Rolls-Royce of motorcycles', the Derby firm sent a deputation across to Nottingham to discuss this impertinence and request Brough desist from its encouragement, but upon entering Brough's Hadyn Road factory, they immediately came across an immaculate assembly area in which spotless machines were being hand-built by men in white overalls and white cotton gloves. It was concluded the sobriquet was well-deserved, and the matter was immediately dropped, the Royce men unaware they had inadvertently visited a special workshop where show machines were being prepared, and not the main assembly hall.

The Brough Superior SS100 was capable of 100mph. It also handled well and was directionally stable. An important attribute, as speed wobbles were a deadly and serious problem at the time for many manufacturers at much lesser velocities. Brough was a friend of Jaguar boss William Lyons, a Brough Superior owner, of course, and like Jaguars, the SS100 certainly had pace, and if not grace, it had elegant lines. Like Lyons, Brough had a stylist's magic touch.

Brough's advertisements were written in trademark period argot, the first ever example coinciding exactly with my birth in November 1920. He was aware of the publicity value in having nicknames for everything. His SS80 line of machines, for example, was inspired by his own bike which he called 'Old Bill'. In the 1920s he was a Gordon Bennett-type daredevil of a man, and in the '30s a man of sophistication and class. He was also the fastest man in the world on two wheels for a while. In the later 1930s the Vincent HRD had become the fastest motorcycle on the market, and, in his forties, as he continued with his philosophy of making what he wanted to own himself, he targeted luxury touring ahead of handling and speed. Brough moved away from V-twins to fours, and his later attempts to build the perfect motorcycle produced machines that were relatively smooth and quiet, but all his later designs flopped in the marketplace. He also made Brough Superior cars which he fitted with American engines because he liked their lazy power. He remained a perfectionist throughout, and would give up on an idea when clear it was not working, scrapping a year's work in a moment.

In wartime the Brough Superior factory prospered by taking on precision engineering contracts and motorcycle production ceased. I called there often, and we frequently discussed his post-war plans for reviving his four cylinder project. He did this, but after a time he gave up and largely withdrew from the motorcycling world. But in the last decade of his life, George Brough became immersed in the newly buoyant vintage motorcycle scene, and a regular at rallies and shows. The last time we spoke was a year before his death, after he had lapped Mallory Park on a sidecar outfit, very much against his doctor's orders!

THE FAR FIELD

I remember my teenage years fondly. Throughout our adolescence, my pal Algy and I pursued our competitive motorcycling hobby on the Far Field at the farm. I recall perfect summer holidays, riding every day until dark, usually through a haze of scorching heat, and then returning home filthy, and not a little bruised, with sunburned foreheads and forearms, to wolf a cold, congealed supper before retiring happy and exhausted to bed.

We purloined Pater's timekeeper's stopwatch (a gold-plated gift from Graham Walker, no less) to see who was the faster; we built up our specials (often lamentable lash-ups displaying merry chanciness in the details of their assembly), which we gave nicknames after war or comic book heroes; and we kept our supply of Mr Pratt's (Charles Pratt became Esso in 1935 – SO: Standard Oil Company you see!) and secret cans of dope under lock and key in the bottom shed, well away from the house (PMS2 was the favoured alcohol fuel of the period – a dirty, cloudy potent liquid, not unlike the home-made liquor we purchased surreptitiously from the incorrigible Dougie Rudd!).

Pater was pally with John Greenwood, Sunbeam's chief designer until 1931, and Ixion's curate, Percy Bischof, who was competitions manager at Marstons after Graham Walker left. He bought two or three machines from them, including an ex-Charles Dance sprinter, which he kept in the top barn. We were not supposed to touch it, of course, but when I knew there was no danger of him returning before nightfall, we would do so.

It was a 1921 side-valve works racer with 'Special' in gold script above the Sunbeam badge on its beautifully enamelled petrol tank. It went like a rocket but was exceedingly difficult to ride, due to its particularly wide handlebars, and complex multiple controls which bristled from its long bars and flat pre-saddle tank. From memory these comprised valve lifter, throttle lever, air lever, hand gear change, magneto advance-retard, clutch lever, and left-hand front brake lever. There may even have been more. The rear brake was the only foot control, although mechanical oiling was carried out using a pedal behind the rider's right boot. George Dance remained my hero, and his 'Go or Bust' motto was frequently inexpertly painted on the tanks of my specials alongside his branded knee grips.

The great Tazio Nuvolari gave up motorcycle racing in 1930 to pursue a successful career as a racing motorist, but it was always Algy's fervent if forlorn hope he would reverse his decision and race on two wheels once again. Algy would frequently place his hands in a bowl of warm water for five minutes before he rode, a violinist's technique he had read Nuvolari adopted to aid throttle control, and in honour of the Flying Mantuan, he would take to our track in Paris-Berlin goggles, a high crown helmet, and a pair of brown leather gauntlets that extended past his elbows. Completing this comical and elaborate raiment was, for some considerable time, a black sweater with the Norton logo reversed out in yellow letters on its front. Knitted for him by his Aunt Florence, it matched one he had seen in hand-tinted photographs of the great man. It was a fine thing, if a little large and baggy. Alas, it became holed from many crashes, and one day his sacred pullover snagged on a bramble just before he set off on his steed, causing it to unpick from the bottom, its speedy unravelment reaching his armpits before he became aware of its sorry plight.

I sometimes wore my Uncle Bof's old two-piece leather racing suit, but it was far too large, and to my horror and astonishment, seemed to be suffering from a process of rapid decomposition and disintegration. Finally, I worked it out. At pre-Great War TTs, they would keep the dust down by spraying the roads with acid from a watering cart. Evidently it worked, but the acid rotted the riders' clothing away. Brought out of long retirement, Uncle Bof's suit looked serviceable at first, but the jacket literally fell apart at the seams, and the trouser legs immediately began crumbling away from the bottom up.

Accidents were part and parcel of our sport, and I caught a packet of trouble and ended up sitting upon my ear on numerous occasions. A memorable instance was the time my brattish young cousin Freddie (motor-mouthed and a quite monumental pest) inadvertently moved the remains of Algy's Norton jumper, unaware I was using it as a braking marker. Inevitably, I crashed spectacularly, fetching up short and hard against the field's low boundary wall, before flying over it in a graceful parabola into Turner Hoof's turnip field. I took an awful honk on my shin, but my kneecap appears to have been the actual point of contact, and it was subsequently found to be cracked. That leg has never been the same since, another reason for my adoption of a stick at an early age.

But while I have taken one or two bad tosses in my time, suffering injuries necessitating the brutal attentions of Nurse Carter in Beedle Cottage Hospital, poor Algy fared much worse. Our racing activities were restricted by law to the farm fields and track, of course, but we would nonetheless venture out into the lanes occasionally, where our chancy manoeuvres would often draw much horn blowing and fist shaking. On one of these sorties we rounded a corner to find the road unexpectedly occupied by Sir Thomas Sly's handsome Rover, and, in deciding not to torpedo it amidships, Algy hurled his machine down a fortuitously sited but bumpy slip-road. So bumpy was it in fact, that by taking this drastic evasive action, he immediately found himself deposited upon his sit-upon, upon which he slid along in a shower of dust and small stones while his machine cartwheeled into the hedge. He rode with a drawing room cushion strapped to his posterior for some time after that.

On another occasion we took our best girls Myrtle and Cora out for the afternoon on our flapper brackets, and a whole series of disasters followed. After stopping for a most agreeable picnic, Algy decided to give Myrtle the benefit of some expert riding tuition, and then, with him having decided she was a natural, they set off together down the lane with his beloved frippet at the controls of his Triumph Trusty. Unfortunately, on the way back she somehow achieved what many decades later became known as a 'power-wheelie', rudely ejecting Algy from his perch on the carrier, backwards onto the road. I should not laugh. Then it was Cora's turn, and she fared no better. Having rapidly developed flying speed on my Chater Lea, she completely failed to make a turn, and hurtled headlong across a triangle of greensward on which a carelessly-tethered shire horse was munching contentedly. Having raised itself upon its hind legs, the poor startled creature naturally bolted, snapping its chain taut across the road just as Algy, following, heeled hard around the corner. He rode straight into it, of course, and was fetched clean off. The poor chap came a terrific box of tacks (he was lucky not to be killed), and the cushion had to be deployed once again.

Then there was the time we used baling wire to tie Algy's carrier to the pig poke in the Rose & Crown yard. The idea was to scrub a new tyre in quickly by spinning it up on the loose surface of the yard, but we only succeeded in pulling the front of the wooden building right off, which in turn caused Rosie the pig and her eight piglets to escape into the village. We spent half a day catching the piglets, and a day and a half rebuilding the shed. The only way we could capture Rosie was to lure her home with Alf's terrier, Patch, with whom she was strangely besotted.

It must have been 1937 when they came to our burgh. It was an unremarkable autumn day and we were, as ever, practising on the Far Field when Pater came into view carrying a can of dope from our secret supply. With him were two other men of unequal size, the larger one was wheeling the old Sunbeam from the top barn, and I recognised him immediately, although with a great deal of surprise, as George Dance. The other was a small, swarthy character pulling on a cigarette, and it was Algy who identified him first. Incredibly, it was none other than Italian racing star Tazio Nuvolari.

We were instructed to complete two laps each of the field, which we duly did, more or less matching our best times. Then Dance, who had been warming the Sunbeam in ritualistic fashion, climbed aboard his mount, tucked away the skirts of his overcoat, thumbed the throttle and set off in a furious rush. At once he was a cowboy on an unbroken bronco. Ruts and small potholes bumped the machine off the ground, and centrifugal force made it jump outwards, but, again and again, violent yanks on the big bars upon landing or in mid air, enabled him to maintain or change direction, and he somehow found time to afford lightning dabs at the carburettor's twin taps.

Next Nuvolari gestured for me to relinquish my machine, a dilapidated old crock built from a Duzmo and an Ace. Both donor machines had Le Vack heritage but it was a perfectly atrocious specimen, with all its components soldiering on well beyond their appointed time. The brakes were foul examples of their kind, the tyres and tubes were worn and weary, and there were terrible sounds of steely argument from inside the engine. It really was the most appalling and antiquated old bus.

Undeterred, Nuvolari wedged his cigarette into the corner of his mouth and climbed aboard. Then, having waddled to the designated start point he winked at my father and thumbed the throttle, whereupon, after a misfire salute, the tachometer needle flew to its maximum and glued itself against the stop, quivering like a guardsman saluting royalty. Bang! Out went the clutch lever and his borrowed steed shot forward like a bullet from a gun. Within seconds the Italian was in the higher of the poor old machine's two gears, and with his silk scarf streaming behind him he opened it out fully once more. The shot-up little bike moved about wildly underneath him as he flew over the rough stuff just as nimbly as any scrambling star, and tore around the bends like a top speedway ace. Nuvolari really stirred the old bicycle up good and proper, and after two extraordinary laps he crossed the finishing line with a huge bang. Upon his shutting off, it seemed, the connecting rod had emerged clean through the top of the crankcase, whereupon several other internal parts were violently ejected. The engine plunked to an immediate and inevitable conk, and my poor old horse shook spasmodically and died on the spot.

Pater checked his stopwatch and laughed. They had both torn lumps off our best times. In short, we had been thrashed on our own dunghill, and I had never seen my father so amused. You can put everything away can't you boys? he said, handing me the Sunbeam and tossing Algy the timepiece, and we watched in awe as three blue-black silhouettes retired to the house in the gathering dusk for a pre-dinner livener.

INTO THE FOLD

My journalistic career began when I was just 12 or 13. I started sending grass track and trials reports to those esteemed motorcycling periodicals, the blue 'un and the green 'un, and as soon as I passed my driving test, I began submitting material to *The Auto* and other illustrated motoring journals. Before long I was invited along to *The Auto*'s offices in High Holborn to meet a young man who would eventually become my boss, a workaholic, alcoholic expat Scot called Murdo Graves. At that time *The Auto* was a flourishing concern with people dashing about all over the place. I vividly remember the long-windowed, galleried newsroom full of famous names in shirts, ties, and sprung sleeve garters, typing in furious, violent spurts of inspiration. I also recall fondly the easy dexterity of the eye-shaded linotype operators; the skill and diligence of the elderly hand compositors; the studied group focus of the stooped stone hands; and the hushed bespectacled calm of the proofreading room. And every Wednesday the giant printing press in the basement shook the whole building. I adored the place.

Murdo showed me the library lined with sacred, canonical tomes; the cell-like scriptorium (a plain, windowless room set aside for writing in longhand); the busy motor workshops; and the bustling photographic department. He taught me the particular value of a good photograph, that people are generally more responsive to images than to text, any proper appreciation of which demands some modest level of education and a longer span of concentration. On numerous occasions during the summer holidays of 1937 and 1938 I visited the capital to assist Murdo in the compilation of a series of pocket explicators (*The Auto Buyer's Guides* – ed). We became firm friends.

They were heady days, during which I fell in love with the trade and craft of motor journalism by which I had begun to earn my bread, petrol and beer tokens. Fuelled in part, it is true, by foaming ale from the Ship Tavern nearby, I became drunk with the notion of chivalry; fascinated by the rhythms of writing; and of motor cars; and by the poetry of mechanised motion. I embraced Murdo's idealist belief that journalism should be as carefully shaped and well written as fiction. An impossible dream, of course, and one that Murdo himself would jettison long before he took over the editor's chair in the mid 1950s. Furthermore, it is an irrefutable fact that the primary objective of a commercial magazine is to gain revenue by gathering advertising. While not exactly outright propagandists, the motoring press was notoriously slow to criticise British makers, its senior figures aware they owed their livelihoods to the motor manufacturers who provided their test machines, and bought the most advertising space in their magazines. *The Auto*'s pre-war editor Harold Bartlett knew he had commercial horses to flog, and an obligation to please those upon whose bounty the magazine depended. When, in one of my early efforts, I described a Lanchester as a hair-shirt heap, he expunged my remarks, declaring *The Auto* must not impair its co-operative relationship with that esteemed manufacturer's advertising department by publishing such a criticism (I bit my lip during his tirade as, of course, Lanchester was owned by BSA at that time). It would not be the last time my copy was bowdlerised. Alas, I have turned out to be infinitely less than my dream of myself. No matter. I hope I have ground out a few worthy chronicles over the years.

What of Murdo? We had a close working relationship for many years, but sadly, like so very many more of my former colleagues, he is now just a series of extraordinary memories. Although a formidable piss-artist who seldom let any deadline get in the way of his appreciation of good food and drink, he was actually a man of some principle, who only rarely let the threat of withdrawn advertising interfere with his telling the truth. He was a fast driver, too. I once tried to keep up with Murdo on the Great North Road (both of us in E-Types), but gave up when we reached 140mph. And it was north he finally went. I think he lived in retirement in Dollar, or some such unlikely Scottish location, and ended his days driving a ferrously-challenged Lancia, which he prevented from rolling off his drive with a breeze block.

THREE WHEELS ON MY WAGON
First published *Motorcycle Review* – April 1975

Are you a photographer? And what do you rest your camera upon to prevent it from wobbling and blurring those precious frozen moments in time? A tripod, of course! As the name suggests, these handy devices have but three legs, so no matter how uneven the surface its trio of appendages will all contact Planet Earth, providing a stable platform while one's victims say 'cheese'.

Possibly for this very reason, a Mr Benz of Stuttgart, the fellow credited with inventing the motor car, gave his new contraption three wheels. Things changed as we raced into the next century. As technology advanced, most means of transport tended to have a quotient of legs divisible by two. Leaving unicycles aside for the present, why do nearly all our cars communicate with the ground in at least four places, when this imposes additional demands on its suspension, chassis and flatness of the road surface?

Simple questions, but unfortunately I am bereft of simple answers and will have to cast my mind back half a century to attempt an explanation. As I discovered all too often in my youth, bicycles have an innate tendency to fall over. Six year-old de Forte would often be pedalling happily along in ruddy health, held aloft by the mysterious forces of momentum and gyroscopes; next he was prostrate in a bloody-kneed heap, wailing for his devoted Mater to wipe away tears.

I doubt 'teenage tearaways' existed in the early decades of the Twentieth

Century, but cometh the day when the Transport Minister deemed one to be of sufficient maturity to ride a motorised bicycle, exactly the same thing happened except at greater velocity. Traffic densities then were such that a dose of gravel rash and bruised pride was the usual result, but pity those who encountered a Clapham Omnibus or other rampant object during their unintentionally horizontal progress.

Happily, pain and impromptu acrobatics could be avoided by attaching an outrigger wheel to our steeds, creating the device originally referred to as 'side carriages', but later known as outfits, chariots or combinations, which one confused with items of underwear at one's peril. While history books tell us that the idea was patented by the Graham Brothers of Enfield Town in 1903, it would be hard to accept that some other bright spark hadn't invented a similar contraption in the previous century.

At first glance the sidecar could be considered a backward step in many respects, as extra weight and aerodynamic drag reduces performance, and extra size reduces manoeuvrability. Indeed, we were effectively regressing to our childhood, as the customary way of learning to ride a bicycle involved outrigger stabilisers, which were removed when the basics of balance were acquired. I can still remember the sense of achievement I felt when I wavered a few yards across the yard at Bales that distant summer. The moment was spoiled rather when my crafty Father revealed that he had contrived to make my single stabiliser fold up, thereby leaving me bicycling without realising it, but overall I was happy to be duped!

At about the same time as that local drama, in the big world outside Bales sidecar outfits were becoming the norm rather than the exception. It seemed that around half the motorcycles in general use boasted a bit on the side, thereby allowing up to five people to travel in or on a vehicle usually limited to rider plus pillion. You will appreciate that a fully loaded sidecar appended to a bike that had only a few meagre horsepower did not provide rapidity nor comfort. All the engine's cacophony of mechanical noise was delivered directly into the passenger compartment, and in some cases the exhaust system outlet was mere inches away. A long trip to the seaside would therefore result in temporary deafness, perhaps with a corollary of hypothermia.

Allow me to illustrate the point... In 1939 when my rattly ohv MSS Velocette was often seen attached to a large plywood and cellophane monstrosity, two new university pals, Alfred 'Archie' Meades, Tom Winchley-Doubleton, and myself decided to take an expedition to the east coast, enticed by a week of glorious May sunshine. The plan was hatched over a game of cards in Reg Kay's shop-cum-shed. We had only popped in for some tobacco and ended up staying all afternoon, as was all too often the case.

Rather than go on three bikes and travel in convoy, we elected to use the Velo complete with wheeled outhouse, the theory being that we could take it in turns at the handlebars, thereby facilitating non-stop eastward progress and a high average speed.

In practice, our progress was anything but continuous, as Hall Green's finest threw tantrum after tantrum, enforcing regular stops to attend the clutch and ignition system. We had set forth at 6am, yet by midday were only just clearing Nottinghamshire and its sprawl of industrial monuments to King Coal. I had never hitherto been impressed by that DH Lawrence fellow, but a slow grind through the desolate landscape he described made me understand. Father met him once, not long before his last illness took hold. I gather that he affected such an extraordinary accent that conversation was difficult. The written word is an entirely different matter, though: from the perspective of age I would recommend *The Rainbow* to everyone and anyone.

Back en route to Boston and its celebrated Stump, which poor, ignorant Archie naively believed had some cricketing connection, the Velo began to behave itself, but we were in a complete funk. To steady our resolve, we stopped at a hostelry and took on board a few fortifying tinctures, only to be ambushed by a vicious wind springing up from the Fenland plain, sapping the 500cc single's energy. As it did to our trio of pilots, whose arm and shoulder muscles wilted in the effort to hold a straight course. While a properly set up outfit can be ridden hands off in neutral conditions, introduce a sudden gust from the nearside, perhaps with an unkind camber thrown in for luck, and one has a recipe for both cliches and disaster.

It would be all too easy to career off the carriageway and disappear into a roadside ditch. Thanks to our Dutch friends who reclaimed the land from the sea, some of these trenches are deep enough to swallow an entire double-decker, let alone a three-wheeled chariot ridden by three Shropshire lads. It would not be a surprise to learn that these drainage ditches became tombs to many unlucky wayfarers.

'Skegness is So Bracing', promotional posters used to say. For once, the copywriters were absolutely correct. We finally arrived in the evening after a fourteen hour slog, quite exhausted. A large fish supper wolfed down on the promenade repaired some of the damage (bought from a smart new fish and chip saloon called The Neptune, I recall – naturally we dared not sit down in the place), but any thoughts of a return journey were forgotten in the remaining hours before closing time at The Prawn and Pilchard, where we enthralled the locals with tales of our adventure.

Unfortunately, there was no room at the inn, so having discounted an attempt to ride home through the night, we were left with two alternatives – sleep on the beach or in the sidecar… At well over 6ft tall, Tom was immediately volunteered to spend the night with the crabs and jellyfish in the lee of a groyne, while Archie and myself plumped for the wheeled shed. I might mention at this point that this homemade creation was a two-storey contraption with a full-length roofrack, which we fancied could be pressed into service as an al fresco bed.

After a short alcoholic argument, I found myself settling down for the night inside the sidecar, cramped and crumpled but reasonably warm, thanks to a vestige of oily heat from the Velo's engine. Archie, meanwhile, had the advantage of being able to lie flat and stare at distant galaxies while listening to the restful beat of the sea. Indeed, he might have enjoyed a peaceful sleep up there, had it not poured with rain at 3am. This might have been hugely amusing, except that the sidecar leaked atrociously and I was equally soaked.

Still, a few hours later the cloud had cleared and the sun rose up out of the grey enormousness of the North Sea into a beautiful azure sky. Tom soon appeared, apparently having slept well once the seagulls had established he had no food about his person.

We wandered around the town until around ten then eyed up the Velo. A pint or three of oil had escaped between Bales and Skeggie, about half of it now unhelpfully lubricating the rear tyre. On reflection, it perhaps wasn't a good idea to wash it off by means of a run down a handy ramp into the sea! The Velo promptly stalled chuffed to a steamy stop, and it took all our combined might to avert a sequel to *Three Men in a Boat*.

A stiff wind whipped in off the sea, riffling the canvas wind breaks, but by this time the sun was up, the tide was coming in, and the shell-spotted beach had come alive. Jingling donkeys plied up and down it, children abandoned their buckets, spades and sandcastles and raced screaming for the advancing line of surf, dogs looked quizzically at the moving edge of the foaming water, and the rumbustious Punch and Judy man was in full spate.

After a detour to Gibraltar Point we headed back west, picking a less arduous route through the Midlands. It only took us ten hours, a magnificent average speed of 14mph! You may scoff, but the jaunt included two punctures, several carburettor fettles and a collision with an errant goose. It was a memorable journey that we three musketeers would often laugh about when we met.

Sadly, in 1941 Archie lost his life piloting a Spitfire (much easier to fly than a Velocette sidecar outfit, he assured us) and Tom expanded his business horizons and was so much in demand that we tended to see each other infrequently as the decades rolled by. Yet, after some gentle joshing about his current ranking in *The Times Rich List*, we would always lapse into nostalgia, the epic jaunt to Skegness being a particular favourite.

Chapter Three

Oh bountiful Gods of the air! Oh Science and Progress,
You great big wonderful world! Oh what have you done?

1940 – John Betjeman

WAR TWO

WE ALL KNEW THAT war was coming, but that did not stop people carrying on regardless, and I went up to Cambridge in September 1938 aware that I was highly unlikely to complete my education without massive interruption. Sure enough, 12 months later war was declared and I did not return for my second year, and indeed, although I did not perhaps fully realise it at the time, I took the decision there and then to chuck my studies for good. In truth, I abandoned the study of law with some relief, not because I was a bad student, but because I was an unenthusiastic one. My heart was not in it. I knew I wanted to be a motor journalist, and I had continued to submit my work and have it printed during my year at Trinity Hall.

It is remarkable I found the time. After the Munich Agreement debacle there was a feeling abroad one had to prepare for the inevitable and to do one's bit, and as well as attending lectures and partaking fully in the social life of a Cambridge scholar (led into bad ways much of the time by my irrepressible and exuberant room-mate Rowley Birkin!), I joined the Cambridge University Air Squadron, and later the University Officer Training Corps. The magnificently moustachioed Air Squadron chief Wing Commander CEW Lockyer was a veteran of War One and a quite marvellous man. He was utterly convinced another war was coming, and as well as teaching us to fly (mostly from Duxford in mustard-yellow Avro Tutors, but also from Abingdon in 160mph Hawker Harts), he forced us to think for ourselves. Lockyer encouraged formation flying, bad weather flying, low level flying, map reading and in-flight orienteering. In conquering the sky I felt elated, uplifted, in fact, and when I saw my first Spitfire I thought it the most beautiful machine I had ever seen, but family tradition would ultimately prove a bigger pull. I deeply regretted disappointing Lockyer, but I elected to join the army.

I signed up for the duration determined to face the goons. The war was predicted to be over in six months, and although I did not believe that for a single second, I was equally determined not to miss out. But my experience would largely be one of frustration, and it would be nearly five years before I saw action. As I have mentioned, I was already working for the motoring press, and because of this I was aware of Herbert Austin's Shadow Scheme and had signed the Official Secrets Act at least three times! Thus, with remarkable and unusual efficiency, within days of registering to join up I was summoned to a meeting at Whitehall and awarded a secret role in procurement and factory liaison which would keep me from direct engagement in the conflict until June 1944. This not only meant I could continue to live at home in Bales, but to facilitate my travelling around the country, I was issued with a warrant entitling me to unlimited travel on the country's railways, and given generous access to emergency fuel supplies.

That is not to say I was not sometimes on the receiving end of Jerry's deadly attentions. One evening in October 1940 I had taken Cora to see *Old Mother Riley Joins Up* at the Futurist in Beedle, and we were queueing to purchase our tickets in its mirrored art deco foyer when the town's air raid siren sounded its warning wail. I immediately bundled my beloved through the revolving door onto the pavement outside, and grabbing her hand, led her quickly around the corner into the grounds of the council offices, where I knew volunteers from Pater's Home Guard unit had been busy constructing shelters for several weeks. As we ran up Parliament Street and into Corporation Street the drone of a lone raider had become ring-tighteningly immediate, and as we threw ourselves down the steps of the nearest shelter, the terrifying shriek of an incoming bomb was so loud as to make me think our time was surely up. The deadly whistle was curtailed by a dreadful crump, and then a deafening bang, and shockwaves rocked the concrete floor beneath our entangled bodies. After a minute or so, I rolled onto my back to a heavenly view of sprinkled stars above. Are we dead? said Cora. No, I responded. There's no roof on the bloody thing.

The following month I was at Austin's Longbridge plant when it was hit in a daytime raid. The blighters were getting bold. Birmingham was heavily bombed, and BSA's Small Heath factory did not escape damage or death, but poor old Triumph fared much worse. From September 1940 to May 1941 the Luftwaffe concentrated a good deal of its bombing efforts on Coventry, and on 14 November 1940, 30,000 incendiary bombs, 500 tons of high explosives and 70 oil and land mines were dropped on the city in an 11 hour onslaught, much of it concentrated on the medieval city centre. Along with the nearby St Michael's Cathedral, Triumph's Priory Street premises were totally destroyed. The sky was lit up all over the Midlands that night. I was making my unsteady way home after irrigating my interior with industry friends by the smoky inglenook of the Merrie Lion in Fenny Compton, and all I could do was park up and watch. Of course, that was the raid that prompted Hamburg being blitzed in retaliation, reportedly sending Hitler into a carpet-chewing rage.

Bales escaped bomb damage almost entirely, and indeed, there was only one significant hit in Beedle (the screamer in 1940 having landed in the grounds of the town's cottage hospital – windows were blown in, causing panic and distress, but no injuries beyond the capabilities of Nurse Carter), but even rural villagers such as us became familiar with sights and sounds of war. The drone of the civil defence siren sounding across the fields, the pulsing harmonics of Heinkels and Dorniers droning overhead, the flashes and bangs of distant exploding bombs, and the heavy claps of Pater's Bofors battery, firing its seemingly impotent response.

Another whistling bomb fell fairly close to yours truly, this time landing in the very corner of the Far Field, where it uprooted an old ash tree and created a crater on the racing line thereafter known to all as the bomb-hole. It landed with a huge thump, then a tremor rattled the farmhouse windows in their frames, shook the plates on the kitchen dresser, and made the teacups swing; and while fine curtains of dust drifted down from cracks in the ceiling, a light sprinkle of dirt and shrapnel peppered the roof. But the biggest bomb to land in these parts exploded in the nave of St Jude's in Beedle (the Patron Saint of Lost Causes!) obliterating everything inside, and laying three of its four unbuttressed walls completely flat. The gimcrack vicarage next door suffered similarly catastrophic damage. The entire front wall and the stairs were blown away, exposing Rev Barnie Wilmott kneeling at prayer at his bedside, as if in a giant doll's house.

An urgent telephone call from our village bobby, PC Sam Thomas, had me shooting over there in my hack Morris Eight, in time to join a small crowd witnessing the poor priest's petrified descent by ladder, clad in nightshirt and sleeping cap, clutching a leather-bound Holy Bible and a threadbare articulated toy monkey. He stayed with us at the farm for quite some time after that, before moving away to live with his sister on the Isle of Wight. An immediate result of his arrival was a sudden swelling of the congregation at St Bede's, and the Rev Jeremiah McShane was in his tub-thumping element until it was decreed from on high that as the senior of our two men of the cloth, Rev Barnie should take over the lion's share of services. Sadly, his last task before leaving our burgh was to officiate at Grandpapa's funeral in March 1942.

It was later that year that, quite remarkably, a Junkers 88 was shot down by Pater's ack ack battery. Or at least he claimed it! Anyway, some of the aircrew managed to bail out, and for 24 hours a German oberfeldwebel was at large in the district. In the end he walked bold as brass into the Rose & Crown to give himself up, and mine hosts Joe and Connie Mallard stood him a pint of foaming ale before PC Thomas and I ran him in. Blackout regulations made driving hazardous at night, and poor old Algy broke his leg that year by tumbling headlong into a shell hole while whizzing along on a bicycle, attempting to beat the 10pm curfew at his training camp. It would have been funny if he hadn't been on my velocipede; an immaculate Standard Sunbeam complete with Joseph Lucas rifle clips which he had borrowed the previous weekend. Algy recovered fully and later served bravely in Greece and Italy.

By 1943 there was a sense the tide was turning, and I agitated more strongly to face the goons. Meanwhile, RAF types started frequenting the Rose & Crown, including a preternaturally tall fighter training instructor by the name of Raymond Baxter. Raymond and I became great pals and he invited me to spend time with him at his finishing school, ie: RAF Montford Bridge. On one occasion we left the drome in his CO's Hillman staff car with yours truly at the wheel and long, tall Raymond lounging in the rear. As we passed the guard block one of Raymondo's chums snapped smartly to attention and saluted the car with a quivering hand, and was shocked to receive a V sign through the open window in return. Later, having picked the Wingco up from a neighbouring base, we returned with the old man in the back, whereupon the same unfortunate fellow greeted our reappearance by running alongside proffering a V sign of his own. The poor chap spent a week in jankers for that. On another visit to Montford, I was given a tour of a Spitfire and through quite spawny circumstances I was invited to become reacquainted with my flying skills. A happy hour was spent in that most marvellous aircraft, ostensibly gently running in a new engine and testing some updated components, but in reality operating at the very limit of my abilities while being coached by Flight Lieutenant Baxter at my wingtip. It's interesting, although the Spitfire and Hurricane have become part of our national identity, Raymond told me they were in fact inferior to the Messerschmidt ME109. Beating Jerry in the air was a numbers game. That and the fact we had better pilots, many of them trained by Raymond over Shropshire meadows. Raymond went back to active service in 1944 and was mentioned in dispatches for his skill and bravery in raids on V2 rocket sites in Normandy. What he did after that is well known, of course. He died in 2006. Another contemporary gone, and I do miss him dearly.

Early in 1944 Pater was proud that he and his men were selected to be sent to London to relieve exhausted anti-aircraft gunners there, and also that I was finally granted my wish and given the opportunity to give Jerry a bloody nose. Having been attached to the Sherwood Rangers, I was posted to Torcross in Devon where I underwent special training as a tank commander in preparation for playing a part in the Normandy Landings (known to us then as Operation

Neptune). Then, on the early morning of 6 June that year, I set sail for Gold Beach on the Normandy coast in an M4A1 'Tommy Cooker' Sherman tank. Yes, dear reader, you did read that correctly. My 400bhp beast was one of a number that floated to France that day (and a good many more that never made it) having been sealed, fitted with a propellor, and buoyed by a canvas flotation screen. The resulting amphibious device was pitifully slow and tricky to steer when afloat, and that day the wind was brisker, and the sea more choppy than anything we had encountered in training. All this made swamping terrifyingly likely, so I was grateful we were only 50 yards or so from terra firma as the peculiar contraption pitched into the drink from the landing craft ramp, with me hanging on grimly atop it, shouting commands to my wonderful driver, a happy-go-lucky Scouser called Derek Harper. I was also thankful to be in the second wave, so to speak, as most of Jerry's big guns had been knocked out by the time we were called upon to make our short and perilous voyage.

The petrol-powered mastodon screamed and roared its way up the beach with old man Dek at the controls (he was at least 35), and Ronnie Prudames and young Chris Dibb loading and operating its 75mm gun and other armaments (Chris was just 19, around five years younger than Ronnie and myself). The Sherman had five forward speeds selected by a large gear stick, and conventional pedals controlled the clutch and accelerator. A pair of substantial 'steering' levers operated brakes which determined our direction by slowing the tank's tracks independently of each other. Quite frankly, I was utterly terrified all day long, but somehow we picked our way through the carnage on the sands and reached a safe haven where we were able to shed our cumbersome inflammable skirt before pressing on inland.

Sadly, by nightfall more than 1,000 of my fellows had perished including numerous Yeomanry chums, and we were to lose many more pals in the following weeks and months as we fought our way across France and Holland, and on through the Rhineland. Hundreds of Shermans were lost to superior German armour, land mines, and the dreaded Panzerschreks (bazooka-type devices), and I have always thought it something of a miracle our Ronson (a grim nickname for Sherman tanks, comparing them to cigarette lighters – ed) avoided the same fate, and that my crew and I all survived the war together. At this point I must make it plain that although I was ostensibly in charge of our Ford Detroit-built battle machine, it was undoubtedly the skill and efficiency of my crew that kept us alive most days during combat. They are all gone now, alas, and I am the last man (just about) standing. I am so glad I took pains to tell them all how much I admired them.

An interesting story concerning Field Marshal Montgomery and Chris Dibb. As we battled across the Rhineland a few weeks before the surrender, we were brewing up after clearing the goons out of a small village, when I was astonished by the arrival of a shiny black, English-registered Rolls-Royce Silver Wraith. Of course, it was Monty's staff car, a 1939 model formerly owned by a famous actress whose name is now beyond my recall. Monty had selected the Royce as his personal transport primarily for its morale-boosting effect on the troops, or so he said. A window cranked down revealing the great man with maps spread across the rear bench, and a panting pet terrier dog on his lap. Hello chaps, he said to our startled group, before calling Christopher across for a private chat. What was all that about? I asked the lad upon his return. Dunno, he said, slurping his cold tea. He just asked me my name, where I came from and what we'd been up to. Dog's breath pongs a bit. Months later Chris told me his parents in Leeds had received a delightful letter signed by Monty personally, telling them how well their son had been doing, and that they should be very proud of him. A kind and thoughtful gesture indeed.

We clattered onto Luneburg Heath a day or two after the surrender, and enjoyed a few days of wild and lurid celebrations, before I was called aside and ordered to sober up, make my way home and report back to Whitehall. No sooner there (having first called in at the farm), I was promoted and flown straight back to Germany, to take on a logistical role involving transportation and anticipated war reparations. The popular wartime wisdom was that brains went into the RAF, suicides became fish-heads (joined the navy – ed), and the dregs went into the army. While that was not generally my experience during hostilities, sadly during this final stage of my military career it was my misfortune to come across some of the dimmest and most abstruse chairborne clots imaginable! But never mind. Things could have been very much worse. With a small team at my command including young Chris, a pair of Bedford trucks deployed as mobile offices, and with a US despatch rider's Hardly-Dangerous and several Willys Jeeps at my everyday disposal, I spent the next 12 months criss-crossing the former Fatherland, and flying back and forth to Blighty while carrying out my new and varied duties. I would remain in uniform until mid 1946.

A return to Cambridge had always been my stated intention, but when on leave in August 1945 none other than Harold Bartlett OBE, Murdo Graves' predecessor as editor of *The Auto*, offered me a staff position on his wonderful periodical, or else a guarantee of regular work as a freelance contributor, whichever I preferred. A liquid lunch with Harold at The Ship secured the latter. Flushed with success, and a not illiberal quantity of Barclay's Golden Hop, I waved him off in his Alvis speed 25, and then, mind made up, jumped in my official Rover and made immediately for home. I aimed to see Cora before my return to Germany the next morning, and I travelled north hopefully, new nylons and packs of her favourite cigarettes in my briefcase, plotting a reconciliation and a new start. But I had no sooner scrunched to a stop outside the middle barn when Pater came bursting through the front door of the house, shouting urgently and waving his blackthorn aloft. The Japs have jacked it in old chap, he said breathlessly, gripping the Rover's door top for support. Get your glad-rags on boy, we're going to the Rose & Crown.

The heaving pub fell quiet at nine and we stood swaying in beery-breathed silence while the King addressed us, his remaining loyal subjects, via the pub wireless. Then came three right royal cheers followed by complete and utter bedlam. And it was while I was on my knees in the scrum helping Pater search for his recklessly tossed trilby that I looked up and saw her, and she saw me, and then I noticed the tall RAF bod on her arm. This is Tristan, Cora said as I stumbled to my feet with the crumpled Lock in my hands. We're getting married. A substantial rock flashed on her finger. Grayling, said the bod, offering me a soft, pink, ground-wallah's hand. Call me Tris. And with that they were swept off in a conga.

A prickly sensation occurred behind the eyes, the firmament becoming momentarily less solid than heretofore. Pleased be pleased for us Wilby, she called over her shoulder as they hopped, kicked and snaked their way to the lounge. What could one say? Actually, for a mahogany spitfire pilot (as Raymond called him!) Tris Grayling was not a bad egg. A long career as a schoolteacher and polytechnic lecturer awaited him, two kids, and a string of isolastic Morrises. He looked after Cora well enough. As for me, demob was serially delayed by bureaucratic forgetfulness, or maybe because I was doing a half-useful job. Whatever, Harold Bartlett kept his word and my freelance career as a motor noter resumed full-time upon my discharge from the British Army in June 1946.

VINTAGE BENTLEY

Cast your mind back if you are able to Christmas 1945 (of course, few now can!), or alternatively travel there in your pure imaginations. The first Christmas Day after War Two fell on a Tuesday, and the previous weekend far flung members of Clan de Forte began gathering at our northern pied-a-terre, a granite mock-gothic pile situated high up on a crag on the east coast of Bonny Scotland.

Actually, Castle Falco in Aberdeenshire was the family seat of my mother's family, the Montagu-Douglas-Scotts, which had been passed down a generation during the war, following the death of her father. Mater's bewitching elder sister Cordelia and her bearish husband Donald Lomax were the lucky recipients (or not, if we were to believe Uncle Donald's incessant bleatings about death taxes, the crippling cost of upkeep, and the blasted Labour Government), and they were our hosts there for the first time that first post-war Christmas.

Also making the trip north for the holidays were Mater's other sisters, my aunts Araminta and Philippa, who travelled from London to Durham by LNER sleeper before being driven up to Falco by Uncle Bof and Auntie Gladys in their newly recommissioned Riley Gamecock. Incidentally, or not, it had always been a constant source of amazement to all in the family, that the exquisitely beautiful Cordelia had contrived to produce so many children despite having a husband who was perpetually abroad on some unspecified business or other!

As if on cue, winter started on the Saturday afternoon with the mercury in the porch thermometer hovering around freezing point, and when we awoke on Sunday morning the crashing sea was invisible behind a frantic swirl of snowflakes dancing against an impenetrable grey curtain of fog, and on the ground a steadily thickening carpet of the chilly white stuff kept us firmly on the warm (relatively!) side of the glass. Scottish Sundays were in any case very different from the English version. Generally, one went to church then celebrated the day of rest by, well, by resting. After a hearty lunch and perhaps an afternoon constitutional along the windswept seashore, further strenuous effort was to be avoided on the Sabbath.

All shops were firmly closed in any event, not that there were any within half an hour's drive, and if one wished to imbibe alcohol one had to travel several miles to a hotel, or else stay at home. That night we did the latter, enjoying a peaceful evening sitting around a splendid log fire, listening to the gramophone and sipping from antique cut glass tumblers loaded with 1924 Strathisla. The Home Service weather forecast had promised more snow, but the grandchildren were tucked up in bed, and we were all safely ensconced in the shuttered drawing room, relaxed, bleary-eyed and cheeks a-glow.

All that is, except for Uncle John, mine hosts' eldest, who was driving up from the English Midlands, and was last heard of somewhere near Abington (the borders village, not to be confused with Abingdon, whence MGs came), where he had managed to find a working telephone. UJ, as he was known to all and sundry, even if he wasn't one's uncle, was roughly the same age as myself and undoubtedly a 'character'. A master steeplejack by trade rather than having become a 'businessman' like his father, he would spend most days up in the clouds, hanging off huge industrial chimneys and church spires. Steeplejacking had been a reserved occupation, and he had spent most of the war erecting transmitter masts and camouflaging factory smokestacks.

Nearer to God than thee, and rather him than me! Bods working in his line tended to have a short life expectancy. In an era not particularly concerned with Health & Safety, some Battle of Britain Spitfire pilots lasted longer. UJ was full of tales involving close encounters with the grim reaper. He told me the final test for apprentices taking their exams was to run around the top of a smoking 200ft factory chimney. The bricks up there were only nine inches across, and they had to run lest they be overcome by fumes. But my favourite story was the occasion where he lost his foothold near the top of a spire, and saved himself by grabbing the lightning conductor, which miraculously lowered him safely to earth as it peeled slowly off its fixings.

When he wasn't beetling about in his boss's faithful Morris Y Series van (he had pretty much unlimited access to the abominable 'pool', the lucky blighter!), John drove a selection of fast and impractical motors. On the death of our maternal grandfather in 1943, he had taken the reins of Beattie, the family 4½ litre Bentley. In actual fact, it had once been Pater's car, but he had sold it to Papa in '39 when he bought his Phantom III. I doubt my Scottish antecedent ever drove it.

After some recommissioning work to correct the effects of irregular use, John was often to be seen in it batting about Brummagem with his ladders and tools lashed on the back. Quite appropriate, really, as Ettore Bugatti famously damned WO's finest as the world's fastest lorries! Apposite, too, was the fact John habitually drove it far too fast while laying a trail of oil and petrol fumes. Of course, I was a little jealous, but it's a fact that at the time no-one really wanted vintage Bentleys. The glory of their pre-war Le Mans victories and Brooklands records had faded, and they were thought of as dinosaurs by most. As little as three hundred quid bagged a runner.

Back to Scotland, 23 December 1945. Sometime around midnight, we were playing 'the game' when there was a sudden commotion at the oak front door. It sounded like some madman was using a battering ram on it, accompanied by much shouting and uttering of oaths. Unsure whether this heralded an attack on our Sassenach enclave, I left the others in the warmth of the oak panelled drawing room, and gingerly crept along the shadowy stone corridor to the main hall. Brushing away an unseen web tickling my face, I paused briefly to consider whether I should don one of the rust-tinged suits of armour dotted along its sides before taking a deep breath and entering the huge, gloomy hall, where a family coat of arms was peeling on the wall, and dusty turkey pattern carpets were draped over baronial chests full of candelabrum and historic pewter tableware.

'Halloo, who's there?' I said, trying not to sound too English. The commotion died down, then there was silence for what seemed like minutes, during which a puff of icy air came in at the ancient door's edge and billowed the heavy velvet curtain. 'Is that you, Wilby?' said a voice. 'Open this blasted door, you idle rotter, I'm freezing out here!'

Yes, UJ had arrived. But minus his beloved car, we learned. To cut a long tale short, he had motored up to within about ten miles of Castle Falco when disaster struck. The Bentley had encountered a patch of frozen slush on a right-hander, lurched sideways and slithered off into a ditch. UJ had no alternative but to abandon the car and complete the journey on foot, fortified (no pun intended) only by a flask of Johnnie Walker's (not wanting to arrive smelling of whisky, presumably). It had taken him four hours.

Next day we set off bright and early to retrieve Beattie. Damage was limited to a buckled rear mudguard and some torn bodywork, so once we'd dug the fresh snow out of the cockpit (UJ always drove without a roof, of course) we only needed to tow her back onto the carriageway. Alas, that proved beyond our capabilities, so we had to enlist the help of one of the friendlier farmers in the vicinity and his little Ford Fergie. As we know Coventry's finest was an incredibly versatile vehicle (still is) and it had no problem dragging two tons of beached Bentley out of a snow-filled ditch.

Possibly unwisely, knowing the hair-raising way UJ drove, I agreed to ride shotgun back to the coast. Those Bentleys can be tricky customers at the best of times, and even the main roads were slippery, so you can imagine how much effort it took to average 40mph in those conditions, in a lorry! Aside from getting used to a central throttle pedal, Pater always said it takes at least 1,000 miles to master the techniques necessary to drive one properly at speed. He had been taught by a maestro, of course, on visits to Captain Birkin's lair in Welwyn Garden. Someone who could cope with a 120mph broadside onto the grass at the end of Mulsanne would have little trouble with a flurry of Highland snow!

Incidentally, it's a common misapprehension, so may I point out that Tim Birkin was entirely unrelated to my erstwhile university room-mate Rowley, whose family was in rubber. In John's case, it was hardly driving as art (we seemed to be facing at least 90 degrees in the wrong direction most of the time!), but after a little more than a quarter of an hour of deafening full-bore plunges, lurid corner work involving frantic heavy arm exercise, and a good number of crunchy downshifts we were home, if not dry, at Falco, overlooking the sea.

Not that the North Sea could be glimpsed more than occasionally through the swirling sleet. The dashed golf course was utterly unplayable, as you might imagine, so Pater and I occupied our time in the workshop, helping John attend to some long-overdue maintenance chores on Beattie. One might say that working on a Bentley four-and-a-half, with its 16 valves and gear-driven cams, is never a chore, but as has been admitted many times, WdF is not a natural mechanic. While fettling the big four that Christmas Eve afternoon I had a sweaty flashback imagining Pater looming over a nine-year-old Wilby, his face going crimson with rage when I accidentally dropped the top contact of a Lodge sparking plug down the threaded orifice one day while working on Beattie in the top barn. 'We'll have to take the head off now,' he said matter-of-factly, while patting his waistcoat pocket in search of his heart pills. Thankfully, he was always very forgiving in such circumstances, and would never beat me, although I believe he once came close when I inadvertently bridged the Phantom II's battery contacts with a Whitworth spanner, setting fire to part of the wiring loom.

While we three worked together that afternoon, it occurred to me that Pater was always rather fond of John, and that in many ways, not least in appearance, John and I were remarkably alike. As the snow swirled all around outside, we set the tappets and ignition timing, fitted fresh sparkers, then removed the massive brake drums to check the linings. They were probably good for another 500 miles, although perhaps not if the roads cleared in January and UJ went Harry Flatters down the other side of Shap, as he was wont. 'The old girl will do a ton-twenty easy. Reckon she'd do 140-per if I had the gears,' he said.

He was probably right. We all chaffed about it at the time, but fate caught up with John a few years later. Heading home from a piscatorial weekend in the Peaks in May 1949, he lost control and Beattie punched a Bentley-sized hole in a dry stone wall on a downhill stretch of A6 north of Buxton. Beattie stayed upright at first, but then hit a saffron-spotted boulder in the sloping field beyond, barrel-rolled, and finally tumbled to a battered, steaming stop, upside-down in a brook 50 yards from the road. UJ was found nearby. He had been thrown clear, but had suffered a brutal and instantly fatal head injury.

The driver of a commercial slogging northwards up the steep slope witnessed the accident in his rear view mirror. At the inquest he said 'seconds before, the big green monster of a thing bristling with ladders, and driven by a grinning maniac', had passed him on the opposite carriageway shifting at a colossal rate, maybe even 100mph. The coroner blamed the accident on 'inappropriate speed', a masterful understatement which I'm sure would have made John hoot with laughter.

With the family's permission I bought the wreck from the scrapper in Matlock, complete with ladders and a trunk full of rotting fish, and trailered it back to the farm. Now it was my turn to become a Bentley Boy.

BEATTIE

The de Forte family Blower Bentley was an early 4½ litre car made in 1927, but with an Amherst Villiers supercharger obtained directly by Pater, and retrospectively fitted by a former Bentley factory mechanic following the firm's demise in 1931. The 4½ litre overhead-camshaft, four-valve-per-cylinder engine had a cast iron block and head. Only 720 4½ litre Bentleys were made altogether, of which 55 were blowers. Pater's 'unofficial' car made 56, and many more have been created since.

Following UJ's fatal smash in 1949, parts were still relatively easy to obtain, and mechanics familiar with them still alive. With help of an ex Tim Birkin man moonlighting at weekends, and other visiting tradesmen and specialists, I rebuilt Beattie over six months or so with an improved close-ratio speedman's gearbox (with Laycock overdrive) and hydraulic brakes, and I had the throttle pedal converted to the right. Crimes against automotive originality? Yes, I hold my hands up, but so is the car's very existence.

The chassis was straightened (essentially two great cross-braced steel girders), and the Van den Plas four-seater bodywork (14.5ft long!) was repaired and repainted in its original British Racing Green. All of the instrumentation is correct for the period, but some of it is not original to the car. Replacement 20 inch wheels, Marchal headlamps, and goodness knows what else were all surprisingly simple to track down (as with much else, it's not what you know, et cetera…), and the car was back on the road in spring 1950.

Following my motorcycle accident in 2011, I realised I was unlikely to drive Beattie again. Reluctantly, painfully, I decided to sell her, and the car is now owned by a long-time admirer, the Florida-based American collector Waverley Scrunge Junior. I doubt he will ever take it out of storage, let alone drive it.

DRIVING BEATTIE

After entering from the passenger side of the car, and having settled into the surprisingly comfortable and supportive pleated driver's seat, one is obliged to go through an arcane starting ritual too tedious to repeat here. But once the black starter button has been pressed and the big four bellows into life, things get very interesting indeed. Getting under way is a matter of selecting low ratio (a gentle crunch is sometimes unavoidable), clutching up carefully, and releasing the external handbrake. Nice footwork should then bring about a rapid departure.

The engine is low revving (redlining at 3,500rpm) but astonishingly free and responsive, and to the accompaniment of a thrilling aircraft-like blare from the exhaust, 60mph is commonly seen in second gear. Then, as speed mounts in third and fourth the long bonnet lifts slightly as the road rushes towards the radiator in the most pleasing way possible. Meanwhile, the mudguards vibrate spectacularly on their stays, and the wheels can be seen visibly rising and falling over the road surface. Tally ho! For once the term 'loud pedal' is fully appropriate, and as speeds increase towards the magic ton, the exhaust's deafening soundtrack becomes a magnificent, full-blooded roar (no other word for it), blending with the dull whine of the gears amidships (also felt as a buzz through the backside!), the mad battering of the wind on one's noggin, and a contrasting banshee shriek from the supercharger up ahead.

Vision is generally first-rate and the worm and wheel steering at high speeds is light, if just a little vague. Braking is good enough too, and double-clutched down-changes bring forth delightful crackles from the superb vocal instrument at the rear (although clash-free cog-shifting can be a challenge). Having said all this, one must never forget Beattie is a powerful animal who will take control if you let her. She can be a bit twitchy at extreme speeds, and it pays to be positive with her or she can get stressed. At all times, but when close to her three figure maxima in particular, you have to let her know who's boss.

But I'm no longer at my best in such a sporting car and capable of being her master. The crude, brutish, pulse quickening joy of driving cars like Beattie is in the past for me now. I am still sensitive to the feel of machinery, I believe, but alas I am not capable of the he-man antics I once was, and my reactions are no longer of the first order. And besides, there are far too many nitwits on the road.

BENTLEY PEOPLE
Walter Owen Bentley, known as WO, was a brilliant engineer, but a quite hopeless businessman. Born in Hampstead, London in 1888, he was the youngest of nine children. One must presume that after WO came into the world, his parents worked out what must have been happening!

A GNR apprentice, he raced motorcycles by fine manufacturers including Rex and Indian, and then he set up in business adapting French DFP cars into racers. During War One he designed rotary aero engines for Sopwith Camel fighters, and soon after it he founded Bentley Motors in partnership with his brother, HM (Horace Milner). His famous race cars culminating with the Speed Six won prestigious races around the world, but his firm was almost perpetually in debt, and had to be baled out by well-to-do backers including South African diamond mine heir Woolf Barnato.

Barnato, whose father had died in mysterious circumstances when he was a boy, inherited a fortune at a young age, and more came his way in adulthood via law suits. He excelled at motor and motorboat racing, tennis, shooting, and boxing, and he played first class cricket for Surrey. As well as stoking massive piles of cash into Bentley's operations over a number of years, Barnato bought up shares and effectively took over the firm, so it was at least partly his decision to pull the plug on Bentley Motors in the summer of 1931, and he may have been instrumental behind the scenes in the company's surprise acquisition by Rolls-Royce at the end of that year. After the take-over, production of all Bentley models ceased, and WO found himself obliged to work for R-R in a consultative capacity. Thereafter for a great many years, all Bentleys were Royces by another name.

But in 1935 WO was set free, and he went to Lagonda as an employee where he designed a new double-overhead-camshaft V12. In 1947 Aston Martin owner David Brown bought Lagonda, and three years later he put a WO designed 2.6 litre six into his DB2 sports car.

Tim Birkin was a fearless *'Boy's Own'*-type racing driver from a wealthy and titled background in Nottingham. Christened Henry, he was called Tim as a boy after the children's comic character Tiger Tim and the sobriquet stuck for the rest of his life. His younger brother Archie was killed somewhat unfortunately while practising for the 1927 Isle of Man TT. He hit a fish van, which brought about a change in regulations whereby the circuit roads were closed to the public during testing (extraordinary that they weren't already). Birkin's Bend exists on the TT course to this day.

In the later 1920s WO Bentley believed in making ever bigger, more multicylindered engines for racing, particularly at Le Mans, which was an extreme test of endurance as well as speed, whereas Birkin came to favour the idea of fitting a supercharger to Bentley's older, smaller 4½ litre four, following the pioneering lead of adventurous Italian manufacturers at the time. WO refused to experiment with a 'blower', fearing reliability problems, so in 1929 Birkin built his own supercharged racer in his workshops in Welwyn Garden City with an Amherst Villiers supercharger driven directly from the crankshaft. Red, not green, the car was a streamlined job rather in the fashion of express locomotives of the period.

After building four more supercharged racers, funded in part by foulmouthed Buckinghamshire millionairess Dorothy Paget, an extraordinarily grotesque and unpleasant creature who, it must be said, was about as comely as the back of a bus, Birkin eventually persuaded WO to make 50 road-going Blowers for homologation purposes so he could compete in the Le Mans 24 hour race in 1930. Bentley struggled to find customers for these cars, and some had to be bodied as saloons, but 55 Blower Bentleys were recordedly put together, of which 45 are claimed to survive.

Birkin made it to the grid at Le Mans, and he went down in motor racing folklore for unnerving German ace Rudolf Caracciola by passing him at 125mph on the grass at the end of the Mulsanne Straight while throwing a tyre tread. Birkin was eventually forced to retire (WO had been right to worry about longevity), but the winners that year were fellow Bentley Boys Woolf Barnato and Glen Kidston in a bigger-engined Bentley Speed Six. Later that year, Birkin finished second in the French GP beating a veritable horde of Bugattis, prompting team principal Ettore's famous comment: 'Le camion plus vite du monde!'

Engineer Amherst Villiers was born in 1900 and it was his supercharger that Tim Birkin's men bolted onto the front of their boss's red race car in 1929, and that was subsequently fitted to factory Blower Bentleys, increasing the 4½'s power output to 175bhp (race cars made 240bhp). Villiers designed Malcolm Campbell's Blue Bird land speed record car in 1927, and after War Two he emigrated to the USA to work on the space programme, before making his name all over again as a portrait artist.

Tim Birkin died of Malaria in 1933, or possibly popped his clogs as a result of a septic burn (opinions differ), Woolf Barnato died of cancer in 1948, and Dorothy Paget (who smoked 100 gaspers a day) died of a heart attack in 1960. WO Bentley passed away in humble circumstances in 1971 (in the 1960s the great and good among the esteemed aficionados of the Bentley Drivers' Club saw fit to present him with an Issigonis Mini to bat about in!). Amherst Villiers, friend of Bond author Ian Fleming, outlived them all, croaking in 1991.

Alas, aside from WO (a charming man) I didn't meet any of them (I came across Dorothy Paget at Rolls-Royce in Crewe on one occasion, but hid under the boardroom table with John Blatchley until she had passed by!), but I did go to Birkin's workshop with Pater as a boy where I recall he treated me to an 'Electric Model Brooklands', a miniature racetrack game that was a forerunner of Freddie Francis' Scalextric. Thinking about it now, I've never seen another. Wish I still had it. I no doubt gave it to Algy.

BENTLEY MARK VI
(First published *Classic Auto* – June 2008)
The most remarkable thing about the Bentley Mark VI was that it was the first Rolls-Royce motor car to be sold with bodywork designed by the firm and fitted at the factory. It was 1946 and the country was on its uppers, having just bankrupted itself beating Jerry for the second time. Steel was strictly rationed, and being seen to be rolling in lolly in times of austerity was not at all the done thing. So Britain's most highly esteemed motor manufacturer took a pragmatic approach when it began producing civilian vehicles once again, after several years dedicating itself to the design and manufacture of the world's finest aero engines.

The famous firm made their new conveyance smaller than those of pre-war design and marketed it as a Bentley, previously a manufacturer of sporting cars driven by raffish types, and a marque that Rolls-Royce had acquired in machiavellian circumstances back in 1931. Previously, the firm's well-heeled customers would take a motorised chassis frame to a specialist coach-builder and have a bespoke body made to meet their requirements. This remained an option for the determinedly individualistic, but the factory-made Bentley was so beautiful and right of line, that most of these splendid post war motor cars were sold with bodies that became known as 'standard steel'.

Despite the efforts of the Attlee government to tax luxury motor cars out of existence, the Mark VI sold well. And although post-war steel was poor and especially prone to infestation by the dreaded tin worm, the car's chassis and mechanicals were sound and robust, and a great many survive to this day. More than a few earn their keep in the wedding trade, and there is no call for anyone to be sniffy about this. Classic cars need regular exercise to give of their best, and summer Saturdays on marriage duty provide the perfect weekly run-out.

I owned a Mark VI for many years, of course, and was pleased to come across a fine black and silver 1950 example at a splicing in the village last month. Quintessentially British in appearance, the car is elegantly proportioned and perfectly balanced. Although very much 1940s new look in its day, its appeal now is largely due to its unmistakeable link with classical pre-war Derby Bentley designs. But late 1930s Bentleys were complex, temperamental machines that could not be looked after by a village mechanic. Dodges and other Americans had been the world's toughest cars before War Two and Rolls-Royce learned a lesson. Consequently the Bentley Mark VI was a strong, simple machine capable of covering high mileages without giving trouble.

The nuptials got under way in St Bede's with a hearty rendition of *Onward Christian Soldiers* and with the driver's kind permission I settled behind the large three-spoked steering wheel and reacquainted myself with the Mark VI's delightful interior which is altogether reminiscent of a rather agreeable sitting room. In retrospect, it can be seen the car marked the beginning of an intelligent shift in design priorities, moving away from the horse and cart model towards greater allocation of space devoted to the passenger compartment. An uncomplicated instrument board and switchbox sits in the middle of the walnut dashboard and hand throttle, ride control and start-run controls mounted around the steering wheel boss, provide what is now a pleasing olde-worlde touch. As does the quick action window lever on the driver's door – perfect for hand signals, not that anyone understands them any more! Up ahead of the long centrally-hinged bonnet, the famous Flying B stands atop a magnificent chromed radiator, behind which lies an in-line six cylinder 4257cc engine of superlative smoothness.

Offered a quick spin round the block, I didn't need asking twice. The torquey engine oozed smooth and creamy power from the off, and the right hand gear lever sliced fore and aft, as if through butter, as I put it through its paces on the back lanes. Fine handling even by today's standards, this Bentley allows all types of corners to be taken with aplomb, and the steering is light and precise. I am afraid when I reached the old main road I couldn't resist a quick blast along Conrod, so instead of doubling back I turned left at the fingerposts and hit the loud pedal. Except that I have to say a well maintained Mark VI like this one is remarkably silent at 80mph (putting many moderns to shame), and the fluttering ribbons were the quite the loudest sound! Upon my return, as the spire of St Bede the Venerable hoved into view and pealing bells signalled I was just in the nick of time, it occurred to me a Mark VI is very possibly the most comfortable car of all time. Altogether the experience was a sheer delight that brought back memories in the most satisfactory manner. I had forgotten what a splendid motor car it is!

I first came across the Mark VI on a visit to Clan Foundry in Belper in the middle part of War Two when, together with other journalists and military procurement bods, I was invited to R-R to test the new Cromwell Tank. Needless to say, I rushed down there like a stoat.

The Clan Foundry sits south of the town twixt the River Derwent and the A6 Derby Road. At the outbreak of hostilities it was a derelict, rat infested, ramshackle collection of buildings, formerly used to turn out grates and manhole covers. R-R transformed it. Montague Tombs of *The Autocar* described Clan as the 'Inner temple' of Rolls-Royce automobile development, 'where Rolls-Royce and Bentley engineers, designers, testers and research workers revolve continuously in their special orbits.' Indeed Chassis Division chief Roy Rumpty Robotham had assembled a brilliant experimental department, housing them in the squash court at the bottom of his garden before transferring to Clan. Chassis development had officially ceased, but in 1943, in an ancient boiler shed at the back of the Clan works, I was privileged to be shown a prototype motor car.

Young John Blatchley, who would go on to become the firm's chief stylist, had been working on the car in secret and he checked we were alone before removing its grimy dust cover with a flourish. It was clearly a test mule and a bit rough around the edges, but it was still a handsome machine and definitely a Bentley. 'We'll get rid of these,' gestured Blatchley waving a hand over the external door hinges on R-R's first complete car, 'And I've got big ideas for the interior.' After becoming chief designer at London coachbuilders Gurney Nutting at an impossibly young age, Blatchley joined R-R at the start of the war and was miffed to be put to work in the aero engine division, where he spent most of his time designing engine cowlings. Not much older than me, he confided that he '…hated everything to do with working on aeroplanes'. But aero engines had become the firm's main business even before the war and Rumpty's motor car styling department spent much time repairing engines from pranged aircraft. Then came the contract to develop the Cromwell tank as a replacement for the unpopular Nuffield-built Crusader.

The sound of Meteor engines firing up in the yard and the clatter of tank tracks on concrete signalled the beginning of test drives and we hurriedly covered the car and left the boiler room only to see both test Cromwells departing through the factory gates behind a bobby on a bicycle. Anxious not to miss out on the fun, I sprinted to a Crusader I spied earlier, languishing in a corner of the yard. Crusaders were unreliable, under armed and prone to catching fire. Furthermore, in early versions gunners could decapitate their drivers by swinging the turret through 360 degrees. Not a good set of attributes for a combat tank! But the Crusader in the corner was special and I knew it. Modified and fitted with a Merlin engine from a Spitfire, it ran on aviation fuel and had been timed at over 50mph in trials at Aldershot in 1941. Yes, of course I could drive it I had assured Blatchley and Wilf 'Hoppy' Hardman, my CO's batman who elected to ride in the turret.

But with the hatch closed it was as black as your hat and I could barely see through the block glass screen. Instruments glimmered in the gloom. The steel sweated. I sweated. And behind me the oil-scented breath of the Merlin was hot on the back of my neck. With the accompanying sound of a cement mixer being cleaned out with half bricks, I selected a gear and then, having a brain geared to the funny side of life, I was suddenly filled with an urgent desire to mash the (very) loud pedal. Wham! An almighty kick in the pants accompanied a shriek like ripped steel from the engine of the beast and I caught glimpses of men running and snatches of tiny, hysterical voices as the tracks pawed the air and the 20 ton beast swayed like a cobra in a 30 degree arc.

Still out of control as the monster crashed down onto the level and shot forwards, I missed the boiler hut by a miracle of God and smashed through the perimeter fence at the back of the works. Then, after speeding across the waste ground behind the Clan at around 40 mph, we plunged down a precipitous drop into the Derwent. Fortunately, the river is stony and shallow at that point and I kept it gunned. Crossing in great gouts of steam, we surmounted a steep hill on the opposite bank as if it were a pimple before disappearing into woodland, flattening a path for ourselves through thick undergrowth. Returning after half an hour of such hooliganism, a maniacal grin had fixed itself on the de Forte phizzog and I had the tingles for several hours afterwards. The official tests had finished and Hoppy and I joined the imbibers in the New Inn on Derby Road. I didn't drive a Cromwell until two years later in the Rhineland.

Rolls-Royce made the best aero engines throughout virtually the whole 20th century. An incredible achievement. The Cromwell tank was finished in time to take part in Operation Overlord in Normandy in 1944. And Bentley Mark VI production began in late 1946, the finished car remaining much as I had seen it, minus the external door hinges. It was for a time, quite probably the best motor car in the world and it was the first time R-R had truly deserved the accolade since the Edwardian Silver Ghost.

I bought a 1950 Mark VI in 1955 and kept it for nearly 30 years. It served me very well, and I regretted selling it for a considerable time afterwards.

Chapter Four

Gabled lodges, tile-hung churches, catch the lights of our Lagonda
As we drive to Penny's party, lemon curd and Christmas cake.
Rich the makes of motor whirring,
Past the pine-plantation purring
Come up, Hupmobile, Delage!
Short the way your chauffeurs travel,
Crunching over private gravel
Each from out his warm garage.

Indoor Games near Newbury – John Betjeman*

TIME OF CHANGE

IN BRITAIN THE POST-WAR 1940s and early 1950s was a time of change, as creeping socialism challenged the values and attitudes of the upper and lower classes alike. The old world order felt under threat, and nobody escaped feeling frightened and bewildered, not least landed families such as my own, and our beleaguered friends among the gentry. My parents' generation alternatively fought the tyrannical forces of change, or else resigned themselves to them, but for this particular de Forte it was a period when, above all else, there was a happy sense of a life coming to fruition, and being lived to the full.

There was a gradual fading into the past of the wartime spirit, and a growing resentment towards rationing and austerity (and the abominable pool!). Do you realise that in 1950 almost half the houses in Britain lacked an indoor bathroom? But five years later one household in four possessed a television, and vacuum cleaners, telephones and twin-tub washing machines proliferated among the masses. Furthermore, it was an age of education and improvement, of talks on the wireless, of good music, and of Penguin Specials, and a feeling persisted that almost all things made in Britain could still be considered a source of pride, not least in the field of transportation.

Diesel trains were coming, but a new express locomotive entering a big city terminus still had soot and sparks flaring from its smokestack, and the screech of its brakes and the hot, steamy breath of its boilers remained part of the powerful symphonic soundtrack of the time. The De Havilland Comet, the world's first jet liner, was developed at Hatfield, Herts. It first flew in July 1949, and within ten years it was flying regularly across the Atlantic (admittedly following a redesign after two catastrophic crashes in 1954). The Fairey Delta 2 became the first plane to break the 1,000mph barrier, taking the world air speed

* 'Indoor Games near Newbury' from *Collected Poems*, by John Betjeman © 1955, 1958, 1962, 1964, 1968, 1970, 1979, 1981, 1982, 2001. Reproduced by permission of John Murray, an imprint of Hodder and Stoughton Ltd.

record to 1132mph in 1956, and thanks to my pal Raymond, I was thrilled to be aboard Christopher Cockerell's hovercraft when it first crossed the channel in 1959, by which time the M1 was open to traffic, parking meters were blighting London's streets, and police radar traps were being deployed on our rural roads.

Fully automatic transmissions arrived on the scene in the 1950s, bringing problems to motorists both here and in the USA. Oldsmobiles and Cadillacs had had them before the Yanks entered War Two, of course (they were never fans of shifting), and clutches and manual gearboxes were largely eliminated from American motoring after the war. But a powerful V8 and exiguous braking is not at all a good combination, and here in Europe our smaller, more frugal engines made insufficient power to absorb the losses. Column shift, however, was an American-inspired craze of which I did approve. Unitary construction was also on the increase, and the future would see long production runs with ever bigger outputs, and fewer fundamental changes.

ONE OF BRITAIN'S FINE IDEAS

As the British Army battled its way across northern Germany during the death throes of War Two, its Transport Corps organised the rounding up and confiscation of thousands of vehicles abandoned by the retreating sausage-eaters, and, following the German surrender, when I was attached to the Corps in an official capacity, I was able to hurtle around in bullet-proof Mercedes staff cars, big bore BMW sidecar combinations, and various kubelwagens and flugabwehrkanonenpanzers. I even drove Panzer and Tiger tanks. But the vehicle that impressed me most was the humble US Army Jeep, made by Willys Overland Inc, a number of which had temporarily fallen into the hands of the goons. In fact I liked them so much I am ashamed to say I stole one.

After the war ended, the dazed and bewildered human flotsam of a continent ravaged by five years of conflict began making its way home. I was granted leave and, amid the chaos and confusion, together with an RAF Sergeant named Passmore, and wearing my army greatcoat stained with the filth of many ditches, and with unkempt hair, unshaven chins and mud-encrusted boots, we drove the pilfered Jeep nonstop across Europe, and blagged our way onto a boat back to Blighty.

Yes, dear readers, I brought it home to Shropshire, and even before I had had time for a recuperative noggin in the Rose & Crown, Pater had put the little Willys to work on the farm (incidentally, the correct pronunciation is 'Willis'). He found it a most useful device. A miniature truck capable of 60mph, it could climb a 40 degree slope and manage 50 degrees of sideways tilt without tipping over. Furthermore, it had an infeasibly tight turning circle and could pull 25 tons. The Jeep was not an iconic symbol of the American war effort without good reason.

When I flew back to my command in Germany I was relieved to find the Jeep had not been missed (I should have stolen Himmler's staff car – it would have been worth millions today!) and it remained in service on the farm for many years, despite being joined by a new Land Rover in 1948, of which more anon.

Returning to journalistic duties after being demobbed in mid '46, I called in on the Wilks brothers at Rover's former aircraft factory, now the firm's new Meteor Works on Lode Lane, Solihull (the Helen Street factory in Stoke Heath, Coventry having taken a severe pasting from the Luftwaffe on more than one occasion). I found the luxury car maker more than slightly moribund. Sheets of aircraft aluminium and tins of paint left over from wartime contracts lay around and car production was at barely a trickle. Although Rover was desperate to get back to producing quality motor cars for Britain's bank managers and headmasters, the Board of Trade wanted small utilitarian runabouts and the famous old firm just couldn't get the steel to build its silky smooth sixes.

Over libation in Maurice's office, the younger Wilks bemoaned the exorbitant level of purchase tax applied to new cars (he would have been apoplectic if he'd known it was to double to 66% the following year!) and told me their designs for small cars were not working out well. Conversation then turned to farming and it turned out Maurice too had a Jeep, which he kept on his farm in Anglesey. 'Why not build a British version of it for farmers?' I suggested. 'And it would sell well in uncivilised parts of the Empire too.' More scotch was poured and I saw the great designer's eyes twinkle as he warmed to the idea.

The Land Rover was launched at the Amsterdam Motor Show in April 1948. Something twixt a truck and a tractor, it was rather similar to a Jeep but with a more agricultural bent. Built on a strong steel chassis, the new four-wheel-drive Rover featured power take off points front and rear, and had undergone extensive trials on working farms including ploughing fields as well as winching, towing and traversing difficult terrain. Out of necessity and expedience its body panels were built from Birmabright aluminium and painted aircraft cockpit green. Basic in the extreme, even the roof and door tops were extras.

Shorter than a Jeep, it was also wider, heavier and faster and shared no common components with the Ohio built vehicle that inspired it, although apparently an earlier prototype had been made on a Jeep chassis with a central steering wheel. This 'centre-steer' device had an engine and gearbox from a pre war Rover saloon model and the driver had sat aside the gearbox tractor-style.

This miniature short wheelbase truck was intended to be manufactured for two or three years to generate cash for building quality saloon cars, but the Land Rover was to remain in production in various forms for more than 60 years.

Series I Land Rovers, as they have subsequently become known, were built until 1958. Purely functional, they have perfect proportions and have a fabulous 'look'. Tough, simple and practical, 218,000 were built and sold around the world. A huge number survive. Driving one is an experience. The suspension is designed for the longevity of the vehicle, not the comfort of its passengers! The teeth rather rattle and the back is sometimes jarred, but it will turn on a sixpence, take terrible abuse, survive the harshest climates and, importantly, somehow keep going when seriously wounded. Rarely will a Series I let its master down.

Many of these early Land Rovers are still working on the farms and estates they were delivered to when purchased new. These vehicles are now rightly regarded as true classics and are becoming sought after by collectors. I was offered £15,000 for Pater's 1948 model just the other week. Not bad for a near 70-year-old truck!

NUVOLARI

The Mille Miglia, for those of you not in the know, was a 1,000 mile race for sports cars held on public roads in Italy between 1927 and 1957 (12 before the Hitler war, 11 after, and one in 1940, which was won by future Porsche race supremo Huschke von Hanstein in a streamlined BMW 328). Tazio Nuvolari, aka 'Il Montavano Volante' (the Flying Mantuan), won the Mille Miglia in an Alfa Romeo in 1930 – his first major success on four wheels – defeating team-mate and arch-rival Achille Varzi. It was the first of his two victories in the event.

Nuvolari often operated as a freelancer throughout the 1930s, but he is most famous for his exploits driving bright red factory Alfa Romeos, despite their declining international competitiveness. In 1935 he greatly upset the sausage eaters by winning the German Grand Prix, fighting back after a botched pitstop and beating a veritable Panzerbataillon of Nazi-funded Silver Arrow Mercedes and Auto Unions (the second of these types the creation of one Ferdinand Porsche, of course). Adolf Hitler considered motor racing victories to be useful propaganda so the German authorities were most miffed. In fact, so confident were they of victory that day at the Nürburgring, no-one had thought it necessary to have a recording of the Italian national anthem to hand. Nuvolari had to supply his own.

But in 1938 the diminutive Italian finally quit Alfa Romeo and joined Auto Union mid-season. That year the regulations had changed. Supercharged engines were limited to three litres, so Mercedes had replaced its 5700cc W125 monsters with newly schemed V12s (the W154), and Auto Union had ditched Porsche's 4360cc, V16 and built new V12s of their own (cars known as Type D).

The front-engined W154 proved the most successful grand prix racing car of 1938. Arch-toff Dick Seaman won the German Grand Prix at the Nürburgring, blithely saluting Hitler on the podium afterwards and becoming the first Englishman since Henry Segrave to receive the winner's garlands in a championship race; and Rudolf Caracciola won the Swiss GP and the title. But Auto Union struggled. Their new 450bhp V12 was not ready for the start of the season, and the team was thrown into disarray by the death of its number one driver, Bernd Rosemeyer, killed during speed record attempts on the new Frankfurt-Darmstadt autobahn (Germany's first inter-city autobahn had opened in 1932 between Bonn and Cologne).

But Nuvolari got the factory back on track by winning the Italian Grand Prix at Monza in September, beating Rudolf Caracciola by three laps, and my pal Algy and I were set to see all these impossibly glamorous men and their magnificent machines in action at the non-championship Grand Prix at Donington Park on 8 October. But sadly, the meeting would be delayed by world events, and only Algy would be able to attend. So when he returned to Bales full of tales of thrills and spills, and of a great victory by his absolute hero, Il Montavano Volante, we sat him down in Grandpapa's chair in the Rose & Crown, and urged him to tell us all about it.

The Germans' sabre-rattling over Czechoslovakia brought about Chamberlain's appeasing trips to Munich, 'Peace in Our Time' and all that. It also meant the 80 lap British Grand Prix at Donington was postponed until October 22, and, to my chagrin, I found I could not go due to commitments at Cambridge. The Donington race, which had been won the previous year by Rosemeyer, was a non-championship event, and Caracciola, already declared champion, did not bother to attend. The Italians were all sulking, having taken a pasting all year, so of the sport's big teams, only French champion Rene Dreyfuss tipped up with his Delahaye equipe to take the fight to four factory Mercedes W154s, one driven by Seaman, and three works Auto Unions.

While practising for the 250 mile race Nuvolari clobbered a deer, breaking some of his ribs, and he had to be strapped up under his cardy. Then, during the race he suffered more beastly luck when he had to pit for plugs (they did that sort of thing in those days), but this turned out to be a blessing because while he was safely off the circuit, an oil slick at what is now Craner Curves, brought about multiple spins, spills and retirements. When Nuvolari got back among the action he drove like a demon, carving through the field, lapping the privateer entries again and again while overhauling the leader, Mercedes' Hermann Lang, and then stretching away to beat him by over a minute.

Miraculously unaffected by the oil that had done for Segrave and many others, Nuvolari put on an exhibition of utterly brilliant, impossibly fast opposite-lock driving. Well, Algy would say that, of course! On the subject of being 'done for', I'm afraid the aristocratic and dashing Dick Seaman was killed as a result of being terribly burned in an accident at Spa the following year, just months before inheriting a stupendous family fortune. He was only 26.

So what has all this got to do with the Mille Miglia, you may well ask (I was wondering – ed). Patience dear reader! When the final entry list for the 1948 event reached the offices of *The Auto* soon before the event, the 167 starters included not only Ascari in a Maserati, and Biondetti, Cortese, and Righetti in Ferraris (all this we had known for some time), but none other than Tazio Nuvolari, a late addition to Enzo Ferrari's star-studded squad. On a whim I persuaded my long-suffering boss Murdo Graves I should get down there, and before he changed his mind I raced home like a stoat to grab Algy as my navigator. That afternoon we set off in a Jowett Javelin, bound for sun, sea and excitement in bella Italia (no, it didn't overheat!).

Nuvolari was 55 by then, and in poor health both physically and mentally. He was depressed: the second of his boys had passed away two years before, aged just 18, and his first had also died young. He would finally stop racing altogether in 1950, and he would be killed by a series of strokes in 1952, but it was his lungs that brought him to the point of death, ruined from vehicle smoke and deadly fumes, and from cigarettes. Blood would often fleck his lips, and in 1946, in a race in Milan, he had steered with one hand holding a blood-stained handkerchief over his mouth.

The 1948 Mille Miglia started at midnight (in a downpour), and the drivers and their riding mechanics bored tunnels through blackness and swirling rain with their headlamps as they raced to the dawn. Rather than spend too much time on my feet in the paddock, I reported the event from a hotel on the circuit. And why not? There was live coverage of the whole race on the wireless, and I had learned long before from old hands (many of them top racing scribes), that when reporting on races such as this, or the Isle of Man TT, it was not only rarely necessary to move from one's barstool, but that as a way of working, it could be surprisingly effective.

Those old timers talked to all the right people as they passed by, and found out all they needed to know. If you do it right you don't have to rush around the paddock like a demented bluebottle or watch with a notepad from the side of the track to find out what's happening at a race meeting. In fact, that is probably the least effective way of reporting a race, particularly when the riders or drivers themselves may not have a full picture. Say a leading driver comes in, his car's running sick but he's got no idea why. If you talk to the team mechanic or owner a little later on he'll say, 'Unbelievable Wilby! We got it into the garage and we found a dratted HT lead was broken. Headline: 'A 10s plug lead cost Stirling Moss victory in today's big race at Silverstone.' People around the driver can sometimes give a news-hound far more information than the driver possibly could. A hard-drinking colleague of mine (most of the racing chaps were enthusiastic bon viveurs!) who had started his career as a crime reporter on a big city daily, was once asked how on earth he was going to write his TT report when he hadn't actually left the bar long enough to have seen anything. He replied that he used to report on murders and he hadn't witnessed any of them either!

Back to northern Italy in 1948. When we awoke from an hour or two of drunken slumber, the sun was up, the rain had cleared, and we ascertained from the staccato croaks of the hotel's wireless (a Ducati, I recall) that the great man was in the lead. In fact, incredibly, he was half an hour to the good. Nuvolari had taken over at the front after Franco Cortese's Ferrari 166S had expired, and the wiry Mantuan was driving like a man possessed. After a rustic luncheon, we sat in the half-light of the half-shuttered, chiaroscuro bar, sipping espresso, ignoring our free measures of the local liqueur (an unutterably foul brown compound), and listening intently to the aforementioned squawking bakelite device (not that we could understand a great deal!). Then the telephone tinkled behind the counter. The proprietario waved his arms and shouted above the radio's frenzied racket. Eccolo! Eccolo! – he was coming. No, in fact, he was here! A disordered scramble and a small table was upturned with a heavy smash as the shadowy, fly-blown bar all but emptied into the blazing bright white sunshine of the town square.

The speakers, clamped to a pole at its corner of the piazza, blared unintelligibly, and above their distorted din we heard the reverberative wail of a Ferrari's approach bouncing cacophonously off the crumbling village walls. Then he came. Men cheered and waved their hats, or else threw them into the air, and women fluttered their handkerchiefs. Nuvolari used tall ratios, and braked little to maintain speed. He cornered by sliding a car, fighting all the while to keep its nose in the middle of the road. He tigered, as we said in those days. Sure enough, that May lunchtime the Flying Mantuan shot through the piazza, drifting as in days of yore, all arms and elbows as he fought the wheel of his open car. A loss of control would have massacred dozens that day, and of course that's what would finish the Mille Miglia in the end (the grizzly deaths of Spanish driver Alfonso de Portago and ten others, including five children, in a single catastrophic crimson hay-baler of a crash in 1957 would prove the final straw).

Nuvolari's Ferrari had been built for the Paris-based Russian aristocrat and part-time racing driver Prince Igor Troubetzkoy, the fourth husband of the stupendously wealthy American socialite Barbara Hutton, and he was scheduled to take delivery of it soon after the race. But it was already considerably shot up by the time it reached us. Nuvolari was always hard on his cars, and in this race, perhaps more than any other, he was driving like a madman, fuelled by grief and a need to reconnect with meaning in his life. The fragile open sports car was literally falling to pieces underneath him. He had hit a bank, swiping a mudguard clean off, and the bonnet had become unattached and flown away over his head, narrowly avoiding killing him and his mechanic, long-time Ferrari man Sergio Scapinelli. Good, he reportedly shouted to him, that will help keep the engine cool. Next the seat had come adrift, and he had replaced it with a sack of lemons.

The telephone tinkled again. This time a friend of the landlord from near Reggio Emilia. Nuvolari had retired. Algy groaned like a wounded animal. Perhaps his brakes had let him down? No, it seemed the suspension had collapsed. Whatever, the car had slewed to a stop and had been left, sagging to one side, ticking as it cooled by the side of the road. The Mantuan had spoken briefly to a priest before going to lie down awhile in the village hospice while Scapinelli telephoned to report their retirement, and order a car to take them to Brescia. Did Signor de Forte and his friend want to go to see him? The proprietario's friend could arrange it. No, we let him be.

Just then there was a most appalling smash and commotion outside. A back-marker had driven a Fiat Topolino Special into the tables at the front of the hotel, collapsing the awning and demolishing a small wall. Miraculously nobody was badly injured and the apologetic driver immediately produced his wallet and peeled off a fistful of notes to pay for the damage and buy drinks all round. Meanwhile in Brescia, Enzo Ferrari took Scapinelli's call and reportedly wept. He later told Nuvolari they would win the Mille Miglia together soon, maybe even next year, but Nuvolari told him to enjoy what glory they had achieved, that at their age there would not be many more opportunities. For one of them this would be all too true.

Clemente Biondetti took the victory in his Ferrari. 'Excuse me for having won,' he said at the prize-giving, justifiably irritated that so much attention was being lavished on Nuvolari, one of 103 non-finishers, while he, the victor after all, was more-or-less ignored. The evening had got to the coffee and cigars stage when I grabbed a word with the wiry Mantuan. He asked after my father, then his beady eyes shone while he recalled his remarkable performance in the Far Field, reliving the event with many a chuckle and much bobbing in his chair, and then he showed great dignity in defeat, as ever, praising Biondetti, insisting he had deserved his victory, and condemning those who had all but ignored him in their speeches. Fortified by adulation, by love, and by food and fine wine, he seemed surprisingly spritely that evening, even athletic, but it was an illusion.

Underneath I could see Tazio Nuvolari was not a well man, and that he knew it too. His doctors would be angry, he said, prickly-eyed and coughing after pulling on a toasty American cigarette, but he would race again just as soon as he could. He hoped to return to England too, explaining he had been invited over to test a new Jaguar sports car for Mr Lyons. In fact, he raced in Italy just a fortnight later, but was too ill to complete the course, and when his pre-war nemesis Achille Varzi was killed at the beginning of July, he reportedly said he felt ready to join him, that it was his time too.

The following day in Brescia, Algy and I were walking down a heaving street in the centre of town when there was an urgent flurry of toots behind us. The crowds parted and an Alfa Romeo saloon crept through the throng. In the rear sat the shrunken figure of Tazio Nuvolari, and as he was driven past us, Algy called out bravo to the great man whose sad eyes sparked in recognition. The maestro raised a hand, thumbed an imaginary throttle lever, and managed half a smile.

PRIDE COMES BEFORE A FALL

The Jowett Javelin of 1947 was an impressive motor car. Capable of 80mph, it had a compact, all-new, 1.5 litre flat-four engine. It steered well, rode well on torsion bar suspension, and had plenty of room for six inside. It had a monocoque body, boasted the first curved windscreen in Britain, and its modern American fastback look (no running boards either) was radically different to the pre-war designs being put back into production elsewhere. Having been brought up in South Africa, its young designer Gerald Palmer was used to colonial roads, and this no doubt influenced him in giving the Javelin given plenty of ground clearance, and a stiff body of stiff construction. Consequently the Javelin proved comfortable on rough surfaces at high speed and was successful in the Monte Carlo Rally. So where did it all go wrong?

I had regular dealings with the Bradford engineering firm in the early years of War Two and the term professional Yorkshiremen comes strongly to mind. Fiercely proud and independent, the firm's senior men were Victorians with Victorian values, but they would fall victim to hubris. The Jowett men did things their own way, which was generally better than that of anyone else, or at least that is what they truly believed. This delusion drove them ever onwards towards self-sufficiency, and this, together with myopic over-ambition, would bring about their downfall.

The Jowett Motor Manufacturing Co went back to 1901 when, from their original factory in Church Street, Bradford, its founders William and Benjamin Jowett began manufacturing stationary engines of various types and for various applications. They built their first car around 1905, and were subcontracted to build motorcycles. In 1907 Jowett moved to new premises where they built tough flat-twin cars and, from 1929, a light van known as penny-a-miler. In the Second War they made capstan lathes; guns and ammunition; aircraft components including coolant pumps for Merlins; flail mechanisms for Shermans, and gears and conversion drives for all manner of tanks; as well as twin-cylinder vehicles for war use.

No wonder the Jowett bods thought they could make anything, and in 1942 they advertised for a designer to scheme them a brand new car. Gerald Palmer responded and the Yorkies went down to Oxford to persuade the then MG man to bring his expertise to the north. They prevailed, and he designed them a nigh-on complete new motor car, and a very fine one it was too. The first Javelin prototypes set off on test into the Yorkshire Dales in August 1944, and I first drove one on a short trip to Ilkley in February 1946. My notes tell me a short engine made for plenty of room in the cab, and positioning the front seat essentially in the middle of the car, made for a commendably bounce-free ride over the tops and down past the Cow and Calf.

By November 1947 full Javelin production had begun. All well and good but after this the Yorkshiremen somewhat overstretched themselves. From 1946 onwards they had been building the 8bhp Bradford van (or truck). It was simple, sweet and charming, but ever so slow (I recall having to jump out and help push a fully-laden one up Chapel Hill in Huddersfield: it just couldn't manage it!). Never mind, they returned high mileages over a long life and thousands were exported all over the world. Then came the Javelin, which was initially well received but not without teething troubles as one would expect. Solving these should have been a priority, but the firm was distracted by preparations for the introduction in 1950 of the Jupiter sports car, the pursuit of a race programme involving a Jupiter single-seater, the detailed development of other new models, and an unwise decision to begin manufacturing its own gearboxes. By this time, their star designer had returned to Oxford's dreaming spires to pen the MG Magnette and Wolseley 4/44 (he had designed the Y-type for Nuffield pre-war).

Although the Javelin's overheating problems were soon cured, gearbox faults further damaged the firm's reputation and sales stalled. Meanwhile, Jowett's body supplier, Briggs of Doncaster, kept churning out painted bodyshells and they had to be stockpiled on waste ground around Bradford. Supply was eventually halted in 1952 and never restarted. Jowett ceased trading in 1954, laying off its loyal and hard-working workforce.

MINOR REFLECTIONS
(First published *The Auto* – January 1959)
We may have never had it so good, but a little more than a decade ago Great Britain was still a bankrupt mess. Indeed, for most citizens of these beleaguered islands, the country was in an even worse predicament than it had been when the war ended, and motorists were particularly inconvenienced. The roads were in an atrocious state, and for the first six months of 1948 no petrol was legally available for private use. A meagre ration was introduced in June, but hardly enough to take one off for a weekend jaunt through our green and pleasant land.

It was frustrating indeed to be in possession of a functioning motor car, yet not have the fuel to bring it to life.

Export or Die was the government's rallying call to industry, and steel was allocated to car and motorcycle manufacturers according to foreign contracts won. Britain owed dollars and needed dead presidents to buy American goods, and this patriotic export drive meant very few new vehicles were available for the home market. So there were very few motor cars on Britain's roads in 1948, and almost no new ones at all, and for those that were able to obtain a new machine, purchase taxes pushed costs to astronomical levels. A few pre-war motors smokily soldiered on, and trams swayed, galleon-like, sparking in the bombed out shattered cities, passing ruined roofless buildings, piles of rubble on demolition sites, and queues on the pavements outside shops with empty shelves. Everything seemed rationed. The air people breathed. Glimpses of the sun. Hope of a better world.

In contrast to the freezing weather and omnipresent gloom, Earls Court reopened its art deco doors on October 27 1948, giving the long-suffering public a chance to see what the struggling industry had in mind for brightening up our future. More than half a million motorists and would-be motorists turned up to gawp, the vast majority, of course, arriving by rail or bus, or by the aforementioned clanking trams, or by bicycle, dodging the bombsites en route. As a consequence, for those fortunates who did have a car and a few pints of precious Mr Pratt's, it was still possible to park within easy walking distance, with no fear of interference by those dratted wardens whose infernal new-fangled clockwork assistants were still a decade from deployment. Some manufacturers even offered test drives from the rear of the main hall, I recall. Carefree times, in some ways.

I was impressed by the Renault 4CV and the Citroën 2CV, but even without the benefit of hindsight it was immediately apparent there were two star attractions on display in the hallowed halls. Bill's boys at Jaguars had pulled off a miracle to create their XK120 in a matter of months, although as we now know, its unveiling at the show was more of an afterthought than the result of a definite plan. No matter. Such was the rapturous response, the model had to be put into production, if only in six-cylinder form (the proposed four-pot twin-cam engined variant ending up being pushed into the background).

Meanwhile, the exhibits also featured a brand new car of more direct relevance to the average Joe Soap hoping to escape the Clapham omnibus. I am, of course, referring to the Morris Minor. Some of us preferred its development name, 'Mosquito', but there was no doubt that the crack Longbridge team led by Alec Issigonis had come up with a winner. Had Issi been in full control his new baby would have included independent rear suspension and a flat four engine, perhaps driving the front wheels. The powers that be in the Kremlin scotched those radical and expensive ideas, so the model emerged from Cowley with various compromises. Most disappointingly, instead of the new engine the car deserved, the first Minors were fitted with the firm's ancient 918cc side-valve four, a dismal device rooted in antediluvian epochs when inefficient long-stroke configurations were forced upon us by a ridiculous and ill-conceived taxation system. But with the RAC HP rating having been finally usurped that year by a flat rate excise licence, penny-pinching by Len Lord was surely the primary reason something more modern was not found to propel the new Morris everyman-mobile, even if a new boxer four was deemed an extravagance (as Gerald Palmer's lauded, but ultimately ill-fated engine in the Javelins on the nearby Jowett stand perhaps proved, although we must congratulate the Bradford men for their efforts).

Insultingly described as a 'poached egg' by a significant person whose name must remain unpublished here, the Minor did at least retain some of its prototype's design features, including unitary construction, making a separate chassis anachronistic overnight. Donkey cart springs and a live axle were the order of the day abaft, and longitudinal torsion beams provided springing for the front wheels, usefully transferring the major (forgive me, dear reader) stresses to the middle of the Minor's floorpan. Unusually, the pedal hydraulics also lived in the same area, contributing to an uncluttered appearance under the bonnet.

While the poached egg appellation must remain a matter for the beholder's eye, one of the Minor's notable features was its above average width. Contemporary rivals such as the Austin A30 were narrower, and thereby hangs a tail, or tale. Minor prototypes were in fact considerably less wide – four inches, to be precise – than the production version. At a late stage of development I called in on Issi one evening and he showed me the current prototype. I dared to suggest the car looked a little narrow. He gave me short shrift, but upon sleeping on the matter he decided his creation would indeed benefit from an increase in girth, and that very morning he swept into the development department, and immediately instructed his astonished assistants to saw the latest pre-production car down the middle, then move the two halves apart until it 'looked right'! Although this last-minute madness probably accounted for some of the Minor's success once launched, it did rather present a problem for the production chaps, as some of the tooling was already made. So now you may gather why the car had a two-piece front bumper! We can laugh about it now, but what a headache it must have been to incorporate a four-inch straight section in the middle of an otherwise curved car. It could never happen today!

As we approach the 1960s, with assurances that we will live longer and prosper, the Poached Egg is, of course, very much still with us, having survived a decade on sale with essentially minor(!) development. Externally, the main changes have been raised headlamps, a one-piece windscreen and larger rear lights. Internally, the cabin is still a minimalist affair, in keeping with its creator's belief that cars shouldn't be so comfortable that their drivers are unable to stay alert ('I would have them sit on nails, Wilby old boy,' he once told me).

Lift the bonnet, however, and it was a different story. Soon after the Nuffield/Austin merger of 1952 (for those too young to remember, the result was BMC, and Nuffield already comprised Morris, Wolseley, MG and Riley), the brand new A-series ohv four found itself playing a Minor role in a major industrial upheaval, consigning Lord Nuffield's side-valve plodder to the Cowley scrap heap. Initially of 848cc capacity, the latest 1000 is actually only 948cc, but we can forgive BMC for this modest exaggeration. Performance is now decidedly more lively, although low gearing still limits top speed to around 70mph. For all its faults, the ancient side-valve bestowed the car with a relaxing gait. For reasons best known to BMC management, the A-series was introduced gradually to different versions of the car at different times. Whether any customers inadvertently took delivery of something they didn't order is uncertain, but I would venture such a scenario would have been entirely possible, if not probable, such was the shortage of supply for the first half of the decade. Delivery of any new car in less than a year was an achievement until relatively recently, so one would have been unlikely to quibble about the engine.

I well remember my first Minor drive in the spring of 1949, when I set forth along largely deserted Oxfordshire roads before dallying with the Fosse and tackling some Cotswold hills. A recent chance to sample the 'fisherman' 1000 over a similar route, albeit in far less pleasant weather (thank goodness a heater is now standard!) was an interesting exercise in nostalgia. Within yards one can appreciate the car's finest feature – its sublime steering. Direct, lash-free and offering wonderful feedback from the chassis and road surface, very few cars can compete in this respect. In truth, I cannot think of anything that answers the helm with such precision. The gear change apparatus is also very satisfying. Having set the beam so high it is inevitable that the Minor is less impressive in other areas. As mentioned, comfort is lacking, and, to be blunt, it is noisy and rather frenetic once clear of urban limits. Lamentably, the same applies to the brakes in some circumstances. Overall, the world has moved on while the Minor has largely stayed still.

And yet… the car has great character, seemingly inherited from its designer, and continues to blow raspberries, both metaphorical and literal, at recent rivals. We hear strong whispers that the small saloon ranks will be swelled considerably in the near future. Ford and Standard-Triumph will have new models, we gather. Will the mighty British Motor Corporation react and introduce a Minor Mark II with more chiselled lines and a cruising speed suitable for our new Motorways? See you at Earls Court in October.

RILEY RMB
(First published *Classic Auto* – March 2010)
There are those who think nothing about how to handle a motor car properly, anxious only to get from A to B. But these dullards are missing out on one of the true joys in life. To drive well at any speed, concentration is required; all the senses are alerted and there is co-ordination of body and brain. When I achieve this I feel part of the great whole. I fit in. Life makes sense.

New fangled driver aids such as power steering and synchro-mesh gearboxes greatly reduce the potential for such satisfaction but real joy can still be realised by the piloting of vintage and what are now called classic motor cars. They are wonderful time machines that take us back to another age when things were very different, and dare I say it, generally rather more agreeable.

One late summer morning a few years ago I was detailed to deliver a 2.5 litre Riley RMB to Raby Castle in County Durham. The early commencement of a dear friend's daughter's nuptuals, in which the cream coloured car had a vital role to play and would inevitably steal the show, as classic cars usually do at these occasions, necessitated a daybreak departure from its village home in Yorkshire's West Riding.

'As Old as the Industry, as modern as the Hour' was once the motto of the Riley Motor Company, but JAC626 looked splendidly old fashioned as the doors of its timber motor house creaked open at sparrow croak that late August morn. That said, there could be no doubt the Riley RMB is still a powerfully attractive motor car. No trailer-borne specimen, the nearly seventy-year-old vehicle revealed in the barn was clearly a regularly used example of the marque, and on the road it would no doubt prove the better for it. The fact its tweed-jacketed and cravatted owner was none other than Riley RM Club Chairman Mr Philip Hallam also augured well.

RMs were the last thoroughbred Rileys and feature the firm's traditional swooping radiator and a distinctive fabric roof. The lines are based on a pre-war BMW saloon owned by an employee who pranged his Bahnstormer and then rebuilt it at the works with a Riley front end. His boss Victor Riley reckoned the hybrid had a certain something so he used it as the basis of his post-war range. It was blatant plagiarism but, as he later explained to me with a chuckle, the goons were hardly in a position to complain about it at the time!

The RM's pressed steel panels are fixed to a traditional ash frame built onto a strong box section chassis. Its torsion bar and wishbone front suspension and steering was inspired by the splendid Citroën Traction Avant, and hydraulic front and mechanical rear drum brakes were perfectly adequate in the 1940s. A pre-war engine that first saw service in the 1926 Riley Monaco saloon provided the urge. A total of 6,903 RMBs were manufactured between 1946-1953 and there were 1,050 examples of the mildly updated RMF which preceded the Pathfinder.

The RM's somewhat ingenious four cylinder engine was originally conceived by Victor's brilliant elder brother Percy who started building cars at 13 and was the mechanical brains behind the Coventry firm. Advanced in its day, it featured gear driven camshafts on the side of the crankcases from which short pushrods activated overhead valves. An RM engine that is out of sorts can be as rattly as a flag collector's box on a poor day, but JAC's well maintained unit emitted only a delightful wuffly noise as it settled to tick-over after I thumbed the bakelite starter. The car's glorious instrument board came to life as I flicked on the panel lights and as air began to circulate in the cabin, the comfortable leather upholstery emitted a quite evocative period whiff which charmed the nostrils no end. Altogether the experience was just so right and full of quality.

After a nod from JAC's sleepy owner, first gear was engaged without fuss and I nosed the Riley's long and elegant bonnet out of its quarters and onto the highway. As expected, the steering was heavy at low speed but once above walking pace, the wheel became light and responsive in my hands. It was not yet 6am so town carriage driving was in order, at least to start with! Nice work with the clutch and throttle, gentle and early cog shifting and smooth braking, having foreseen the necessity for slowdown or stop, led to a smooth and quiet passage through rural villages en route to the Great North Road.

And, after pausing at a junction, by way of a test I started in top and accelerated gently to 60mph without using the low gears at all. A Royce or Bentley are the very best motors for this stunt but the Riley's flexible engine boasts the longest stroke of any post war car, and the stupendously torquey RM performed the feat with aplomb. A passenger would have been quite unaware anything unusual had occurred.

But then, quite suddenly, the imps in me came out to play. Down went the loud pedal and I began to tear around the swervery at full chat. Cornering was not without roll, but the Riley was up for the challenge and a demonic grin soon fixed itself on the de Forte phizzog.

The rack and pinion steering was fully up to the job and the Riley's suspension performed its task of tying the big car to the road but Blighty's by-lanes are increasingly ill-maintained and on one appalling patchwork apology for a road I hit a series of bumps and was was rather caught out by a fourpenny one. Unplanned arm exercise followed and there was, I am ashamed to say, a squeal of tyres as the rear end hung out over the white lines upon landing after a donkey back bridge. Flushed with embarrassment as I thought of the verbal clout

I would have received had JAC's owner been on board, I knocked it off a little until I reached the A1. Upon reflection, a Riley RMB handles perfectly well, but in truth the smaller, faintly pug-like RMA is a better town and country lane car than its longer and larger-engined brother.

Where the 2.5 litre car really excels is on the open road. 'Magnificent Motoring' was another Riley advertising slogan and the RMB is certainly a car for those seeking adventure on the King's Highway. Sharing the Great North Road at that early hour with just a handful of plodding merchants and an occasional modern allowed me to slip the big Riley off the leash. With a 2443cc engine producing almost 100bhp the RMB is a quite outstanding goer, and with its seven league boots fully on, a true ton can be seen on the clock. For covering long distances at speed, it is still a capital motor car.

A long run in a good car going its best on the Great North Road has a marvellous tonic effect and can change a mood of blue depression to a feeling of being one of fortune's favourites. As the road flies towards the radiator, the strain brought about by the unseemly tempo of modern life drops away, and approaching Scotch Corner your correspondent felt such a sense of wonderful well being that I must confess I began carolling like a lark!

Those of my generation may be becoming thin on the line, dear reader, and while most of my contemporaries are reduced to mumbling incoherently through toothless gums, I am sure that somewhere in their minds they are still young and vibrant. I know that in essence I am unchanged from the teenage boy who drove his dear Uncle Bof's Riley Gamecock on that historic road before the second war. In the RM on that summer morning in 2006 I was eighteen once again. That is the power of a fine classic motor car.

WOODIES
(First published *Classic Auto* – November 2008)
Between Wars One and Two, one of the most useful vehicles on the farm in Bales was the family's hard-working Jennings-bodied shooting-brake. Modelled on the estate cars father had seen coming into fashion for carrying guns, rods and bods on Scottish sporting estates at the time, it sported a timbered utility body built onto an accident salvaged Rolls-Royce 20HP limousine chassis bought cheaply from a scrapyard in Stafford (its first owner, I recall, was the crash-prone pioneer motorist and aviator, Sir Roderick Cholmondeley-Ker). Part van, part bus, part car, this marvellously practical machine was used for taking us away to school, running errands in the village, carrying hay and equipment around the farm and, at various times, transporting sickly or injured creatures to Spates, the town vet. And, after a cursory clean-out, it also often did duty picking up visitors and their luggage from the railway station in Shrewsbury.

The first shooting brakes were open horse drawn carriages used to convey shooting parties into the countryside and when motorised versions followed, wood remained the principal material of manufacture. Seasoned ash was the timber of choice due to its splendidly springy properties, strength and light weight. Station wagon, of course, is an American term coined to describe hotel courtesy transport used principally to ferry guests to and from railroad stations. Station wagons of this type gained in popularity on both sides of the Atlantic throughout the 1930s and became known as Woodies. Incidentally, the correct singular spelling is Woodie. A Woody is a woodpecker or an eccentric Hollywood film director, not a motor car! In time, mass produced Ford V8 Woodies imported from Canada introduced the concept to the British hoi polloi and soon even modest Morrises and wee austere Austins were being rebodied as 'estate' cars to provide utility motoring for the many.

In the Second War, many vans, ambulances, and suchlike conveyances were needed on the home front and the cheapness and availability of timber made Woodie conversions commonplace. Furthermore, commercial vehicles attracted a decent quantity of Mr Pratt's petroleum. And to get hold of the precious juice, many more perfectly healthy saloons were pushed into coach-building and joinery shops by their civilian owners to have their rear portions cut off and replaced by wooden hindquarters, after which they were driven smugly home.

Most Woodies were made to order and individual customer specification, so there was a great deal of variation in design. Long-established coachbuilding firms deployed time honoured skills in the manufacture of many finely crafted creations, but crudities and bodge jobs also abounded. My good chum Algy Tomlinson commissioned a wartime Woodie on a Daimler chassis from Tom the village carpenter who, it must be said, was not a bright fellow. Left to his own devices while Algy was away fighting the goons, the lumpen nitwit made the body frame and panelling entirely from fine English oak.

The car certainly looked natty enough, but it weighed two tons and drove like a stinker! Held rigid and unable to flex at all, the once benign and accommodating Daimler chassis frame took on handling and road-holding qualities of unsurpassed dreadfulness. My sainted aunt, it was a complete deathtrap! Like all young rip-stitches home on leave, Algy drove with the loud pedal on the boards (he would have done better to have heeded the blanket 30mph speed limit applied to all 'commercials') and it seemed the rebodied beast would kill him more surely than the sausage eaters.

The tyres slithered and fought for grip, there were no guiding sensations through the steering wheel or seat, and the back end of the car often broke away completely without warning. Fortunately, while bouncing wildly along the track to visit me at the farm one summer's day, the rigid body snapped the chassis clean in half. The contemptible creation was later broken for scrap, its body remaining on the farm for many years as a hen hut.

Nevertheless, as a motor car it outlived Pater's poor 20HP which he had given to the RAF for the duration. While parked on the perimeter of a fighter aerodrome somewhere in Norfolk, having just dropped off some visiting bigwig, Jerry came low along the main runway and dropped a land-mine straight through the sunroof. The dear old thing was blown to smithereens but amazingly the mascot survived intact and was returned in the post. It sits on the mantelpiece in the dining room at Bales to this day.

Punitive post war purchase taxes, from which 'commercials' were made exempt, and the continuation of rationing made utilities even more attractive in peacetime and, until legislative loopholes were closed in the mid 1950s, there was a Woodie manufacturing boom. Pent up demand for new cars could not be satisfied due to steel shortages and compulsory export quotas, so to circumnavigate the rules many folk purchased rolling chassis from car manufacturers and had them bodied in wood by a coachbuilder of choice. Additionally, several established motor car manufacturers including Alvis and Lea Francis, supplied large numbers of chassis to approved bodyshops, and then listed their factory endorsed shooting-brakes alongside the saloons in their official sales blurb.

But as the 1950s wore on, better times saw the end of tax breaks for utilities and an easing of restrictions on the supply of standard cars. This, coupled with the motor industry's move to unitary construction (no more separate chassis on which to build alternative bodies), brought an end to the Woodie story. Apart, that is, from a post script provided by the hugely popular Morris Minor Traveller. Built originally for travelling salesmen, this once ubiquitous wooden framed motor car was manufactured from 1953 to 1971 and a quarter of a million were sold.

Remaining Woodies deserve to be preserved, but very few have survived. Wood is quite possibly the worst material with which to build a motor vehicle body and in the first half of the 20th century, effective preservatives had not yet been developed. Woodies' exposed wooden frames needed revarnishing every couple of years to stop rot taking hold. Unsurprisingly, this tedious task was rarely carried out and consequently most Woodies never saw the 1960s let alone the end of the millennium. Woodie survival rates are pitifully poor and wooden bodied utilities found slumbering in sheds and barns tend to be woodworm eaten, crumbly and semi-collapsed, with coachwork completely beyond effective restoration. And the few that have continued to be driven are often held together by myriad tie rods, screws and angle irons.

But happily there is a club keenly dedicated to restoring and recreating these characterful and individualistic motor vehicles. Formed several years ago, the

Woodie Car Club has its own website, and a fine book entitled 'British Woodies from the 1920s to the 1950s' has been written by enthusiastic club chairman Mr Colin Peck and published by Veloce.

Reading Mr Peck's capital little book I was astonished to discover there is only one roadworthy Austin A70 Hampshire still in existence. These sweet little utilitarian shooting-brakes were frequently used by television companies as outside broadcast support vehicles as well as by motor racing teams, and I well remember seeing several of them parked together in the paddock at big race meetings at Silverstone in the 1950s. Bread and butter jobs they may have been, but I'm sure many older readers will have similarly fond memories of these once popular commercial vehicles from a bygone age. It really would be a pity for this small but significant part of our motoring heritage to be lost forever. Good luck to Mr Peck and his friends!

JAGUAR MARK FIVE
(First published *Classic Auto* – September 2002)

Possession of a Jaguar motor car used to be a signal achievement and one of the most desirable things in a man's life. As well as providing an exhilarating means of transport, a Coventry cat was a beautiful object to behold and envious looks just add to the pleasure. There is absolutely nothing wrong with a bit of showing off!

Now there have always been chaps who have considered Jaguars to be a tad vulgar, but under autocratic boss Sir William Lyons, the midlands firm built motor cars which gripped the imagination of millions of motorists by the magic of their name alone. Alas, this is no longer the case! Bill Lyons' stylish cars were always sold at a price that would appear to invite certain bankruptcy, but in fact the man was a genius. By underselling his more mundane domestic opposition and exotic foreign rivals alike, Lyons' oft repeated trick was to offer dramatic looks and stimulating performance at a relatively attainable price.

When the art deco style Jaguar XK120 sports car was introduced to an astonished world at the Earl's Court Motor Show in October 1948, the firm's other new model at the exhibition was rather put in the shade. The pretty little two seater was to become a landmark car in Jaguar's illustrious history and it is still revered today, but in those post war years, the comparatively staid Mark V saloon which first appeared at the same time, was far more important to the Coventry firm's immediate future and precarious bank balance.

It was hardly surprising the little XK attracted all the plaudits. Apart from its show-stopping appearance, its stupendous new double overhead camshaft engine, which was to remain in production for more than 35 years, and went on to power such Jaguar classics as the Mark II, XJ6 and E-Type, delivered mind-boggling performance. As was usually the case for us motoring scribes when writing about Jaguars, superlatives were the order of the day when I filed my copy for the show issue of *The Auto*.

The Earls Court bash just two years later saw the first public appearance of the gargantuan Jaguar Mark VII which spelled the end for the Mark V (there was no Mark VI, of course, there being a contemporaneous and rather successful Bentley with that particular moniker). Consequently, the Mark V was a stop-gap model made for just three years. Today it is rather a forgotten Jaguar, which is to do it an injustice.

When motor car production resumed in 1945 it was essentially revamped pre-war models that creaked off Britain's assembly lines and modern replacements were desperately needed, not least by Jaguars of Coventry. The firm's colossal 1950s saloons were still on the drawing board and the hairy-chested XK motor that was to propel them existed only on the test bench. There was little money in the bank and old Bill was in a bit of a bind.

His solution was to produce a modernised version of his pre-war type cars, still powered by their old fashioned six cylinder engines in 2.5 and 3.5 litre form, but with a new chassis and state of the art suspension. It was a compromise. 'Export or die' was the clarion call of British manufacturing in the post war years and Jaguar needed to earn US dollars to fill its coffers and help revive the near bankrupt British economy.

The new model may have looked similar to its immediate post war predecessor (the Mark IV, logically enough) but in fact it had no shared panels and boasted many newfangled features such as faired in headlamps and push button door handles. And, by virtue of its suspension design, it drove better than any Jaguar before it. But would Lyons' instinct for style and Jaguar's value for money policy make the car a success?

Surviving British Mark Vs are rare beasts indeed and it was with the greatest of pleasure that I learned of the availability for demonstration of a fine 2.5 litre saloon example at Kettle's Emporium in my home village of Bales. On approach, one's first impression of SLO 226, which was first registered in 1951, is of a baroque coach. Very 1930s in appearance rather than 1950s, this large motor car has graceful, flowing lines well suited to its well polished gunmetal grey paintwork. The Mark V is certainly an eye catcher in the 21st century.

If it is pretty on the outside, the interior is an olde worlde delight. The large cross spoked steering wheel features a charming Jaguar head on its prominent horn push, and the pretty walnut dashboard features exquisite art deco lettering on its dainty dials which are bathed in a delicate violet glow at night. There is walnut garnishing throughout the cabin, unpleated leather upholstery fore and aft, and a mohair roof lining. As in most Lyons Jaguars, occupants are made to look and feel important in such splendid surroundings.

Under the side opening bonnet (this was the last Jaguar to be so equipped), the 2.5 litre pushrod motor has Jaguar stamped on its block and it was indeed made at the Jaguar factory, but it was cast from 1930s tooling purchased by Lyons during the war from the extraordinary Captain John Black at the Standard Motor Company. The Mark V is a big car with a chassis made from two whopping great steel girders and the 2.5 litre version is a little underpowered, but SLU's willing motor started easily, revved sweetly and performed adequately throughout the test, bowling along at 60mph without fuss. But as I recall the 3.5 litre version was not exactly a racehorse between the shafts either. Lacking the outright urge of the new XK powerplant, the old overhead valve straight six was nonetheless quite capable of a steady 70.

The Moss gearbox is slow to operate but crunch free in skilled hands and its action suits the car, the hydraulic drum brakes are out of the top-drawer and there is no need to apply a heavy boot. Besides, if anyone gets in the way, the Mark V has a horn of nautical volume and tonality! Some transmission whine is audible as the driver's ear becomes attuned to the car and there is a little lost motion at the steering wheel, but not enough to affect control. When driving some elderly motor cars it can be difficult to ascertain whether one is enjoying a vintage experience, or merely contending with vagueness caused by old and tired components!

The Mark V rode like a battleship on any sort of decent surface and on dreadful B roads, which would be a disgrace in a third world country, the suspension soaked up bumps and floated over potholes with aplomb. Your tester was kept alert as the soft cross-ply tyres kicked on white lines and tramlined on road repairs, but a twitch of the large cross spoked steering wheel soon brought her back into line. And when I threw on the coals and began to push on through the twisty bits I was impressed how the car stuck to its line, and by the absence of pitch and roll. This is by virtue of its fine independent front suspension inspired by Citroën's Light 15, and designed by Jaguar's engineering chief William Heynes.

As the revolution counter swept around the dial, in my mind I found myself back in the 1951 Monte Carlo Rally when I rode with privateer Irish racer Cecil Vard in his 3.5 litre Mark V. Dubliner Vard, and his Hibernian chums finished third overall in the Monte that year, a feat made all the more remarkable by the fact he swiped the car from his mother-in-law's drive and drove it across Europe to get to the start line!

The flickering orange fuel warning light snapped me out of my reverie and it was time to find some juice and head for home. The big car's fuel consumption clearly plummets with hard use, but then again 1950s Jaguar owners were not normally kept awake at night worrying about petrol bills! Upon returning to base I noted the test car's working sunshine roof (a standard factory fitment) and inspected the substantial toolkit in the fold-down boot. Incidentally, the Mark V was the last Jaguar with such a feature.

In conclusion, reacquainting myself with the Mark V was a very great pleasure. This rare Jaguar has immense charm, quite gorgeous looks and offers extremely pleasant, comfortable motoring even today. But find one if you can! Only 1,661 2.5 litre saloons were ever manufactured and most were sent across the pond.

Fortunately for Jaguar the bigger-engined version sold in far greater numbers and the 1949-1950 financial year saw record profits, up 149 percent on the previous 12 months. The turnaround was mostly due to the stop-gap Mark V. Bill Lyons' strategy had clearly worked, and his elegant blend of old and new was just the ticket. The interim car earned thousands of US dollars and underpinned the firm's even bigger successes in the 1950s and 1960s. It was a crucial car in Jaguar's history.

ROLLS-ROYCE SILVER CLOUD
(First published *Classic Auto* – January 2008)
In 1955, the Rolls-Royce Silver Cloud and its Bentley equivalent, the 'S', were launched in a new era of optimism. Rationing had finally ceased and it was once more socially acceptable to spend one's loot on items of style and luxury. Rolls-Royces were again rightly trumpeted as the finest cars in the world and in July 1957, less than a month after our test car, Silver Cloud TRW 585, was delivered to its first owner, Harold MacMillan told us all we had never had it so good.

The new Rolls-Royce Silver Cloud succeeded the Silver Ghost, Phantom, Wraith and Dawn, and when approaching the car from any angle there are unmistakable signs of its glorious tradition and breeding. It is an evolution of pre-war styles; the handsome gothic radiator, unchanged for 50 years, and the graceful, sweeping lines of the bodywork give this splendid gentleman's carriage great presence and majesty. Its 'standard steel' coachwork was finished by artisans at the Crewe factory, the body panels having been made by the Pressed Steel Co Ltd in Oxford, but no matter. Bespoke coachwork was still available from a dwindling number of specialist builders such as HJ Mulliner, James Young or Park Ward for chaps fortunate enough to be able to afford something even more exclusive, but the factory-made car is still enormously beautiful. Despite its enormous size, it is elegant, balanced and aristocratic. Time has not diminished it.

Designed to be equally suited to chauffeur or owner driving, which was itself a reflection of changing times in the 1950s, the Cloud is 20 percent longer and 5½ inches wider than the models that preceded it, dimensions which may give present-day owners problems finding adequate covered storage! It is also a high car and its interior floor is almost completely flat. As a result, entry and egress can be achieved with decorum. The passenger compartment is the epitome of comfort: the wide rear seat contains a generous centre arm rest, the upholstery is carried high to form padded headrests which envelop the occupants, and lights in the rear quarters allow reading without disturbing one's driver. There are exquisitely polished pull-down picnic tables and an ample carpeted luggage locker accommodates the largest cases. The front bench seat sports separate front arm rests so a passenger can travel in comfort without reducing the driver's elbow room – handy in the event of some unplanned arm exercise when 'pushing on'!

The Rolls-Royce Silver Cloud is a hand-made motor car of extraordinary quality, with cost clearly an afterthought. The interior is trimmed in good taste, and perfection of detail is to be observed in all respects. The dial-type instruments and gauges are clearly seen and read, the dashboard and door garnish rails are furnished with well matched walnut veneers, and the pile carpet and fine English hides are of the first rank.

It had been some years since I had driven a Cloud, and I was pleased to accept an invitation from my old pal Elmley Greenidge to test drive a 1957 model he had for sale for this feature in *Classic Auto*. A quick shufti in the Greenidge workshops in Shrewsbury revealed all was tickety-boo with this fine example, and it was time to get cracking. Enjoying the ride in the back, and keeping a beady eye on yours truly, were Mr Greenidge himself, and my long-suffering housekeeper, Martha, whom I had taken along as a treat for the afternoon. The Royce (never a Roller) moved off smoothly without slurring its automatic gear changes, and we were soon passing through Shrewsbury, drawing admiring glances from the populace. For such a massive coach, TRW was surprisingly manageable around town and not at all difficult to drive once one has adapted to its great size. Just as well as I had to swerve around several gormless nitwits crossing the road to get to Darwin's statue. Natural selection at work, eh! On the open road a Cloud has good acceleration despite its bulk, and mechanical quietness and lack of wind noise make it deceptively fast. So much so, it is easy to find oneself tooling along at highly illegal speeds!

Developed from that of the Bentley Continental, the 4887cc six cylinder engine in the Silver Cloud provides ample urge, although it was replaced in 1959 by a larger American-inspired V8. Until relatively recent times it was Rolls-Royce policy to be highly secretive about the performance of its engines, simply stating that power output was 'sufficient'. However, aided by several glasses of a very fine malt, which I had brought from the cellar in Bales, I did once persuade R-R chairman Lord Hives to admit to a figure of 178bhp for the Cloud.

More significantly, time has proved the over-engineered unit to be capable of a quarter of a million miles' service if properly maintained.

The Silver Cloud has an automatic gearbox, pandering to the American fashion of the time, which changes gear itself without regard to the driver's skill or intelligence. No bad thing in many cases! A manual gearbox option was not offered and this raised motoring scribes' hackles at the time, including mine, but in truth, the Hydramatic system, as fitted to 1950s Cadillacs and made under licence from General Motors, goes about its work unobtrusively and is, on the whole, quite delightful. But it is possible to override the Hydramatic's 'brain', holding on to first gear up to 22mph, second up to 34mph and third up to 63mph. Incidentally, with a heavy boot it is possible to spin the wheels on a V8 Silver Cloud, quite something for an automatic car, although this is not something I would attempt with the owner present! I recall leaving black lines up the road outside the Rose & Crown in Bales in a borrowed Cloud II in '59. Impressing some Popsy or other no doubt!

Free from vibration and bounce on good roads (soft tyres help), the rear seat passenger's experience is of near silent wafting progression. In fact, at 70mph on the M6, the loudest sound I detected from TRW was the incessant twittering of the bods in the rear! Back in 1955 much was made of the fact the 100mph Silver Cloud was the fastest motor car to bear the Rolls-Royce name. Poppycock! Pater's 1939 12 cylinder Phantom regularly saw the ton up on its silver plated Warner speedometer, but I will concede the Cloud may well have been the first 100mph closed Rolls-Royce motor car. Sadly, second class road surfaces, once only experienced in backward parts of Europe, are now all too commonplace here in Blighty and my rear seat passengers were sometimes made all too aware of the unsprung mass of the rear axle below them when travelling quickly on patchworked A and B roads. A two position switch on the steering column selects either 'firm' or 'soft' rear damper settings, but in reality the difference is minimal and the generous foam overlay and substantial spring case of the rear seat base can become tested to the limit.

Power steering became standard equipment on the Silver Cloud in October 1956 and Rolls-Royce's new hydraulic system brought great joy to chauffeurs everywhere. Previously a chore, parking was made easy, yet 'feel' was retained when the car was on the move. In fact, above all else it was exactness of steering and stopping that put Rolls-Royce in a different class to other cars in the 1950s. A two ton car needs damned good binders and when properly set up the Silver Cloud's huge cast iron drums are about the best that such brakes can be, boasting 240 square inches of braking surface. The firm's venerable mechanical servo (designed in 1919!) lags at walking speeds, causing some frightening parking moments, and it is always good policy to engage gear with the handbrake safely deployed, but when it really matters the car can be hauled down from high speed without any snaking, squealing and shuddering, and attendant and unwelcome pong! Fine de-misting wires set in the rear window was an advanced feature in the 1950s and the device still works well on TRW, but the car's over-elaborate heating and ventilation system performs poorly by modern standards. I found it hard to keep the screen clear and provide a comfortable environment for my passengers and frequent fiddling with the blasted thing is the only option, as deafening wind roar is the result of opening the windows at speed.

Frederick Henry Royce was a fine British motor engineer and it is down to him that his company became a universal synonym for excellence (and remarkably, this is still the case despite the firm's embarrassing bankruptcy in 1980, and subsequent cataclysmic catastrophes such as the fitting of BMW engines, which eventually led to a total takeover by the dratted sausage eaters). Royce perfected convention rather than inventing the unorthodox. A driven man, he had a capacity for taking pains, carried out uniquely exhaustive tests, took great pride in craftsmanship and brought a perfectionist attitude to all that he did. The Silver Cloud was released 22 years after his death, but the exquisite line and form of the car, and its exemplary driving behaviour, are a testimony to his values, and remain so to this day.

The Silver Cloud is essentially quite simply engineered, but sophistication is not necessarily an attribute. Uncomplicated, cultured and refined, the first generation Cloud is a very fine motor car indeed. Royce's personal motto was: 'Whatever is rightly done, however humble, is noble,' and in the 1950s the thoroughly British Rolls-Royce Silver Cloud was the most carefully made car in the world. In June 1957, TRW 585 cost Mr Godfrey Umbers, mill-owner of Huddersfield, £4,796.10s.1d inc purchase tax, the cost of a street of terraced houses in that industrial town. Today it is worth many times that. But whatever its value in the market, the huge prices paid for coach-built cars on the same chassis will make it seem a bargain. The 'standard steel' Rolls-Royce Silver Cloud is a quite charming motor car of extraordinary quality that satisfies the senses and easily justifies the cost of purchase. It is just a shame it is too long for most chaps' motor houses in this modern day and age!

Chapter Five

Let's say goodbye to hedges,
And roads with grassy edges,
And winding country lanes:
Let all things travel faster,
Where motor car is master,
Till only speed remains.

Inexpensive Progress – John Betjeman*

CITROËN TRACTION AVANT
(First published *Classic Auto* – June 2007)

YOU WILL NOT BE surprised to learn that André Citroën was a Frenchman. We all have our crosses to bear, but he had no choice in the matter, I understand, his family having moved from the Netherlands to Paris in 1870, some five years before his birth.

As such, there should rightly be a couple of dots above the 'e' in his surname. I am at the mercy of the typesetter of this fine publication as to whether this nicety will appear in print, but linguists and pedants will be interested to know that the family name was plain Citroen when they lived in Amsterdam. The dieresis was only added upon reaching France, perhaps to avoid confusion with lemons. As the surname was ultimately derived from the Dutch for that very citrus fruit, as sold by grandfather Citroen in his market stall, one wonders why.

No matter; André was a clever chap in so many ways, with a flair for engineering, business and promotion. His less useful traits included laziness and a weakness for gambling. After leaving the groves of academe, Citroën's early success was built on a type of double-helical gear, apparently inspired by a chance sight of the dismantled wooden guts of a water mill while on a train journey to visit the Polish arm of the family. After adapting and patenting the idea, he set up in business to produce steel gears with a distinctive herringbone pattern, which have the advantage of being quiet and producing no side thrust.

Thus was born Citroën's fortune and the double-chevron company motif. With a thriving and very profitable business, no doubt our hero could have lived a life of gay Parisian leisure should he have so wished, but immediately after the Great War André decided to diversify into the automobile market. He wasn't

* 'Inexpensive Progress' from *Collected Poems*, by John Betjeman © 1955, 1958, 1962, 1964, 1968, 1970, 1979, 1981, 1982, 2001. Reproduced by permission of John Murray, an imprint of Hodder and Stoughton Ltd.

particularly interested in cars, but he could see that everyone else would be, either now or later.

The Type A Citroën motor car duly appeared in 1919, a not particularly adventurous design that became successful because it was cheap, thanks to the application of mass-production techniques, as pioneered by Henry Ford. One futuristic feature, however, was a set of pressed steel wheels, then a fairly recent Michelin innovation.

In the 1920s Citroën became one of the top half-dozen motor manufacturers in the world, employing tens of thousands of workers in factories dispersed far and wide. Few people were unfamiliar with the name, at least partly because since 1925 it had been emblazoned in thousand feet high lights on the Eiffel Tower. Those who missed that unsubtle message might also have seen 'Citroën' sky-written by passing aeroplanes, a technique some say invented by him for the purpose. Whether they found a way of adding the all-important dieresis, I know not.

In contrast to the flamboyant marketing, the cars were still quite staid, selling because they were relatively cheap, well-equipped and available through an extensive network of dealers. The patron wanted the next generation of Citroëns to be bought for their innate quality. If a car were good enough, he reasoned, it wouldn't go out of fashion and therefore could be kept in production for much longer after recouping the initial investment.

The Traction Avant was that voiture! Inspiration came from a variety of sources, including the 1931 prototype built by American manufacturer, Budd, which just happened to have front wheel drive and a unitary construction bodyshell (aka, usually incorrectly, 'monocoque'). Citroën already had business links with the company, and had earlier bought Budd's patent for an all-steel body, so it's likely that ideas had been buzzing through brains for a while before the TA project began in earnest in 1932.

Astonishingly, after appointing gifted designers, André Lefèbvre and Flaminio Bertoni, to develop the concept, it took barely a year before the car was unveiled. A popular misconception is that the Traction was the first with front wheel drive, unitary construction, independent suspension and hydraulic brakes. Not so! All those things had been tried many years before. For instance, the Lancia Lambda made from 1922 featured a unitary body and independent rear suspension, while Alvis back here in Blighty had produced front-wheel-drive models in 1928, with DKW of Germany not far behind. Still, one has to give Citroën credit for being brave enough to put all these elements together, and in such a short time.

One also has to hand Monsieur Citroën un grand brickbat for insisting that his new car should have an automatic transmission, a novelty that appealed to lazy motorists like himself but had far too many teething troubles… literally.

Unfortunately, the general economic climate and the cost of developing such an avant-garde (no pun intended) automobile put the business under extreme financial stress. In desperate search of a cash injection in early 1934, the TA was shown off to prospective lenders. It's reported that all was going well until the delicate automatic gearbox disintegrated, resulting in immediate disinterest from those considering ploughing more money into the company.

Bankruptcy loomed, and Michelin, the largest creditor, took control and promptly pensioned off the company founder. In a cruel twist, André Citroën became ill and died the following year, along with his million watt advertising hoarding on the Eiffel Tower. Strangely, or not, his car business continued virtually as before, with the controlling Michelin men letting the design team get on with launching the Traction, minus its troublesome automatic transmission.

Faced with such innovation, people were suspicious. Arch rival Peugeot declared that the car would be unstable without rear wheel drive and dangerously weak without a traditional chassis. Citroën responded by launching a TA over a cliff to land on its nose, resulting in so little damage that the doors could still be opened normally afterwards. Any other doubts about functionality were well and truly answered in 1935 when François Lecot managed to drive an incredible 400,000km in 400 days in a Type 11.

Mention of which reminds me that although all Tractions share the same basics, they were available in a baffling number of variations, with a deeply confusing selection of names. To give a taster, the first model, powered by a 1303cc engine, was the 7A, which was almost immediately succeeded by the 7B and 7C, each with slightly raised capacity. Then there was the 1911cc 11, and the 2867cc, six-cylinder 15. The numbers usually refer to the French system of fiscal horsepower rating (CV, standing for 'Cheval Vapeur'). But sometimes they don't, because the 15 was actually a 16CV!

To add further bewilderment, the initial 7CV was called the Super Modern Twelve in Britain, while the 11 was called the 15, not to be confused with the French 15, which was actually a 16CV. To make things crystal clear, I should also mention that the French 15 (16CV) is often called the Six, because that's how many cylinders it has, of course.

Beyond that, a choice of wheelbase lengths and body styles were catalogued, including the Commerciale, which has a justified claim of being the world's first hatchback. Perhaps for the sake of our sanity it's just as well the proposed 3.8 litre V8 never made it into production.

One of Citroën's many satellite factories was in Slough, as immortalised for all the wrong reasons by John Betjeman (Come, friendly bombs et cetera!). Apart from the obvious steering wheel relocation, British TAs differed in trim from the French version, by having leather upholstery rather than cloth. A chrome radiator grille, semaphore indicators and 12V electrics were other identifying features.

Changes to the steering mechanism and drive shafts were made early on (a major obstacle in providing front-wheel-drive in those days was the problem of transmitting power to wheels that had also to be steered, explaining 1000km greasing intervals). In the last years before War Two, the car also gained a set of distinctive broad-spoked wheels known as pilotes.

Understandably, production dwindled after 1939, although the occupying Germans appreciated the Traction's abilities, it's gathered. A superior mode of travel to Hitler's People's Car, we can be certain! No time was lost in restarting manufacture in peacetime. Some essentially minor alterations were made, but the model carried on into the 1950s, looking increasingly quaint compared to the new breed of American-influenced autos. The year 1954 gave us a taste of another future, when the rear torsion-bar suspension was supplanted by a hydro-pneumatic system, which was to appear on the groundbreaking DS scheduled to arrive the following season. The last of some 750,000 Tractions was built in July, 1957.

Notwithstanding my loyalty to an even more ancient motor car, I must admit that familiarity had made me slightly contemptuous of the big Citroën by the mid-1950s. Like everyone else, though, I warmed to it again in more recent times when the model made regular appearances on our television screens in the hands of Inspector Maigret. Always a rare sight on UK roads, a great number continued to be used as everyday transport in France right up into the 1980s, when the unfortunate word 'classic' entered our lives. Over 25,000 were assembled in Slough (the bombs landed on Birmingham and Coventry instead), but not many seem to remain and values have risen accordingly.

The scruffy example I tested for *Classic Auto* in modern times was a late French model that had not long been rescued from a long period of idleness in an outbuilding on a Welsh farm. After a static quarter of a century, it had needed only minor work to make roadworthy, and sensibly the new owner had resisted the temptation to destroy the car's character by embarking on a 'restoration'. Blemishes abounded on the grey bodywork, but it was an eminently usable machine, as proved by a recent trip to Arras for the model's 75th anniversary celebration. A jaunt of a mere 800 miles may not have impressed Monsieur Lecot, but we are all much older than we were then!

I first caught sight of the Citroën closer to home. Wearing its rusty patina with pride, it looked splendid, and attracted far more attention than the ranks of cosmetically enhanced cars nearby. Few shapes are so stylish or evocative. De Forte is emphatically not a Francophile, but his eyes misted with the memories of a lost age; of Charles Trenet, Edith Piaf and a time when motoring – and life

– was such great fun. The word 'icon' is grossly overused these days, but the Traction Avant deserves the appellation.

NASCAR ADVENTURE

In July 1955 I was glad to be invited along by Triumph man Edward Turner on his annual trip to the west coast of the United States, but I am afraid Edward was always far too fond of his own voice, and after a solid fortnight in his company I was desperate to get away. A NASCAR (National Association for Stock Car Auto Racing) race meeting at Bay Meadows in San Francisco provided an ideal opportunity for escape, and promised to to be a first-rate subject for a colour feature in *The Auto*. So while Turner was whisked off somewhere salubrious for the weekend by Triumph distributor Bill (JoMo) Johnson, I made my way north from Los Angeles on Highway One.

Whenever I ride over long distances, I find the de Forte mind splits into two modes, a higher one which philosophises as I go along, and a lower one which is concentrating intently. I can't separate the two, and without them both one couldn't motorcycle in the same way. Thus the long, bend-swinging ride along the spectacular Pacific seaboard on a borrowed Triumph Thunderbird afforded plenty of thinking time. The Johnson Motor Corporation (JoMo) was Triumph's official importer and distributor for the whole of the USA from its smart headquarters on West Colorado Street in Pasadena. Originally built as a car showroom, the futuristic concrete and glass building was an attractive showpiece with floor-to-ceiling plate windows, a bright, spacious sales area, modern workshops, and well stocked stores. Above all, it was clean, modern and presented a new image for motorcycling. To Britons in the 1950s, there was a feeling that in the USA the future had already arrived. Films and newsreels projected a technicolor picture of a different, happier, sunnier, more glamorous world than that endured in dull, grey, rain-lashed Britain. They appeared to offer the possibility of a better life and better times ahead, and by 1955 there was just a glimmer of hope that an exciting American-style consumer society could be coming our way. Despite its vulgarity and brashness, I loved being in the United States.

The Bay Meadows race track in San Mateo, California, was a one mile oval, although in reality more like a paper clip in shape. Principally a horse racing track that first opened its doors in 1934, it was built on a former airfield in a southern San Francisco suburb. The famous thoroughbred Seabiscuit raced and won there before War Two. When it closed in 2008 it was California's oldest horse racing track. There is housing there now, inevitably.

I arrived on Saturday evening just as qualifying finished for the following day's 250 mile NASCAR Grand National feature race, and after parking the

Trumpet and introducing myself at the race office, I left my riding integuments there and began acquainting myself with a new sport. Arrayed in the paddock were Buicks, Olds, Oldsmobiles, Dodges, Hudsons, and Studebakers, but I was most of all drawn to the smart and well organised Mercury Outboards Chrysler equipe. The gargantuan C-300 Chrysler saloon of one Tim Flock had just been announced as having achieved pole position for the following day's big race, but leaning against it, and accepting joshing backslaps, and heartfelt handshakes from his fellow competitors with laid-back southern good humour was another Flock, Tim's elder brother Fontello, known to all as Fonty.

At that moment young Tim was on the other side of the country, winning a NASCAR 100 miler in Syracuse, New York in an outwardly identical car. Then, remarkably, he would fly coast-to-coast with his redoubtable team manager Carl Kiekhaefer, millionaire owner of outboard motor manufacturing company Mercury Marine, in order to race at Bay Meadows the next day. The journey, which would involve a helicopter ride, a hop to Chicago in a chartered light aircraft, and a scheduled flight to San Francisco, had been organised and financed by Kiekhaefer, who was keen to see his driver pick up Grand National championship points at both venues, and garner a good deal of publicity in the process.

I was drawn to the Flocks. Like their team boss, as I would later discover for myself, they were fiercely competitive and more than a little crazy, but unlike Kiekhaefer, they also manifested a zany sense of fun, which sometimes clashed with the Mercury chief's puritanical side. Tim (actually Julius) Flock was born in Alabama in 1924, the youngest of three racing brothers, and his big sister, Ethel, raced too (Tim later told me their daddy named her after the petrol he put in his taxi!). A few years before, Fonty informed me, Tim had competed in eight races with a tame rhesus macaque as his co-driver. Wee 'Jocko Flocko' had his own uniform and a custom seat, and his name was sign-written on the car's roof, but the joke came to an abrupt end during a race when the inquisitive primate pulled the chain to open the tyre wear observation hatch in the floor, and stuck his head out under the car. Having been whacked in the phizzog by a stone, the little creature went totally berserk, and Tim had to make an unscheduled pitstop to let him out. This monkey business cost him second place and a significant wad of prize money.

Big brother Bob Flock was a race promoter in Atlanta, but also an accomplished racer, and Ethel Mobley, the boys' sister was another formidable driver, who had raced at Daytona Speedway, beating champion drivers and all her brothers except Tim. Like many other stock car stars of the 1950s, the Flocks had started out in Sunday afternoon moonshiner events. The histories of moonshining, or bootlegging, and stock car racing are closely intertwined, and

Ethel explained that home brewers had been active in the southeast as far back as the 1700s. Various governments had tried to impose taxes, and the activity was clamped down upon during the civil war, but moonshining had continued to thrive in isolated mountain communities, and had boomed again during prohibition.

Indeed, bootlegging became an important means of survival during the depression for many folk in remote communities, and it was then that the moonshiners started racing along dirt back roads, hauling liquor in nondescript looking (stock, in fact), but heavily adapted cars using special components. Specially strengthened whiskey cars (the US spelling appropriate here!) could carry up to 180 gallons of liquor in tanks hidden under their floorboards and rear seats. Truck springs kept them from sagging, the engines were hotted up with twin carburettors to outrun the county sheriffs, and the lights were wired with an off switch so they could be extinguished when expedient. The young kids who drove these cars at night knew every bend, and the limits of their machines, and when the post-war period brought the beginnings of stock car racing, these young men in Ford V8s, and Chrysler Hemis became American stock car racing's first stars.

The Flock family ran a moonshine business from their home in the backwoods of Georgia, and all over the southeastern United States, similar operators in adapted cars raced through the night running illicit alcohol along dirt back roads from country stills to distributors in the big cities. For fun, and for bragging rights, the runners would race each other in fields on Sunday afternoons. At the end of the 1940s Daytona Speedway boss, big Bill France saw an opportunity and organised a stock car race series on a regional, and then national basis. NASCAR was born.

Carl Kiekhaefer had first arrived on the NASCAR scene at the Daytona beach-road race earlier that year, having transported a brashly sign-written white Chrysler C-300 down to Florida without anyone to drive it. Tim Flock, the 1952 Grand National Champion, was suspended and he watched the car arrive while sunbathing on the beach, but Kiekhaefer paid his fines and the happy-go-lucky Georgian started on pole and finished second in the 140mph race behind the Buick of Glenn 'Fireball' Roberts. But Roberts was disqualified for a technical transgression, and Kiekhaefer's team scored the first of 52 NASCAR wins in two championship-winning years.

Styled by the forward looking Virgil Exner, the 5.4 litre Chrysler C-300 was a huge luxury car, 219 inches long, and 80 inches wide. It was a new model, rushed into production in time for the Daytona race, but actually something of an amalgam of existing products. Boldly painted with his own and company names emblazoned all over its bodywork, Kiekhaefer's brand new machine was built as a racer with heavy duty taxicab and truck components, a racing exhaust, twin four-barrel carburettors, and a special camshaft and other permitted trick parts in its 'Firepower' Hemi V8 engine (the Hemis featured domed pistons and other technology developed for aircraft in War Two). Astonishingly, Kiekhaefer's car retained its Powerflite automatic transmission, but upon Tim's (unsurprising) insistence, he persuaded Chrysler to build a special 'stick shift' unit for its next outing.

Kiekhaefer was a perfectionist and a workaholic, and he brought a new professionalism to American stock car racing. He hired only the very best drivers, used transporters rather than have the cars driven to the track, kept his machinery looking smart, and introduced timed pitstops. His large, well organised crews featured dedicated engine, chassis, and brakes men, and a two-man refuelling team, all clad in immaculate white overalls. In fact, everything about his operation was spotless. Having his own moniker on the cars together with the Mercury name was perhaps a mite vulgar, but what the heck, it was the American way, and he backed all this up with a highly effective advertising and marketing programme.

Was he tough? Fonty laughed. Tough as hell! He fired people who didn't even work for him! A fellow given two weeks wages in cash in lieu of notice for sitting down on the job turned out to be the Coca-Cola delivery man. At the race track, and in his factory he was dictatorial and a fanatical, but he paid his drivers a good wage, gave them bonuses, and let them keep every cent of their prize money. Was he a little crazy? As nutty as a fruitcake. He would take over a whole corridor in a hotel and keep the drivers' apart from their wives at night; post armed guards at his test facility; spy on his opposition in the outboard industry, whom he referred to as 'the enemy'; and destroy his rivals' marine engines in symbolic and ritualistic ways, burning them on a bonfire in front of his staff and then dancing around it.

The next morning there was a knock on my motel room door at 6.30am. It was Fonty Flock. Late last night Kiekhaefer had telephoned from Chicago O'Hare to tell him young Tim had won the race at Syracuse, and to meet them at San Francisco Municipal at 7am with Tim's car. Did I want a ride over there in the Chrysler with Ethel?

Howdy. The passenger side door was bolted up solid, so I was obliged to climb somewhat awkwardly through the window aperture, and then drop down onto the softly sprung front bench seat. The rest of the luxury interior had been stripped out, I noticed immediately, even the instrumentation. Expensive-looking aeronautical oil pressure, and oil and water temperature gauges were angled up at the driver from below the dash, and a large tachometer (calibrated precisely to that engine on Kiekhaefer's dyno, Ethel later explained with an illustrative blast on the (extraordinarily) loud pedal) was bolted onto the top of the dashboard. Various neat holes had been cut in the floorpan with inspection lamps mounted to shine directly into them so the driver could to judge 'tire' wear. Are you ready, boy? said Ethel, having waited patiently for me to finish looking around the car. Then brace yourself, and hang on tight.

Boy could that girl drive. We rocketed away from the motel, fishtailing and spraying grit into the swimming pool as polka-dot curtains twitched and paunched men in boxer shorts shook their fists in trellised doorways. We raced down an avenue of under-lit gum trees as Sunday paper boys and early morning dog walkers dived for cover behind them. Then I found myself slithering helplessly across the seat as, with a violent shriek of tyres, we hurtled around a sudden right-hander, shot up a short ramp, 'aired-up' momentarily, and then catapulted, the big beast twitching in every sinew, onto the shiny new freeway, leaving suburbia behind and below us.

The wheels have been widened, laughed Ethel as I picked myself up off the floor, and the shocks are heavy duty, as are the brakes, the axles, and the drivetrain. The chassis has been braced, and the engine has been blueprinted and balanced, and everything inside it has been polished with toothpaste. Impressive, huh? And with that we blew past an XK120 like it was standing still. Kiekhaefer's people were 'right particular', stripped every car to the last nut, and then rebuilt it, fixin' all the mods, and spending hundreds of hours on the engine alone. Kiekhaefer had two workshop sites, and hear tell there would soon be one in the south too; and he moved spares and personnel around every day in his private plane. He was an uppity individual, but impressive sho' nuff, Ethel said as we swung off the freeway. Why was the car so deafeningly loud? Ethel grinned. A pair of darn tootin' four-inch diameter open pipes run in a straight line from a purpose-built manifold, straight through the trunk, and exit out the back panel of the car.

A few minutes later we screeched to a stop at the airport where a small group stood waiting for us. Cripes sakes, where abouts you been? Held up by stop 'n go lights? scowled a smallish, heavily-built man in thick-rimmed glasses. It was Carl Kiekhaefer. Pay no mind, said Tim Flock, greeting his sister through the driver's window. We just got here this second. Who's this? Ethel explained about her shell-shocked English passenger, and Tim in turn told her why she and the C-300 Chrysler had been summoned. You need to go find a guard rail and scrape it good down its full length, right on the swage line from here to here. You got that? It seemed the New York car had picked up such an injury, and the world had to believe the same car was about to try to win races on consecutive days on opposite American coasts. With that Tim signalled to the three other men with dirt-streaked faces who had been standing in a huddle behind the marine millionaire, and they began shuffling off to get a cab to a breakfast diner, and then on to Bay Meadows. Who were they, Mr Kiekhaefer? Losers, he said, deadpan. In a generous act of sportsmanship, the taciturn tycoon had flown three of Flock's main championship rivals across the country with him. Now that got my attention. Could I be granted an interview sometime today? Talk to me when we've won the race, he growled.

You hankerin' for a drive? asked Ethel as we swung back out into the Sunday city traffic. Er, no, why? Could be your only chance, and with that she pulled onto another hidden freeway ramp, jerked the taped steering wheel to the right and clanged against the steel barrier on my side of the car. With a shrill of tortured metal she ran along the rail, its rivets bumping along the Chrysler's bodywork, sending a shower of orange sparks flying through my window and singing the hairs on my forearm. A further snap on the wheel flicked our tail off the steel with a 'ching', and then there was a chirp, and then an outraged shriek of protest from the fat tyres, as we moved from scantily grassed verge to warm, grippy asphalt, and then lunged, sharking onto the freeway looking for prey. That should do it. Now, you drive, and she immediately slid along the seat towards me. Moments later, having quite involuntarily played my part in a miraculous manoeuvre rather akin to castling in chess, I found myself at the wheel of the great white beast.

My word! To say Mr Kiekhaefer's garish 350bhp Chrysler packed a wallop would be a gross understatement. Bottom end torque? Rather! Top gear roll-on gave this hedonist a kick in the plus fours like no other, and in really applying the heavy boot, the needle on the revolution counter whipped instantaneously clockwise as the big V8 displayed that indefinable readiness to rev which distinguishes a truly happy engine. Moreover, as the needle hurried rapidly around the dial, mighty eruptions of fire under the bonnet turned to a thunderous boom in our wake, as the big V8 lunged forward to velocities well in excess of 120mph. But with plenty left! The enormous thing possessed utterly preternatural and quite demoniacal energy, and no doubt managed to impose itself on the notice of everyone within a mile radius, not least those poor potterers whose gentle Sunday morning run to the beach, or perhaps to church, was so completely smashed, so utterly shattered by the seismic shock of our passing.

Eventually aware that Ethel was no longer laughing hysterically at me, nor convulsing at the horrified and terrified reactions of the aforementioned dawdlers, but had instead begun hollering urgently in my ear, jerking her thumb rearwards and stabbing her finger at some distant point ahead, I came dimly to surmise her meaning. Time to leave. I chopped lanes rightwards, and shifted to the middle of the car's three forward ratios to slow a little for the exit ramp 'over yonder', before ripping around a tight corkscrewing right, the big car clinging like a postage stamp as we spiralled back down towards the everyday stop and go of suburban Sunday morning San Francisco.

At the bottom of the ramp the traffic lights turned treacherously red, but the patrol car my co-driver had so keenly spotted joining the super-highway in urgent if forlorn pursuit, had evidently failed to notice our strategic departure from it, and we chuckled impishly as it wailed on obliviously, impotent, overhead. What else to tell? Nothing of great note as I drove decorously from then on, but I can vouch that nothing, but nothing, in its time would have held that Chrysler in a getaway from the stop and go lights (as Kiekhaefer had so quaintly put it), or the pub for that matter. What fun it would have been to have demonstrated its prowess to Bolster and co outside the Cock in Coventry, or the Rose & Crown in Bales! Yes, Tim Flock's car was vulgar and brutish, but it was also impressive in its single-mindedness and honesty of purpose, and powerfully attractive for its eagerness, and its peerless, stump-pulling power.

Back at the track, I made a friend of the young man superintending the refreshments in Kiekhaefer's well-drilled team (I noticed he never sat down when his employer was present!), and he proved a most useful guide to the machinations of NASCAR and of the mechanics of the Mercury Outboards equipe. The Grand National series had begun in 1949, although called Strictly Stock Series in its first year, and most races were held in the southeastern USA, often on dirt ovals of a quarter or half a mile in length. In the 1960s, paved 'super-speedways' would come to dominate, but in 1955, 40 of 45 races took place on dirt. The dirt tracks were particularly hard on the drivers and the cars. Dust got into the cars' engines and killed them, prompting Kiekhiefer to invent and perfect paper air filters to keep it out of his Hemis. But it still got on the inside of windshields, and of drivers' goggles where running sweat turned it to streaks of mud. Tim Flock's face was still grimed from Syracuse when he arrived at Bay Meadows, having had no time to shower or shave. Like most of his fellows, he was a hard and determined man, and American stock car racing in the 1950s was a rumbustious and dangerous game. Deaths were not uncommon, and even in those carefree days, public unrest was beginning to be stirred up by do-gooders.

As I found out that July afternoon, NASCAR racing is a contact sport; violent, bone-jarring, and a gruelling test of endurance for man and machine in front of baying crowds. Heavy cars like the Mercury Outboard Chryslers were good for bumping and barging, but needed more powerful engines to shift their weight. Fonty had qualified Tim's car at a fraction under 80mph. Fonty was, by all accounts, a spectacular driver, nicknamed the Crackup King because of his propensity for spectacular accidents, but on the Bay Meadows dirt track that day what struck me the most about his brother Tim was his smooth, no nonsense style. He circulated again and again, gunning past his rivals using his power advantage, or else passing them in the turns, getting inside and underneath them, then pressing against them through the bend. This prevented understeer taking his car outwards, enabling quicker cornering, and facilitated a sling-shot onto the 'straightaways'. Including pitstops (directed by Kiekhaefer himself), Flock averaged 68mph over 252 laps (there was a scoring error), and lapped the entire field as he streaked to his 13th win of the year and his second in 24 hours.

After the Flocks pocketed the impressive winner's cheque, threatened colourfully to come over to 'Yoorp' to kick everyone's ass at Aintree and Silverstone (I had been goading them, I admit), and set off home together to Georgia, the pugnacious Mr Kiekhaefer took me to a diner; and over root beer and steak and eggs, and to strains of *Rock Around the Clock* played repeatedly on the juke box by pomaded and bobby-socked youngsters, he told me about himself. Elmer Carl Kiekhaefer, was clearly a determined and hard-working character. Born in 1906 in Wisconsin, he was from a farming background but had trained as an electrical and mechanical engineer. In 1939 he bought a defunct engine manufacturing plant with the intention of using it to manufacture dairy equipment, but found 300 outboard engines lying around. Did he scrap them? Heck, no. Kiekhaefer fitted them with better crankshafts, rebranded them and found a new buyer. That led to his forming Mercury Marine, a company which made him his stupendous fortune (and is still a leading manufacturer of outboards to this day – ed).

But before designing and building his own outboards, he had already developed two-man chainsaws for the American army and radio controlled drones of various sizes used for artillery practice targets. In fact, by the end of War Two the Kiekhaefer Corporation was the biggest chainsaw manufacturer in the world. Most were used to cut down jungle in the Pacific theatre, of course, but I was able to tell him I had come across them in the Rhineland in '45, and jolly good they had been too, and that I had heard from gunnery types that the two-stroke flat twin drone was also an exceptional thing. Under the shaded booth lights, the glints on his glasses served to magnify a slight smile. Now, with the American leisure boom showing no signs of abating, Kiekhaefer told me with no little pride he now needed a Goodyear cycle-motor to get around efficiently in his huge outboard motor factory in Cedarburg. And did I know he had also bought an alligator-infested lake in Florida which he called Lake X and used as a secret test facility? He had spent big, building staff accommodation, workshops, seawalls, and piers on the 1,400 acre site. Surely I had seen the publicity photographs from the time he used a Mercury outboard to tow an elephant around the lake on waterskis?

Kiekhaefer had dabbled in Mexican road races, but he had nevertheless been an unfancied outsider with an untried car when he had arrived at Daytona that February. Fonty had told me that at that point reigning champion Lee Petty was already looking good for a second successive National title, so when Oregon backwoodsman Hershel McGriff declined the opportunity to drive the C-300, and a Mercury agent introduced Kiehaefer to Tim Flock, surely that had been a sizeable stroke of luck? Not so, said Kiekhaefer dismissively, signalling for more root beer as the steaks arrived. There were up to a dozen drivers capable of winning the championship, and whoever prevails will have the best car and support team. It costs many thousands of dollars to develop my cars, to prepare them each week, and to transport them around the country. Meticulous preparation gives a driver the confidence to push hard on every lap, and my pit crews keep them going during the race. That is what I bring to the table.

These guys could not win a championship on their own, he said. In fact, by running multiple entries in the bigger races later in the season, it will most likely be me who decides who will become 1955 NASCAR champion. And next year I plan to run as many as seven cars in a race, and to have depots around the country. You see, like the cars, I see the drivers as interchangeable. I reward them well, but I don't expect them to get any big ideas. I pay them to do what I say. Besides, the Flocks can drive sure enough, but like all moonshiners, they lack discipline, he added harshly. I try to keep them away from it, but hell, those boys make liquor out of any-damn-thing. Corn, wheat, rye, seed cane, sugar liquor; and they make fruit brandies too – apple, peach and banana. Did he not drink at all? I asked. I have a beer once in a while.

I asked him why he was spending so much money to conquer NASCAR. Let's just say I have ambitions in the automotive world, he said coyly. Was it true that despite his unique and close relationship with Chrysler, he was backing other teams to provide blocking. No comment. Did he plan to experiment with lighter cars? Yes, watch this space. And with that he parked his eating irons and dabbed his lips with his paper napkin. I've got a plane to catch, he said. My own. I fished for my wallet. No, you stay there, I'll get the check. Call me if you're ever in Wisconsin.

TAKING STOCK

Tim Flock would go on to rack up five more victories on his way to becoming 1955 NASCAR Grand National champion in his Chrysler C-300, clinching the title on October 30 in Hillsboro, North Carolina. Kiekhaefer's Chryslers would win 22 of 39 races they entered that year, and bring about irreversible and major change to stock car racing in the United States. Tim won the first race of the 1956 season too (actually held in November 1955), but he quit Kiekhaefer's team after just three races. Flock appreciated being well remunerated but found working for Kiekhaefer too stressful, he told me years later. He resented the regimentation, the tough testing schedule, and the strict driver conduct rules; and he didn't like being told who should win.

Buck Baker was the 1956 NASCAR Grand National champion in a 5.8 litre Mercury Outboards Chrysler 300B but Kiekhaefer's dream had started turning sour. NASCAR founder Bill France resented the publicity Kiekhaefer and his cars attracted, which left him and even NASCAR itself in the shade. In an effort to regain the limelight, he used his officials to try to hound Kiekhaefer out of the sport. Every part of a NASCAR race car had to be 'stock', or at least available to the public, and France bent the rules or turned a blind eye to help people he wanted to do well. But he clamped down hard on Kiekhaefer's Mercury Chryslers, instructing his technical men to run a tooth-comb over them at every opportunity. Further, France is alleged to have been fond of using the pace car to Kiekhaefer's disadvantage, to have ordered fuel tampering, and once to have arranged a crash to take place at the pit entrance, blocking it when he knew a Mercury car needed to come in. For his part, Kiekhaefer did his best to make France apply his own rules consistently and across the board. The bespectacled tycoon felt needled, and France felt NASCAR wasn't big enough for both of them. It was war.

At the beginning of 1957, Kiekhaefer pulled out of motor racing, but not because France defeated him. He quit in dismay because the public had started booing his cars. He considered himself the last of the independents, a plucky privateer, yet the fans had begun to loathe him for his efficiency, for being so successful, and for making the sport less unpredictable.

Perhaps he also saw that soon even the best funded independents would be unable to compete. During 1956 Ford and Chevrolet had woken up and started spending big to beat him, and with no Mercury Outboards runners on the grid the following year, the Detroit factory teams dominated the sport. In the short term, France subsidised small independents in order to put on a show, but drastic change was needed. He came up with a single carburettor rule, a masterstroke which forced Ford and Chevrolet out of the sport – something they were actually glad of, as it enabled them to back out of their expensive battle with dignity – and which would have crippled Kiekhaefer's Chryslers. My guess is he knew it was coming.

What were those automotive ambitions Kiekhaefer mentioned? Did he wreck them one day in 1956 when, having become enraged by Ford crowing about a victory which he himself had masterminded, he fixed a special Ford engine up to a fuel line and revved it until it blew itself to smithereens? We will never know, although rumours have since surfaced that he was discussing selling Mercury Marine to Mercedes.

DREAMING SPIRES
(Diary extract – 13 November 1957)
Second early start of the week for excursion to Oxford to see my old friend, AI(*1) who wanted to discuss some devilish new contraption he's been working

on recently. Jack Frost had visited in the night, so spent first few miles peering through letterbox-size slot in screen. With little vision available, nearly flattened Bob, our ever-disrespectful postman, when he materialised suddenly on his cycle. Perhaps if he stopped that dratted whistling for a minute he might be better able to keep out of the way. Took evasive action and skilfully avoided a collision, but the incident made me more sure than ever that heating equipment jolly well ought to be standard fitting on a £500 motor in this day and age.

Took the usual route through Black Country and Brummagem, where I must have seen over a thousand motor vehicles in half an hour. Soon the country will be completely ruined, I fear. Passed Fort D at 9.25am and picked up A34 to Bardsville(*2), then onward to Banbury, where I should have found use for a cock horse to thread through the melee! One would never know that petroleum is in short supply. Lovely run through leafy Warwickshire countryside to Oxford's dreaming spires, where I encountered all too many dreaming bicyclists. Might expect varsity chaps to have more brains than slothful Bob, but they seemed equally unable to concentrate on the task in hand, so I often had to sound horn to make swift progress.

As usual, met AI at the Trout, a pleasant hostelry near Cowley factory. He was his usual ebullient self, rattling on about various pet projects of the moment. During the war I had to suffer his enthusiasm for ridiculous powered wheelbarrows and other chimeras (he assumed I wasn't in cahoots with Lord HH, evidently!), but a few years later he consulted me many times about the Mosquito(*3). Contrary to rumour, the late decision to widen the car by four inches was originally my suggestion. Dear Alec tends to 'forget' these things, of course.

The latest ADO car is naturally still on the top secret list, so Len Lord would probably shoot me if he were aware of my involvement. It's going to be a tiny machine, scaled down in all respects yet still able (alleges Issi) to accommodate four adults plus luggage. I playfully suggested he should use a rear engine, as any mention of a car with even the remotest similarity to a Volkswagen makes AI apoplectic with rage. He laughed about it later!

In fact, the Morris Microbe is destined to have a lightweight two-stroke engine. You mean you're copying DKW, I teased. No, Wilby, he thundered, it is an entirely novel design, and at some time in the future all manufacturers will be producing cars built on a rhomboid base, with a flat-twin two-stroke engine mounted under the floor driving the middle wheels.

As the conversation drifted on into the afternoon, by which time we were both somewhat scotch squiffy, I outlined some of my own theories again. All the details were set down in 1938 diary, so there's no point in repeating myself here(*4), but I genuinely believe this rhombus plan is misguided and told him so. Look, Issi, I said, forget this damned diamond nonsense – put the engine across the car in the front, driving the front wheels. To save space, stack the crankshaft above the gearbox and use small wheels (the Microbe has 12-inch side wheels, admittedly, but the leading and trailing ones are as big as my Bentley's). As I explained, with the aid of sketches on a paper napkin, the finished car need only be ten feet long; a true miniature.

AI eventually conceded that my ideas had some merit, and it will be interesting to see how BMC's small car develops. Arranged another Cowley rendezvous for May, by which time Alec promised he will have a prototype for me to try. If so, let's hope he chooses a different route from the factory, because his horrid little Microbe (a name that I sincerely hope will be changed for production) will become a see-saw on that humpback bridge on the edge of the village, and what happens to the steering then, eh!

Homeward journey took only three hours. Although it's fashionable to believe that drinking alcohol before driving is unwise, I find my concentration greatly improved by a moderate intake, particularly in winter, when one would otherwise feel uncomfortably chilly. 'One for the road and half a dozen for the motor' is sound advice, certainly.

It is surely noteworthy that my best ever time for Greenfirth-Bales(*5) was achieved early on NY's Day, 1953, when I had consumed almost a full bottle of my favourite malt libation and rather a lot of Clive's rather excellent punch. Incidentally, that 2hr 28m record could easily have been better, because I was obliged to stop for several minutes on the outskirts of the Potteries to dislodge a Keep Left sign that had somehow become trapped in my nearside front wing.

Going farther back, it's indisputable than most Brooklands class records were set by drivers who were so comprehensively oiled that they were barely capable of walking. Once installed behind the wheel they were truly magnificent. For instance, having been in the Clubhouse knocking back doubles since early morning, Archie F-C(*6) took his 8 litre Snardly Napier Special round at 124mph with absolutely no trouble. Mind you, he only realised he'd done it three days later. Great times.

Notes
*(*1) Alec Issigonis, of course, whom I first met before WW2, when one frequented Shelsey and Prescott.*
*(*2) Stratford-Upon-Avon, obviously, but my youthful self evidently preferred silly nicknames!*
*(*3) Later known as the Morris Minor.*
*(*4) A Modern Mini-Car for the Common Man', described in July 1938 entry.*
*(*5) Family friends Clive and Mary Temple lived in Oak House in Greenfirth in Yorkshire's*

West Riding, and for a great many years I was a frequent visitor to that spectacular, if soggy part of the Pennines.
(*6) Archie Fiennes-Clinton. Splendid fellow. Shot down over France in 1941, aged 26. Tragic waste.

BENTLEY ANTICS
(Diary extract – 24 April 1958)

Simply splendid day in God's own country! Up at dawn to extricate Beattie(*1) from her temporary quarters in the top garage at Oak House. After months of inaction one anticipates trouble, but she soon cranked up and bellowed menacingly in the early mist. Formalities over, I ate one of Mary's hearty breakfasts (condemned man; I should say not!) while listening to some Elgar on the Third, clobbered up and set off into the yonder.

By jove it was nippy up on High Moss at 7am, but Yorkshire on an April morning is such a glorious, glorious place to be! Once the old girl's lifeblood had warmed through and I could give the motor some stick, we were fairly flying. My eyes streamed and my leather helmet threatened lift-off as the sinews of the ancient way unwound at a cracking rate. Stupendous. Still snow in the hollows at 1,500 feet, and the standing stone near West Nelly End pointed a portentous finger through the swirls of low cloud, but what a way to travel, what pure joy!

Reaching 'Bevel Straight'(*2) the sun's orange orb seemed to be sitting upon the horizon, drawing me onward, willing me to go faster. Some say I should know better at my age, but who could resist a flat-out blast in such heaven?

Down went the loud pedal to the floorboards, and four and a half supercharged litres took up the challenge with a deep roar of satisfaction. 70mph, 80, 90... The double-O came up a mile or so before we had to slow for the sharp left-hander heralding the descent. Overshoot here and you will shortly be meeting your maker in the valley far below. Steeling myself, I kept my foot firm down. At 110 she faltered briefly before unleashing a few more horses and accelerating again. At 115mph my headgear surrendered to the slipstream and disappeared(*3), bumps pounding through the chassis, wheels hardly in contact with the ground. I could barely see nor breathe, and Beattie was shaking fit to bust. My nerve finally gave out just shy of 120, leaving precious little space to haul anchors down to 60, which is pretty well the maximum one might entertain here without inspecting the scenery on the exit from the left-hander.

It was as well we had the world to ourselves this morning, for I found myself unable to hold her on the nearside carriageway. After a certain amount of unplanned arm exercise, we emerged part sideways, but still heading more or less in the right direction. A prang would have been inevitable if anything else

At 115mph my headgear surrendered to the slipstream, and disappeared.

had been around. Moments later, Ronald D's Minor chuffed into view, straining up the bank from Skagsdale, no doubt en route to Blackbridge market. He smiled as we passed, but best not dwell on what might have happened if he had been a hundred yards further up the road.

Heart was in my mouth for hours, so had every excuse to imbibe stiff one or four in the Bay Horse at lunchtime. Arrived back glowing!

Notes

(*1) Beattie, Pater's old Bentley, BTT 40, sold but then rescued from the scrapman's clutches in '49. Not bad value for a fiver!

(*2) Thanks to Romans dead and gone, the road here runs true as an arrow for two miles. The local speedy set nicknamed it Bevel Straight back in the '30s after an incident involving a thrown propshaft when testing there before weekend meetings down at Donington. I'm referring to the original Donington Park circuit, of course, not that twiddly thing they use now.

(*3) Sometime around 1963, Dick Barucco had a spot of bother with his '59 XK on Bevel and was obliged to stop for some roadside wrenching, to use a dreadful Americanism. While pondering how to stem the flow of petrol from his front SU, he happened to catch sight of a rather battered object in a ditch nearby. Yes, it was my old flying helmet, somewhat the worse for wear, but eminently fit for further service. One always took care to fasten the straps securely after that incident!

Chapter Six

And now you live dispersed on ribbon roads,
And no man knows or cares who is his neighbour,
Unless his neighbour makes too much disturbance,
But all dash to and fro in motor cars,
Familiar with the roads and settled nowhere.

Choruses from *The Rock* – TS Eliot

WHITE HEAT

PATER'S LAST VISIT TO the Rose & Crown was in 1960, just a week before he died, around five years before his favourite poet and contemporary, TS Eliot. He looked small in the captain's chair by the fireplace, a chair he once amply filled. That chair became my chair, but his presence remained, as it does to this day, his face looking out from faded motoring photographs on the pub wall.

The 1960s was a time of Tupperware parties, of Hugh Johnson telling the aspirant middle classes all about wine, and of DIY. A pre-war apprentice I came across at Daimler called Barry Bucknell was to blame for the last of these. He came to fame on television in the 1950s, but the DIY craze he spawned didn't take off until the following decade, by which time he was busy inventing the mirror dinghy. I bought one, of course. He had a lot to answer for! The 1960s was also the period when university education began to become universal, rather than a luxury, when polytechnics proliferated, and some began to have ambitions of becoming universities, and when idealistic middle-aged lecturers such as my ex's beau Tristan Grayling, began breezing about in beards and safari jackets. Men whose grandchildren would consider attaining a degree to be entirely commonplace.

The spread of TV and radio allowed stories to be brought into our homes with unprecedented immediacy, bringing about the beginning of newspapers becoming clever purveyors of comment and entertainment rather than news; skilfully mixing and manipulating facts with opinions. MacFisheries, Boots and Timothy Whites notwithstanding, the 1960s high street was still largely free of global chains. Every community was different, and special, and nowhere was like everywhere else. Consequently everywhere was still interesting.

Car ownership doubled in the 1960s, encouraging the lower orders to move about, but in 1967 Raymond Baxter introduced us to the breathalyser on *Tomorrow's World*. The writing was on the wall!

MINI

Ting-a-ling went the telephone one bright and blustery Friday morning in May 1959. What ho! It was none other than my good pal Alex Issigonis. Get down here Wilby old boy, he said. There's something I need to show you. Of course, I knew exactly what it was: Issi's new mini-marvel was ready for test.

Grabbing toast and slurping PG Tips as I gathered myself together, I assured dear Hector he would definitely be getting a walk just as soon as I returned, before jumping in the Bentley and rushing down to Longbridge like a stoat; but not before popping in at MacFisheries in Beedle armed with Martha's shopping list. Aha, I thought as I arrived on High Street, the gods are smiling: herewith the perfect parking spot. No such luck. Hidden behind an unattended Scammell coal lorry was a dratted Heinkel bubble car parked head-on to the kerb, and I was forced to collapse my trafficator and abort my approach. A Mini, I would later come to realise, would have fitted perfectly in the limited remaining space beside the diminutive post-war product of the Heinkel Flugzeugwerke, but in the Mark VI, of course, I had no chance, and was obliged to park around the corner and walk 200 yards or more to collect my weekend groceries.

As I did so I passed a Goggomobile slung half on the pavement outside Terry's All-Time, a 24 hour 'caff' on Market Street, and no doubt inside that insalubrious establishment at that moment sat a grimy coal delivery man perusing the *Daily Herald* and partaking of a 'full monty' (of course, I am referring to what our French friends call a 'crise cardiaque sur une assiette(!)', ie: the full English breakfast, so banish unsavoury thoughts of sausages of another nature!). Saints alive, the confounded things were everywhere! Bubble cars, that is. They had become popular in Britain as a result of the so-called Suez Crisis of 1955. With fuel in short supply, private motorists had once again been restricted in their usage, with ten gallons the monthly maximum. BMW Isettas, Heinkel Kabines, Messerschmitt KR200s, and push-me pull-you Zundapp Januses started appearing on every high street, not just Beedle's. They offered low cost, short range motoring, and ease of parking (hah!), and they were light, lively, fun (according to some), and cheap to buy and run. The so-called crisis had now largely abated, but there was no sign of an end to the micro-car craze, and that was what the Mini was all about.

BMC Chairman, Len Lord (soon to be Sir Leonard) was an irascible bugger, and he hated bubble cars. 'We must drive them off the streets by building a proper miniature car,' he opined. 'A miniature car capable of carrying four adults and their luggage.' (Profanities have been omitted in this sanitised version of events!). It was the same thinking as that of Herbert Austin, whose magnificent Seven had seen off the abominable cycle cars of the 1920s, and suppressed the sales of sidecar outfits to boot. Alec Issigonis had left Morris after the BMC merger, afraid that he would lose his autonomy in such a sprawling organisation. He flitted to Alvis where he set about designing a luxury car together with my old Cambridge chum Alex Moulton, but when the project was parked, Len Lord asked Issi back, and soon afterwards commanded him to burst the micro-car bubble.

I knew more-or-less what to expect, having discussed the project with Issi in its early days and, dare I say it, supplied him one or two ideas. Then I had driven a development car the previous autumn, albeit only within the confines of the Longbridge plant. But I was nonetheless impressed by my first acquaintance with the finished product parked outside the admin block and awaiting my attention that May morning. Unlike that prototype, this bright red, brand new Mini was not hand-built, but neither was it truly a production car. It was, in fact, part of a test batch built on the production line, and it would be another three months before the line was fully functioning, the dealerships were sufficiently stocked, and the car was officially launched. Why was I so privileged? Len wants you to persuade your boss to write one of your in-depth features to coincide with the launch, said Issi, and he wants *The Auto* to take a car on long-term test before the end of the summer. He handed me the Mini's keys, and it was then I noticed Len Lord's menacing figure as he looked down at us from his office window in the Kremlin.

Drawn from Issi's own pen (he was actually a first-rate technical artist, and endearingly proud of his skills), the Austin Mini Minor before us, registered number WRO154, was a small car with tiny wheels and cheeky looks that sat low to the road, but unlike the aforementioned micros, and the new and much lauded Fiat 500, it was very much a proper car with its engine in the right place, and a remarkably spacious interior laid out in a conventional fashion. Furthermore, it was absolutely without ostentation or undue ornament (as was Issi's way). It was also damn clever.

The engine was not advanced (it had first been used in Austins in 1951), and indeed there was little absolutely new about any of it, it was the intelligent putting together of its components in a way that made for fine handling and allowed so much space for the occupants, that made the Mini such an efficient driving machine, and a supremely practical car for carrying people of all shapes and sizes, and their goods and miscellaneous gubbins. The Mini was only ten feet long (smaller than an Austin A35), and eight and a half of those were taken up by the human compartment, into which the box pressings containing the car's ten inch wheels encroached very little, and only at the very corners.

It was front-wheel-drive, so there was no propshaft tunnel either, but the real masterstroke could be put down to Jack Daniels. No, not the Jack Daniel's whiskey company in Lynchburg, Tennessee, I'm talking about the quietly spoken former MG man and first-class draughtsman of that name who was perhaps Issi's most trusted collaborator at Longbridge. A long-discarded front-wheel-drive Morris Minor prototype being used by Daniels on an everyday basis served as a permanent reminder to the pair of the space-saving benefits to be gained from mounting an engine transversely, but if the engine goes in sideways, what of the boite de vitesse? Issi tried a compact BMW-style flat twin with a gearbox in the same housing, but found it too coarse and vibratory, but then he had a brainwave! Combine the engine and gearbox, yes, but put the box underneath (as we had once discussed) and have the engine and the gears running in the same oil.

Adopting front wheel drive presents further problems to a designer in that the leading wheels need to go up and down as well as steer, and the Mini's wee ten-inchers (Issi had asked Dunlop for eights!) demanded an unusual type of universal joint. BMC's solution was the Birfield joint. Originally designed by a Czech way back in 1926, it was still being made in limited numbers for use in submarines. Propshaft manufacturer Hardy Spicer was soon commissioned to make them by the thousands, enabling Minis to be driven and steered with commendable smoothness. To Issi's disappointment, Alex Moulton's radical designs for hydrolastic suspension system had proved too expensive for the new car (they would be adopted in 1964 following its successful deployment in the Austin 1100 two years earlier), so the first Minis had simple rubber cone springs. Subframes front and rear took stresses off the body at the suspension mounts and insulated the passenger compartment from engine noise and road thrum, Issi assured me (to a degree Issi, to a degree!).

Wee Red One, as I came to christen WRO, was a De-Luxe model, and so benefited from bright trim around the wheel arches and along the bottom of the car; and opening rear windows, meagre loose carpeting, two-tone upholstery, a weedy crackle-black heater and other interior 'extras'. The non-adjustable front seats were exiguously upholstered in two-tone fashion (although they were to prove surprisingly comfortable), and provided a very upright seating position; and the steering column rose upwards at a steep angle. Together this gave a bus cab look to the driving position, but helped make the most of the space in the cabin. There were no seat belts in those days, of course. A good job, as the driver would be unable to reach forward to operate the choke and electrical switches. The doors had sliding windows, and their absence of inner skins added elbow room (a pull-cord took care of opening – something of a vintage touch, I thought!). A flat floor further added to the feeling of space, and out of it protruded an extremely long and thin gear lever. There was no instrument board. Instead, a central pod containing a large circular speedometer (which itself incorporated a fuel gauge and tiny, beady warning lights) sat atop an open parcel shelf which ran across the full width of the bulkhead. This was a most useful feature that would come to prove indispensable for many owners, likewise the capacious storage tubs built into the bottoms of the doors.

Oh, how wickedly Issi had chortled upon my arrival whereupon I had parked the comparatively colossal and veritably vintage-looking Mark VI alongside the diminutive embodiment of modernity that was his Mini. Amazing to think its supposedly 1940s new-look, yet really fooling nobody olde-worlde body style had been in full production just four years previously (although, of course, the R Type had an altered boot). Take it for the weekend insisted the car's proud designer, opening the driver's door to allow my entry. Alas, I cannot, I replied. I have a big car stuffed to the gunwales with immoderate supplies of wine and groceries, and I'm picking up a family of four from New Street before heading home (the Temples were down for the weekend). Nonsense old boy, he said, before swivelling smartly through 90 degrees and stalking off to the works, returning moments later with two slim wicker hampers. We're having these made specially. Now watch this. With that Issi began busying himself loading the contents of the Bentley into the Mini without compromising its seating capacity. The custom-made baskets were filled and then slotted neatly under the rear seat, and the door bins and bulkhead shelf were put to full and good use. There, said Issi, patting me on the arm while wedging a complimentary bottle of most excellent Bordeaux from his office into the passenger door. The boot is free for their luggage, and if they've got big cases, you can leave it down on its wires and strap them on. Right, be off with you. Come back to collect your dinosaur on Monday morning!

That was all very well for him to say, but where was the blessed starter button? Ah, on the floor by my heel. The battery was under a mat in the boot, and the power cable ran under the floorpan. Why divert it for the sake of conventionality? They did eventually. It felt strange at first, of course, after the Mark VI, no matter that I had by then tested literally thousands of cars of all types and sizes, but once I got into the swing and sway (not that there was any of the latter to speak of!), I quickly came to adore the wee thing. To get straight to the point (why break the habit of a lifetime? – ed) it handled better than any road car I had ever driven before. Quite a statement, but not in any way an exaggeration.

The car's centre of gravity was propitiously low and central; its rack and pinion steering was absolutely state of the art; the clever independent suspension, though a little hard, did its job admirably, tying the car to the road;

and despite its small wheels, the car gave an excellent ride even over atrocious surfaces. I soon found it went around bends at any speed without any fuss at all, whether under power or on the overrun, and pushing hard through the lanes later in the weekend I discovered to my great delight I could slide it under full control, even on the bumpiest bends. Adding to the pleasure, gear-changing was snappy, and the car's light weight (1,380lb) made for nippy acceleration despite a bantamweight power output of just 38bhp and a minuscule capacity of just 848cc (larger engines were fitted to prototypes, Issi told me in confidence, but so well did the car handle, Len Lord had been concerned about the average Joe Leadfoot becoming encouraged to exceed his abilities).

How to judge it? According to its inventor, the big idea had been to make ordinary folk mobile, and with the cheapest model set to sell for just under £500 it was certainly affordable and priced to sell. So was it a utilitarian runabout? A car to take on the bargain basement Ford Pop? Yes, but it was much, much more than that. It was enormous fun when driven fast, as I have already waxed lyrical, and it was eager and full of personality, but how did it fare as a practical car? Well, the provisions made it home intact, and Temples senior and minor were transported to and from the railway station in reasonable comfort so yes, it passed that test. If the Mini had a weakness at all, it was as a long-distance machine, and for that can be forgiven. The rubber suspension and subframes did absorb road noise, it was true, and top gear was set tall, but I did not need to journey to John O'Groats to realise it would provide a harsh and tiring environment on long trips. I would also add that the gearbox hummed just a tad, and the tiny brakes were perhaps not quite up to the standard of the rest of the machine. Then again, we all know what Herbert Austin said about good brakes only encouraging bad driving! In conclusion, the Mini was a motor car based almost entirely on the principle less is more. Tiny, yet roomy. Practical, yet a driver's car. Handy for parking too.

Tooling up and preparing the assembly lines was a feat of organisation that was carried out in double-quick time, and the Mini was launched on 26 August, 1959. A week beforehand journalists were invited to my old stomping ground, the MOD's Fighting Vehicles Research and Development Establishment (FVRDE) at Chobham in Surrey. The site featured various measured and specific gradients, a banked oval and a skid pan. I knew it like the back of my hand, but the racing driver Paul Frere put me to shame, plunging through the dips, ripping around the banking and wriggling through the sinewy snake section like a man possessed. In Frere's hands the Mini proved itself a rally car in the making. Its small size and low weight, its low centre of mass, its relatively wide track, and its responsive steering and first-rate suspension made it fabulously agile, yet remarkably stable. The speedy Belgian declared himself impressed.

Sales were a little slow at first, as the middle classes took to it rather than the lower orders. People didn't seem to know what to make of it, and it didn't help that BMC sold it as two almost identical models, the Austin Se7en (made at Longbridge), and the Morris Mini Minor (at Cowley). After a while these became the Austin and Morris Mini, and later, simply, the Mini, and soon more than a few conspicuously famous folk came to buy the car as a fashion statement, and for fun, and finally it was bought by ordinary people as a practical car, just as Issi intended. To drive a Mini would be to cock a snook to all and sundry, and the car became an expression of classlessness.

By 1961 sales had taken off and the little car was outselling all other BMC offerings. The previous year had seen the arrival of Mini vans and shooting brakes. These were ten inches longer than the saloon with a wheelbase stretched by four inches, and the van payload was quite remarkable (the battery and spare wheel were hidden away under the floor). The Post Office bought them by the thousands, as did small traders as commercial vehicles did not attract purchase tax. We had one on the farm for a while, and it was a most useful machine. It had double rear doors and its loading level was conveniently low. When empty it would sit tail-high due to its stiffer suspension rubbers. Sadly, it met its end on a moorland road one wet and foggy night when Algy ran off the road to avoid hitting a bedraggled Shropshire ewe.

The Mini was not without its faults. There was no fresh air heater until 1961 (earlier cars' heaters just recycled humid air), its ventilation was not the best, and misting was a bind, not helped by the rear windows not opening on the cheaper models. The floors leaked, making the carpets soggy, the sliding windows stuck, whistled and let in draughts. The engine's orientation led to early problems with cracked exhaust pipes, and the distributor, sited just behind the grille, would get drowned by heavy rain and spray until measures were taken to shield it. More seriously, in sloshing around the gearbox as well as the engine, the oil took a beating it wasn't designed to tolerate. We were at the beginning of a new era, and cars were not being maintained in the same way as in the past. Oil changes could be left too long with expensive consequences. More seriously still, it was not a good car to be inside in the event of a big shunt, and Len Lord had been absolutely right, maniac drivers did try too hard to use up the generous margin they had been given, occasionally with fatal consequences.

But never mind the negatives! A Mini being used to the full might have upset empurpled onlookers, shaking their fists from behind their garden gates, but a speeding Mini was usually safer than it looked, and what was so wrong with folk enjoying themselves as they went about their everyday business, as long as they picked the right time and place? The Mini was a supremely competent little motor car that was fun across country, fun in town, and even fun in city traffic.

It made me proud to be British and I salute it. It is just such a shame it was sold so cheaply that for many years BMC failed to make a profit from it.

MINI COOPER

The Mini proved popular among racing drivers, who had them tuned, and Ferrari designer Aurelio Lampredi apparently said if it didn't look so awful, he'd shoot himself. A backhanded compliment indeed! Issi, John Cooper and I competed together on occasion in the late 1940s, and it was at the Brighton Speed Trials many years later that John and I persuaded him to give Cooper a shot at building a Mini-based special, just for the heck of it. Cooper converted the A-type engine to 1000cc, improved the gearbox, added miniature disc brakes made specially by Lockheed, and then did further work with Jack Daniels at BMC. The Mini Cooper duly appeared in mid 1961 and it went on to become successful in world rallying and saloon car racing, and the flow of royalties from BMC to Cooper kept the racing firm afloat. The Mini Cooper was exclusive at first, but many thousands were made in the end. I told Issi it could have potential for sales, and how right I was, as 25,000 Coopers were sold up to early 1964.

The Mini Cooper was clearly a good underdog car but not quite good enough to take the rallying world by the scruff of the neck. By this time BMC was fully behind John's efforts and a decision was made to build an 1100cc version of the engine using materials of superlative quality. The result was a motor that was fast and strong, yet docile enough for urban pottering, and with further improvements to the brakes, tyres and steering made for a competition car that was an absolute cracker. It was called the Mini Cooper S. With Aaltonen, Makinen and especially Paddy Hopkirk leading the way, the giant-killing S won the Alpine, Tour de France, and Monte Carlo rallies, despite the best efforts of the dratted Froggies, and there were also numerous wins in international saloon car events. My pal Raymond Baxter drove one to 43rd in the 1964 Monte Carlo. Hopkirk won, beating Bo Ljungfeldt in a Ford Falcon, with Erik Carlsson third in his Saab 96. You might consider it amazing Baxter even got in a Mini, but it was part of the car's genius that even the preternaturally tall can lounge in it!

The French were hated for allowing modifications to their own drivers' supposedly standard production cars, and for setting unreasonable handicaps in their favour, while penalising minor infringements by foreign manufacturers who tended to enter more exotic machinery. By the time of the 1966 Monte Carlo, Minis had already won two years running, and the dratted Frogs were hopping mad when the first three cars home were Mini Coopers. First they challenged the validity of the torquey 1275cc version of the Mini's engine, and were decidedly cheesed off to find more than 5,000 units had been sold to the public. Then they stripped the Abingdon cars down to the last nut and bolt, and measured every component, before deciding at the very end of the process, that the headlamp bulbs were of an illegal type, or some such tosh. They gave the winner's award to Pauli Toivonen in a Citroën (of course), whose crew I had seen swapping its bulbs at the end of the event. In 1967 BMC returned and I was pleased to report in *The Auto* that Rauno Aaltonen won in a Cooper S by a country kilometre. But ever faster cars were being allowed to compete, and the Minis were getting harder to win in, so in 1968, as Leyland took over, the BMC competitions department at Abingdon closed its doors for the last time.

BMW IN PERIL

In December 1959 BMW had been a company in trouble. With the return of prosperity in Germany, motorcycle sales had collapsed almost totally, and the company's cars were not the right models to carry the firm forward into the bright white heat of new decade ahead. Mercedes made a takeover offer and a BMW shareholders' meeting was arranged to discuss it. Pater was a long-time Mercedes shareholder, his relationship with the Stuttgart concern dating back to the Gordon Bennett Cup in 1903, and having survived two world wars. In 1959 he was too decrepit to travel (sadly he would pop his clogs the following year), could I go across and use my press credentials to find out what the devil was going on?

Upon arrival in Bavaria, I met with my pre-war motorcycling friend Alex von Falkenhausen, a remarkably fortunate and talented fellow. As well as designing and competing on motorcycles, Alex had been part of the team responsible for the mercurial BMW 328 sports car. During War Two, his house was bombed but his beloved 328 racer survived. He had hidden it from the advancing Yanks in his in-laws' barn, first taking its wheels off and burying them under a rose bed (so it couldn't be towed away in the event of discovery), and then covering it with horse blankets and a stack of rusty farm equipment. After the war, von Falkenhausen opened his own garage where he tuned 328s and constructed 328-powered racing cars. His AFM racers (Alex von Falkenhausen Munich) built from 1948 onwards were excellent and successful machines, although only a handful were ever made. Another lucky and talented chap, Hans Stuck, was his main driver.

Stuck was born in Switzerland but grew up in Germany. A War One veteran, Stuck bumped into Adolf Hitler while out walking in the woods one day in the 1920s (I kid you not), and later he persuaded Herr Wolf to back the Auto Union race programme, bagging a works drive on the back of it. That's not to say Stuck was not a fine driver. He won grands prix, and he was a crack hillclimber. After the war, Germans were banned from driving racing cars until 1950, so he took out Austrian citizenship. He was past his best, but still capable of winning, and the following year (1960) Stuck (aka: the Mountain King) would win the German hillclimb championship for the last time, aged 60, in one of Fritz Fiedler's little 700s (of which, more anon). Later he became a Nürburgring instructor, and he taught his personable son Hans-Joachim how to drive impossibly fast round the place. Sadly, in yours truly he had far less malleable material!

In 1954 Alex von Falkenhausen rejoined BMW, and in 1957 he became the firm's head of engine development. There was no better man to tell me what had been going on, and I looked forward to getting all the inside gen as we repaired to a restaurant for dinner. It was crazy, said Alex as we settled down to enjoy a pre-dinner Pils, after the war Germany was on its knees and the whole country was living hand-to-mouth, but BMW had used its share of Marshall Aid to build big luxurious cars that were totally wrong for the times. The bulbous 501, and subsequent V8-powered 502 and their derivatives became known in Germany as the Baroque Angels, and although heavy price cuts and increasing general prosperity brought a degree of eventual success, by the end of the 1950s their day was surely done.

BMW big boss Hanns Grewenig was a U-Boat captain in the Kaiser war, and in the 1920s he had had connections with Ford Germany and GM. He was the man responsible for brokering a somewhat incongruous arrangement whereby BMW built Italian micro-cars under licence. The first one appeared at the Frankfurt Motor Show in 1955. An odd-looking contraption with a front-opening door which carried the steering column, it became known at home as 'Das Rollende Ei!'. Quite. It was, in fact, a modified version of the Isetta, the original bubble car which had appeared in 1953. The micro craze was born of high fuel prices, the Suez crisis and all that, and the Isetta was the creation of Italian Count Renzo Rivolta, a man who made his fortune making fridges in Milan. BMW ditched the Isetta's 9bhp two-stroke engine, and fitted their rolling eggs with R25 motorcycle engines producing 12bhp, together with four-speed motorcycle gearboxes to drive their twinned rear wheels. The BMW bubble car could achieve 53mph, return 43mpg, and it could be parked end-on, allowing egress straight onto the pavement. In 1958 BMW Concessionnaires in Brighton had started making the dratted things (drove one, rolled it, loathed it), and a four-seater 600cc version was developed with a car-type rear axle.

These economy vehicles were actually quite big sellers for BMW, but they brought meagre profits, and now, as prosperity increased apace, BMW were in seriously deep doo-doo. Motorcycle sales had collapsed utterly (everywhere you went in the factory they were parked up and mothballed, and manufacture had long since ceased); the Isettas had been a stop-gap; and the oversized Angels had never been the right cars for their times, and were now ready for replacement in any event. The new Michelotti-styled 700, a rear-engined, two-door monocoque coupe based on the 600 had just been launched. It would tide the firm over, but medium-sized cars were what was really required. Company chairman Dr Heinrich Richter-Brohm knew this, and von Falkenhausen and his pals had begun its development, but the firm had no means to bring the design to production. In fact, BMW were in debt.

When the tomatensuppe had been slurped and we were scoffing the rindersteak, Alex topped up our wine (the cat's whiskers, of course, German red is so underrated), and brought the story fully up to date. BMW's bankers had tried to force a Mercedes take-over, and the board had recommended acceptance, but at tomorrow's meeting I could expect a spirited resistance from dealers and shareholders alike. There was a market for well-made, well-priced, medium-sized saloon cars, and BMW was the firm to make them. Further, there was a Bavarian tradition to be preserved, an attitude sadly lacking in today's world of globalised takeovers, massed sackings and rapacious international asset-stripping.

The following day I was glad to have Alex beside me as a translator, as the last of a number of clearly quite persuasive presentations rose to its tub thumping peroration. We had already heard how the 700 flat twin was likely to be a success, that orders for it were coming in strongly, and now, whispered Alex, it seemed dodgy accounting had been revealed. Uproar! Then the dealers and shareholders argued successfully for a short postponement, during which time the Mercedes offer expired. Among those listening intently to all the impassioned speakers was high-powered industrialist Dr Herbert Quandt. The poor man was almost blind from childhood disease, but he was never poor in a financial sense. In fact, he was one of the wealthiest men in Europe. The Quandts got rich making Imperial German Army uniforms in War One, then diversified into mining, battery manufacture and engineering, and when daddy Gunther Quandt popped his clogs in 1954, the family owned 200 companies, as well as ten percent of Mercedes and 30 percent of BMW. It is only relatively recently that it has come to light the Quandts used Jewish slave labour in their factories during War Two.

As the meeting broke up and Dr Quandt was led away in the heaving throng, he was already deep in talks with his bankers, and he soon took action to ensure an independent future for BMW. Against the advice of his advisers, he increased his shareholding in BMW to 50 percent, and as a result a financial solution was found. Alex and his chums duly got to build their new motor car, in fact a whole series of highly successful medium-sized cars known collectively as the BMW 'New Class' saloons, and jolly wunderbar they were too. Incidentally, it was around about the time of this story that Herbert Quandt married his secretary Johanna, who became his third wife. Mrs Q still owned a huge number of BMW shares right up to her death in 2015, and she died one of the richest women in the world.

Back home in Bales at the close of the 1950s, Pater wanted to know if he was now, de facto, a part-owner of BMW. Father, I shouted into his ear trumpet, he was not, but he should be glad of it, and that as an act of solidarity and support for Alex and his chums, I had pledged to instruct Tibballs & Whitney, de Forte stockbrokers since days of yore, to purchase us a modest quantity of shares in BMW, proud builders of those Bavarian Mechanical Wonders.

ALEX

Something of an aristocrat, my friend Alex von Falkenhausen was born into a military family in 1907, and married a baroness. I first came across him when he won a gold medal at the ISDT in Llandrindod Wells in 1937 on a works BMW R5 with an ingenious rear suspension he himself had designed, having been asked to do so by none other than Adolf Hitler.

Alex was one of a small group of engineers who made BMW a force in motorcycle racing at the end of the 1930s, but I found him quiet and modest, and a man of decency and integrity. In 1938 his plunger-type suspension concept went into series production, and it would be revived in 1949 (even though BMW had lost all the tooling and drawings during the war). I spent time with him at the TT in 1939 (won by Georg Meier on a supercharged BMW) and again at the ISDT in Salzburg at the beginning of September. The event was abandoned, of course, when war was declared, and we bade each other what might well have been final farewells, before I dashed for the Swiss border at Lake Constance with the British Army team.

In August 1942 Alex followed German front-line troops into action near Stalingrad on an R75, to see first-hand the problems experienced by army motorcyclists. He found their machines were being disabled and destroyed by liquid mud, and that bureaucratic incompetence was preventing replacement parts reaching the front. Having returned to Munich to kick backsides, he developed protective shrouds for the R75, and a periscope affair for its air filter. After this, although he designed a one man tank, and helped develop a Panther tank powered by a BMW 132 radial aero engine, he worked on bikes in secret whenever he could.

By 1945 his Munich home had been destroyed by bombing and he had taken digs in another part of the city. He avoided recruitment by Home Guard fanatics by reporting to two units, telling each he was enlisted by the other. Finally, Alex rode his R75 towards the Americans, intending to join his wife and daughters in Leonberg, where he had hidden his 328 racer. After finding a rogue SS unit guarding a stash of stolen brandy at his in-laws' home, he hid in a tower until they fled from the Americans, to whom he then gave himself up. After grilling him and fooling about on his BMW for a few days, the US soldiers eventually left him in peace to exhume his buried racing car and get on with the rest of his life.

He was a remarkable man, and one I am proud to have called my friend. After a long and successful post-war career at BMW, he retired in 1976. Alex died in 1989, and I miss his intelligence and enthusiasm to this day.

JAGUAR E-TYPE
(First published *Classic Auto* – July 2004)
Some time in September, 1960, I had occasion to visit my chums at Jaguars, where a very special machine was waiting for appraisal. The prospect of a new model from Coventry was exciting, to put it mildly. Hard to imagine now after recent sorry events, but in those days the Cat people were riding the crest of a wave. Indeed, Sir William Lyons and his team seemingly could do no wrong (although the recent takeover of Daimler may not have been obviously beneficial!).

Swinging through the Browns Lane factory gates after an invigorating blast down from Shropshire along largely uninfested roads, I spotted a car-shaped dust sheet in the parking area, directly under Bill's lair. The contours were very low, very long and obviously of sporting intent. I'll admit that my nosiness overwhelmed my sense of propriety, causing me to sidle over and lift the corner of the cover. Alas, a tantalising glimpse of a rounded flank was all I managed before being rumbled: 'Stop right there, de Forte, or we'll have that old banger of yours towed away to the junkyard immediately!' With the air of an apple-scrumping schoolboy caught in the act by the local bobby, I swivelled round to see the towering presence of service chief Lofty England marching towards me. The mock-martinet tone of his voice softened as he approached, his face dissolving into a smile. 'Knew you wouldn't be able to resist having a shufti if we left it out here... the innate journalistic instinct, eh?'

After putting up with yet more teasing at the expense of my 'old banger' (how they'd have laughed if they'd known that vintage Bentleys would be worth millions in the next century!), we adjourned to the office for tiffin. Somewhat inevitably, the rest of the boys gradually homed in to join us. And as the afternoon wore on, tea was replaced by a rather stronger libation, and we were all feeling distinctly merry by the time the main workforce headed home. (Incidentally, the vast majority were on bicycles: wages were such in those far-off days that very few could imagine owning the fruits of their labours.) Despite the absence of that fanciful modern concept, 'Global Warming', the evening air was still distinctly sultry when we eventually trooped outside to inspect the new arrival. The wraps came off with a flourish, and there it stood in all its glory: E-Type, or XK-E, as our colonial cousins insisted it be known. Reposing in oblique sunshine, the car looked strikingly splendid. I was taken aback by its beauty. Some details were not finalised on this pre-production roadster, but who could have doubted that Jaguars had produced yet another winner?

The offer of a strictly off-the-record spin was eagerly accepted. Dropping into the snug cockpit, surrounded by leather and figured aluminium, I thumbed the starter and heard the big 3.8 litre six cylinder engine gurgle into life through its triple SU carburettors, a prod of throttle clearing its lungs with a satisfying rasp. Vvvrrrrmmmm. I couldn't help grinning as I felt the whole car rock sideways through torque reaction. 'Exhaust's a bit throaty on this one – we'll quieten it down a touch for the great unwashed,' said Lofty, anticipating my next question. He also admitted that the power output of this particular example may have been slightly in excess of the figure to be catalogued, which was similar to the outgoing XK150S's 265hp. Ah, yes: 'Bliss was it that dawn to be alive, But to be young was very heaven'. Our friend Wordsworth nailed it, to use the contemporary argot.

Threading gently out through the suburban contagions of Coventry, my disco volante felt entirely happy at 30-40mph in top gear, the revolution counter needle hardly stirring from its stop. Used thus, the E progressed with almost total silence save for a whoosh from the tyre treads. Even the exhaust contrived to stay subdued when dawdling. Above all, though, I remember the car for its astonishingly compliant ride, courtesy of new independent suspension. While the model's predecessor, the XK150, betrayed its age and live rear axle by becoming wayward on occasions, the E's double-wishbone set-up, developed directly from racing experience, offered limousine-like comfort. Moreover, as I was shortly to discover, the chassis handled wonderfully at high speed. Truly, the best of both worlds, and this itself was a good enough reason not to christen the model 'XK160', as had been intended originally.

After skirting Lady Godiva's home city to the south we picked up the old A45 coach road, the pace picking up as we plunged into glorious green countryside and traffic dispersed. A scintilla of extra throttle made the long bonnet rise with feline grace, the speedometer rushing past 60mph with contemptuous ease. There was good reason to be heading this way. An early strand of Britain's much-delayed motorway network began near Dunchurch, about ten miles of largely empty dual-carriageway appended to the old A5 at Crick. Wily Sir William liked to claim Minister of Transport Ernest Marples had built this new superhighway expressly as a development facility for the Midlands car industry. A slightly dubious notion, perhaps, but there's little doubt that the M45 was a handy place to test a car's high-speed mettle!

A trace of mist was rolling in off the meadows as we crossed the unofficial 'start line'. After overtaking a dawdler who seemed alarmed by the novelty of a road with no junctions for so many miles, I was finally able to give the Jaguar its head. Reaching 5,500rpm in third launched us past the ton. Then into top (without much help from the dratted Moss gearbox, one of the car's less marvellous features), foot to the floor, and 110mph... 120mph... 130mph with a mellifluous trail of acoustic spume in our wake. And although I thought it prudent to straddle the central white line, she tracked straight and true at such elevated velocities.

Acceleration was waning now, but we had motorway to spare for an assault on the magic ton-fifty! A mile or so later, the needle on the big Smiths dial was still nudging higher, 150mph looming. Speeding in an open car is truly exhilarating. Trapped in a screaming vortex, head buffeted, eyes streaming: I can only liken it to travel in an early aeroplane, or perhaps the first few moments of a parachute jump, before the canopy opens (the latter tends to follow the former!). We clocked 152mph that distant day. Possibly the instrument exaggerated by a few percent, but I do know that we despatched eight miles of tarmacadam in well under four minutes, in an era when most vehicles were lucky to do it in ten. Arriving back at Browns Lane, the return leg enlivened by a dice with a determined bod on a Triumph motorcycle, no doubt a tester from the nearby Meriden factory, I had never been more impressed by a car.

Reader, I bought one. As soon as RHD production examples became available, I signed on the dotty line and a red drop top became mine. The best £2,000 I ever spent. Many E-Types have passed through the de Forte stringbacks since. Apart from a ferrously-challenged V12 automatic, I liked them all. But original is definitely best, as I re-discovered nearly half a century after my first drive, when the chance to sample an early 3.8 litre Series I arose. Sadly, my aged bones dropped into the cockpit with less alacrity than in 1960, but once ensconced the cabin was as appealing as ever. Pressing the starter summoned the past in my mind, yet failed miserably to do the same in reality. Alas, the open roads we enjoyed then are now a seething morass of inhumanity.

Yet, pushing the loud pedal lightened my gloom. A bid to clock 150mph again would have no doubt resulted in a period of incarceration in one of HM's hotels, so I did my best to keep tight rein on the six cylinder beast. But my best fell short, and I must confess that I gave in to temptation a couple of times when goaded. Thus, an upstart in an Audi, of all things, learned that an old motor driven by an even older gent would not necessarily be driven at molluscs' pace! Exiting a roundabout, the blighter pulled out to overtake. I waited until he was alongside, then floored it in third. Soon he was a straining silver dot in my mirror. A drag race is one thing, but it would be folly to presume that 1961's ultimate could match 21st century chassis technology. Fortunately, the road was straight. By current standards, the E has modest roadholding and will be

...the return leg was enlivened by a dice with a determined bod on a Triumph motorcycle.

embarrassed by whippersnapper hatchbacks in the twisties. No matter, because driving pleasure comes from a car's feel, sound and handling feedback, more so than ever now that speed is deemed to be so socially unacceptable.

The E-Type is an automotive icon, of that there is no doubt. But is it suitable transport for stylish chaps, one might wonder? Of course it is! While in the second half of the 1960s Jaguars generally attracted the wrong sort of clientele, personified by that ghastly Simon Dee character, the marque later recovered its dignity, if not its profitability, and any fellow of taste should be proud to be seen in one now.

BRISTOL 407

In the aftermath of War Two, the BMW factory in Munich was in the American occupation zone. In poor shape, having been bombed to smithereens, it was set to be demolished with everything half-useful being shipped to the US of A. This seemed to me a wasted opportunity. So, after making sure my pre-war chum, Alex von Falkenhausen got his hands on a few 328 engines and choice pieces of special equipment, I made contact with one Harold Aldington.

Aldy, as he was known, had been a wheeler-dealer in motorbikes in sarf London when my Uncle Bof first came across him in the 1920s, and years later, while I was at Cambridge, he sold me my Velocette. By that time he and his brother Don (DA) ran their own garage and had taken over the ailing Frazer Nash concern. The Aldingtons also imported BMW motor cars, selling them as Frazer Nash-BMWs. Aldy and DA had Air Ministry jobs during the conflict and beyond, so we kept in touch, and it was easy enough for Aldy to set up a trip to Munich, as I suggested, in order to meet me, pronto, at the ruined BMW plant.

He flew over in a Stirling bomber, returning that night with armfuls of plans while eagerly looking forward to the delivery of a truckload of 328 two-litre engines which I had immediately despatched, signed off as war reparations. At my strong suggestion, BMW's senior engineer Fritz Fiedler set off for Blighty too. A thoroughly decent chap, and one of several a BMW motorcycle men involved in the design of pre-war BMW cars, Fiedler would come to modify and develop the 328 engine for the Bristol Aeroplane Company. For after a few words in the right ears, it came to pass that Aldy purchased the rights to build BMWs in Blighty, and to use the 328 engine, and he wasted no time entering into a manufacturing agreement with Bristol, who were looking to diversify, having grown fat on wartime government contracts. The car which ended up as the Bristol 400 was unveiled at the 1947 Geneva Show, but by then the Aldingtons had both fallen out with, and sold out to, the south-west aeronautical concern.

The 400 was a beauty. Reminiscent of pre-war BMWs, its origins were plain to see, but Bristol's metallurgical expertise and aircraft manufacturing standards made for a fine and up-to-date motor car. The 1950s was the heyday of long-distance rallying in Europe, and in these the Bristol performed reasonably well. Bristols sold from the company's only showroom in Kensington High Street. They were exclusive and expensive, with controls and seating adapted for the purchaser rather like Brough Superiors.

The BMW-based four which Fiedler developed, powered Bristols until 1961, then Chrysler V8s took over engine duties. Built from that year onwards, the Bristol 407 was the epitome of 1960s smartness, and the first Bristol model following the motor car division's full separation from its aero company parent. The 407's beautifully finished coach-built, two-door aluminium body was mounted on a formidable separate chassis of great strength, and it was powered by an intelligently-modified 5.2 litre Chrysler V8. This was connected to a three-speed automatic gearbox, as might be expected, but push-button selection of the lower gears enabled engine braking, and there was a handy kickdown feature too. The engine was remarkably compact. Indeed, despite there being two rather clever thermostatically-controlled cooling fans under the bonnet, Bristol's designers found room for capacious storage pods in the front wings, in which were housed the spare wheel and a substantial battery. Inside, heavy-pile carpet sat atop generous felt underlays on a sound-proofed floor, and comfortable cushions adorned fully reclining seats (handy for catching some shut-eye on a long journey!). Quality walnut veneers faced the instrument board and door cappings, and a fine array of dials, while functional, also pleased the eye. That said, inside and out it was clearly a car of the very highest quality without unnecessary ornament or ostentation.

My estimable colleague LJK Setright always said a Bristol was a car one had to grow to appreciate. He argued one had to learn its moods and its behaviours before pushing it to the edges of its generous comfort zone. Well, I found straight away that while the 407 was a bit ponderous at low speeds, the steering and suspension apparently tightened as the speedometer needle got among the bigger numbers, and while a degree of oversteer was discernible, the car really excelled on long, fast corners, sliding just a little at the rear. I discovered quickly too that although the gearbox prevented wheel-spin, acceleration was quite remarkable for such a heavy car, and the Bristol's natural cruising gait was best found at a languorous 100mph.

CORTINA REFLECTIONS
(First published *The Auto* – October 1962)

Large post-war Fords have been named after either winds, government representatives or celestial divisions, for some peculiar reason. I can see that that the first two are linked by being responsible for giving us much hot air, but is there a connection between motor cars and that non-scientific nonsense known as astrology? Doubtful, but ours not to reason why, as the poet once said. For whatever reason, from 1950 we had Consuls, Zephyrs and Zodiacs in the big saloon class, all notable for Ford Dagenham's deployment of the compact and effective MacPherson strut front suspension system.

Despite what some people at Ford will insist, Earle Steele MacPherson's eponymous contribution to automotive history has been around in essence for some time. He designed something like it for General Motors during War Two (he spent the Kaiser War in Britain working on aero engines), and in any case it appeared in near-finished form on the French Ford Vedette the year before the Consul et al were launched upon us. Earle, a direct, straight-talking and clear-thinking Yank whom I came across once or twice at industry soirees, never pretended otherwise, perhaps explaining why he died peacefully in his sleep a few years ago at a good age, rather than living with a guilty secret gnawing at his conscience and a stomach ulcer.

The Mark II version of the Con-Zeph-iac unveiled in 1955 was a worthwhile update based on the same straightforward mechanical recipe as its predecessor, but with shameless American styling and an even more commodious interior. Much as I admire Citroën's curvaceous Goddess – an ostensible direct rival – the big Ford was just as clever in its own simple way, and in truth was far more a car of the future than the Gallic temptress released the same year.

To put it another way, although mechanical malfunctions are unwelcome in any circumstances, given the choice, de Forte would prefer to fail to proceed in a DD ('Dagenham Dustbin', as the current argot has it!) rather than a DS. Certainly, if I had to fix whatever had gone wrong myself, I would much more fancy my chances trusting to luck in a Zodiac, or being given fair wind in a Zephyr.

Of course, we have the RAC and the AA for those occasions (breakdowns, not dustbins), but can even the brightest and best trained patrolman be expected to fix a hydro-pneumatic system on the Biggleswade by-pass? Not on your nelly! And that is not a trivial concern, because an un-pressurised Citroën is a brakeless beached whale that cannot be towed nor loaded onto a recovery vehicle by normal methods, so one would be well and truly up that creek without a proverbial paddle. Please don't remind me about what happened to me in that loaned DS in the Massif Central back in '58!

My reference to the new swathe of tarmacadam diverting the Great North Road around the Bedfordshire market town of Biggleswade was borne of recent direct and painful experience. Having behaved herself so well over summer, poor old Beattie blew her head gasket while making haste on this new and featureless diversion, and I was stranded alongside it for many hours, not least because the attending RAC patrolman's BSA tradesman's combination also conked to an inglorious halt while en-route to Bedford to fetch a suitable replacement. Saddened though I would be to witness the end of an era, isn't it high time the last of those plonkingly primitive sidecar buses were replaced with something much more modern? A fleet of Issigonis's new Mini Minor vans would do very nicely.

Rotten luck for all those in peril near Biggleswade, but while waiting and listening to a fine performance of the Op.10 Chopin etudes on the Third, I mused upon how such situations could be averted. Instead of the traditional trudge to find a telephone box, it would be wonderful, would it not, to have an on-board communication device. While I fear for the effect on road safety through driver distraction, would it not indeed be a great convenience to summon help through the ether, merely by erecting a 20ft telescopic antenna on the roof and connecting it to a wireless transmitter? Such technology exists, I am told, and in a crate barely the size of a suitcase. The battery box is apparently of similar dimensions, and setting up the apparatus only takes about ten minutes in clement conditions, after which one would be able to send a Morse Mayday directly to the chaps at RAC HQ in the Mall.

Or dare we dream about the possibility of a telephone that one could carry in one's pocket? A space-age fantasy at present I grant you, yet a pal of mine in the GPO's research centre assures me that given the breakneck pace of semiconductor miniaturisation, such things will become common in our lifetimes. Trials using radio telephones built into shopping trolleys are already under way in the SW1 area, I am informed.

Once the patrolman (a kindly sasquatch of a man, with a phizzog mashed to rawness by exposure to wind and rain) had fixed his blasted Beesa and returned with my new top gasket, he proved to be an amicable cove with an obvious talent for his work. The blood-orange sun sloped down to rest, and in gathering gloom he made short shrift of the decapitation, then expertly bolted the head back down by feel rather than using a torque wrench. Because he used skill and a fine sense of touch rather than rely on an easily-fooled calibrated device, he identified that two bolts were close to being stripped of their threads. For some reason writing that sentence brings forth an enduring image of the ladies of the Folies Bergere, but the new Ford Cortina awaits us (eventually – ed) so let us save such indulgences for another occasion.

By 7pm the engine was back in one piece. Although my role had merely involved passing the required tools or parts in the correct sequence, rather in the manner of an assistant surgeon (the Mark VI's under-bonnet inspection lamp would have been such a boon!), he saluted my efforts before we headed our separate ways: he to his depot in Harpenden, your scribe up the Great North to a dinner engagement in Stamford.

With my RAC friend's wise counsel, 'Try to keep her below 3,000, Sir, or those threads may let go completely,' echoing in my ears, I behaved myself for an hour or two, noting that the A1, as we're obliged to call it now, has more by-passes than through roads these days. If this trend continues, it might qualify one day as a motorway, and if so won't motorists be somewhat confused by there being two M1s. What do you say to that, Mr Marples? A bit of forward planning at the MoT might not go amiss, I feel.

Urban 30mph limits notwithstanding, leisurely progress is normally an exercise in self-control rather than enforcement, but on this occasion I had neither excuse nor need to speed. As the Bentley's handsome Marchal headlamps swept the roadside and road ahead, casting ever-longer dancing shadows as blue-grey evening turned to inky-black night, I mostly followed the old highway, travelling back into the past and taking in sights that were once familiar on my jaunts to the frozen north. Pity the poor owners of petrol garages, milk bars and commercial transport cafeterias, whose livelihoods vanished overnight once the bulk of traffic had been diverted along a series of loops that look like wandering caterpillars on my complimentary *Austin Road Atlas*.

In my reverie the question I kept asking myself was whether I would rather have been at the wheel of my Mark VI (although highly unlikely to have broken down), or more pertinently the new Cortina that had been in my charge that morning. Comparisons between a Cricklewood fire-breather, a bespoke product of Crewe's finest craftsman and a mass-produced Dagenham saloon are odorous at best (quite how massed we will have to wait a few months to find out, Ford have been stockpiling them in anticipation of great demand), but they all have four wheels and an internal combustion engine, ultimately producing similar results.

First, what's in a name? Cortina? Not a wind, diplomat or mumbo-jumbo star sign, but actually that Alpine town in Italy where the 1956 Winter Olympics were belatedly staged (war having scuppered the original date, you will recall). Why? Why not, as Terry Beckett and his men will rejoinder, having made an eleventh hour decision to rip the Consul 225 badge off the bonnet. Cortina sounds a lot less dull, granted, although perhaps not to Spanish speakers, who won't want to drive around in a 'curtain'. En passant, Mr Beckett told me during development the new Ford was codenamed Pontiff, or some-such, and for a long time big boss Sir Patrick Hennessy was rather keen on calling it the Caprino. But that plan had to be consigned to the dustbin when caprino was discovered to be Italian slang for goat manure!

Fellow motor noters present at the preview were not entirely convinced that the new Ford is exactly what Britain needs in a new and supposedly exciting and prosperous decade, preferring to ignore most of the car's technical attributes and concentrate instead on making clever comments about the rear light assemblies, of all things. 'Ban the Bomb' indeed! Mercedes use round three-segment lenses, so why the brouhaha?

Of course, we've all heard the Cortina owes its existence to internecine grappling by the global arms of Ford. So while it's Curtains for Blighty, the Germans will get the front-wheel-drive Taunus. Nothing adventurous on the menu there then, except... Except, well, everything, really, because as with the outgoing Con-Zeph-iac, the engineers considered the whole car as one, not an assemblage of separate entities that may or may not fully complement each other.

To this end, former aircraft engineers from Bristol were involved in the design of the unitary bodyshell (monocoque, if you please), with the result that each and every element is only as heavy as it needs be to perform its function. Whilst that may feed ill-informed rumours that Fords are flimsy tin boxes, the truth is that the complete structure is immensely rigid and strong. In fact, although some of my younger colleagues may scoff, in hotted up form I predict a bright future for the Cortina as a racing car. In many other cases, probably including most BMC products, I'll wager, monocoque bodies are vastly over-engineered in some areas, and woefully under-specified elsewhere, thereby resulting in curate's egg-boxes!

It's no surprise to see that Ford's Cortina uses Mr MacPherson's struts once more, in harness with a simple leaf-spring live rear axle. Coils with more comprehensive location were considered, I understand, but it is reasonable to assume that Ford customers are more interested in overall running costs, so simplicity has been key. Likewise, the 1200cc base model is propelled by a development of the Kentish ohv four already seen in the Anglia. Would an overhead camshaft engine help the average chap in his daily driving? Not in my book. In the Motorway Age I believe he gains more from the short-stroke configuration, allowing his Cortina to whizz along the M1 at 70-80mph at 5,000rpm without fear of con-rods emerging through the bonnet.

Which brings us once more to our travels and travails on the Biggleswade by-pass, I'm afraid. I daresay my patrolman friend would be able to repair an ailing Cortina without recourse to a heated workshop, or a manual, or a clairvoyant, or even a bag of special tools. He would have merely lifted the lid, located all the vital parts immediately, and proceeded to find a simple and effective solution. For purely mechanical malfunctions, the local blacksmith could have repaired those 'primitive' leaf-springs in a trice.

Some say it's dreadful Americanisation, but I also approve of Ford's continued belief in steering column gear changers. It frees up so much floor space! The Cortina is a smallish saloon, but at a squeeze, there's room for six in it, with the bonus that the capacious luggage boot could swallow all their bags and suitcases. Much as I admire the Mini and its minor genius of a designer, even Issigonis wouldn't pretend that there was room for much more than socks, Y-fronts and a toilet bag behind the rear seat.

Furthermore, BMC's little wonder has much else to commend it, but cramming things into a small space costs money, and the intelligence is that they built the car, then set a price they believed would make it attractive to buyers, rather ignoring the sordid matter of needing to make a profit to stay in business. Fords, on the other hand, costed the Cortina's every nut, bolt and ball joint, then set a price yielding a decent margin, some of which will no doubt be ploughed into the development of the next Cortina incarnation (the California, perhaps?)*

In this instance the baseline is £639, not much more than a Mini. A normally reliable source suggested that the Cortina would still make more financial sense if the prices were reversed! Indeed, whispers abound that Mini Minors are actually being sold at a loss. If so, we must fear for BMC's future.

* The 1960 Winter Olympics were held at Squaw Valley, Northern California.

A WHITE CHRISTMAS
(Diary extract – 25 December 1962)
Spending the holidays rattling around on my own in Bales suddenly seemed a rather dull thing to do so I gave the Greenfirth-ites a tinkle after the Home

Service farming report first thing on Christmas morning, rather hoping to blag myself an early invitation to God's county for a few days' fine festive cooking and Yorkshire hospitality instead of driving up for Hogmanay as is the norm.

It was still dark but thankfully Clive and Mary were up and about bright and early as per usual and, good egg that he is, Clive immediately invited me to join them and the children for Christmas luncheon at 3pm. It was snowing steadily in Greenfirth, according to Clive, who was no doubt standing in his dressing gown looking out across the garden from the fine panelled hallway at Oak House while he barked amiably at me down the blower in his usual gruff fashion.

We had both heard the doomy Met Office forecasts warning of blanket snowfalls sweeping southwards across the country but a dusting of the fluffy white stuff was not going to prevent me from getting to grips with a slap up feed and Mary's fluffy roast potatoes really are the best. Soon I was packing father's Rover while swigging tea and cramming toast and Frank Cooper's finest into the old cakehole.

A Rover 100 may not be the ideal tool for the job, a skinny-wheeled front wheel drive car being by far the best bet for vehicular sorties on snow and ice, but beggars can't be choosers and all that. The four wheel drive Land Rover is still going strong despite 14 years' hard use on the farm(*1) and it truly is the 'go anywhere' vehicle Rover's copywriters claim, but it's a bit parky under a canvas tilt, and brilliant though Maurice Wilks' marvel is, it is not eminently suitable for distance work or driving at speed. I needed to make a degree of rapid progress before hitting the approaching blizzard.

Beattie(*2) is a game old girl but an open racing car was hardly the right machine for the task either. What is more, she is still suffering from the mystery misfire that has been plaguing her since her last hillclimb outing at Loton Park in September(*3). So in the unusual event of there being no press loan hack skulking in the de Forte motor houses it was a case of the proverbial Hobson's Choice for yours truly(*4). It's been two years since Pater's death but I still can't bring myself to sell his last motor car, delivered new in summer 1960, six months before he popped his clogs. Just as well.

'Hurry up old man!' I had to wait an eternity for the normally cheerful but strangely belligerent Harry Haynes to switch the pumps on at the village garage. Lazy bugger – I had to drive over the bell wire 20 times before he emerged in his pyjamas to open his forecourt hut. Was he going to spend the whole morning in bed?

I settled into the Rover's comfy bench seat and with Hector's chin upon my knee (*5), as much to get himself into an ideal position in front of the heater blower as an act of devotion to his master, we set off briskly. But maintaining a decent lick became increasingly difficult. Flakes of snow began hitting the windscreen near Stoke-on-Trent and we were soon fully under the snow belt. Visibility was down to around ten feet or so on the road from Macclesfield to Whaley Bridge, and it was on the high point of this vertiginous switchback B-road that the normally surefooted Solihull saloon gave a warning lurch as, for the first time, it found compacted snow rather than slush and Edgar Hooley's (the inventor of tarmacadam – ed) under its Avons.

From then I had to be on my mettle and with the quarter-light ajar to direct an icy blast at the de Forte phizzog in aid of concentration (much to Hector's disgust) it was a case of applying the rules of winter driving: no involuntary sudden steering movements, smoothness on the throttle, intelligent selection of gears, judicious use of brakes and bags of anticipation at all times.

Having passed only a venerable army surplus 20 ton Foden six wheeler along the way (its skilled driver finding time to give a cheery wave as I overtook, despite working hard at the time to make good use of its alternative ultra-low ratio box on a particularly slithery section) I reached the most challenging leg of the journey, the ascent of High Moss, without great incident.

High Moss is not the site of the BBC's northern television transmitter without good reason. Its summit is 1,750 feet above sea level, and even at the start of the climb from Skagdale on the Manchester Road, the snow was whirling wildly and the drifts were banked high against the stone walls. The road would soon become unpassable. We had to get a move on.

As the aforementioned Foden pilot would have agreed, momentum is vital when making uphill progress with limited resources, whether of grip or horsepower, so I was not best pleased (to use an appropriate Yorkshire-ism) when a group of dimwits leapt into the road in front of me waving their arms around like windmills just as I got the torquey Rover settled comfortably into a third gear run at 25mph and was making firm if fishtailing progress.

When it became clear I was not going to stop they scattered among their abandoned vehicles at the roadside and there was much colourful language as I saw them in my mirrors picking themselves up and dusting off the neige. Hector, of course, swore back, bouncing up and down on the well sprung rear seat cushion. Why do people always expect others to be constrained by their own limitations?

Maintaining my rhythm and concentration I drew on all I'd learned from Ronnie Adams(*6) and co at the Monte over the years and we wagged and wheelspinned our way to the top. Pausing at the Yorkshire border to clear accumulated snow and ice from the headlights, we were met by amazed transmitter staff who left their station to greet us. The last vehicle to make it up from the Derbyshire side had apparently been their own Land Rover SII station wagon some three hours earlier.

The poor blighters were resigned to being snowed in for the foreseeable so I gave them a bottle of malt intended for Clive and asked them by way of thanks to ring same requesting he set off immediately to meet me for a livener at the Bay Horse(*7). Half an hour hence, having given the brakes a jolly good cooking and experiencing several one or two hairy lock to lock moments on the descent, we joined him at the bar. And it was still only 2.30pm when we scrunched onto the drive at Oak House an hour later. Needless to say by that time I had come to hold Pater's last Rover in rather high regard.

Peter and Susan rushed to greet Hector and their Uncle Wilby and while Clive carved the festive bird there was time for present distribution – a charming Steiff teddy bear from that delightful toy shop near the Nürburgring for Susan and a splendid clockwork scale model of a Ferrari by Schuco for Peter, who also received a few more motorcyclist autographs for his collection (Bob McIntyre, Derek Minter and the remarkable SMB Hailwood).

After a splendid roast dinner far too lavish to mention in the hearing of the peasantry, washed down with 1957 Chateau Neuf de Pape grabbed that morning from the cellar in Bales (the first duty of any wine is to be red, as Alec Waugh so correctly states in his most amusing book on the subject), it was time to doze in front of a roaring sitting room fire before the Dunnills, Whitakers and other agreeable neighbours called round for an evening of charades and several turns of 'the game'.

While snowflakes the size of dustbin lids fell on the Yorkshire landscape outside (everything's bigger and better in Yorkshire, the natives will have you believe), Hector stretched himself out on the hearth rug, tooting gently, Peter set about building a Meccano Beattie, and Susan and her mother played ultra-competitive and high-scoring Scrabble. Clive fell asleep under yesterday's *Times* while I sipped his best malt and caught up with the latest *Auto Sport*. Top hole!

Notes

*(*1) It is still in service 55 years later at the grand old age of 69. Not bad for a vehicle that has worked almost every day since Pater bought it in 1948.*
*(*2) My adored blower Bentley. See diary extract 24 April 1958.*
*(*3) Pipped into second that day by a chain-driven Napier, I seem to remember.*
*(*4) Thomas Hobson ran a horse rental business in Cambridge at the end of the 16th century and became famous for the strict rotation of his livestock which gave hirers no choice in the animal they were offered. He died aged 86 prompting John Milton to declare 'he had bin an immortall carrier.' Odd thing to say about someone who had just kicked the bucket!*
*(*5) Since my boyhood several de Forte house dogs have been Hectors, and all these have been terrier-type mongrels.*

(*6) *A fine rally driver and famous winner of the Monte Carlo rally in 1955 in a Jaguar Mark VII, for any youngsters reading this.*
(*7) *Splendid hostelry tucked away down an alley in the centre of Greenfirth.*

LESS IS MORE

I am not a devotee of supercars. Never have been. Pointless. And not just modern ones. Looking back through my 1963 diary, I see I tested a Morgan 4/4 and an Austin Healey 3000 in the same week, declaring afterwards that I had much preferred the little Morgan.

I always liked the Worcestershire company's pre-war three-wheelers. Yes, they were crude, but I adored the low-down urge of a big V-twin Matchless or JAP, and the handling characteristics of a skittish three-wheeled device with a low down centre of gravity. They were honorary motorcycles, of course, and I blagged a drive in them whenever I could, delighting in the seat of the pants fun of the things, drifting them happily all day until the spokes broke.

The first Morgan 4/4 arrived in 1936, with 4/4 meaning four-wheeled (Morgan's first such), and four cylinders (as is still the case today), and in 1955 the Malvern men hit upon the look that would define the breed. Even today all Morgans retain something of their 1950s cars' appearance, and of course it has become part and parcel of the marque's charm, but sadly larger-engined Morgans have become almost caricatures, no longer retaining the flimsy grace and delicate style of scale of early 4/4s or Plus 4s. The present-day 4/4, however, appears to be a car in much the same spirit as the delightful sports car I tested in February 1963.

Britain was gripped by one of the worst winters of the 20th century when I assayed the little Morgan 4/4. Some main roads had been cleared, but many were slippery with ice, and on an afternoon trip to Buckinghamshire it began to snow again heavily. With the celluloid side screens down for the sake of visibility, I pressed on, using my frozen phizzog to sense minute changes in air temperature and therefore gauge the likelihood of treacherous black ice.

Despite the conditions, and the fact the lightweight car was powered by a small and rudimentary Ford pushrod engine of just 1340cc, the Morgan 4/4 was a joy. The little car danced around corners like a quickstepping ballroom beauty, sliding under my full control, spinning little, and finding purchase without undue snatch. Bends were taken in sensational, long drifts, felt through the backside and fingertips as in days of yore. But soon we were enveloped in a downright blizzard, and snow soon carpeted the frosty tarmacadam. I steered a serpentine course uphill to reduce gradient and improve traction, but soon the game was up and I had to give best to the constantly falling snow. I spent the next two nights trapped in an agreeable village inn near Aylesbury (splendid old ale brewed on the premises, I recall), before a helpful farmer dug the ash-framed Morgan out of its yard with his David Brown 30D, enabling me to complete my freezing journey to visit my friends, the Baxters.

The maximum speed attained in the 4/4 on either driving day was barely 90mph (with the canvas top down, and protecting myself from snow with an open umbrella!), but there can be no questioning the Morgan's sports car credentials. It was a genuine sporting machine, and quite thrilling to drive despite its decided lack of oomph. A considerable performer in its own gentle way, and I loved it.

The Austin Healey 3000 on the other hand, which it seems I tested for the same issue of *The Auto*, I found to be a bit of a brute. Its 130bhp engine had good torque characteristics, true, but this flexibility wasn't enough to overcome some serious negatives. I found it had a heavy clutch, a ponderous gearbox with far from foolproof synchro that only an expert could rush, and that it manifested a disturbing scuttle shake when tramping on. But of far more concern was that while it was a fine enough car at slow speeds, it was actually a very fast car indeed, and furthermore most buyers were attracted to it because of that very fact.

Not a problem in itself, of course, but the big Healey was far too tail-happy for my liking, and I found it unpredictable and highly dangerous when operated at the top of its range, especially in the wet. While I could drive the responsive Morgan with vim and verve, hanging its rear end out with gay abandon; managing slide and counter-slide in such a brutal and capricious animal as the 3000 was not at all fun. Big engined beasts are fine for pointing and squirting, but it is balance that flatters the driver, and that is a quality which is usually to be found in much smaller packages.

DODGY GEEZERS
(First published *Classic Auto* – April 2002)

So you want to buy an old banger, as we used to call old motor cars in the days before 'classics' had been invented? What should you look for, apart from a psychiatrist? Apologies, dear reader, but given my chequered history of vehicle ownership, I am probably the worst person to proffer advice.

Put simply for the uninformed, buying a vintage or classic car is at least as dangerous as walking blindfold through a minefield surrounded by bears, bandits and boobytraps. I've been messing around with old jalopies for more years than I care to remember, yet still make the same silly mistakes. Fortunately, in my earliest dabblings the dropped clangers were comparatively painless in financial terms, and during the immediate post-war era it was possible to unearth – often literally, in the case of vehicles that had been buried for safe-keeping in gardens throughout the land – a bargain banger for a few shillings. That's not a great deal of dosh, even allowing for a few thousand percent RPI adjustment to scale it up to present-day values.

Given some backyard bodging, these dormant wrecks could often be persuaded to move under their own steam again, at which juncture one could either drive the treacherous contraption (MoT roadworthiness tests were decades away, of course), or sell it on for a modest profit to another mug. Said mug would be unlikely to complain, as petrol was still rationed, and he'd be unable to travel far or fast enough for the wheels to fall off. I mean that quite literally, as it was by no means a rare affliction in that innocent era.

Moving on, as the '40s turned into the '50s and '60s, the Luftwaffe still cast a shadow over the used car trade, as London was festooned with bomb site dealerships, managed with great creativity by old-fashioned cockney spivs with wide-shouldered jackets and pencil moustaches. Undoubtedly, some of these chaps were involved in petty crime, and were no strangers to Her Majesty's hospitality suites. However, for the most part they were likeable, if roguish, characters who did their best to keep their penurious punters happy.

One of my favourites, operating from a rubble-strewn spot 'up west', where a small flat would now cost several million pounds, was Dave Davidson (evidently his parents were short of imagination when it came to christian names), known to me as Dee-Dee. His rocky pitch always contained an interesting selection of motors, often of continental and therefore exotic provenance. Whence these came I preferred not to imagine, but I well remember the occasion when a pre-war racing Alfa Romeo appeared in the line-up, a slightly incongruous sight in the circumstances.

Perhaps fortunately, I didn't buy that Latin lovely, but I couldn't resist others, including a Bentley, sundry Jaguars and a particularly eye-able Alvis. On each occasion Dee-Dee would insist on clinching the deal with a spittle-laden handshake, and the assurance that, 'You won't regret it, Rocket, old son.' By the bye, I'd been a customer of his for at least five years before the penny dropped about his nickname for me. Originally I had naively believed it to be some sort of complimentary reference to my somewhat brisk driving style!

It must have been in spring 1963, emerging as we were from a long period of snowbound stagnation, when a young colleague on *The Auto* took a fancy to a rare car he'd spotted on Dee-Dee's lot, and he took me up to town specifically to take a look at it. It was hard to miss the rare red and white Ford Zodiac convertible, its nose nestled up close to Dee-Dee's faithful brazier (scorched paint or chrome work was of less concern than a cracked cylinder block caused by a frozen cooling system!), and we parked the Mark VI right next to it. Dee-Dee immediately abandoned a spotty youth looking longingly at a rust-holed

Vauxhall Wyvern, and, with his hands stuffed deep into the pockets of his sheepskin, bustled across the lot while greeting me with all the enthusiasm of a salesman who can spot a sale from fifty paces. 'Welcome to our 'umble emporium, Rocket, me old son, and you too young man. Just the motor for you this is. Lovely straight one lady-owner job wiv a tuned engine and all the extras… Just watch this!'

With that he leaned in and flicked a switch somewhere on the dash panel, and in a series of sudden jerks and spasms, and with an accompanying soundtrack of electrical whirrs and clonks, the hood rose eccentrically and theatrically in the air, and then suddenly collapsed, folding itself as it did so back into its stowage compartment behind the rear seats. 'Like magic, innit?' said Dee-Dee, surreptitiously shoving the crumpled roof a little further down into its cubbyhole. 'It'd be great for impressin' the ladies, and we wouldn't want yer to trap yer delicate pinkies doin' it by hand, would we, me old son?'

Now, while I've never been keen on superfluous gadgetry, I do detest standing in the rain trying to erect the Heath-Robinson tent-like structures that most car manufacturers foisted upon us as hoods, so I was actually mightily impressed. Trying unsuccessfully to appear nonchalant, I nodded secretly to my young companion, and gave the rest of the Ford a quick once over. All seemed well, and the six cylinder engine purred like a well-fed kitten, to use one of Mr D's favourite expressions. En passant, the idea of a push-button roof was as old as the hills even in 1963. Most notably, Peugeot offered one in the '30s.

Dee-Dee's innate salesman's instinct proved infallible, and my friend soon found myself handing over a wad of fivers in return for the two-tone Zodiac and customary slippery handshake. Dee-Dee had assured us the paperwork was all in order, but when the log book made an appearance (strangely enough almost the second the deal was clinched) it revealed that while the one lady owner claim was true, he had neglected to mention the five previous male title-holders. 'Sorry, Rocket, that part must have had the pages stuck together…' Yes, of course it did.

Still, I wasn't too concerned, for the car was fairly priced and I was happy for my friend to take possession. Or at least I was until he flashed me urgently on the way back to the office, and then appeared apologetically at my driver's window asking me if I'd mind awfully taking a listen to some strange and disturbing noises coming from somewhere underneath his newly-purchased Dagenham dustbin.

Oh dear, oh dear. The rear axle howled like a tone-deaf banshee (I understand that some banshees were quite musical) at 25mph, at which speed the propshaft sounded as though it were about to fly loose and break through the floor at any moment. While I could have chipped Dee-Dee down a score, to use his own street vernacular, and lived with the howl, I'm afraid the clonks and vibration were a long way beyond the English pale.

By the time we had returned to the Bentley the frightful commotion from below had grown steadily worse, so I led us back to discuss the matter with the man whose rickety shed-cum-office boasted a garish sign offering 'The Cheapest Cars in West London: No Sensible Offers Refused'. The following year a stormy night changed the last word to 'efused', prompting much ribaldry among fellow traders concerning Dee-Dee's Rs blowing off, but I digress.

'Back so soon, Rocket? Don't tell me yer want that 'illman as well?' No, I did not. My colleague wanted a driveable Ford, ASAP. We both knew the score. Dee-Dee's official warranty may have only lasted as long it took for the wheels to revolve three times, but he also didn't want to lose a regular customer, particularly one engaged in the trade of motor journalism. Besides, as he had told me more than once, he was an honourable man. 'It's the public wot are messers, wasting yer time and then trying to part-ex cars with HP on 'em.'

'Don't worry me old son, me chief mechanic will fix it in a jiffy,' said Dee-Dee laying a paternal hand on my colleague's shoulder. 'Leave it wiv us. Must admit she did sound a bit noisy when you drove up.' A masterful understatement.

There was actually only one resident mechanic, Sid. A pugnacious character who spent most of his life putting eggs into leaking radiators and shoving putty into holes in rusty bodywork. Or vice versa. 'Better go to the stores tonight and fetch a new prop for Mr de Forte,' commanded his boss. Did I detect a conspiratorial wink as he said it? Probably, but I cared mostly about him fixing my pal's stricken Zodiac, not how it would be done.

A taxi delivered us to Dee-Dee's lot next morning, where, to my relief and surprise, the Ford appeared to be ready. Had I underestimated Sid's abilities? 'See how we look after you here, Rocket. Sid worked on it for you all night.' were Dee-Dee's parting words, as we set off back to the office with the top down. Mercifully, the transmission was now silent.

By coincidence, less than a mile away we found ourselves waiting at traffic lights on an arterial road directly beside a Ford main agent. On the pavement outside, a selection of smart second-hand Zephyrs and Zodiacs were basking in the watery spring sunshine. One, a blue saloon, had its bonnet raised and was surrounded by a gaggle of sales staff in heated discussion. Additionally, a pair of overalled legs stuck out from underneath at amidships. As we waited I could not help but overhear that it seemed this particular Zodiac had a problem. The car had been fine yesterday, but now its transmission was making the most terrible noises. As the lights changed to green and we glided away, four pairs of eyes swivelled round to observe our smooth and silent departure. 'The stores,' indeed!

Chapter Seven

I'd like a nice blonde on my knee
And one who won't argue and nag.
Who cares to come hooting at me?
I only give way to a Jag.

Meditation on the A30 – John Betjeman*

MOTORING TYPES OF THE 1950S AND 1960S
(First published *Classic Auto* – June 2006)

TRUE PIONEER MOTORISTS SUCH as my dear Grandpapa were inevitably rather well-heeled, and as they tore around the countryside, Mr Toad-like, in their large and terrifying contraptions, they looked down on the fleeing commoners they passed with undisguised arrogance and disdain. More than a century later, the owners of Teutonic Bentleys and ugly new Range Rovers sporting absurd and depressingly daft registration plates, attempt to communicate a similar message of superiority to the great unwashed.

The motor car has always projected the status of its owner, and in mid twentieth century Britain, the maker's badge on the radiator grille was a particularly reliable and subtle indicator of social status. Of course, a man's individual taste and personality could influence his choice of conveyance to a degree, and a touching degree of old-fashioned loyalty ensured a clapped out family jalopy would often be replaced by one carrying the same emblem of marque, but, generally speaking, society was conformist and everyone knew their place.

Fords were for those of the penurious stratum. Cheap and cheerless, most Dagenham dustbins became total heaps: nasty little things finally driven into the ground by the most irksome erks. A chap had to reach Austin and Morris level to achieve any degree of respectability. Interestingly, although these two manufacturers' popular products were of broadly similar standard and character, and the two companies actually merged in 1952, people rarely transferred their allegiance from one to the other. Later, in the 1960s, devotees of Fords and Vauxhalls were split by a similar theological divide, Ford having moved up the pecking order by virtue of its Cortina, the first production motor car with a truly

* 'Meditation on the A30' from *Collected Poems*, by John Betjeman © 1955, 1958, 1962, 1964, 1968, 1970, 1979, 1981, 1982, 2001. Reproduced by permission of John Murray, an imprint of Hodder and Stoughton Ltd.

effective heater! At last one no longer had to dress up in a greatcoat to travel in winter.

Austins were dour and austere, the car of the puritan, but they were utterly dependable. 'You buy a car but you invest in an Austin,' proclaimed the company's slogan. This was taken as gospel by the factory's most devout and dedicated devotees, but was also true of the equally worthy Oxford-built Morris. Both reflected a solid and most definite Britishness.

Although once Britain's largest motor manufacturer, Wolseley had always attracted a staunchly middle class clientele. The Wolseley 6/90, which had a smart interior featuring a surprisingly natty formica instrument board, was the last real Wolseley to be built before the Coventry marque disappeared in the 1960s. Apart from being bought by most of Britain's police forces, these handsome Wolseleys were bought by the sort of suburbanites later to buy Volvos. Only a handful now survive, but several more are immortalised in British B pictures, heeled over tyres a-screeching and Winkworth bumper bells a-jingle chasing cockney villains in Jaguar Mark VIIs. Meanwhile, long-legged Riley RMs offered 'Magnificent Motoring' for cravatted gentlemen and their ladies.

Owners of most minor marques were trying too hard to be different, small Hillmans were frivolous and gutless, and Captain Black's Vanguards, Pennants and Ensigns, despite carrying noble names on their brows, were also standard fare for humdrum types.

French cars of the period were primarily built for peasants and the Italians made tinny, unreliable rust buckets. And although most of us no longer hated the sausage eaters, apart from being jolly expensive, German cars were just too Teutonic to sell in any numbers. American motors, of course, were bloated and vainglorious, but almost indestructible and not at all unpleasant to drive for those of us fortunate enough to sample them. For most Britons, however, they were rarely seen outside a picture house.

Rover's patriotic owners were the epitome of sobriety, discretion, respectability and decorum. Like their motor cars, they were modest, unassuming and almost uniformly reliable. But Rover drivers were also astute. The Solihull saloon was an exceptionally well engineered conveyance, and some upper middle class families drove nothing else for three generations. In the 1960s the advanced Rover P6 attracted smart young executive types and the future looked bright (or tobacco brown), but takeover by the Leyland Motor Corporation and subsequent nationalisation saw the company struggle to maintain its identity. Remarkably, the Rover mystique and good name remained largely intact throughout the dark years of British Leyland, which is why, of course, it was chosen as the new name for the ailing giant in 1986; the myriad other marques in the group having had their names sullied and reputations destroyed by the nationalised monster.

A 1950s Rover man would think of a Jaguar as tasteless tat. Indeed, Sir William Lyons' cars were built to a price but they looked fast standing still and attracted attention as a honeypot does bees. And of course, Jaguar hatred is rooted in envy. Vulgar extroverts, flashy spivs and nouveau riche upstarts were especially drawn to Bill's powerful and beautiful cars even before War Two, as well as speed merchants, with unscrupulous and unethical types such as black marketeers, bookies, property developers and second-hand car dealers among their undesirable number. As a serial Jaguar owner myself I must confess to membership of the above club on at least two counts!

Many now consider the Jaguar Mark II to be the archetypal 1960s villain's car, but the less fashionable and commercially successful S Type gave the same remarkable performance while offering better, certainly more roll-free, handling and a considerably more voluminous boot, which provided a space that came in particularly handy for hurling ill-gotten loot, and even a dead body or two. Consequently it was an S that was usually stolen as a getaway car by sawn-off toting bank robbers and diamond thieves. But larger gangsters found all Jags somewhat difficult to get in and out of in a hurry, especially hauling swag and clutching a shooter, and from the mid 1960s Ford Transit vans proved themselves more practical for crooks in a number of obvious ways.

As the 1960s swung on, seismic economic and political change saw the end of many of the great names of British motor car manufacturing, and the age of homogeneous plastic modernity was almost upon us. At the same time, Issigonis's clever little Mini proved to be a car that could cross all social boundaries, and where my dear chum Issi led, others followed. By that decade's end, although it was still possible to determine a chap's wealth, personality and social standing by the make of car on his driveway, it was becoming a much more complex art.

FORD CORTINA AND MORRIS 1100 RETROSPECTIVE

In my column in the October 1962 issue of *The Auto* (reproduced in the previous chapter of this tome under the heading Cortina Reflections), I wrote about the new Ford Cortina following its launch in Britain in September that year.

Cortina was the name given to a series of mid-sized cars that fitted into Ford's range between its distinctive little one litre Anglias, and larger six cylinder Zephyrs and Zodiacs. What was the point of it? To make good profits, of course, and to refresh the company's image to boot. Well, it achieved both of those objectives, and a million units were sold by 1966.

I also discussed the Issigonis Mini, which was a huge seller throughout the whole of the 1960s and beyond, but not a great success financially. Issi's next project was the four door Morris 1100 which was, in fact, released a few weeks before Ford's Cortina. A true Super Mini, it was also a super seller (getting on for two million were produced over 12 years), and it proved far more profitable than its smaller stablemate. Like the Mini three years earlier it was a thoroughly modern motor car. Front-wheel-drive (of course!), and likewise powered by a transverse engine with an in-sump gearbox, it also featured front disc brakes, and Issi's clever hydrolastic suspension linked fore and aft, which he designed in conjunction with his chum Alex Moulton (a thoroughly good egg incidentally, and a bright-eyed contemporary of mine at Cambridge).

The 1100 was also sold as an Austin variant, and a 1300cc version of both models soon doubled the range. Styled by Pininfarina and of pleasingly balanced proportions, the car has actually aged rather well, but it was never really fashionable, is unsought after by modern collectors, and not least due to its fatal attractiveness to tin worm, it is as rare as the proverbial rocking horse poop today. Deceptively spacious, to borrow the estate agent's stock phrase, it could accommodate five in comfort despite being a small car. Indeed, my neighbour and insurance broker of many moons, a father of three strapping boys, had seven of them in succession as company cars, driving nothing else over a 14 year period, although he did finish off with a flourish, choosing, in 1972, a snazzy orange twin-carb GT model with a black vinyl roof. Mind you, he always wore the same patched jacket, worked in the same office all his career, ate the same sandwiches for luncheon every weekday all his life, and took his brood to the same boarding house in Bognor Regis every August for his holidays.

The 1100 didn't change much over the years either. There was a minor restyling job in 1967, gearbox revisions in 1968 gave it synchro on first, but there was no development as such, and the model was replaced by the unloved Austin Allegro in 1973, a car that made such a negative impression upon the British motoring public, it was voted the country's worst ever by readers of a national newspaper. Actually, I don't concur: a contemporaneous brown Morris Marina which had seven new clutches in the six months I had it on long-term test and broke down on me five times would get my vote (and that was a factory-prepared car!).

The Ford Cortina was a conventional front-engined, rear-wheel-drive saloon (estates came later), but sharp and good looking in a modern way, and it sold at a great price. The Cortina was pitched to undercut Issigonis's Morris 1100, and it was also cheaper than the Farina-refreshed Morris Oxford and new-style Vauxhall Victor, both released the previous year. It was a car for the masses and a jolly good one too. A rep's car, and a family conveyance, it was roomy, practical, reliable, and looked like a proper car should look, although I have to say I was not struck on the interior. Meagre instrumentation with a mean strip speedometer (the column-mounted revolution counters in sporty versions always seemed to me something of an afterthought), lots of painted metal, a bench front seat, and thin rubber mats on the floor.

The Cortina range soon expanded, and the interiors became a little less austere. I drove a GT for a few days in 1963 (fantastic value at around £770), rather liking the fact the badging was discreet. A bit of a Q car? Not really, but it offered sports car performance by the mediocre standards of not too many years previously. The GT was special, Ford's publicity blurb told me. It had a special high compression head, special valves, special inlet and exhaust manifolds, and a special twin-choke Weber carburettor. It was powered by a 1500cc pushrod four mated to a sweet, all-synchro four speed (on the floor) box with a light action. It sat tall, I noted at the time, allowing good visibility. The ride I found a tad harsh, but the car's lightness and rigidity made for handling that was altogether good. It also went like the clappers. According to my notes I squeezed 100mph out of it down Conrod bringing it home on the first night. Keen, no doubt, to get to the Rose & Crown before closing time! It stopped well too, and the brakes were fade free through the lanes. Discs at the front, drums behind.

All things considered, the Cortina was a winner, and I was correct back in '62 to have predicted a bright future for it as a racer, although to be honest I already had an inkling then that Colin Chapman's clever chaps at Lotus were developing a twin-cam engine for it, and that they were working on the suspension too. The Lotus Cortina of 1963 had light alloy bodywork assembled by Colin's boys, trick suspension (coil springs at the rear were later changed to leaf), and a Lotus twin-cam engine. It was built for saloon car racing, but even the cars sold to Joe Public were good for 110mph. In 1964 the mercurial Jim Clark was British saloon car champion in a Lotus Cortina taking eight wins in JTW 498C (I have a photo here on my wall), and the following year he won the Welsh Rally with that indefatigable automotive author and historian Graham Robson as his co-pilot.

By the way, thank goodness I have several of Mr Robson's books here to hand while I write these reminiscences. Someone once said something along the lines that the daughter of truth lives at the bottom of a very deep well, and that with every year that passes, the effort to disentangle her from accumulated rubbish becomes ever more difficult. Quite, and it is a lamentable condition of old age that mental qualities become impaired. Not least the mechanism of memory. I stare into the past and the de Forte grey matter reiterates apparently truthful data, which is, in fact, wholly erroneous. I look again and there is no variation. Reliable compilers and chroniclers such as Mr Robson are invaluable in jogging the memory onto a different track.

Also in 1965, the Lotus Cortina won the European Touring Car Championship in the hands of Baronet Sir John Whitmore. Now a sports psychologist, Sir John was a product of Eton and Sandhurst who inherited his Essex seat in 1961, the year he won the British Saloon Car Championship in a BMC Mini. Pressed hard on the track, Cortinas would lift the inside front wheel to an alarming degree. The crowd would gasp, but Clark and Whitmore plainly knew exactly what they were doing. A farm boy like me, Jim Clark was a kind of driving genius, unlike me. He was also modest and reserved, but he always found time to talk to spectators and lesser mortals on the grid. Like many others around the world I am sure, I was affected rather deeply when I heard he'd been killed. I feel a tad melancholy thinking of him even now.

Later Cortinas featured fascias of a more attractive design, and a quite fabulous heating and ventilation system, called aeroflow, with eyeball swivel vents in the dash. I say fabulous because, by golly, it worked. It really was very much the best system I had ever come across, and the first with head level ventilation. Thank goodness its principles were soon unblushingly copied by manufacturers all around the world. A game-changer, as the tiresome Top Gear obsessed herberts at the Rose & Crown would put it in the dull argot of today.

Heaters had been either non-existent or pathetic since motoring's earliest days. The unit in my E-Type at that time was not far short of useless, and there is a story about Bill Lyons from a few years before that is worth repeating here. A disgruntled American XK customer apparently dragged Sir William down to the basement car park during a New York motor show to prove the ineffectiveness of his car's Smith's heater. 'See, nothing,' said the man, having started the already warm engine and opened the quaint black metal flaps under the dashboard to facilitate airflow into the cabin. Sir William, a non-smoker asked one of those present for a lighted cigarette, and proceeded to hold it in front of these little doors. The column of smoke rising from its burning end bent over ever so very slightly. 'You see,' said the Jaguar patriarch, 'it works perfectly well.' The exasperated owner ventured that winter temperatures in New York were consistently 15 below freezing. 'Wear an overcoat,' said Sir William, departing.

Heavy clothing was still necessary for cold weather driving well into the 1960s, even in saloon cars, and misting was another bugbear. Side windows or quarter-lights had to be open to prevent steaming up, while the occupants shivered in overcoats, hats and scarves. I could never bring myself to smear a raw potato across the inside of the windscreen to keep it from frosting overnight, though there were those that swore by it. In my childhood Pater would drive in a cashmere overcoat, and Mater would heat house bricks in the range and then wrap them in old woollies so we could hug them under our travelling rugs, or rest our feet on them. Overnight a de Forte motor car would be drained of water, and an eiderdown would be placed over its bonnet, covered with a heap of dunny sacks and topped off with a tarpaulin. In the morning, hot water was heated in a saucepan in the house, and carried across in a stone bottle to be poured into the radiator. If possible an engine would be turned over by hand before using the self starter, and only when an engine was running happily would cold water be added. You can see why some folk didn't bother with that daily palaver during a cold snap, and simply laid their motors up for the duration.

ALVIS REMINISCENCES
(First published *Classic Auto* – March 2007)

Douglas Bader could be a disagreeable old cove, but only towards those who didn't meet his standards, or couldn't operate at his level of heightened urgency. This applied to sluggard motorists as well as dimwitted superiors in the RAF, and the legless ace piloted his Alvis motor cars rather as he flew his Hawker Hurricanes.

Travelling with Bader was a startling experience. With his left tin leg shoved well out of the way in the passenger footwell, he used a cupped hand to aid shifting his substitute right peg back and forth between throttle and binders. What he lacked in feel and subtlety of touch, he made up for with bravery, alertness and lightning reflexes. Pulling out into oncoming traffic to pass the potterers, he would simply floor the loud pedal and shout, 'Make way for the quality!' Nutty as the proverbial fruitcake though he may well have been, Bader's automotive battle cry was utterly apt. This is because, above all other considerations, the Alvis Engineering Company made gentlemen's motor cars of the foremost rank.

A manufacturer of fine and imaginative cars since 1920, Alvis also made a name for itself designing and building military vehicles and aero engines. Car production ceased in 1967 but, despite several changes of ownership, the fighting vehicle division still exists to this day. Pre war Alvis cars were fast, stylish and brilliantly innovative. The firm built a front wheel drive Grand Prix car in 1926 and two years later applied the technology to a road-going model. Most of the firm's technical drawings from this period were lost in the Coventry blitz of 1940, along with much precision tooling and manufacturing equipment, but the front-wheel-drive blueprints survived and my good pal Alec Issigonis spent many hours poring over them to good effect when he worked for Alvis in the early 1950s.

After the goons were defeated, Alvis settled down to building sensible and solid sporting saloons, and a new chassis and six cylinder 3.0 litre engine were introduced in 1950. Alvis had its own foundries and precision engineering shop but the business was far from self sufficient. Its cars were always coachbuilt by bodywork specialists, but these concerns were in increasingly short supply after the war and finding reliable and economical body suppliers was a problem that would hamper the company for more than 20 years. But it was not all doom and gloom. Swiss master coachbuilder Hermann Graber produced some quite exquisite designs on the new chassis, and from the mid 1950s the best of these was licensed and used as the model for all future Alvis cars. After a few early cars were bodied somewhat expensively by Loughborough coachbuilder Willowbrook, a more businesslike deal was struck with Park Ward of London, a firm by then owned by Rolls-Royce.

Between 1958 and 1967 Alvis worked with Park Ward to produce around 1,500 of these handsome sporting saloons and coupés. They were craftsman-made motor cars which were well received by the public and motoring hacks alike, but ultimately the high retail prices necessitated by the cars' laborious and costly production process could no longer be sustained. The firm, which was taken over by Rover in 1965 and subsequently sucked into the British Leyland abyss, made its last motor car in 1967.

It is many years since I have driven an Alvis 3.0 litre, so it was with great pleasure that I learned of the whereabouts of a fine Park Ward example tucked away in a secluded Pennine village near Greenfirth. And I only had to mention to the owner I was working for *The Classic Auto* and a morning of do-as-you-like driving was soon arranged.

8213KR is one of just 95 TE21 drophead cars built, of which 88 are said to survive. First registered to a lady doctor in Kent in July 1964, KR was sold two years later to little known thespian Malcolm McDowell, who later achieved fame playing juvenile delinquents in the films *If* and *A Clockwork Orange*. McDowell kept the Alvis for many years, taking it with him to Beverley Hills where the climate and lifestyle was perhaps rather kinder to the car than to its owner. The pale gold TE21 eventually returned to Blighty in the 1990s, whereupon it was reunited with its British registration plates and began to enjoy the pampered existence of a highly valued classic car.

The test took place on a fine autumn morning, so KR's mohair ragtop was collapsed without fuss and the tonneau cover was quickly and easily fitted before I jumped into the well-upholstered driver's seat. The immaculate six cylinder engine fired immediately on the key, and, while the semi automatic choke sucked away audibly for a minute or two until the owner deemed the old girl ready for take off, I had a chance to take in my surroundings. Delightful contrasting timbers and smart clocks and controls made for a tasteful dashboard and the original cream leather seats and door cards were complemented by a smart new carpet. The wood rimmed steering wheel sported the glorious Alvis Eagle motif on the horn push, and the car's factory fitted wireless with discrete speaker and other details were also pleasing to behold. All in all the car's interior exudes quality, and is quite the perfect cockpit for a retired RAF pilot; I was reminded why Douglas Bader was so fond of his Alvises (he had four) and had slipped into something of a daydream when I felt a hand on my shoulder. It was time to go!

Wiping an errant nostalgic tear from the de Forte phizzog, I clicked off the choke and nosed the Alvis clear of its sleepy village home and onto the King's Highway. On the road, the car's modern power-assisted steering system is a delight. It is smoothly progressive in operation so low speed manoeuvring is almost effortless, and at high velocities the device is utterly imperceptible. Quite brilliant and completely unlike the horrid floaty devices of the 1950s. A two pedal model as preferred by my old chum Bader, KR features a Borg Warner automatic gearbox with a natty slide control device with which the driver can override the box's hydraulic brain to bring together or space out its shifting points. Some say a degree of torquiness was lost as Alvis developed and tuned the 3.0 litre lump over the years, but I found the lazy burbling power of this 130bhp version of the motor to be quite delicious. And once a lazy mood has passed, shifting the gearbox control lever to what may now be termed sport mode, and throwing on the coals, brings about acceleration of no less urgency than a contemporary Jaguar saloon.

Although I opted not to reach the three figure speeds recorded daily by Bader, the car was comfortable cruising at 70mph on the motorway and wind noise, considering we were topless, was minimal. Tractable and docile in town, the Alvis featured disc brakes all round and the car crouched down to a dead stop without fuss. Proper motoring in every regard. All too soon my sortie was complete and it was time to return to base for photographs. While snapping pics of this charming and pretty car, which is little different in appearance to the Graber originals from which it was developed, I asked its owner to reflect on its enduring appeal. 'It's stylish yet unpretentious,' was his reply, 'and it offers an opportunity to experience a piece of England that otherwise no longer exists.' Hear hear!

Incidentally, my last memory of riding in an Alvis with Bader may be worth repeating here. We were tooling through Buckinghamshire on the A40 on a wild, wet and windy night, on our way to a POW reunion dinner at RAF Northolt (I was Bader's invited guest), and had picked up a soggy beatnik hitch-hiker, who turned out to be in obvious need of a good bath, and whose incessant 'yeah man' twittering soon proved rather tiresome.

The scruffy erk then made the mistake of asking us where we were going. Seizing an opportunity, Bader reacted in an instant. 'To meet up with some people I was in prison with,' he calmly replied. Some time then passed before our whiffy back seat passenger spoke again, asking finally: 'Like, why were you in prison man?' 'For killing people,' came the legless one's honest and immediate response, and with that he turned to fix him with his best toothy grin. An expression of ineffable fear struck across the erk's face, and he decided with some urgency that he had, in fact, already reached his destination.

MGB MATTERS
(First published *Classic Auto* – April 2007)

Being dismissed from a company you founded and nurtured for more than a decade must be bruising to the ego, to say the least. But that's exactly what happened to dear old Cecil Kimber, the man behind MG cars, who was given the order of the boot in 1941. In one version of history this came as a result of the way he went about procuring contracts from the WD (War Department – ed). In another, it was because he disobeyed a directorial directive to sack an errant worker. Either way, far worse was to come, because having lost his job, just four years later Kimber lost his life in an unfortunate and rather silly train accident in a tunnel outside Kings Cross station. He was 56. A sad end for one of the key figures in the pre war British motor industry.

As every man and his whippet will tell you, MG stood for Morris Garages, the Oxford branch of William Morris's nascent automotive empire. Or did it? I have to point out that my old pal Cecil used to say that MG – or M.G. as we used to write it – didn't actually stand for anything at all. This was probably a little mischievous of him, but is apparently substantiated by original documents relating to the firm's early years. In 1923, Morris Garages started a little sideline, fitting rakish new Raworth bodies to modified Cowley saloons. Customers appreciated the effort, because by 1924 Kimber had branched out on his own, establishing MG as a marque with the soon-to-be-famous octagonal badge blazing the way. The early cars weren't too sporty, but as the '20s roared on the name became synonymous with speed and technical innovation.

The first Midget appeared in 1929, the year the company moved out to a new factory in Abingdon. In accordance with the firm's publicity slogans promising 'Safety Fast', here was a high-revving little sportster that could literally run rings around all sorts of grown-up machines with much larger engines, as Pater discovered on far too many occasions when dicing around in his Bentley! Unfortunately, while the cars were undoubtedly marvellous, MG suffered along with the world economy as we headed into the 1930s. By 1935 the company was in Queer Street and was bought out by – yes, the Nuffield Organisation, aka William Morris.

Kimber stayed on at Abingdon, but found himself in the embarrassing position of being an underling of Leonard Lord, who had a deserved reputation for being somewhat less than diplomatic with his minions. Lord by name and nature's first bombshell was to close down MG's competition department, ending the Octagonal reign in racing and record-breaking. 'Stop racing and make money,' was his typically blunt message to the workforce. To this end, he insisted that future models would be simple and affordable... and hopefully profitable too. Hence the 1936 debut of the Midget TA, a Morris/Wolseley-based creation with a more tedious specification than had gone before. Crude or not, at £222 it was irresistible, and went on to spawn a series of sports cars that became increasingly important to MG's success, particularly in post-war America.

The mildly updated TB appeared just before the hapless Mr Chamberlain waved his useless bit of appeasement paper in front of newsreel cameras, and after a busy war making armaments, the Abingdon concern soon resumed production of cars with the TC. Export or Die was the industry's mission in those days, of course, so a large percentage of the factory's output went across the pond. This became especially true with the succeeding TD, which was designed with left hand drive in mind. America fell in love with MG, and by the early 1950s thirty times as many were sold in the US than here in Blighty.

The TE never happened for fear that it would be nicknamed 'Tee-Hee', so the TD was replaced by the TF in 1953. It was wider and less spartan than its predecessor, but still had a pre-war mien, which was exactly what some luddites wanted. However, for others it was out of step with a world awakening from the stultifying effects of War Two. Rationing was finally ending and a bright young Queen was on the throne. Furthermore, branded, higher-octane petrol was returning to the forecourts and fun was back on the agenda. By this time MG's pre-eminence was under threat from within and without, in the form of the Austin-Healey (also a product of the British Motor Corporation, following the 1952 amalgamation of Austin and Morris), and Triumph TR2, so a completely new car was long overdue.

Then in 1955 came the MGA, a curvaceous, modern machine powered by a 1500cc version of the B-series engine first seen in the 1947 Austin A40. The performance was already better than the TF, and the subsequent installation of an 85bhp, 1588cc four promised to improve matters further. More power was now available, at least, that was the theory. In practice, the complicated engine rarely functioned long enough to find out, and the revised twin cam would be short-lived. My road test example expired in a cloud of oily steam almost within sight of Abingdon, I recall, as I mashed the loud pedal in an attempt to verify the claimed 115mph top whack while en route to Banbury. If the factory bods couldn't make it work, what chance had one's local village garage?

BMC revived the Midget badge in 1961, and a year later, after sales of 100,000, the A was replaced by the B. All jolly logical. While using many of the same mechanical parts as the outgoing model, MG's new roadster was quite advanced in its construction. Rivals from Austin-Healey and Triumph still relied on a separate chassis, but the new B featured a unitary bodyshell, which was a rather daring and clever notion for an open car at the time.

Designed by modest Abingdon stalwart, Syd Evener, the shell relied on its double box sills and transmission tunnel for strength, not the Bailey Bridge off-cuts favoured by the opposition! The structure was thus impressively rigid, so the B was largely free from dreaded scuttle shake, and allowed its suspension to do the work of absorbing bumps and keeping the wheels in line. Admittedly, the live rear axle and front wishbone set-up (which had its roots in pre-war Wolseleys) needed all the help it could get, but remember that we motorists had fairly low expectations in those carefree days. It wasn't a Jaguar E-Type, after all! As the new B was no lightweight it needed a beefier power unit than the A just to keep pace. BMC's no-expense-dared solution was to enlarge the group's long-suffering ohv four once again, this time to 1798cc. This necessitated a change in cylinder arrangement, using siamesed bores, but the bottom end stayed pretty much the same, with only three bearings supporting the crankshaft. 95bhp proved to be more than enough to cause distress in that department, resulting in the introduction of a five-bearing engine two years later.

I exaggerate only slightly by saying that development ceased at that point! The MGB did change in detail virtually every season, but basically the same car was still going down the production line until 1979, when Abingdon became a casualty of crazed axeman, Michael Edwardes, who had been appointed Chief Executive of BMC's sickly child, popularly (or should that be unpopularly?) known as British Leyland. It is my sad duty to report that the last MGBs made were decidedly inferior to the first, being slower, less economical, and having in 1975 lost their handling poise to US regulations that obliged BL to raise their headlamp height and lumber the poor things with a huge pair of black plastic buffers. Consequently, in the later years the B and its Italian-designed GT offshoot had become something of a joke. What purpose a sports job that could be seen off by all manner of humdrum saloons?

To be candid with you, reader, I never cared much for the MGB when it was in production, nor the people who usually owned them, who were wont to wear flat caps and talk far too loudly while propping up the bar in country hostelries. By and large, they preferred blathering to driving, especially of the spirited sort. Cecil Kimber would not have been amused. As was inevitable, large numbers of these original octagon worshippers have now retired to the great concours meeting in the sky – or perhaps the devil's sump. The remaining faithful few and most new devotees come across as more interesting company, having largely realistic views of their motoring charges.

The owner of the splendid 1964 B roadster I tested for *Classic Auto* was a fine example of the 21st Century breed. He is not unaware of the model's failings, but can come up with convincing arguments as to why these are of no great importance. Bravely, he let your scribe lever his ancient limbs into the snug leather cockpit for a drive. Musing as to why later versions were kitted with garishly upholstered seats reminiscent of striped deckchairs, off we went, crunching gently into the non-synchro first gear. After a brief struggle with the hood, a device as obstinate and recalcitrant as the tent I used as a schoolboy and from which it was no doubt a direct descendant (that's one thing BL did improve in later years), I delighted in the distinctive deep and fruity gurgle of the exhaust as we wandered off into the shires.

Too many Bs are ruined by worn suspension and rotten, floppy bodyshells, but when all is well they steer lightly and accurately and provide a most rewarding drive, if not a fast one. Although the ton is achievable, it's about all you can expect in normal circumstances. And pity our colonial friends, who had to make do with a paltry 65bhp in the emission-controlled era. Back in 1966, the home-brewed solution for slowness was to drop in a beefy 3-litre six; the MGC, no less. That didn't work very well, so various specialists tried the aluminium Rover 3.5 litre V8 instead. Much better! But alas, BL contrived to launch their official V8 MGB in a fuel crisis, making a double blunder by offering it only in GT coupe form. With half a million sold, the B was to become the country's all-time top-selling open two seater, but only a few thousand V8 variants ever left the factory.

Still, I must admit that speed has become less important to us all these days on our increasingly overcrowded and potholed roads, so 95bhp and 35mpg with the wind in one's follicles can be a more pleasurable proposition than it was in the 1960s. A jolly good wheeze, in fact. I'm bound to say it's more than a little ironic that after the Brits had completely abandoned the simple, mass-market ragtop, it was left to the Japanese to step into the void. Mazda's pretty little MX-5 is in so many ways what the MGB should have become, if only BL/Rover had been a tad more far-sighted.

A HOLIDAY ADVENTURE!
(Diary extract – 26 June 1966)
When I was a boy I knew every car and motorcycle that roared or rattled through Bales by sound alone. And vehicles from the village I could tell apart even if they were the same model! Jim Berry and Charlie O'Rourke's identical Morris Commercials could be differentiated by the pitch of their whining back axles.

So I was immediately alerted this morning, having just stopped for juice in Kristinehamn(*1), when a new green Saab 95 burbled rather than crackled onto the old fashioned petrol station forecourt where I was standing with the R69S I was testing for the blue 'un. By its pulses I reckoned the little wagon had a four-stroke V under its bonnet and everyone knows these splendid little cars, driven so expertly in rallies all over the world by my good friend Erik 'on the roof' Carlsson(*2), are powered by barely adequate, in-line two-stroke triples. Was this a home-brewed special or something new from Trollhättan? Time to find out!

So while the attendant fussed around the Saab, I tackled the driver, making direct eye contact and speaking slowly and loudly, as is always the best policy when communicating with foreigners of any sort. But, despite understanding the Queen's English perfectly well, I am sure, the impertinent blighter turned shifty and feigned ignorance to avoid answering my questions. After a muttered conversation in their own incomprehensible and peculiar lingo, the pair retired to the forecourt hut, closed the door firmly behind them and watched me from behind twitching curtains. Clearly, the intriguing little car would not run again until I was off the scene. Time to make myself scarce.

There had been no chance of a proper shufti, but the car definitely did not have the distinctive whiff of a two-stroke about it, and neither native appeared to have added any lubricating agent to the petrol. A surreptitious glance inside the car had revealed a technical manual of sorts, and Saab headed graph paper on a clipboard on the passenger seat. Clearly this was a factory job!

After donning gloves and bone dome I fired the Bee Em and made haste until I was well out of sight. Then, using a gentle throttle I made a series of left turns on minor roads until the petrol station came back into view. The little green estate was still at the pump, so I parked the Bavarian instrument discreetly behind some pines and sat doggo. The Saab's pilot soon emerged, and after looking furtively up and down the road several times, the uncommunicative Swede jumped in his little green estate and tooled off along the lakeside road at a fair old lick.

He set a hot pace but what a fine atmosphere disturber the R69S is! After some glorious bend swinging the Saab was soon within striking distance, but I held back to avoid putting the wind up its driver. After several miles the finned estate swung off the main road onto a forest track and I was suddenly struggling to keep up. BMWs do not make the very best off-roaders(*3), and the teeth rather rattled in the de Forte bonce as the Saab began snaking away from me, handling like the rally car to which it was related. And by now one thing was absolutely certain: at no time had I detected burnt oil in my nostrils, or heard the familiar ring-ting-ting of an expansion chamber exhaust system.

The car finally pulled up in a clearing surrounding a large wooden building, and where another 95 estate and no fewer than six 96 saloons were untidily arranged. Rather than pull up at a distance and snoop about on foot I pressed on and scrunched to a sudden stop behind him, yanking late on the binders and leaping off the Bee Em before he even had a chance to get into the building.

But before I could confront the chap once more, the house door flew open and with much nationally uncharacteristic shouting and arm waving a group of highly agitated Swedes rushed out and began manhandling me. They wanted me to leave immediately and were prepared to use force if necessary. It was a dicey-do but then a calm and familiar face appeared in the doorway and with just a wave of the chap's hand the babbling ceased and the norsemen retreated. The senior bod was none other than former aircraft engineer Gunnar Ljungström, the brains behind every Saab car since the first 92 back in the 1940s. 'de Forte if I'm not mistaken,' announced the distinguished Swede in perfect English. 'What a turn up (turnip!) for the books. Please come in.'

Apologising for the overexcitement of his fellow countrymen, Ljungström led me through the old house past telex machines, telephones, typewriters and drawing boards and into a kitchen where pistons and conrods lay on the table and strong coffee was brewing on the stove. From there we entered a large garage area where several more 96s were being fitted with small V4 engines. Elsewhere, boffins in white laboratory coats were microscopically analysing and measuring the component parts of a disassembled motor. I was told to sit down, given a mug of supercharged coffee, and, while his men returned to work around us, Ljungström gave me the pukka gen about what was happening in this remote timber complex deep in the pines.

It seems as far back as the introduction of the 96 in early 1960, Ljungström and colleague Rolf Mellde had been urging the company to develop a four-stroke engine, but because Carlsson, Moss and others were winning rallies all over the globe using two-stroke power they could not convince the top brass of the need to act. The problem also stemmed from the fact that all Saabs have to have an in-built and unique character, known in the factory as 'Saab spirit'. For this reason, to many Trollhättan-ites, abandoning the quirky front wheel drive two-stroke was utterly unthinkable.

But the Saab chiefs were clearly badly out of touch with their customers. Powering the front wheels had been made acceptable practice worldwide by the success of Issigonis's Mini, and the Swedish public was falling out of love with the little 'stinky toy' two-strokes it had once held so dear(*4). Sales plummeted and the company began slipping quietly into crisis. At the eleventh hour, Ljungström and Mellde's view prevailed, but by now there was no time to develop a new engine. A suitable unit would have to be obtained from outside and made ready for production without delay, but everything had to be kept top secret because a leak would kill stroker sales completely and bankrupt the firm. Ljungström drained the last of his coffee and wiped the back of his hand across his chin. The solution, he explained, was this covert op in Kristinehamn dubbed Operation Kajsa. I had gatecrashed the party.

The 1500cc German-built Ford Taunus V4 was chosen for the job(*5) and a carefully selected employee called Gillbrand, announced to his colleagues he was leaving the company for family reasons, but in fact drove secretly to northern Italy in a Taunus-powered Saab 96 prototype. The trusty then drove it day and night on Dolomite passes, racking up 80,000 tough kilometres in just a few weeks.

The test went well and a bogus company was set up to order further engines, rent the concealed timber complex in the forest and to purchase clutch casings, electrical systems and miscellaneous ancillaries. By now nine Saab chaps were in the know and they were all gathered here in the woods to build and test more V4 cars, analyse Gillbrand's much travelled engine, rewrite workshop manuals and plan the production line switch-over.

After dining on meatballs of uncertain origin and pungent but strangely addictive pickled herrings, the beer and home-made schnapps began to flow. I was made to swear a solemn Viking oath to keep the V4 project a secret, and then Ljungström and his pals sketched out the next stage of the plan.

It seems the V4 fitted the 95/96 engine compartment very well and linked up easily to the transmission so no large scale assembly line prep was required. The annual factory shutdown period was due to start and 40 reliable individuals had been hand-picked for summer holiday work at the Trollhättan works where many complete cars minus engines and brakes were stockpiled in readiness. These were destined to become the first V4 production cars, but no-one suspected as there had been a disc brake supply problem and the drones thought they were coming in to fit stoppers to the unfinished cars.

Next week the nine exhausted Operation Kajsa engineers would return to Trollhättan, and during the holiday month, they would work together with the trusties to complete as many four-stroke cars as possible ahead of the V4's official announcement, which would coincide with the return of the rest of the workforce and the factory's restoration to full capacity(*6).

I was more than slightly pie-eyed when at 2am Ljungström and I raised our glasses in final toasts to the future success and prosperity of Svenska Aeroplan Aktiebolaget and to 'Saab spirit'.

After three hours' kip on the sofa under a blanket I gulped down some stewed coffee from the stove and tottered out into the silvery dawn light. I felt a bit woozy for a moment after swinging down on the BMW's somewhat awkward starting lever, but started to feel better as the German machine warmed through, shaking off the morning dew as it did so. Clearly I was still somewhat schnapps squiffy but I had to be inside the Arctic Circle by nightfall and needed to press on. Pale and anxious faces appeared at the windows as I clunked into first gear and turned to leave, but they had no need to worry. Their secret was safe with me(*7).

Notes

(*1) Kristinehamn is a tiny town on the shore of Lake Vanern, 250 kilometres from Oslo, Gothenburg and Stockholm. A baffling totem pole-like sculpture by Picasso stands on the lake shore.

(*2) Carlsson was a motorcycle racer who taught himself how to drive on unmade roads in a 25 horsepower twin cylinder 764cc Saab 92. He learned to keep the revs up and the wheels in line, steer accurately, and find the shortest route through any bend. Driving Saab 93s and 96s in the late 1950s and 1960s, he won or was highly placed in dozens of major international rallies, including the Monte Carlo, East African, Baja, English RAC, the Tulip Rally in Holland, and the Thousand Lakes in Finland. And he married Sir Stirling's equestrian sister Pat who became his co-driver.

(*3) Of course, this was long before the German firm's gigantic Paris-Dakar adventure bikes could be found on the pavement outside every British high street cafe.

(*4) 28,894 two-stroke Saabs were sold in Sweden in 1964, 26,046 in 1965 but just 18,963 in 1966. At the insistence of die-hards, two-stroke sales continued alongside the V4, but this ended in 1968 after only 28 were sold on the home market that year.

A two-stroke must be loved and cared for otherwise will let you down. As motorcycle racers know only too well, if oil is not mixed with the petrol in the correct quantities two-strokes are likely to nip up pronto, with disastrous consequences. Frequent failures, usually due to owner error, were making Saab's engine replacement policy cripplingly expensive, according to Ljungström.

(*5) The Taunus engine was initially designed in the USA for the abandoned 'Cardinal' small car project, before being passed on to Ford's European subsidiaries where it was further developed before appearing in Britain in the rear wheel drive Corsair, and in Germany in the front wheel drive Taunus. The secretive Scandinavians were amused when I told them Ford had used Saab 96s as test mules during the engine's initial development in the USA.

(*6) The plan worked well. The target was met, and, when the V4 was officially launched on 2 August the company had 600 cars ready to ship to dealers.

(*7) I kept my word, and a crate of Swedish schnapps and a box of pickled herrings arrived in Bales at Christmas for many years.

LAMBORGHINI

As I have already recorded in this volume (page 84 – ed), I was sitting in a roadside hostelry in Italy in May 1948 when a car came through the wall. It was the Mille Miglia, and a Fiat Topolino-based special of some sort crashed out spectacularly at three-quarters distance. The driver bought everyone a drink, and many years later he entertained me in his home and his wife cooked me dinner. That man was Ferruccio Lamborghini.

Lamborghini was an irrepressible character; strong, stocky, engaging and frequently smiling. On the factory floor, working with his men, he was approachable and popular. A former mechanic himself, he was from a farming background, having been born of peasant stock in the Lambrusco grape growing region of Italy in 1916. Bologna was the nearest industrial town. Lamborghini studied engineering there, and in War Two he was an airforce mechanic, ending up as a British prisoner of war in Rhodes. But he spent very little time locked up: he was too useful to the British army, repairing their trucks.

Back home in 1946 he built his parents a tractor out of scrap components and then he came across a quantity of abandoned British armoured cars which he set about converting for sale as vehicles for agricultural use. To advertise these machines he would organise pull-offs in town piazzas. His business prospered, and by 1952 he had a proper factory, manufacturing vehicles powered by diesel engines of his own design. By 1962 Lamborghini had already accumulated two fortunes, one from his tractor and agricultural machinery factory, and another from manufacturing heaters and heating equipment. His love of cars made him set out to build a third. Incidentally, to this day I've got a Lamborghini in the bottom barn. People don't believe me, but it's true. It's an oil heater!

Lamborghini's cars were not necessary. They were not practical transport. They were built for pleasure, for speed, for delight in operation, and for satisfaction in ownership. His cars were often badly finished, unreliable and insufficiently tested, but when a car is great art, when it is pushing boundaries, when it is brave and pure, I can forgive it almost everything. A motor car's function is to carry people happily, and Ferruccio's did that.

It was the summer of 1967 when I went to interview Ferruccio Lamborghini at his villa on the Adriatic coast. I blasted there straight from speed testing Fiat Dino Spiders, and I had been granted the use of one for the week. The Turin giant had its own private stretch of motorway for speed runs, built parallel to the Milan-Turin autostrada by arrangement with the government. What chance BMC?

He came to meet me in the village near his property and guided me to the villa, driving a dusty Fiat 125 box. He wore working clothes and as soon as we entered his home he kicked off his shoes and slipped into carpet slippers. But it was not that he was above being ostentatious, or didn't like to spend his money. Later he showed me his quite magnificent turquoise, wooden hulled Riva Aquarama speedboat powered by two Lamborghini V12s. I liked him straight away. He was tough, strong and open, ready to laugh.

During dinner I asked if he considered himself in competition with Ferrari. Was it true he had been snubbed in some way by old man Enzo, left cooling his heels in the corridor outside his office at Modena? No way. Not at all. But it was true he was shocked to discover an expensive clutch part he had needed for his own Ferrari was, in fact, identical to that which he already used in his tractors, and which could be bought elsewhere for a fraction of the price. Ferrari lived to race, said Lamborghini, and his road cars were just a way to make money, whereas his aim was to build the perfect GT car. Fast, yes, very fast, but refined, luxurious, and much, much more comfortable than any Ferrari had ever been.

Later, over brandy. Did he do any development testing himself? Had he ever raced? Ah yes, he had entered the Mille Miglia once but it had ended embarrassingly. He had crashed through the wall of a hotel. He knew his limitations. It was only then that the centesimo dropped, not that they used them any more! We chuckled together as we remembered that day. He still drove with a heavy touch, he admitted, candidly. He left the serious development work to others.

Later I lay awake while the sea beat below and the sea air filled my room. In the morning I awoke early, but Ferruccio had already left for work. After a delightful breakfast of coffee and cakes on the patio overlooking the shimmering Adriatic, I made my way to his fabulous and futuristic new factory. It was still not 9am. I found him on the factory floor, spanner in hand, oil on his forearms, working with his men. Laughing together, three of them were hanging on a wrench trying to shift an obstinate nut. Come here, you try!

New Zealander Bob Wallace was his chief mechanic and development driver. He was out testing, but he would soon be back for his breakfast, and then they had things to show me. Wallace was a dry, laconic man, and so incredibly young. Everyone there seemed so young, I noted, and so talented. They all seemed under 25. He had let his young men get on with things, and the result had been the Miura.

While waiting, I took the opportunity to cock an eye at the internals of a Lamborghini V12. The story was ex-Ferrari man Giotto Bizzarrini was offered a generous fee to design it, but had chosen instead to be paid by the bhp figures he achieved. Working at first in the corner of the Lamborghini tractor factory, a 3.5 litre V12 four-cam was running on the bench in May 1963. It was a developed from existing drawings for a 1.5 litre grand prix engine Bizzarrini had already schemed for Enzo Ferrari. It made plenty of power, and Lamborghini's design chief, former Maserati engineer Gian Paolo Dallara then refined it for road use, and it duly appeared in the first Lamborghini production car, the 350GT of 1964. My esteemed colleague LJK Setright claimed this accepted version of events is great bosh, asserting it was commissioned from Honda. With the greatest respect, I do not agree.

Wallace returned and a Miura was prepared and taken outside for my use. Just launched, the Miura was the world's first mid-engined road-going sports car. Painted in wonderful bright colours and just stunning in every way, it was a car that would force Ferrari to up his game. No matter that it was fragile, noisy, and temperamental, it was impossibly glamorous, and arguably the most visually exciting car ever. It was a road car that looked like a racing car.

The Miura chassis was first shown to the world in November 1964. It was just a tub with holes in it, but as every schoolboy since Alf Tupper knows, the Gorgonzola treatment makes for lightness, and it always looks sophisticated and high-tech. It didn't have a name yet, or any sort of body, but the orders started coming in. The body design was entrusted to Bertone's Marcello Gandini, just 25 at the time (that age again!), and he came up with an exquisite and rather delicate set of curves, not unlike those of the British Lola of 1963, a mid-engined prototype Le Mans racing car which had already spawned the he-man Ford GT40. The Lola had a sheet metal monocoque hull, and its front and rear bodywork were just hinged bins: a capital idea that would be adapted for the Miura. Giorgetto Giugiaro's work could also have had an influence on Gandini – he of folded paper and so much more – and it is said Nuccio Bertone himself finished the Miura design, having sent his over-excited young charge away on holiday to cool off.

In March 1966 there was a second debut for the Miura, this time in Geneva, and suddenly beautiful people everywhere wanted one. At that time it was still being called the P400, but it had its beautiful, seductive body, and soon it would be the Miura, named after a ferocious bull. The intention, according to Ferruccio, was to make a couple of dozen or so and then move onto something more commercial. Installing Bizzarrini's V12 sideways had solved all sorts of logistical problems. It meant the cockpit could be further back, and the occupants would have plenty of legroom. Of course, five years earlier Issi's Mini had a transverse engine too, albeit at the front of an everyday runabout, and yes LJK, so too did Honda's Formula One car of 1964. Technical difficulties with the clutch housing and the transmission, and a lack of adequate tooling, made the car expensive to build, but the factory was prepared for production and the first customer car was ready for collection in early 1967.

My Miura's Bertone body was vivid in lime green, set off by matt black detailing trim, including its alluring Twiggy eyelashes, and its quattrocento loveliness invited the eye. The cockpit was cramped, and poorly finished (disappointing, considering its price tag of £8,050 in the UK); the switches confused me, there was no seatbelt, and nowhere for luggage except the passenger seat. But at that precise moment I did not much care about these things. I wanted to be off! The Bizzarrini V12 barked into life behind me, prickling the hairs down my arms and on the back of my neck, and then settled to a comfortable burbling tickover at just 800rpm. Oops! I blipped the throttle more heavily than intended, and a delivery man pushing a trolley across the car park visibly jumped up into the air, upsetting his pile of parcels onto the ground. I stifled a grin as I raised a palm in apology, but the accelerator action had been heavy and insensitive. Not good. And moments later I discovered the clutch was reminiscent of the infuriating and unhelpful device in Mater's 1924 Austin Seven. The confounded thing was either in or out, with nothing whatsoever in between. Not good either, and it took two attempts to get under way.

The pedals were well placed in a roomy footwell, but the throttle was awkward, as well as heavy, and the clutch was leaden, as well as tricky. Despite this, the car was quite manageable in traffic, and once clear of the dawdlers in their Topolinos, acceleration was incredible, the gear change sublime, and the soundtrack from behind most exquisite. The brakes were up to the task but, you've guessed it, heavy, wooden, dead. No servo required in such a machismo car, of course, for men only, despite its epicene outward appearance.

Fast roads opened up ahead promising sweeping bends, and beyond that I knew they tightened and climbed sinuously and through sequences of hairpins affording tantalising, virtiginous glimpses of the curve of a bay and distant twinkling sea. The Miura's four Weber carburettors were in bang-accurate tune and I was dialled in too. Time to get a move on, to start to push. Despite her clumsy foot controls, the Miura rewards a delicate and sensitive touch. Arrive too fast and lift off, I discovered, and she will step out; give her too much heavy boot, and she will try to spin. So be on your mettle, give her your full attention (as you must a motorcycle), and treat her kindly, and then she will give you all she's got.

Noise does not always produce locomotion, but when I gave the Miura the works she responded, bristling in every sinew, proving herself an outstanding goer as well as imposing herself on the notice of everyone on the hillside down to sea level. Rear visibility was awful, and the cabin was too hot and too noisy, but I drove her on until the grilling sun went down, a great red flaming ball in the western sky. It was then I found out the lights were woefully inadequate for a car of such prodigious performance, and it was as a result of this that the next morning I observed skid marks of my making which stopped just short of a deadly, craggy drop!

I returned to a factory in darkness, but Ferruccio himself was waiting to lock up. He had told me they sometimes put special engines in test cars, but when I asked him about my Miura he just shrugged and smiled. So I am not sure if she was a standard car, but by golly she was searingly fast. I told him I was in love with his motor car, that it was more authentically beautiful than any other sports car in the world, and that its sweet looks may never be matched. I told him this, and also that his car was a handful on bumps, that it could be twitchy, that it was temperamental, and that the front end went light and flighty at extreme speeds, but he knew these things. What I did not tell him, because I did not want to hurt this generous and courageous man's feelings, was that it was still, in truth, a prototype, that it was unacceptably badly finished, that the driver controls needed refining, and that from front to back, if it were ever to be a true production car, there was still a great deal more work for his talented young team to do.

The Miura S followed in 1969 with added interior features and refinements, improved rear suspension, and better brakes. It was even faster. Then came the Miura SV of 1971 and 1972, which was perhaps the ultimate, and getting close to something finished and worth the money, but it lacked the Lesley Hornby peepers. I drove one, it was white, and it was a better car than my green one, if not quite as powerfully attractive, but it was already rusty with less than 1,000 kilometres on its clock.

I had been introduced to Ferruccio Lamborghini two months before I became his house guest. In May 1967 I met Princess Grace at the Monaco Grand Prix (she was interested in buying a Rover and Spencer Wilks sent me over to show her a P6). Meeting her was a magical experience (an utterly charming, impossibly glamorous and elegantly beautiful woman). Before the race she was driven around the circuit in the Lamborghini Marzal show car (nowadays, I suppose we would call it a 'concept car') and at a function that night she asked me if I knew Signor Lamborghini.

The Marzal (named after another fighting bull) was a true four seater built on the Miura chassis, and designed wholly by Marcello Gandini, who was clearly given free rein. Singularly stunning, it is among his wizardest and most joyous work. The car was powered by a transversely and rear-mounted two litre straight six. Half a Bizzarrini V12, in fact, and it made a more than respectable 175bhp. The engine configuration avoided both overhanging at the rear and undue compromise in the design of the cabin.

The Marzal's distinctive bodywork was silver, and so was its futuristic interior, even its sculpted and comfortable leather seats; and octagon motifs and honeycomb patterns abounded inside and out, featuring on the Campagnolo wheels, and dominating the dashboard. The windscreen was vast, and it had a glass roof, making the interior light and bright, and there was also a considerable amount of glass in the car's massive, gull-wing doors, an attribute which left Ferruccio Lamborghini less than fully impressed. The doors' transparent lowers meant a lady's legs could be ogled by all and sundry, including those of the princess. He had a point. But minor niggles aside, the Marzal was just so gloriously modern, so fabulously futuristic, and so wonderfully optimistic. Cars like this made the world a better place.

The Marzal concept was never developed for production, but instead Gandini was commissioned to return to his drawing board and keep some of its features in mind while drawing up a more practical Lamborghini four-seater. The result was the Espada, and excellent it was too. The Espada, which made its debut in

1968, was a fabulous GT car. Comfortable, a pussycat in town, and blisteringly fast on the open road, 1,200 of them would be sold over ten years, by the end of which time it had been developed into something finished, something almost commercial, but it would be killed off too soon just like the Miura and so many other promising Lamborghinis which were rushed into production and cancelled prematurely.

Other 1960s models included the 400GT, the Islero, and the Jarama, but the Espada was my favourite. Eye-catching, and to my eyes still exotic today, it had plenty of space in the back, and offered very comfortable seating for four adults. It was altogether fabulous, actually, and much underrated, not least as a repaying car to drive. Driven timidly through long corners the front end drifts out, but this can be controlled easily by keeping the power on. Do this positively and progressively and an Espada holds a line quite beautifully. As for sharp turns, if you lift off suddenly the back end swings out, but that can be trimmed easily by pressing the throttle pedal down again. Antithetically, booting the loud pedal brings the tail around into spectacular oversteer.

The Miura was cancelled before its replacement, the Countach was ready. The Countach was originally intended to be a driver's car, and I know Bob Wallace devoted many hundreds of hours to making it so, but it would come to evolve into some sort of ridiculous machismo machine, an anathema to me, and therefore something of nugatory interest, I'm afraid. It became really rather silly.

By that time the bullish Ferruccio Lamborghini was no longer at the helm. In 1969 he had started yet another engineering and manufacturing company, this time making hydraulic valves, and he would make a success of it and hand it over to his son, Tonino. But as he built up his hydraulics operation, his other businesses became overstretched, and were beset by cancelled orders and labour problems. He sold the tractor division in 1972, and accepted offers for the car company from two Swiss investors. Things had got out of control. He was no longer enjoying life, and he'd had enough. In 1974 he retired to a run a vineyard near Perugia, where he would live peacefully for 19 years and make excellent wine. He had a private collection of his cars there to remind him of his bold adventure, but sadly the Marzal was not among them.

BMW 2002

In the glorious summer of 1966, in the immediate aftermath of Alf Ramsey and co's famous victory over the Deutscher Fussball Bund, I was commissioned to write a series of 'state of the industry' pieces about the two nations' leading motor manufacturers. Start with the sausage eaters, said *The Auto*'s long-standing editor Murdo Graves while pouring himself his second whisky of the morning. In fact, make it BMW. What are the Muncheners up to in their 50th anniversary year?

At the Frankfurt Motor Show in 1961, the BMW 1500 had been revealed to the public for the first time. The first of the factory's Neue Klasse saloon series, it was a middle market machine, and not without a few wrinkles that needed ironing out, but it was clearly a car of quality and understated style, and it represented a turning point in the firm's fortunes. Of monocoque construction, it featured MacPherson struts at the front, and semi-trailing arm suspension to the rear, and a revvy new vierzylinder overhead-camshaft engine designed by my pal Alex von Falkenhausen, who had become BMW's head of engine development in 1957.

Alex had telephoned me in early 1960. Money man Herbert Quandt and his advisers wanted the New Class car to be a 1300, whereas he was pressing for a 1500 and winning the argument, but the engine he really wanted to build was a two litre. What to do? My dear fellow, I told him, the solution was obvious. Make it enlargeable, first to 1800cc, and later to a full two litres. A total of 3.5 million New Class cars would be eventually built, and von Falkenhausen's strong and gutsy motor, which utilised a five bearing crankshaft, and featured an unusual combustion chamber design, would power the factory's saloon car range until 1988. Quite some going. It also formed the basis of a number of successful racing engines, culminating in the incredible 1500cc turbo used in Nelson Piquet's 1983 world championship winning Brabham BT52 which produced 800bhp, so von Falkenhusen definitely made it up-scalable!

But of course all this was in the future as I approached Munich Airport in a Lufthansa Boeing 707 on a sunny afternoon in August 1966. What I did know was BMW had dropped the Isetta bubble car in 1962, that 1963 had seen the last of the bulbous Baroque Angels, and that the rear-engined 700 had done an admirable job as a stop-gap, carrying on until the previous year. I knew too that the New Class saloons (pluralised here because an 1800 had soon followed the 1500, and the two-litre option had arrived in 1965) were completely new and truly first-rate motor cars that were selling like the proverbial hot cakes all over Europe. So well that in 1964 the company had paid the first shareholder dividend since 1943 (extraordinary they had managed it then).

Newly introduced in 1966 was a short-wheelbase, economy, two-door version of the car that was lighter, shorter, faster, and reputedly better handling. Better even than an Alfa, according to the odious Otto von Schoffl of *Deutsch Weg und Strecke*. I had packed the de Forte stringbacks. BMW design chief Wilhelm Hofmeister, he of the kink, not the drink, had redesigned the interior and added some external tweaks, but most of the running gear was the same as the four-door saloons. At first the 1573cc '1600' motor was being used to power the new two-door model, and it had been called the 1600-2. It was proving the most successful car of the firm's 50th anniversary year.

I knew Alex von Falkenhausen competed (and won) in hillclimbs driving the New Class saloons so it was no big surprise that he picked me up from Munich airport in a new two-door car that had clearly seen recent action. But what did take me by surprise was its neck snapping performance. What's in this thing? I asked. He flashed a smile, shifted down a cog, and shot up the tree-lined drive to his house.

This, he said later, is the future, as he lifted the bonnet to reveal a two litre version of his vierzylinder marvel. I got the special shop to build this for me, he continued, and Helmut (Helmut Werner Bosch, BMW product planning supremo) had one made too. We didn't know until they were both in the workshops at the same time! Next year a twin carburettor version of the 1600-2 will be in our product range, then a two litre like this. Do you know why? he added rhetorically. The Americans.

They are crazy, said Alex, as if by way of explanation but without actually shedding any light on the subject. Particularly the Californians. What was he on about? Polluted air was getting trapped above Los Angeles. Did I know they were thinking of boring an enormous hole in the Santa Ana mountains so westerly winds could blow through it and push the smog out over the Pacific? I did not, although it conjured up an extraordinary image. Since the first clean air act there in 1963 they've become obsessed with exhaust emissions, he continued, and emissions restrictions on imported cars will be stepped up again in 1968. The 1600-2 is already struggling to meet their requirements, but the two litre engine from the four door saloon has been set up for the American market so we can put it straight in the two-door just like this one. Simple. Now you drive, he said, dropping the bonnet with a reassuring clunk.

The two litre car was much better than the 1600 I drove later in my visit. Just as fine handling, but effortlessly fast. It was a sporting car and a family car combined, and it did both things well, remaining highly practical as well as being great fun. I liked the interior space (spartan, plasticky, yet somehow sophisticated), the big windows which made for good visibility (the Americans would complain about sunshine overheating the cabin, but that wouldn't be a problem in Blighty!), the good brakes, the grippy tyres, the doors that fitted and closed with teutonic precision, the comfortable yet supportive seats, and Alex's lusty engine which made plenty of smooth power despite being fed by just one carburettor (a twin carb version would apparently not be clean enough). A precise gearbox made keeping the motor on the boil a joy (60 in second, 80 in third, that's mph), and the controls were light and precise, although the steering was perhaps a tad slow, and a deal of energetic arm exercise was required to keep everything on course once enthusiastic cornering got the tail hanging out. Not that it was ever a problem. In fact, it was a hoot. The handling was Alfa-like, and the car was altogether wunderbar!

The Americans would think so too, and the fast, lightweight two-door car, which BMW would call the 2002, got rave reviews upon its release in the USA in 1968. 'One of the best ways to get somewhere sitting down,' said my irrepressible American friend David E Davis Jr of *Car and Driver*, and I see from perusing my bound copies of that estimable organ that David went on to add the little Bavarian wonder refuelled the American male's '...unshakable belief that we can meet and marry a pretty girl who will expertly cook, scrub floors, change diapers, keep the books and still be the greatest thing since the San Francisco earthquake in bed'. He was a card, and I do miss him very much.

Emission controls did take a toll on the 114bhp 2002, but a smart, lightweight car with a big engine and a big heart proved a mighty package, and the model sold well for eight years in several variants. As David astutely observed in 1968, the car was a giant killer. It was not flashy or overtly sporty, but it was 'a devoted servant of man', and 'beautiful when doing its job'. He recommended it to intelligent buyers who would take pleasure in beating Porsches in a sensible family saloon car. Absolutely! Meanwhile, *Auto Bild* called it a whispering bomb. Odd. I prefer David's analogies.

I was quite smitten by the 2002. I liked its handling, its agility, its use of McPherson strut front and semi-trailing arm rear suspension (front and rear anti-sway bars were optional). I liked its subtlety, its unpretentiousness, its simplicity, and its complete lack of ostentation, although later cars afforded a little luxury, coming with softer seats, and a padded steering wheel. These later variants included a three door hatchback which appeared in 1971 (Michelotti at work again) with split rear seats (a novelty then), as well as a twin carburettor model, and devastatingly quick fuel-injected big-valve versions which were not officially available to our American cousins. A Christmas card from Alex in 1968 contained the message: 'I'm going to build a turbo!' and the following year a turbocharged racer making 280bhp took four wins and the 1969 European Touring Car Championship. Then in 1973 the 2002 Turbo became the first turbocharged production car from a European manufacturer.

The New Class cars, but most especially the 2002, put BMW back on the map in Europe, and established the marque in the USA, although they were generally regarded there as 'economy cars', and my German friends were appalled when I told them most Americans of my acquaintance thought BMW stood for British Motor Works!

It is interesting to me that BMW developed the New Class against the odds, at least partly due to the car enthusiast culture of the firm. This enthusiasm even included its partially sighted and therefore non-driving chairman Herbert Quandt. It was reflected by his bold decision-making, and his tactile approach to assessing new models and designs. Focus groups, market segments, competition analysis, et cetera, all have their place in the car business, of course, but creativity is stifled because so much is predetermined before the first line is drawn on a designer's Macintosh. This is a big problem in my view. That and the fact that car people in car companies live in perpetual fear of the dreaded bean counters.

JAGUAR COMPACT SALOONS – SAVING THE BEST UNTIL LAST
(First published *Classic Auto* – June 2009)

The Jaguar Mark II, so-called compact saloon was launched in October 1959 at a launch event in New York, and simultaneously at the British Motor Show at Earls Court in London (an occasion which also featured the debut of another great British car, the Mini), and a special show car was prepared for the later New York Motor Show featuring gold plated brightwork instead of chromium plate. The 2.4 and 3.4 litre compact saloons manufactured by Jaguar from 1955 to 1959 had been a huge sales success for the company, but as the decade neared its end, the march of time and competition from other manufacturers necessitated a redesign. The resultant Mark II version was not only a significantly superior car but was also so attractive in appearance it has come to be recognised as one of the greatest classic cars of all time.

Jaguars had pulled off another masterstroke when they unveiled the model known retrospectively as the Mark I. By using the basic mechanical components of their enormous luxury saloons in smaller unitary construction bodies, wily old Bill Lyons could offer a small car with all the expected grace and pace of a big Jag, but minus a portion of the space. At first the only model offered was a 2.4, powered by a short-stroke version of the firm's all-conquering XK six, but inevitably a 3.4 soon followed, to the great delight of cops and robbers alike.

Criticisms levelled against the retrospectively named Mark I cars had included concerns that its narrow rear track made fast driving unsafe and that its large window pillars, which resulted in a lack of window area, affected visibility to an unacceptable degree and gave the car an old fashioned, heavy look. The interior was also considered dated. All these faults were addressed and rectified in the new Mark II, which boasted improved handling and visibility, as well as fantastic looks inside and out. Curvaceous and beautiful, the compact cat was arguably an instant classic, and as the years rolled by, young men in the 1970s who had admired them as boys in the 1960s found them affordable to buy, if not exactly economical to run, and they were also a big hit with bank robbers and the stunt unit of Euston Films! Then, in the 1980s, the model was at the very vanguard of rapidly rising classic car values.

As with most cars, a great number of modifications were made to the Mark II during its production run which was extended to nearly ten years by the 240 and 340 derivatives which were introduced in 1967, but the fact almost all the changes were of a minor nature demonstrates how altogether excellent the car was from the start. Major changes between the Mark II's launch and the introduction of economy measures in 1966 in anticipation of the XJ6 were restricted to the introduction of power-assisted steering as an optional extra, and improved automatic and manual transmissions.

Both Mark Is and IIs were heavy to park, so it was significant that from 1960 onwards this chore could be reduced; and from 1965 the latest Borg Warner three-speed automatic gearbox changed up and down more smoothly than the same company's earlier type which it replaced. But in my view the most significant change came later that year, when in September 1965, the execrable 'Moss box' was jettisoned in favour of Jaguar's own all-synchromesh boite de vitesse. Although robust, the Moss gearbox had a crash first gear, a heavy, slow action and inordinately long travel between its first two ratios. The Jaguar replacement, which was already in use in the company's Mark X and S-Type saloons, could hardly fail to be an improvement, and was mated to a revised self-adjusting clutch. Incidentally, in case anyone needs to know, the unlovely-looking S Type, which featured independent suspension from the E-Type, was intended to fill a perceived gap between the Mark II and the gargantuan Mark X, although it ended up being much closer in size and appearance to the former.

As Jaguar rationalised its saloon range in advance of the 1968 season, the 3.8 Mark II was dropped and the remaining 2.4 and 3.4 versions were refreshed and renamed as the 240 and 340 respectively. These cars have always been cheaper and less sought after as classics than so called 'proper' Mark IIs they were derived from, and that is not entirely fair. The seeds of the 240's unpopularity were sown many years earlier when the 2.4 litre model in the original Mark II line-up was found to be rather sluggish and underpowered compared with the sporty 3.4 and fire-breathing 3.8. Then the aforementioned cost-cutting measures, introduced as Jaguar battled to fend off the competition while the XJ6 was finished and launched, did it further harm, and finally, in a drive to keep sales alive by offering better value for money, Jaguar perhaps sent the wrong message by slashing the price of the new 240 to an incredible £1,364, virtually the same amount as the original 2.4 in 1956, and more than £200 less than the Mark II's launch price in 1959.

To achieve this miracle Jaguar changed the upholstery from leather to Ambla vinyl (Jaguar's own astonishingly leather-like, man-made material), jettisoned the cute picnic tables on the backs of the front seats, simplified the chromed mouldings on the door pillars, replaced the fog lights with horn grilles, and fitted cheaper horns while they were at it. Headlining and sun visor materials were also changed for budget alternatives and lower quality carpets were specified.

But most obviously, the Armco-like wrap around bumpers were replaced by slim affairs with smaller, more modern overriders, and this is how these cars are most easily recognised. Further economies included discontinuing metallic paint options and using plastic hub cap badges, and a plastic tool box replaced the wood and metal version previously specified. In accordance with changing tastes, the interior wood trim on these later cars was lighter, and featured less prominent graining than that of its predecessors.

Thus Jaguar's 240 and 340 saloons were dated and tainted from the start, correctly perceived as cheapened stop-gap models introduced to extend the life of the Mark II, which was itself heavily based on the Mark I design from the mid 1950s. Therefore they were cars that always existed out of their own time, and they were made to look even more ancient when the sophisticated and long-awaited XJ6 was launched to much acclaim in September 1968. At this juncture the 340 was immediately discontinued, but the 240 remained on sale until the following year with the last one being built in April 1969.

But there were improvements too, not least in the form of a number of significant mechanical updates, and that is why the humble 240 might be considered the best value Jaguar Mark II of all. The short stroke six was given SU carbs like its bigger brothers instead of Solexes; and updated with a lighter crank, clutch and flywheel, an E-Type style straight port cylinder head, and new ribbed cam covers like those of the forthcoming XJ6. A new distributor and improved cooling completed the changes and power was boosted from 120 to 133 horsepower. Peak torque was also improved, though it was moved further up the rev range. This, combined with the improved breathing efficiency of the unit made the 240 engine a revvy, sweet-sounding unit that produced rich, creamy power and rewarded spirited driving, while improving the engine's torque characteristics to boot. Jaguar's smallest saloon could now reach 100 mph without effort for the first time.

So as a driving car the 240 is possibly the wizardest Mark II of the lot, and it is perhaps only now beginning to receive the appreciation it truly deserves. The 1969 example I tested on its 40th birthday for *Classic Auto* in 2009 featured leather upholstery, wire wheels and overdrive which were all desirable optional extras. Furthermore, to some eyes the narrow gauge chrome bumpers, based on the S-Type but not dissimilar to those on the E-Type, work even better with the car's beautiful body than the chunky armco guardrail-like affairs fitted to the earlier model.

Indeed, the 1969 Jaguar 240 proved to have a very different character to the 1964 3.4 Mark II saloon I had assayed just a few weeks before. The short stroke engine's naturally revvy nature and comparative lack of bottom end torque, combined with fairly low gearing meant the engine had to be worked hard and plenty of cog swapping was needed to make brisk progress and avoid bogging down. But the lightened and upgraded 240-spec engine revved freely and happily, and the gearbox on the car was super-sweet so I really enjoyed driving and getting reacquainted with the once unloved Coventry cat.

The 2483cc short-stroke six immediately feels and sounds different from its larger relations; equally growly, but smoother, more sporty, and with a higher pitched tone; and bowling along behind a large slim steering wheel while looking down the bulging bonnet at a bobbing leaping cat mascot I have found to be one of motoring's great and enduring pleasures.

The overall gearing is low, but third is still needed on most gradients, although it must be said there is no hardship whatsoever in keeping the engine on the boil. Thank goodness the dratted Moss box was jettisoned three years earlier! Pressing on in the lanes can provoke the live rear axle somewhat, and the heavy, low-geared steering requires plenty of frantic arm twirling on sharp corners, but that is all part and parcel of the classic experience and one soon becomes accustomed to it. People who are still sniffy about Jaguar 240s and 340s need to wake up and smell the Classic 20/50. The 240 in particular is a real driver's car, and in my opinion it is as attractive to look at, and special to be in, as any 'pukka' Jaguar Mark II.

Chapter Eight

In a car you're always in a compartment, and because you're used to it you don't realise that through that car window everything you see is just more TV. You're a passive observer and it is all moving by you boringly in a frame. On a (motor)cycle the frame is gone. You're completely in contact with it all. You're in the scene, not just watching it anymore, and the sense of presence is overwhelming.

Zen and the Art of Motorcycle Maintenance – Robert M Pirsig

HONDA CB750/4 FIRST IMPRESSIONS
(First published *Motorcycle Review* – April 1970)

THANKS TO THE EARL of Denbigh, aka Rollo Feilding, my eccentric friend and occasional racing rival on two and four wheels (some of those races rather naughtily conducted on public roads, when I sincerely hope no-one was looking), I have now ridden the new Honda CB750. In his capacity as grande fromage of the motorcycle retailers' association, old Rollo can pull extremely forceful strings when necessary, and in this case it was of great importance to him that he should take delivery of the first 750 available in the UK.

Don't tell anyone, but it is in fact the very one that amazed the herds at the Brighton show last April. Dealers could sell thousands, if only any bikes were available here in Blighty. As yet there are none, with all production being shipped to the States, and I gather there's already a healthy black market in the US of A, with people prepared to pay twice the retail price to jump the queue.

Although there can be few with the merest inkling of appreciation for fine and significant motorcycles still ignorant about this magnificent machine, allow me to run through the basics. Firstly, as with any Honda-badged motorcycles made in the last couple of decades, its remarkable 736cc four-cylinder engine is an overhead cam job, utilising a tiny roller chain.

Power is the product of torque and rpm, of course, so all things being equal, an overhead-camshaft engine is likely, or has the potential, to propel its attached bicycle to higher speed and offer greater acceleration. Furthermore, siting the cam as close as possible to the cylinder head and combustion chambers generally confers an additional advantage, in that the valves can be kept in control more successfully, because there is less reciprocating mass to upset. As a result, it's reasonable to expect an engine so equipped to be capable of reaching higher rpm without fear of unwanted assignations between poppets and pistons!

All you historians out there will doubtless be salivating at the prospect of citing umpteen instances of this not necessarily being true, but please don't bother writing in to tell me. Long experience of the dangers of entering into correspondence with readers means the only letters I read these days are those warning me that the farm's electricity supply is about to be terminated. Although many in my home village survived without such fripperies until the late 1920s, I am officially lily-livered and have no wish to travel back in time.

Speaking of which, my pedantic pen pals will also be itching to tell us that four-cylinder motorcycles have been around since the dawn of infernal combustion, and that Mr Honda is not altogether breaking new ground, as some have deluded themselves. It is true. FN, Henderson and Indian were at it in the early years of the century. The difference is that these pioneers placed their engines in line with the wheels, whereas our Far Eastern friend Soichiro has turned the motor through ninety degrees, solving some problems but also introducing several new ones. Evidently, most of these have been well and truly licked, as one would expect from a manufacturer with such long and fruitful experience with four, five and six cylinder multis in motorcycle grand prix racing.

The CB750 unit is comparatively tame, revving 'only' to 8,000rpm, nowhere near the fanciful figure of 20,000rpm predicted by one or two of my colleagues. Nevertheless, while the rumoured 100bhp fire-breather did not become a reality, this most civilised motorcycle is able to produce 67bhp without strain. Curiously, the stroke is quite long. One assumes this was a ruse to reduce the motor's width (one of the endemic problems mentioned). For the same reason, perhaps, the five-speed transmission is more complex than expected.

Aside from the engine, the rest of the bicycle is unexceptional: the usual assemblage of mostly tubular steel frame, telescopic forks and pivoting rear suspension. Much attention has been given to the large stainless steel rotor and hydraulic brake caliper, but these dullards must realise that disc brakes have been used on all but humdrum (pun intended) cars since the 1950s? Hardly earth-shattering news, what?

Unfortunately, or not, space and deadlines are tight and we will have to return to matters mechanical another time. Motorcycles are much more than the sum of their parts, and the proof of the proverbial is in the riding. Heading out of Surrey's gin and Jag belt atop Rollo's prized possession on a prematurely springlike morning, the big engine burbling between my knees, I felt like the luckiest chap alive. Out in the countryside, my nostrils were being rammed full of scented warmth, urging me to ride faster and faster. Childish though it may seem, I was soon actively searching for another vehicle to 'blow into the weeds' as our colonial cousins so colourfully put it.

Performance figures reveal that we were unlikely to encounter much that would put up a fight. Motorcycles have barn door aerodynamics, so the big bluff four won't best 125mph unless conditions are very favourable, but acceleration up to the spoilsport limit, foisted on us by that Barbara Castle harridan, and onwards to the magic ton is simply ripping. Literally, it took my breath away, leaving it somewhere on the Hog's Back near Guildford as I diced with an enterprisingly driven Jaguar 3.8 saloon.

Realisation that we were not far from where Mike Hawthorn lost his life in a similar car caused me to complete my ride at a slower pace. As much as its speed impressed me, the CB750's ability to loiter along at under 50mph in smooth silence was as much a tribute to the genius of Honda's engineers. And need I mention that upon my return after four hours in the saddle, not a drop of escaping oil besmirched the engine. It is my sad duty to report that when I rode a new Triumph Trident triple last year it left an oleaginous calling card every time we stopped.

The future is here.

HONDA DREAMS

Soichiro Honda was an extraordinary and mercurial man. He was an extrovert, an eccentric, and a vigorous autodidact who created an industrial giant out of next to nothing. I first came across him when we shared a table in a fish and chip saloon called The Lighthouse on the Isle of Man during TT week in 1954. He didn't speak English, and I certainly didn't speak Japanese, but I nonetheless found him fascinating, and with the help of inventive sign language and drawings on paper napkins, a great deal was discussed (although I recall there was much fruitless probing of the de Forte mental archives!).

Astonishingly, nearly 20 years later, while I was on a trade trip to Japan, he recognised me and called me over from my party during a guided tour of his breathtakingly advanced factory in Hamamatsu. After much bowing and hand-shaking, he invited me out to luncheon.

Of course, it was a seafood restaurant and he wanted to see if I would eat raw fish. Having passed that test by polishing off various types of sushi and sushimi (some of which smelt like dead Hun), I waited while the red shirted maverick flirted with the kimono clad waitresses and then went into the kitchens to thank all the chefs one by one. Upon his eventual return, he ordered more beer, and then the ebullient Japanese industrialist sat back in expansive mood and through his hard-working and beautiful interpreter Namika, he told me about history, strategy and forthcoming tragedy.

In the early 1970s, Honda founder Soichiro Honda was still at the helm as president of his eponymous company. The son of a village blacksmith, Honda was entrepreneurial as a young man. He repaired cars and motorcycles, and owned a motor dealership. He also raced cars. In 1936 he became a piston ring manufacturer, and during War Two his company produced piston rings and aircraft propellers. After the bombs Honda sold up to Toyota, and then in 1946, in a wooden shed in Hamamatsu, the sprawling city which had absorbed his home village of Komyo, he began his new venture manufacturing motorcycles.

As has been well documented, Soichiro Honda started in motorcycle production by fitting bicycles with army surplus two-stroke engines designed to power generators. His fledgling firm built its first complete motorcycle in 1948, the 98cc Dream appeared in 1949 and Honda's first four-stroke was designed in 1951.

As the business grew and prospered he spent time studying the motorcycle market in the USA, and in 1954 he came to Europe, looked around the Triumph factory and visited the TT. After each of these visits he resolved to raise his company's standards, and the very best American, Swiss and German machine tools were purchased and installed in the company's expanding factories, making intelligent use of the soft loans that were available to him from the American Government. Of course, America wanted Japan to rebuild itself as a successful western-style economy, its greatest fear being that communism would become established if that were not the case.

I sipped my Sapporo patiently while he continued to tell me things I already knew. The NSU-influenced Benly entered production in 1953, and a 350cc version followed in 1955. The Super Cub arrived in 1958, the same year Honda opened a new Tokyo head office. In June 1959, after proving its product by selling hundreds of thousands of its small, well-made motorcycles at home in Japan, Honda entered five machines in the 125cc event at the Isle of Man TT races. One rider fell off, the others finished sixth, seventh, eighth and eleventh, and Honda won the team prize.

The first Hondas had come to Britain in 1958, the year before the 250cc Honda Dream started rolling off the production lines. By then Soichiro's Honda Motor Company had become Japan's largest producer of two-wheelers and was already building more bikes per annum than all the surviving British motorcycle firms combined. But Edward Turner and other myopic senior figures in the British motorcycle industry were all utterly convinced the Germans and the Italians posed a bigger threat to their livelihoods. Japan, under US occupation after the war, was naively considered an export market.

Rebuilt with American help, Japan's economy was growing rapidly, but the only British machines sold there were acquired by motorcycle manufacturers whose engineers took them apart most carefully and scrutinised them for ideas. Like most rapidly emerging economies before and since, Japan was going through an intense period of copying and piracy, but foreign motorcycle designs were not just copied; they were improved.

Indeed, years later Honda UK boss Gerald Davison said to me: 'The Japanese are great developers but they're not great innovators, and I've often said to their faces, if I gave you a blank sheet of paper and came back tomorrow it would still be a blank sheet of paper, but if I gave you a drawing of someone else's design and came back in half an hour, you'll have done it better. Almost all of their culture they've got from the Chinese and modified it to suit themselves. That's really what they've always done; they've taken other people's ideas and improved on them.'

But the Honda 50 Super Cub was not a copy of anything. Not built to appeal to motorcyclists or even potential motorcyclists, it was essentially a commuter machine for people who needed an economical way to get to work. It was an instant success during a motorcycle sales recession and nothing from Blighty came close to matching it.

The Super Cub was attractive and colourful. It had a reliable and willing engine, it was capable of 43mph and could return 200mpg, its scooter-style frame was easy to get on and off, its large 17 inch wheels gave stability, and its automatic clutch made it simple for beginners to ride. It could even be ridden one handed. The Super Cub had clean, uncomplicated lines, it offered a degree of weather protection, its engine and chain were hidden away, it was easy to clean, it was easy to park, it was quiet and smoke free, it didn't break down and didn't leak oil, it was cheap to run and insure, its unburstable engine ticked away merrily like a Timex watch, and it would suffer the most terrible abuse and keep coming back for more.

Honda's first foreign subsidiary opened in June 1959 on West Pico Boulevard in Los Angeles, California, in what is now the Korean district of the city. It was a modest, white, two storey building with American Honda Motor on the sign. Soichiro told me how Honda's first American sales reps were sent out in Chevy trucks with a Honda Cub lashed on the back. Their instruction was to persuade someone to take the bike on consignment, and they targeted lawnmower repairers, drug stores, hardware stores and sports goods outlets ahead of motorcycle shops.

More than 750,000 Super Cub 'step-thrus' were sold in 1959 alone, and by the start of the 1970s the figure had exceeded six million. Honda had become the world's biggest motorcycle manufacturer by far, and the firm's success had been built on the non-enthusiast, ride-to-work market. The phenomenal financial success of the Super Cub and its derivatives underpinned Honda's growth and development throughout the 1960s and into the 1970s.

Namika was looking at her wristwatch and the manageress had long since finished cashing up, but Soichiro drained his glass and signalled for two further beers. He was in the mood to talk, and there was much more he wanted to say. Newcomers to motorcycling were not frightened or overwhelmed by the Cub, he explained. They learned that bikes were fun and once confidence was gained and it was time to trade up, they found larger Hondas were also relatively easy to handle. By 1961, Honda had 500 dealers across the USA to meet that need. The enthused autocrat twisted an imaginary throttle and in his mind he swept down a Californian canyon road. Motorcycling had exploded in popularity in the USA, and where America led, other countries followed. Honda was growing the world motorcycle market.

Then he turned to the future. That giant industrial conglomerate Kawasaki had just brought out the Z1, their 900cc double-overhead-camshaft CB750-beater, and Suzuki was rumoured to be following suit, but his best engineers were spending all their time struggling to build motor cars, and the Honda Motor Company was finding it difficult to respond to these threats to its hegemony.

I said I was hoping Honda would upgrade the CB750 to 1000cc with double overhead cam, but he waved the suggestion aside. There was no chance of anything like that with the limited resources available at the time. The car side of his business was beginning to occupy all his best men.

Really? Honda's earliest cars were really just four-wheel motorcycles. They were cheap, but they were also pretty basic. The Japanese car market was very unsophisticated in the 1960s, so selling them at home wasn't too much of a problem. They were reliable enough, typical Honda, but they had terrible fundamental problems and were simply not of a good enough standard for the more discerning European or American buyer. I remember seeing hundreds of them sitting in rows in London's docklands, slowly rusting to oblivion.

There was a 360cc car and a 600cc model, both with underpowered twin-cylinder air-cooled motorcycle-type engines. To have enjoyed driving one of those early cars it would have helped to have been stone-deaf; they were noisier than flying a Spitfire with the hatch open, and the heater was just a flap that allowed the hot air in the engine compartment to come into the cab with all the attendant fumes and everything else, so in the winter you either froze, or choked.

I laughed as I reminded him of this, and then impersonated the racket they made, pretending to fly Supermarine's fabled fighter plane, but my attempt at humour was clearly ill-judged. I had committed a terrible faux pas, and his face darkened visibly. Don't mention the war? No, not that. There was nothing wrong with air-cooled cars, he shouted, banging the table. It was the only way to go. Why could no-one see it? He looked left and right, checking nobody could overhear him before he sat back down and continued. His voice dropped to a whisper, and consequently so did Namika's. He was about to lose control of his company, he said, calm again for a moment, his eyes glistening and looking straight into mine. We were pinioned in the moment. It was altogether ineffably sad. Then he snatched up a knife and brandished it rather closer to my face than was comfortable, before adding, close to tears, that 'they' were going to move him sideways. That there would be a coup. That he could not prevent it. He dropped the knife with a clatter and left the table. Say nothing about this, said Namika.

It was not many months after this astonishing lunchtime revelation that Mr Honda was made the company's supreme advisor. He waved the Honda flag, and represented the company with a smile, but only as an ambassador, and with no specific or strategic role. He visited Europe quite a lot, and I met him in London once or twice. He was jovial but he seemed smaller, somehow diminished.

I heard they were still very frightened of him back in Hamamatsu, particularly in R&D. He did have a very short fuse! He did not suffer fools, and more than one Japanese has told me how he would whack a man on the back of the hand with a spanner if he made a mistake. Shocking, but apparently those stoical and devoted chaps took it without complaint, just stood there bowing and apologising. Even the management went to some lengths to keep things from him. Mr Honda hated two-strokes and would rant on about them at the slightest provocation. When the company was developing crankshaft compression racing engines in R&D, he saw them and made a derogatory comment, but he was told don't worry, they're just for lawnmowers. He was not interested in lawnmowers and let it drop. They fobbed him off.

But the engineers in R&D had felt a terrible restriction because old Soichiro had such very fixed views. There could be no two-strokes, and no water cooling, which included cars. His argument about water cooling was if you're dealing with a symptom, you're not dealing with the problem itself. There must be another way. He wanted to make air cooling more effective rather than have to pump water around an engine, so back in the early 1970s all the exciting new 1300cc, front wheel drive cars they had coming out had to be air-cooled with an air jacket system. They were noisy, and ended up carrying so much soundproofing they became front heavy.

It was hopeless. There was an impasse and something drastic had to happen because Mr Honda absolutely forbade water cooling. Then there was the amount of resources the car side of the company required, and the fact Honda could not simply recruit a fresh crop of engineers to free up capacity for motorcycle development. The Japs were completely locked into their job for life system, and changing firms for a bit more money wasn't the done thing. Honda couldn't lure the staff they needed from elsewhere, so they had to do it all themselves.

The top people in R&D said Mr Honda had to go. He's too obstructive, we're not going to make progress. I don't know how it was done but suddenly the great man was put out to grass. This was, I believe, 1973 and it enabled Honda to produce the first Civic. A silly name but a damn good car which was an instant success. It was water cooled, of course, and everything was right about it.

I admired Soichiro. He was almost entirely self taught, but he was actually an unusual kind of genius. He always tried to see the root of the problem. This was the philosophy he preached, not just to deal with superficial issues but to find out why a problem had occurred. He was down to earth, he drank working men's drinks, he never forgot his origins and he always identified with the ordinary man. That was one of his real strengths. He was also a bit of a playboy, he was very humorous, he told dirty stories, and he had a great sense of fun. Above all, he was an enthusiast, and he inspired those around him to work hard, to think, but also to have fun.

Back in the early 1970s the Honda UK headquarters in Chiswick was always a happy place to go to pick up test bikes, or attend press conferences. I think that had something to do with the firm's founder and patriarch, and his personal philosophy. Now, I am told, in the firm's offices in Swindon, everybody is very serious, nobody ever smiles, every door has to be unlocked to pass through it and locked up again afterwards, and there's an atmosphere you can feel as a visitor which isn't very pleasant. Back in Soichiro's time the company was full of enthusiasts, and everybody really seemed to enjoy what they were doing. Business can, and I think should, be enjoyable, and there are always ways to achieve that.

HONDA GL1000 – ON A WING AND A PLAYER
(First published *Motorcycle Review* – August 1975)

If I only had a brain, lamented the scarecrow in *The Wizard of Oz*. Those of you who have achieved anything close to de Forte's great age will recall that this spellbinding piece of Technicolor whimsy was released just a few weeks before War Two began (actually a little later here in Blighty. I saw it at the Futurist in Beedle in Christmas week, 1939). Can I have been the only one who has thought that if only our leaders had brains we might not have spent the next six years burying our dead?

On a purely selfish level, I can also blame Mr Hitler for my stalled musical career. In 1943 the position of principal trumpet with the Halle appeared to be mine (Barbirolli was at school with Uncle Bof's boy, Edwin), but for various fairly obvious reasons the deal went up the Swannee without a baton. Lack of practice owing to my becoming active in hostilities from that year onwards meant that my embouchure was never quite the same again. Alas, when peace finally returned the reality was that my playing fell substantially short of the standard required for a newly re-invigorated, and re-established major symphony orchestra.

Some readers may well be wondering what this has to do with Honda motorcycles. Patience, my friends! Apart from the fact that I would never have stumbled into journalism had the Nazis been playing cricket, the connection is, of course, wings. Honda's emblem is a wing, gold or otherwise, as was Herr Hitler's.

Unfortunately, the association is so strongly embedded in my conscience that the merest mention of Honda's new 'superbike' makes me think of the war. As a corollary, I am prompted to shuffle over to the long-suffering Bechstein and bash out part of Harold Arlen and EY Harburg's anything but brainless score. 'With the thoughts I'd be thinking, I'd be another Lincoln, if I only had a brain,' indeed.

You will therefore understand why I choose to refer to Honda's latest marvel by its model number, GL1000. First seen at last year's Cologne show, the 999cc GL started life as even larger machine with a flat six engine. Perhaps because conspicuous consumption of fuel and natural resources is hardly fashionable in this decade of oil crises, the production version features a more modest water-cooled flat four with cylinders integral to the crankcases, and overhead camshafts driven by toothed belts.

While this may be a first for motorcycles, it's already old hat in the car world. As far back as 1960 the German Glas concern in Bavaria was the first to develop belt-driven cams (which was why BMW acquired the Dingolfing company in 1966), and a host of others followed, Ford, Fiat and Vauxhall being prime examples. These reinforced 'rubber bands' have both advantages and disadvantages. On the plus side, they are quiet and don't elongate as they age, like chains (the 'stretch' in a chain is, of course, a lengthening resulting from cumulative wear in the bushes, not deformation of the metal). On the negative side, belts have a shorter life and if improperly tensioned can suddenly shred their teeth, possibly occasioning a catastrophic collision of valves and pistons. A well-designed 'non-interference' engine will not suffer such grief, however.

Perhaps the main reason for motorcycles to stick with chains is a matter of space: to achieve a reasonable service life, belts need to be run on larger and wider pulleys. It's interesting that when Honda's twin cam CB450 twin was released some engineers were quick to point out that its tiny crankshaft sprocket (the only practical way to fit the necessary gubbins in the cylinder head: remember that unless a two-stage drive is used the camshaft sprockets are twice the size of the one on the crank) was asking for problems. As we now know, the Black Bomber did often suffer valve-gear trouble. Whether this was a direct consequence of the chain trying to jerk round a small sprocket, or just a result of the general complexity of the camshaft drive and the speed at which it operates, I know not.

In most other respects the GL1000 engine follows normal Honda practice… except that it is liquid-cooled (Soichiro will not be pleased!). Pedants will tell us that all engines are ultimately air-cooled, with the liquid merely being a more efficient vector in the initial quest to disperse heat. Be that as it may, the flat four designers' goals were 1) smooth running from tick-over to WOT (wot? Wide Open Throttle, of course!) in the harshest of conditions, and 2) silence.

Mechanical noise can be suppressed by surrounding the cylinders with water jackets, a fact that only Porsche engineers seem not to realise.

Also to this end, the GL has an elaborate, vast and extraordinarily heavy underslung exhaust system, a U-shaped edifice that does remarkably well to keep out of the way of luggage, pillions, and the road surface when banked over. At any speed and at any revs, only a distant murmur emerges from its twin pipes. Some people call this a demerit, but why anyone would want to be fatigued and deafened after a long ride escapes me. Let them eat cake and buy Harley-Davidsons!

Thanks to the horizontal cylinders and aforementioned exhaust, the GL's centre of gravity must already be unusually low, and Honda made sure of it by putting the petrol tank in the middle of the wheelbase, under the seat. What appears to be the 'tank' is in fact a plastic dummy hiding a storage compartment. We must assume that the big beastie's commendable low speed stability and surprisingly good handling balance are at least partly due to these measures. If ever a motorcycle disguises its weight and size on the move, this is it, but as de Forte's wheezing revealed, however, no amount of Hyacinth Hippo nimbleness will help a stationary Winger if he is daft enough to park his beast nose-in to the kerb. In the absence of a reverse gear, I suggest asking a fit passer-by to help push, or pull. Failing that, there's always a friendly police constable or the Fire Brigade. For once I wished for a full-face helmet, if only to cover my abashment.

Yet, once rolling and pointing in the right direction the GL is a delight, very probably the smoothest and most silent two-wheeler ever assayed under the de Forte fingertips. It is the antithesis of most motorcycles. Some of my fellow typewriter pounders have grave misgivings about this, and rhetorically ask why one wouldn't buy a £1,600 car instead. I believe they are missing the point. Vincents and Velocettes stir me. Nortons and Triumphs are part of my soul, but flying along on the Wing took me to a new dimension. No matter what the speed there was no feeling of effort. Even at 100mph the sense was of a horizontal version of free-fall parachuting, as if Honda had found a way of redirecting gravity.

My colleagues have also been less than complimentary about the GL's handling, complaining that cornering at quite modest speeds caused sparks from the undercarriage, and indeed I managed to wear away both sides of the centre stand during my two day test, and there were no feet left on it at all by the time I'd finished! Happily, this is of no concern to typical customers, except, perhaps, when fully loaded. While the Wing has a fatter rear wheel and tyre than the norm, it has a limited ability to cope with two diet-fearing adults and their chattels. Some sort of self levelling system to assist the somewhat ordinary suspension would be a welcome addition. Otherwise, I liked the bike. It is a heavyweight, long distance express. Reliable, durable, strong and capable of reaching 120mph fully loaded, and of delivering high speed cruising for hour after hour.

Forget the naysayers, I predict a long future for Honda's latest 'superbike'.

FIZZERS!

It was early one weekday evening during the long, burning hot summer of 1976. I had been dictating some urgent copy through to *The Auto* (such a tiresome business, thank goodness for electronic mail!), and was just replacing the receiver while simultaneously reaching for the scotch decanter, when the telephone rang in my hand. It was young Prudence Mallard, daughter of my old school classmate Frank, a dim boy turned tedious monologuist, and now second generation landlord of the Rose & Crown. Mr de Forte you must come quickly she said. A gang of yobbos are zooming round the car park on motorbikes, and taking it in turns to race each other to Beedle chippy and back. Old Dr Cooper nearly got knocked over coming across for his whisky Mac, and they've frightened Miss Termagant's cat. Dad refused to serve them and now they won't go away.

I went along to see what all the fuss was about, arriving at our village hostelry just as two delightful little two-stroke motorcycles flashed into its car park, ridden flamboyantly by youngsters in half-face helmets, streaming scarves and flapping flared trousers. The wee bikes were Yamahas, I discerned as they pulled up in the car park alongside another half a dozen similarly smart small machines. One Yamaha was purple, the other orange, and they joined an already varied line-up comprising two Suzukis, a Honda, a Gilera (goodness me!), a yellow and black Garelli (another blast from the past), and a peculiar Minarelli-powered charmer called a Fantic. My word, what pleasant little motorcycles they all were, and how curious they all sported bicycle pedals and red and white learner plates.

Can you talk some sense into this lot, Wilby? said Frank, emerging suddenly from the pub, while waving his arm in a broad gesture which encompassed the mini motorcycles, and their eight spotty young owners, all of whom now stood smoking vigorously in surly silence. They're underage, and they're frightening my customers away. Leave it with me, I said, not knowing at all what I was going to do next. First off, I asked the boys how old they were, to which they all simultaneously smirked or sneered while continuing to stare steadfastly at the tops of their rubber-soled boots, as has always been the way with teenagers since their invention in the 1950s. I pressed on nonetheless. Why haven't any of you passed your tests? No point, said one lad. Two-up means going slower, and the test is meaningless once you're 17. It was then the penny dropped. This was the so-called sixteener sports moped generation I had heard the chaps talking about in the office at *Motorcycle Review*. And the two little Yamahas were the famous Fizzers (actually Fizzies

– ed) that had boosted importers Mitsui's sales figures so mightily since their arrival in Blighty three years earlier.

Conservative MP John Peyton's sixteener law which came into force in December 1971 had had unexpected consequences. The legislation's declared intention was to reduce accidents by restricting 16-year-olds to pedal assisted shopping mopeds and raising the age for riding 'proper' motorcycles to 17. But Peyton's legislation, which was, of course, designed primarily to put newcomers off the idea of riding two-wheelers altogether, ended up fuelling a boom. For half a generation aged 16 between 1972 and around 1979, owning a moped was as influential a part of their lives as being a modernist or a rocker had been in the 1960s. The world's motorcycle manufacturers exploited Britain's new regulations by building super little 50cc performance motorcycles for the British market. These exciting 'sixteener specials' or sports mopeds were equipped with pedals purely as a token gesture to comply with the law, and they conferred magical freedoms upon their owners, both real and symbolic. And a social revolution was taking place. For many sixteen-year-olds the sports moped proved to be far more than a stopgap before getting a proper motorcycle, or learning to drive a motor car. Bonded together by their shared and restricted two-wheeled experience, there was great camaraderie among these young riders, and the intensity of their moped year hooked a whole generation into biking and, for some, influenced their brand loyalty for life.

How often do you ride? I asked my little gang. Every day. Where do you go? Youth club. Chippy. Here. Where else is there? Tell you what lads, I heard myself saying, come with me. And with that I gestured for them to follow, and after much prodding of kickstarts and making of white smoke, I began guiding them, rather as a hen does its chicks, and the little flotilla buzzed its hazy way slowly through the village to the farm, and then bumped and burped down the track to the Far Field.

The change in the law had been a long time coming. At the end of 1967, a full four years before Peyton's sixteener law came into effect, a petition of over 27,000 signatures was handed to the then Labour Minister of Transport, Barbara Castle, at Downing Street in protest against her declared intention to restrict 16-year-old motorcyclists to machines of under 50cc. From the beginning of 1972 the sports moped, the new breed of 50cc machine that came into existence as a direct result of the Peyton legislation, became the primary machine of fledgling motorcyclists' new-found independence.

Previously the BSA Bantam had been the country's favourite first bike, but, coincidentally, Bantam production had ended during 1971. The Bantam, which, like so many other small motorcycles around the world, was a modified version of the excellent pre-war German DKW RT125, was an unremarkable two-stroke utility machine which aided mobilisation after the war, and sold well for many years afterwards, primarily as a cheap and cheerful way to get to work (remarkable I had to work so infeasibly hard to persuade the smug denizens of Small Heath to consider the project at all!). Its engine was a mirror of the DKW unit, it had a BSA designed frame and it handled well enough, but it vibrated ineradicably, pogoed over bumps, and its reliability was not the best (whereas Yamaha's first-ever motorcycle, the estimable YA1 'Red Dragonfly' which was released the same year, and which was also greatly influenced by the DKW, featured significant design improvements over the 1930s German original, and proved strong and reliable).

Over time the Bantam became ever more dated and no more dependable. In fact, later Bantams were generally even less trustworthy than earlier ones, while lightweight Japanese machines came along in the 1960s, which appealed far more to spirited youngsters and serious commuters alike. But around half a million BSA Bantams left Brum over 23 years. Not numbers to be sniffed at, and for many thousands who began their motorcycling careers on one, memories of pushing home after a seizure or other disabling breakdown became forgotten, while fond recollections of a simple motorbike that put a smile on their faces and a song in their hearts endured.

Once at the Far Field with my young charges, a madcap couple of hours of two-wheeled competition followed. The racing was not especially fast, it must be said, but a great time was had by all. I organised heats and a final, and we rounded off the evening with a few flying laps each on Old Thunderer (a Rudge speedway iron I dragged from its resting place under a tarpaulin in the middle shed). Then, while the reborn Rudge stood happily against the fence by the house, tinking loudly as it cooled, its downpipe a glorious dull maroon, we stood talking motorcycles in the darkling garden, with Martha superintending the refreshments, having prepared ginger biscuits, a tray of glasses and a gigantic jug of iced lemonade.

The boys' 50cc machines were without exception thoroughly competent little motorcycles. They were attractive, sweet handling on the road (from their hair-raising stories of derring-do, they must have been), and appeared to me to make just enough power for a beginner. The lean, lively Yamaha fizzers (from their proper name, FS1-E) possessed a particular 'rightness', and were arguably the all-round best of the bunch. The Suzuki, fetching in pale blue, was a slightly bulbous copy of it. It had an extra gear, and was a smidgeon faster. The Garelli, a raucous yellow and black thing called a Tiger Cross, emitted a raspy roar while simultaneously clattering as if a tablespoon were being agitated in a tin biscuit barrel. It was rapid sure enough, but the lad spent a lot of time kicking it! And the stubby orange Fantic Motor, a TI, growled its way around the circuit in the fastest time of all. The Honda (a four-stroke, of course), was terribly slow at first, but I soon sorted that by whipping it up to the workshop and slicing half an inch off the bottom of the carburettor slide! The Gilera was well made, but also disappointing in the performance stakes. I suspect it had tiny ports. Open them up and it'll fly, I told its crestfallen young owner.

Perfect if only by happy accident, they were super steeds for those teenage lads (Gary, Barry, Andy, Dave, Phil, Steve, Russ and Pete, according to my diary). In that awkward period of transition from adolescence to adulthood that coincides with leaving school and beginning to make a way in life, riding these bikes felt terribly grown up, and awarded their riders instant credibility. Most sports mopeds, certainly those made by the Japanese, were far more reliable than the Bantams and Francis Barnett Plovers they superseded, and DIY motorcycling maintenance for beginners effectively disappeared overnight (apart from de-carbonising the two-stroke models, of course). Sports moped sales rocketed and dealers sold insurance and HP by the pad, but not everyone was happy about the burgeoning moped scene, its social significance, and beneficial boost to motorcycling as a whole. Sports mopeds gave freedom and independence to hundreds of thousands of British teenagers and kick-started a massive mid decade motorcycle sales boom, but just a year after that happy night in the Far Field, the Callaghan Government enacted further legislation which redefined the moped, and spoiled the fun at a stroke.

At 10pm the boys buzzed happily down the track and away. I still see some of them around. One chap became the foreman at Quickfit in Beedle (a most handy contact), another a police motorcycle training instructor, and a third became quite a well known politician, I won't say of which persuasion! But I'm sure they have all joined the massed ranks of misty-eyed middle-aged men, who have come to regard their sixteener year as among the happiest of their lives.

ABOUT JOHN

Incidentally, John Peyton, the Tory MP for Yeovil who served as Ted Heath's Transport Minister from 1970 to 1974, and was ultimately responsible for the aforementioned misguided legislation in 1971, was regarded in the motorcycling press as autocratic, brusque and off-hand, and he came to be seen by bikers as something of a hate figure. I have it on the best possible authority, that his patent dislike of motorcycles was due, at least in part, to his having fallen off one while ineptly learning to ride it on an army officer course in Flanders in 1940, and that subsequently, due to his injuries, he had been taken prisoner from his hospital bed by the advancing Germans. Hah!

BMW MOTORRAD

BMW's new 1977 motorcycle range was not centred around a new engine type, as had been rumoured, nor was it in any way exotic in mechanical engineering terms. It was a stage in an evolution, as was the BMW way. The German company's development work was about making their flat twins more civilised, not stretching their performance, and it is a German characteristic to insist on content over form, but for some time BMW's motorcycle division had been becoming more fashion and style conscious.

The smoke grey and psychedelic orange finishes on the sporting R90S model on sale since 1973 had been deliberately aimed at attracting moneyed young executive types, and they had been suitably well received. The R100RS which replaced the R90S had an enlarged capacity of 980cc, bore having been increased from 90mm to 94mm, and the effect was an increase in torque rather than top speed. Bing carburettors replaced the Italian Del 'Ortos of the R90S, and cast alloy wheels were available as an optional extra, and there were a number of engineering improvements too, but the obvious difference between the outgoing and incoming models, and the most attention grabbing feature of the new /7 series in general was, without question, that the RS was fitted with a spectacular and quite unique full fairing.

I had flown out to Bavaria in 1976 to attend the retirement party of one of BMW's most loyal servants, my good friend Alex von Falkenhausen, and on the morning of his big day, I was afforded the opportunity to have a test ride on a prototype machine. The official /7 series launch the following year would be blighted by torrential rain, and TT racer Ray Knight of *Motorcyclist Illustrated* would be the only journalist brave enough to ride the R100RS to its limits, but it was on a beautiful autumn morning with clear blue skies that Alex collected me from my hotel and took me through the factory to the motorcycle development department.

The R100RS's integral fairing has been designed in a wind tunnel, explained Alex as I caught my first sight of the extraordinary and futuristic-looking machine which was standing by the workshop doors. The fairing is highly aerodynamically effective, he went on, demonstrating airflow using his hands. It was designed to stabilise the bike at speed, keep the front wheel pinned down at all times and to resist the effect of crosswinds, as well as provide weather protection and reduce rider fatigue. The development bods are claiming it reduces wind resistance by five percent, front wheel lift by nearly 20 percent, and side wind sway by a remarkable 60 percent, and it also aids engine cooling. I am hoping to get one as my leaving present! he added with a wink to designer Hans Muth who was hovering nearby.

I was already bowled over. The extraordinary looking wedge shaped fairing was assembled from seven parts but looked as one and seemed wholly integral to the machine. Below its windshield it incorporated a comprehensive set of instruments including a clock, and short, low bars promised a sporting riding position. Many BMWs were ridden over great distances (always a BMW forte) and this new aerodynamically tested fairing would enable BMW riders to stretch their touring range still further. The firm had reinvented the sports-tourer.

Having donned the de Forte bone dome and my hooked Kett racing gloves (no need for thicker or more expensive types, those cheap beauties gave the very best feel) I ventured out for an hour or two aboard the ice blue prototype (it would be the primary production colour). The machine behaved perfectly in city traffic, I discovered, and the brakes and the horn proved particularly effective, and soon I was speeding through the Bavarian countryside. I say speeding because almost every time I stole a glance at the speedometer I was surprised to discover I was riding in quite considerable excess of the legal limit, but while the Bavarian Wonder Bike was undoubtedly capable of sustaining high velocities all day long, it did not at any point feel particularly fast. Further, while corners of all types came and went without fuss, the R90S was a machine that calmed the rider, bringing out one's latent grown-up (better that way around!), and bend-swinging, not ear-holing was the order of the day. The fairing was doubtless a factor in this, contributing to a quite extraordinary sense of stability and engendering a feeling of utter imperviousness.

The most useful electric clock kept me from venturing too far from base (remarkably, when the same timepiece had appeared on the R90S, it had been the first on a production bike since the Ariel Leader), and I returned to Munich on the autobahn where I tried my utmost to bring up 200kph on the speedometer. I failed, just, and interestingly getting down under the bubble made no difference to my attempt. Dare I say it, despite the fairing's impressive aerodynamics, I had to conclude the R90S was a fractionally quicker motorbike. I was also disappointed to find that while the fairing protected me from wind blast and crosswinds, the absence of a supportive air cushion eventually began to tell in the form of chronic arm fatigue, and I was glad to swing off on the ausfahrt and trundle back to the Bayerische Motoren Werke headquarters through the gentle ebb and flow of the suburbs.

Over luncheon in the factory cafeteria I added further criticisms to the verbal list I passed on to Hans and Alex. The fairing had amplified pushrod rattle (not a flattering feature in an era of whisper-quiet Japanese double-overhead cam fours!), and the oil dipstick and filler neck looked all but inaccessible. Had I used the steering damper? No, I had not needed it. Nor had I been required to top up the juice. They told me in Otto Normalverbraucher's hands the R100RS would return 50mpg, giving a touring range of 250 miles. I had no reason to doubt them.

When the R100RS went on sale worldwide the following year, the price in many markets was equivalent to three 1000cc Kawasakis. Was it worth it? Clearly not, but that was not the point. It was a bike that did something of which no other machine was capable. Arm-ache notwithstanding, it was the world's best long-distance motorcycle. It could lope along easily and safely all day long at near three figure speeds, doing it day after day, and keeping on doing it for many years after every Kawasaki Z1 was scrapped, mothballed, or else consigned to an Arizona salvage yard awaiting restoration and resurrection in the early years of the next century.

Flying home from Munich the next morning, nursing a not inconsiderable hang-over and a restorative large gin and tonic, I considered the R100RS's recent lineage. Following War Two the BMW factory got by the best it could making bicycles, pots and pans, kitchen utensils. No motorcycles over 250cc were permitted to be manufactured, and it was not until 1947 that development began on new models. These brought a modest profit, but by the mid 1950s Germany's speedy return to economic health had seen the demand for motorcycles fall into drastic decline on the home market, and scooters were all the rage across the rest of Europe. By the end of the decade BMW had so many unsold machines they did not know what to do with them, and they littered every corner of the works.

In 1960, following Dr Herbert Quandt's successful financial rescue, the company started building motorbikes again, but there was little new development, and the 9 in the R69/9 of 1968 indicated a ninth set of minor revisions. The R69 models were in any event re-workings of pre-war designs. They had old-fashioned Earles forks and outdated frames and engines, and they were, quite frankly, both long in the tooth, and toothless, but the Bavarian firm's flat twin was based on an aircraft-type unit and when properly looked after it was strong and reliable. The engine was suitable for redevelopment and improvement.

The New Class cars revived the firm's financial fortunes, but during their development BMW became an auto-focused business and motorcycle development was ignored. Then, as ever more space was needed for the manufacture of these new cars, senior executives wondered whether motorcycles needed to be part of the firm's future at all. The Beautifully Made Wonderbike was threatened with extinction, but Alex and the firm's other motorcycling men persuaded their superiors not only to continue making motorcycles, but to produce a whole new generation of BMW bikes.

In 1964 the august and aristocratic Hans-Günther von der Marwitz, then aged 37, joined BMW to take charge of the project. A sporting motorcyclist who owned an AJS 7R, von der Marwitz was not a fan of the traditional low slung BMW with heavy controls. He was an engineer who test rode machines himself, and he wanted BMWs to handle like Manx Nortons. BMW's top brass had made a good decision. The new BMW /5 series was launched to great acclaim in the USA in 1969, and the first year of production was completely pre-sold. It was impossible for British journalists to get a machine for magazine testing, let alone for the British public to buy one, so in 1970 I flew PanAm to California to meet a wonderful young man called Cook Neilson, the editor of *Cycle* Magazine, who had pulled strings so I could assay an R75/5 for *Motorcycle Review*. Upon arrival in sun-soaked LA, I made my way north to *Cycle*'s newly acquired offices in Westlake Village a small town a short distance from the Pacific, and hemmed in by the Malibu Hills and the Santa Monica Mountains. It was close to Los Angeles, yet with easy access to ocean and canyon roads and dirt trails. Ideal for motorcycle testing.

A shiny, black R75/5 stood outside, 'gassed up' and ready to go against a bleached suburban backdrop wobbling in a haze of heat. Although a proud and noble instrument, and largely adhering to a BMW's traditional prescribed form, it must be said that my first impression was that it was hardly an exciting looker. The new bike's massive power egg was inclined upwards at the front, and its silencers were inclined upwards at the rear. This gave it a somewhat broken back appearance, but while I found this unattractive, I knew I would likely uncover beauty of a different kind in the BMW's functionality, strength, loyalty, and promised longevity. Further, an incongruous slimline petrol tank boasted chromium panels on its sides and was unrecognisable from those of /5 Series machines I had seen in Europe. An experimental job, Cook explained.

According to the factory data sheet, the R75 weighed 421lb (considerably lighter than the R69), had a 110mph maximum, and put out 57bhp. An electric starter motor, originally designed for the Opel Kadett, was fitted as standard. The bike's flat twin engine looked familiar, but in fact it had little in common with its predecessors. It had lighter cases, its internal layout had been inverted, and all its key components had been made significantly stronger than ever before. BMW had invested in crank forging equipment, and the new crankshafts were designed to be adequate for years to come. The big ends and con rods were the same as fitted in the firm's car engines. Consequently, they were unstressed, with massive built-in reserves of strength and fatigue resistance. BMW's trademark shaft drive had been retained, of course, alloy wheel rims were fitted as standard, and the bike was fitted with a new and very powerful twin leading shoe front brake, the brake lining material having been developed for Porsche and BMW racing cars.

With a friendly pat on the back, young Cook bade me farewell and returned to the air-conditioned coolness of the *Cycle* offices, but at that moment, as I sat astride the machine, pulling on my new Kett gloves, even though the midday temperature was such that I could feel the cracked mosaic pavement beneath the soles of my boots, and the leaden heat on my black jacketed back was oppressive almost to the point of asphyxiation, I would not have swapped places with him for all the aqua pura in his water cooler.

A touch of the starter button and I felt the boxer's pistons shoving the bike

I can't recall ever enjoying myself more on a motorcycle.

left and right on tickover, the minuscule tachometer flicking spasmodically in the headlamp cowl. A clunk into gear, the low centre of gravity made it easy to manoeuvre, and then I was away. I liked the seating position straight away, so obviously designed by a motorcyclist, I thought, and soon I was free of Westlake's light industrial zone and canyon roads beckoned, and I was filled with an urgent desire to twist the grip off the bar. How did the bike perform? Well, apart from in the halcyon years of my youth, I can't recall ever enjoying myself more on a motorcycle.

The big BMW (it wouldn't be considered big now, of course!) changed direction easily and gave good ground clearance, positioning the tall engine's camshaft under the crank having altered its centre of gravity and raised its cylinders. It also handled superbly, and roadholding was first class, the bike proving commendably stable, and able to stick firmly to its line. In short, Hans-Gunther and his men had produced a fast touring motorcycle that cornered like a racer, and a machine as at home on fast, sweeping turns as tight, twisty hairpin climbs and descents. I rode the canyons for hours, and then tried a dirt road or two (it managed with aplomb – why not develop a scrambler version? I later told von Falkenhausen), and on the shimmering Freeway 100mph came and went at an early stage of the game. Not that I stayed at such heady velocities for long. The California Highway Patrol take a dim view of such antics, as I know from bitter experience! I returned to the canyons once more, climbing to enjoy a breathtaking vista as the sun began setting with unbelievable splendour behind the twinkling cobalt blue magnificence of the Pacific, and then I rode on until the light drained from the sky, and violet evening began darkening into cool black night.

Through all this, and mostly in supersaturating dusty heat, the engine performed magnificently, producing plenty of urge across a generous powerband, so concerns about the gearbox containing only four ratios proved unfounded. Likewise worries about the machine's lack of a front disc brake. The brakes, having been properly bedded in by Cook and his men, were simply second to none. Ah, you say, but you have already mentioned the BMW gearbox clunk. Well, silent changes were possible, I found, but it was a skill that needed effort and practice, but once remastered, it became second nature once more.

The large and amiable security man waved me into the *Cycle* Magazine workshops, at that time still under construction, and as the bike sat ticking in the semi-darkness and I gathered my possessions and made ready to leave, I decided the R75 was going to go down in history as one the finest BMW motorcycles ever built. So competent, so well rounded, so superior, so royal, and the most extraordinary thing about it of all was it had not been built on a work bench by experienced and dedicated technicians as had been the case with the R69. It had been put together by lumpen nitwits who did not know one end of a motorcycle from the other! The /5 Series BMWs bore the stamp of a practical mind in more ways than one. Incredibly, they had been deliberately designed to be assembled by unskilled labour in a new semi-automated factory at Spandau in Berlin, and still be brilliant enough to take on the hordes of meretricious marvels from Japan.

The air hostess tapped me on the shoulder. Would I please sit up straight and fasten my seatbelt. We would soon commence landing at Luton Airport (twinned with Spandau!). Drat! I had been dreaming (and drooling!). I have never forgotten my long-suffering but ever stoical English master Captain Geoffrey Peacock telling the Remove never to end a piece of writing with the line, 'I woke up, and it was all a dream'. Thankfully, such an unsatisfactory denouement would have no place here. The imperishable memory of that afternoon in Southern California has stamped itself on the de Forte mind in an adhesive and indelible way, and the dream recounted in these pages is an entirely faithful reproduction of actual events. Reader, I stand by every word! The following year I visited Allan Jefferies' new BMW emporium in Yorkshire's West Riding and rode away on an R75/5 of my own. I still have it, and sadly it is now the only remaining two-wheeler in the middle shed here in Bales. Over time I came to call it Apollo, and it has now achieved a mileage wholly appropriate to the sobriquet!

Chapter Nine

Before the Roman came to Rye or out to Severn strode,
The rolling English drunkard made the rolling English road.
A reeling road, a rolling road, that rambles round the shire,
And after him the parson ran, the sexton and the squire;
A merry road, a mazy road, and such as we did tread,
The night we went to Birmingham, by way of Beachy Head.

The Rolling English Road – GK Chesterton

HISTORY LESSON

BRITAIN HAD ENJOYED THE benefits of cheap Middle East oil since before War Two, but now the towel-heads (apologies – ed) began flexing their muscles. Prices were rising and inflation, the buzz word of the decade, was the result. Meanwhile, successive British governments struggled to run the country's nationalised industries, and internationally, Britain was seen as a country in decline; very much the 'Sick Man of Europe'. Trade unions were at the height of their power, and their leaders were among the national personalities of the day, not least my good friend and gourmand, the elaborately moustachioed Tom Jackson, whose Post Office workers suspended postal deliveries for 47 days in 1971 forcing me to telephone my copy through to *The Auto*.

Rolls-Royce's financial problems led to nationalisation by Ted Heath's Tory government, and in 1973 the Motors division was separated and privatised. Inflation raged as foreign goods became increasingly expensive due to oil prices, and in May interest rates soared to 13 percent, their highest figure since 1914. Then the Yom Kippur War started a full-blown oil crisis, causing shortages and driving fuel costs ever higher, and when the miners started an overtime ban in late 1973, street lighting was dimmed and all television transmissions shut down at 10.30pm.

As petrol became harder to obtain, fuel vouchers were distributed (although not used), and one kept one's car topped up. I was glad of Colin Haynes' 'regulars only' sign outside the village garage. A temporary maximum national speed limit of 50mph for all roads, including motorways, was introduced on 8 December, and less than a month later came the three day week. Factories were affected more than offices, blue collar workers more than white. By the end of the following decade, of course, many areas of Britain would have no factory jobs at all! Power cuts to conserve coal stocks caused lengthy evening black-outs, and we read by candlelight, huddled together around paraffin heaters, or retired early to our beds.

Master politician Harold Wilson was returned to Downing Street and gave the miners most of what they wanted. A huge public expenditure programme followed, and the 70mph speed limit on motorways was almost immediately restored. But in another oil crisis, petrol prices rose once more, and national speed limits were imposed once again, and November 1978 saw the start of the biggest labour stoppage in Britain since the General Strike of 1926. The strikes during the so-called 'Winter of Discontent' were haphazard and anarchic, and reached a peak during freezing, snowy weather in January and February 1979. Britain reeled in chaos as hospital workers, gravediggers, lorry drivers, council workers, train drivers, nurses and rubbish collectors all stopped work at various times.

The strikes ended in March, and then in May the formidable Margaret Thatcher led the Tories to the first of four consecutive General Election victories. But ironically, in as far as these things can be measured, 1978 is now regarded as a high point for happiness and contentedness among the British population. The difference between the richest and the poorest in society was at its narrowest. Britons have never had it so good again.

TRIUMPH STAG

Triumph Snags, as my learned chums in the trade used to call them in the 1970s, were awarded their unsolicited and inglorious epithet for very good reason: a car hidden in a roadside cloud of steam would invariably be a Stag with an overheated engine and an even more overheated owner, and everyone who drove Triumph's stylish new GT car in the 1970s was probably on first name terms with his local RAC patrolman. Meanwhile, the justifiably maligned but not wholly incompetent BL concern somehow managed to produce other V8-powered vehicles that were perfectly reliable and rarely apt to impersonate boiling kettles. What on earth was going on?

Well, reader, you will not be surprised to learn that the story of the Triumph Stag is both long, tortuous, and really rather sad. Here we sit, a good many years since the last one rolled out of Triumph's Canley factory, lamenting another heroic failure produced by the nationalised colossus that was British Leyland. After a break of many summers, I drove a Stag again a few years ago through a beautiful, if chilly, autumnal Salop landscape. While the V8 growled its unique and euphonic sounds, the shadows of clouds slipped silently across the fields, the watery sunlight flashed through the tree branches overhead, and the air swirled with a trillion kaleidoscopic leaves. True to its co-creator Harry Webster's original stratagem, the Triumph Stag was a unique niche product which successfully opened up a new market sector for itself. In its first year it was well received and sold strongly. The car drove and handled reasonably well, had pleasingly simple lines and made a sensational sound. Hood down, heater on, that relatively recent October day, I could think of few better ways to motor than in that comfortable two-plus-two. Based on all the evidence before me, the Stag should have sold a million, especially in the US market in an era when a V8 under the hood almost guaranteed success.

But of course it did not. In fact, history records that only 25,877 were ever built and after the initial enthusiasm faded the last cars made in 1977 were hard to shift at any price, thanks to a deserved reputation as a vehicle that broke down about as often as it moved. Particularly devastating was the fact our American cousins failed to take the Stag to their collective bosom, thereby torpedoing any realistic hope of large volume sales. Although there was a minimally modified 'Mark II' version, one had a definite sense BL wished to kill the model off ASAP once the engine's cloven hoof had become so damningly apparent, and this was more than ever the case once the full effects of the 1970s fuel crisis hit home, obliging high flyers and hoi polloi alike to consider smaller engines and reduced performance.

After being declared bankrupt in 1939, the Triumph Motor Company had been bought by Standard in 1945 and the firm enjoyed a reversal of fortunes, mainly because chief engineer Harry Webster designed an interesting and varied range of cars. In recognition of this, Standard traded as Triumph from 1959 onwards. The Triumph Stag began to take shape in the mid 1960s when renowned Italian car stylist, Giovanni Michelotti asked Webster for a spare vehicle to use as the basis of a show car at the Turin Motor Show. Webster and Michelotti were friends and had worked together on a number of projects including the hugely successful and profitable Triumph Herald which had been launched in 1959. In mid 1964 Webster sanctioned the despatch of a well used Triumph 2000 saloon race support car for Michelotti to work with, on the understanding Triumph had the option of using the design themselves if they liked it.

In June 1964, Triumph 2000 registration number 6105KV, which had supported the Triumph Spitfires racing at that year's Le Mans 24 hour race, was driven to Michelotti's studio in Turin. The Italian designer retained the drive train and suspension and shortened the floorpan, but completely replaced the four-door saloon body, changing it into a four-seater two-door convertible. When Webster visited Michelotti and saw the car, he was so impressed he persuaded the Triumph top brass to buy the design, and consequently the car was never exhibited at the Turin show. Webster was convinced a Grand Tourer would be a profitable addition to the Triumph range and that the car would sell especially well in the USA. He hoped to target young executives. 'Someone who wanted something different, something sporty but with creature comforts.'

But Triumph had other priorities. It was not until early 1966 that work got under way on the grand tourer project under the code name 'Stag', and development of the car into a production vehicle was not straightforward. Like most things BL, the Stag suffered an extended gestation period. When Michelotti first came up with the idea of creating a grand tourer based on a shortened version of the 2000 saloon floorpan, it was a few years after Leyland rescued the company, but a few years before it was hitched to its former deadly rivals, Rover, in a shotgun marriage brokered by the big bosses of newly-founded behemoth BL. The new '2000 / 2500 GT' was scheduled to be launched in 1968, but the plan fell apart, thanks to turmoil and strife within the new regime.

It was eventually decided to move the Stag upmarket by jettisoning the saloon's straight six, and using a doubled-up version of the new Triumph modular overhead-camshaft engine that had taken shape in conjunction with Saab. Miraculously, the slanted four cylinder version, displacing around 1800cc appeared in the Saab 99, more-or-less on time, but Triumph was a company in crisis. Somehow its planners had to gear up for production of both the four and its related V8, which was basically a pair of the same cylinder banks appended to a single crankcase at 90 degrees. Initially the V8 was going to be a 2.5 litre with Lucas petrol injection (as (in)famously seen on the TR5!), but as time rumbled by it was decided to increase torque by adding more cubes, and three litres and twin carburettors became the chosen spec. Looking forward, there was space enough in the bore and stroke to enlarge swept volume to around four litres, with the additional possibility of four valves per pot achieved through devious means as per the later Dolomite Sprint. Indeed, 200bhp or more should have been on the cards. If only! In reality, the standard three litre with Stromberg carbs mustered rather less than the promised 145bhp at 5,500rpm, and it wasn't long after the first Stags went to paying customers in 1970 that 0bhp at 0rpm became a far more likely proposition. Not £1,522 well spent.

As mentioned, overheating was the main issue. It seems crazy, but one problem was that the aluminium cylinder heads hadn't been properly torqued down in the factory. Unusually, the heads were clamped to the (iron) block by studs and bolts at different angles, so it wasn't simply a matter of tightening to so many lb/ft and going off for another tea break. A rigorous process had to be followed. More heartache was caused by engines that were left full of swarf from machining operations. Bad news, and worse still when allied to reports that cylinder heads were made out of an unsuitable type of aluminium alloy, while some crankshafts were apparently not hardened correctly, causing rapid wear. That in turn led to oil starvation of the camshaft bearings, timing chains, et cetera. Worryingly, the oil pump itself was shared with the four cylinder cars, so there were question marks as to whether it could ever be up to the job. There was also a weakness in the timing chains which meant they sometimes 'stretched' (of course, this is really a misnomer – lengthening is actually due to wear in the links) and jumped a link, upsetting the valve timing with catastrophic consequences. Further, the water pump, which was located between the V of the cylinders, was mounted too high so a drop in coolant level left it running dry, and the poor manufacturing quality of the cylinder heads exacerbated the problem. In any event, the cooling system was barely adequate for the job, and as the engines became older, if aluminium additives were not used in the anti-freeze, the waterways would become blocked. Additionally, cylinder head corrosion would cause further blockage and even water leaks. All this also led to hot running, causing excessive wear and blown head gaskets.

In a nightmare scenario, the proud owner would drive gently for a few months with swarf gradually blocking the oil pump pick-up, causing a vicious circle of attrition. Meanwhile, the already strained cooling system would silt up. Then, with the engine by now run in and gleefully given more stick, it would promptly overheat and the cylinder heads would warp. Obviously, there was no easy solution. Skimming the heads without addressing the fundamental causes was doomed to failure. A complete new engine, preferably clean inside and made out of the correct materials, was the order of the day. Some unlucky punters had a whole series of replacement V8s, only for each to suffer the same steamy fate.

This is exactly what befell Andreas Bishop, a near neighbour, and Rose & Crown regular here in Bales, who took delivery of a Stag soon after the launch and almost immediately regretted it. By the end of 1970 Bish had visited the local Triumph agent so many times we joked he should be given a personal parking space by the service manager. Unfortunately, the joke began to wear thin after six months or so, and after Rowley Birkin had a word with him at my behest, Bish threatened British Leyland with legal action. The details are now lost in the steamy mists of time, but the eventual outcome was that the Stag was replaced by an utterly reliable, if rust-prone, Datsun 240Z. After a lifetime of buying British, another customer had defected, probably permanently. Triumph addressed some of the Stag's problems in early 1972 by redesigning the water system, although the waterways within the engine were unaltered, but the problems persisted and the engine's reputation for overheating and self destruction were soon accompanied by criticisms from America about poor build quality, gutless transmission and a lack of steering 'feel'.

Such was the strife of Stag ownership that a cottage industry developed, either offering to fix the original V8 or supplanting it with something better. The deep irony was that many felt the best engine for the job was the Buick-based Rover V8, which had become available when the Triumph V8 was still on the drawing board (did it ever truly leave it, one must ask). By 1977, when the

Stag was put to rest, there were plenty of second-hand Rover lumps available, and despite BL's assurances it didn't fit the engine bay, that was proved to be quite evidently untrue. Indeed, none other than Spen King, who took over responsibility for the Stag's development when Harry Webster was redeployed in the Austin Morris division, assured me when we fell to chatting during a coffee break on one of our long motorcycle rides together after his retirement, that the Rover engine would indeed have fitted, but BL simply did not have the capacity to build the engine for Stags as well as for Rovers and Range Rovers. Part of the problem with the Stag engine was the bloody-minded Triumph workforce, he told me candidly. It was simply not made very well.

One notable knight in shining armour was Anthony Hart, whose Fulham-based garage could work wonders with the Triumph V8. With a background in historic racing, HRS (Hart Racing Services) rapidly became the go-to place for Stag expertise. 'Give Your Stag New Hart!' ran the magazine advertisements. Assuming you began with an engine with correctly torqued heads, and that wasn't full of filings, the gospel according to Tony was simple enough, and could be summed up thus: 1) Stick to the 3000 mile / three month service intervals, 2) Always use the correct quantity and type of antifreeze, 3) Change the timing chains at 25,000 miles, before they 'stretch' and start flapping around. Now then, that doesn't sound too onerous, does it? But apparently it was beyond some bloodthirsty Stag hunters, who preferred to transplant Rover V8s or Ford Essex V6s. The latter move obviously robbed the car of its aural identity, but worked surprisingly well – at least, it did until its oil pump cannibalised itself, which must be considered a form of poetic justice!

Later there were signs that the tide had turned, with some converted cars being reunited with Triumph's own V8, and it's interesting that Stags now have a way above-average survival rate, despite suffering from the usual bodywork corrosion issues that blighted all automotive offerings of their era. My theory is that many of the cars with blown engines were barn-stored rather than scrapped, ready to re-emerge someday to a sunnier, better cared for future. Internal politics, neglect and cost cutting caused problems with other models in the Triumph range, and the marque's increasing reputation for fragility sent it into a long decline culminating in the death of the name in 1984. But my drive in a well-restored thirty-year-old Stag in late 2010 demonstrated that Triumph made a potentially great machine, in many ways a superior one to contemporary BMWs and Mercedes. If only, if only…

MATTERS RELIANT

For many years motorcycle sidecar combinations had been commonplace on British roads. A hard up young motorcyclist who gained a wife and family would fit a sidecar or trade his solo in for an outfit or combination, and continue riding. A motor car would come later. But, said many, sidecars took all the fun out of motorcycling. They ruined bend swinging, and they were uncomfortable. Miserable, freezing cold family outings would be spent with driver and passengers shouting themselves hoarse, their voices drowned by the beat of the engine or snatched away by the wind. They were obstreperous, treacherous contraptions requiring quite different techniques for turning left and right, they were apt to skid, and the 'chair' was prone to lift, especially when empty, often with disastrous consequences. In short, they could be damned dangerous. By the late 1950s, sidecars were on the wane. A general rise in affluence began to make the small car affordable, and for the impatient or penurious motorcyclist, there was another option – the three-wheeled car.

Something of an oddity in world motoring, British three-wheeler cars came into existence mainly due to an historic anomaly in British driving licence legislation and classification. For a great many years following the issue of the first drivers' licences in 1903, nearly all three-wheelers on British roads had been motorcycles with sidecars, or else Morgan-type trikes, and for this reason a British motorcycle licence entitled its holder to drive a 'three-wheeler' as well as a 'bicycle'. Taking advantage of this fact, from the 1950s onwards, small fibreglass-bodied cars started to be produced. These were generally four seaters with automobile steering wheels and standard floor-mounted brake, clutch and accelerator pedals, and all their other driver controls were also laid out in the same way as in conventional motor cars.

For many young motorcyclists with a new and growing family such a three-wheeled car was a logical choice. It was a way of keeping everyone reasonably warm in winter, and there was no need to invest time and money taking driving lessons. Additionally, road tax was cheap, fuel consumption was miserly, depreciation was surprisingly low (fibreglass you see, the bodies didn't rot away!), and, of course, there were only three tyres to wear out!

By the 1970s three-wheelers were also starting to appeal to penny-pinching motorists looking for an economical way to stay mobile. In an attempt to attract more such converts, Reliant of Tamworth in Staffordshire, by far Britain's biggest producer of such cars, spoke to their long-time collaborators Ogle Design (the styling house responsible for the look of the BSA/Triumph triples in the late 1960s), and asked them to come up with a more modern design as a replacement for their ageing Regal saloon and van range. The result was the Reliant Robin, perhaps the best known three-wheeled car of all time.

Owning a three-wheeler has always been a way of being different, but although there was, perhaps, a slight degree of ironic appeal, it was never a way of boosting one's street credibility. Cars of the 1950s and 1960s such as the

Preston-made Bond Minicar and Reliant's Regal always had something of an image problem. They were a bit like 'invalid cars'. They were not proper cars. They were, in fact, the proper car's poor relation. They had a wheel missing. They were a bit odd. They were objects of derision and the subject of jokes. They were good for an easy laugh.

Despite its cleaned up looks, the Robin was no different. Television comedian Jasper Carrott, who had a hit 45 in 1975 with a song called *Funky Moped*, told a joke on his show about a Reliant Robin driver, desperate to gain the kudos of a speeding ticket, who drove flat out past a speed gun cop stationed at the bottom of a steep hill while making roaring engine noises at the top of his voice out of his open driver's window. The cop turned to his colleague and announced: 'I got the number Sarge... Chassis number.'

Those who plied the A5 during the second half of the twentieth century will have been well aware of the Reliant factory at Two Gates, Tamworth. Originally a boot factory and a bus garage, in later years the plant expanded over both sides of the old Roman road, so the production process involved stopping the traffic and pushing half-finished rolling chassis across Watling Street! Not an inconvenience in the post War Two period, but becoming a challenge by the closing years of the 1950s!

In its '70s heyday Reliant was the largest independent car manufacturer in Great Britain, enjoying the Royal seal of approval from HRH Princess Anne, who owned a succession of Scimitars and even, it is alleged, some three-wheelers, although it seems that the latter were only used by underlings on the estate. Still, it was jolly good of her to support a British company.

Sadly, the entire Two Gates area is now a housing estate (albeit named Scimitar, and with roads bearing the monikers of other Reliant models), and the A5, or London-Holyhead trunk road, has become a wide dual-carriageway sweeping majestically through the countryside towards Wales. What went wrong? As usual, there were multifarious reasons for Reliant's demise, just as was the case with British Roverland and its other former incarnations.

Reliant grew from a very small acorn indeed, circa 1934 in a back garden shed in Tamworth, where a Mr Tom Williams thought it would be a good idea to make his own version of the newly defunct Raleigh Safety Seven (a V-twin-powered passenger three-wheeler, of which fewer than ten are now believed to exist). Williams went on to buy up all the suitable Raleigh parts he could get his hands on, and to develop his own ideas for economy vehicles, and in 1935 he began to sell commercial trikes called Reliants, propelled by 600cc JAP singles. Improved V-twin models followed, and by 1938 the 747cc Austin Seven engine was Williams' engine of choice. Then, when Herbert Austin's little sidevalve ceased to be made the following year, Williams took the bold step of building his own version designed in-house by his pal, former Raleigh man Tommo Thompson.

The minor matter of War Two scuppered Williams' plans for improving his vans and developing passenger vehicles, and his men were put to work building motorcycle frames and jet engine parts instead, but by 1946 Reliant three-wheelers were back, and in the early 1950s the Regent and Prince Regent made their debuts. In 1953 these vans were joined by the Regal, which catered for passenger travel, and two years later by a four-seater version. During the late 1950s the firm's long-established ash frame and aluminium panel method of construction was gradually supplanted by the use of a new wonder material called GRP (aka glass-fibre).

Inevitably, Reliant had their eyes on the much larger four-wheeled market, and the firm helped set up car manufacturing plants in Israel (Autocars) and India (Sipani). The Sussita (Arabic for mare) was a four-wheeled workhorse which was exported by Reliant in kit form for assembly by Autocars in Haifa. It was a big success, and the Carmel saloon soon followed.

Williams died in 1964, whereupon the ever-helpful Ray Wiggin became MD and began steering the company to greater things. Ten years later turnover had risen from around £700,000 to £20m, and Reliant had become a household name, thanks mainly to its distinctive three-wheelers, but also the Scimitar GTE, a fast and powerful motor car which introduced a new concept that is with us to this day. It is a matter of great regret to me that the badges on current grand touring estates tend to be either that of Audi or BMW. Under Wiggin's stewardship, four-wheeled versions of the firm's tri-cars were developed, small economy cars called the Rebel (1964-74), and its successor, the Kitten. But throughout this period and beyond, Reliant's bread and butter business continued to be its successful three-wheelers.

I have mostly happy memories of Reliants both three and four-wheeled. The Two Gates factory was only an hour from Bales, so I always gladly accepted Mr Wiggin's invitations to sample test vehicles and see the production process in action. Inspired by Maserati or not, the Ogle designed GTE was undoubtedly a trend-setter and deserved its success. Some disliked the old-fashioned separate chassis and live axle, but in practice it worked very well. A well located rigid rear axle is invariably preferable to the geometric gymnastics of a poorly designed independent rear end. BMW proved as much beyond doubt! For another instance, the Triumph TR4 was often more steadfast than its independent rear suspension 4A replacement. On the same tack, the later Capri 2.8 handled marvellously with nothing more than cart springs to keep things in line, thanks to Rod Mansfield's expertise. I choose those examples for a reason, because the TR range donated its compact double-wishbone front suspension to the Reliant cause, while the Scimitar eventually benefited from the German equivalent of Ford's Essex V6.

The injected V6 cured a perennial Scimitar foible caused by heat build-up under the bonnet and a silly cooling system. Not often an issue in frozen Britain, admittedly, but in hot weather Scimitar wielders often fell on their swords when filling that enormous 20 gallon tank. Let me explain. A five minute stop was perfect for causing petrol vaporisation in the carburettor, sandwiched as it was in the Ford Vee, resulting in an engine that stubbornly refused to re-start. Owners resorted to all sorts of weird and woeful cures (and perhaps sinecures), but the ultimate solution was fuel-injection, not a bodyshell full of holes or extra fans.

I had no such problems when I took a handsome brown and beige GTE across Europe to Austria in November 1978. Surely just the sort of trip for which the Tamworth touring machine was most ideally suited.

The Scimitar has an interesting history. The first Scimitar body started off as an Ogle design for Daimler, intended as a sports saloon body for Edward Turner's V8. Nothing came of the commission and when Jaguars took Daimler over at the end of the 1950s the idea was dropped. Reliant then picked it up, adapted it to fit their Sabre sports two-seater chassis, and, as per the Sabre, tucked a Ford Zephyr straight six under the bonnet. The car made its debut in 1964, and in 1966 it became Essex V6 powered. Around 900 cars in total were made.

Scimitar GT owners were often discerning types. They appreciated its simple, tough mechanicals, its smart yet unconventional looks, its reliability, and the fact that due to its fibreglass body, it could live outside at a time when almost all cars rusted away overnight if you even parked them over a puddle. Prince Philip had one and he commissioned Ogle to build him an estate version as a one-off. Everybody was pleased with the result, and in due course the design was developed for production by Reliant's former Lotus and BRM race engineer John Crosthwaite, working closely with the Ogle bods. The finished GTE hit the road in 1968 and created quite a stir in automotive circles. The three litre Essex V6 shoved the GTE along at 120mph, and it was a highly comfortable and immensely practical motor car. Other manufacturers ogled it, and went away to their drawing boards, and many imitations were spawned. Meanwhile, in 1970, the Queen and Prince Philip bought one for Princess Anne's 20th birthday. She must have liked it, because she went on to own eight more.

In late 1975 a new version of the GTE appeared that was longer, wider, and considerably more luxurious inside. I tested one over Christmas that year, and called in with it to visit my wartime pal Raymond Baxter and his delightful American wife Sylvia in their fabulous home in Denham (played a peculiar version of table tennis called Pong, on his television set, I recall. A marvel at the time, and strangely addictive!). The interior was also roomier, and the car had gained power steering and other improvements including a power increase (to 135bhp), although extra weight dulled any advantage. From 1979 onwards, as the Essex engine approached the end of its life, GTEs were fitted with Ford's German-built 'Cologne' 2.8 litre V6. Although not as torquey as the Essex lump, it was smoother and more free revving. From 1980 a convertible car called, logically enough, the GTC appeared on the scene. Only 400 or so were built and they are relatively desirable today (I say relatively as none of Reliant's underrated GT cars have particularly high values as 'classics').

With its modern-looking body and chunky Wolfrace wheels, the GTE was more than handsome, but more importantly it was a car for those who go forth seeking adventure. The Scimitar was a quite fabulous machine for carrying people and luggage over distance, and I had to transport these things across France and Germany to Austria back in 1978, as well as two dogs and several sets of skis, having picked up some French industry pals and their pooches in Poitiers. The simple combination of a strong chassis and lightweight body, made for a fast, fine handling machine (the suspension was stiffened up, I believe, after the first few face-lifted cars in 1975). Whatever, my notes reveal I found the GTE swept round fast corners with aplomb, as well as performing quite adequately on the twisty stuff. The rack and pinion steering was quite high-geared, but that presented no problems, and a small steering wheel suited the behaviour of the car. The brakes performed perfectly (the only rude smells coming from the canines aboard!), and I also praised the urge and surge of the torquey Essex V6 mill. While I suggested an automatic box would suit the GTE, as with Bill Lyons' XJ6, I found the manual ratios well matched to the engine's power characteristics, and by flicking the overdrive in on second and fourth, managed 26mpg for the trip. Not good by today's standards, but the huge fuel tank meant we could press on for hours at a time.

Best of all, of course, the Scimitar was wonderful for fast cruising, and by 1978 motorways and dual carriageways criss-crossed Europe making transcontinental travel a speedy business. And while we cruised past the Beetling herrenvolk on the two-lane autobahn, we sat in absolute comfort at a noble 100mph, able to relax and appreciate the Reliant's considerable extra refinement over the honest mediocrity of the products of the big volume manufacturers of the day such as Ford, or Vauxhall. In its time, the cockpit of a Scimitar was an altogether pleasing and stylish place to sit. The leathercloth seats were comfortable, there were no creaks and rattles (so often a problem with fibreglass construction), and the reassuringly old-fashioned cockpit featured a fascia crammed with a fine array of traditional black dials. I liked the Scimitar GTE. Its virtues were real and rare, it was potent yet restrained, its solidity was pronounced, its comfort and quietude were appealing, and its reliability was commendable too.

From looking further back in my diaries, I see that I tested a Reliant Regal 21E saloon for *Motorcycle Review* in October 1972. The *Review* carried regular ads for Reliant's three-wheelers, and I was encouraged to test the subjects of them from time to time by the *Review*'s advertising manager, Arthur Paige, not least because the issues which carried such tests would attract plenty of extra advertising from Reliant's many dealers.

At the time of the Regal test, Reliant was celebrating the manufacture of its 100,000th three-wheeler or tri-car. The firm had made Regals since 1953 and moulded fibreglass bodies since 1962. The shells were bolted to steel chassis. Previously aluminium bodies had been fitted over a wooden frame. The Regal at this stage had a 700cc engine, up from its earlier 600cc specification, and the pushrod motor was accessed from above via a tiny trap door. Its crunchy boite de vitesse had no synchromesh on the first ratio, and the synchro on its other gears could be beaten by changing quickly. Nonetheless, the car's light weight meant it could move reasonably rapidly if thrashed, and was capable of 70mph.

But flogging a Reliant three-wheeler was perhaps not a good idea. The Scimitar was a fine handler, but the tri-cars were another kettle of piranhas entirely. They couldn't lean or be drifted, and, in the wrong hands, they had a tendency to flip over. Rapid changes of direction, or sudden braking or gear changing in corners could bring about this most alarming result, and my sage advice to self was always to take it steady around bends until I really got to know the feel and limit of any three-wheeler machine. The Regal was also badly affected by crosswinds on motorways, and its suspension, which was necessarily stiff to prevent roll, was quite hard over bumps. The car's cost in late 1972 was £770. Not particularly cheap to buy but cheap to run, was my conclusion. At the time Two Star petrol was 32p per gallon and 60mpg was considered attainable. Road tax was low at just £10.

The Bond Bug was a two-seater, three-wheeler sporting microcar which was styled by Ogle Design. Bond Cars Ltd, which had changed its name from Sharp's Commercials in 1963, was taken over by Reliant in 1969, and Reliant commissioned Ogle to come up with a fun car aimed at a young market which it would manufacture itself in its Tamworth plant, but using the Bond name.

The resulting Bug was outrageous and exciting in appearance, an absolute hoot to drive and a highly individual thing to have parked on the drive. Magazine advertisements for the Bond Bug were headed: 'Dolly Bug. There's never been a car like this for pulling the birds' and contained the line: 'Provides pilot type excitement as you thrust the urge along!'

The Bug had an aerodynamic wedge shape and its futuristic fibreglass body was riveted to a welded steel box section chassis designed by the estimable John Crosthwaite. It had no doors and the roof canopy lifted up to provide access for driver and passenger, rather in the style of a jet fighter. The engine was Reliant's own venerable pushrod design, available in various states of tune but its performance exceeded that of the Regal and its successor, the Robin, due to the car's light weight. With the exception of a few promotional vehicles, Bond Bugs were all bright orange.

Bugs were quirky and peculiar to drive but once one became acclimatised they really were great fun when given the spur. They were well engineered, but finish was poor and they were rattly, draughty, cold and uncomfortable. They were also expensive and, in general, Bond Bugs appealed to motorcyclists rather than car drivers. The Bug was only in production for four years before it was squashed (sorry, I couldn't resist that!), but has a cult following, and there is a buzz about them to this day.

In 1973 Reliant launched the Robin saloon. Broadly an update of the Regal, it was another product of Reliant's long-term relationship with Ogle Design. Like the Regal before it, the new Robin was powered by the firm's venerable Austin Seven-based engine. Titter ye not! Despite its ancient origins, this all-aluminium four-cylinder motor was extremely light and it could be tuned to deliver quite unfeasible levels of performance. It had a long and successful career in motorsport. Early Robins had 750cc engines and a new all-synchromesh gearbox, but the car was still only capable of 70mph and the box remained somewhat notchy. From 1975 onwards the Robin came to be powered by an 850cc version of the engine, and it was then that I was invited to the factory and offered the opportunity to be the first tester to try the newly uprated three-wheeler.

Not far from the factory gates at Cannock I discovered two things: first, thanks to its flyweight construction the 850cc Robin was quite a Q-car, able to out-accelerate many unsuspecting vehicles of its generation. The second discovery stemmed directly from the first, in that I inadvertently reached a considerable velocity before noticing that the road didn't continue in a straight line. Yikes! As time-served sidecar pilots know only too well, the secret of tripodal survival is Don't Panic! One might be obliged to turn the steering wheel, but braking while doing so is almost certainly a bad idea. This transfers weight in an unhelpful direction, quite possibly resulting in an inverted trip into the scenery. As a corollary, Robins and their Regal ancestors often had scratches on the roof, but they were sturdy vehicles and could shrug off a slide or two. Hitting solid street furniture was a more serious problem.

Fortunately, I resisted the temptation to stamp on the binders, and as I exited the corner in one piece, further sage advice for driving a Reliant came to mind. 'Always enter a corner at the right speed, in the right gear and always brake or change gear before changing direction... never while taking a corner.' Actually, the Robin's smaller, quite natty alloy wheels made it more stable than a Regal, I ascertained, and it was less easily provoked by lurid corner work, but it would still pick up a rear one during spirited attacks on the swervery.

A final point concerning matters dangerous. From data compiled by insurance companies, it is actually a fact that Reliants had a consistently low claims rate, thereby confirming that road safety is not about crumple zones and airbags, nor indeed ultimate roadholding and handling. As an unusually wise politician once remarked, people start behaving responsibly when you give them responsibilities. That, and as I've always said, albeit sometimes to howls of outrage, motorcyclists generally make better car drivers.

Back to 1975. The interior of the Robin was all new and thoroughly modern and my test car even had a radio, although at speed it was too damn noisy in the cabin to listen to anything of any subtlety. Because of the hard and bouncy nature of the suspension, I found it nigh on impossible to keep a steady throttle setting on potholed roads (it would certainly be impossible today!). Fitted with myriad extras including a heated rear window, the Robin did not seem especially cheap, but the car became as commonplace on British roads as the sidecars once were that it displaced. Reckoned to resemble a whistle and nicknamed the plastic pig, the Robin remained in production until 1981, and it was also made under licence in India and Greece.

As well as being popular with the penurious, Reliant three-wheelers were also bought by motorcyclists obliged to give up bikes through injury, and I once came across a Regal van driven by one such invalided rocker which had been fitted with a tuned Vauxhall Viva engine. Having placed breeze blocks in the back to aid weight transfer, this comedic leather jacketed hooligan would make his Regal rear up on its back wheels and wheelie under heavy acceleration. On the flanks of this fantastical vehicle seen roaming the roads of Shropshire looking for an audience in the mid 1970s was sign-written the legend, 'Plastic Rat'.

But a Reliant three-wheeler's strongest appeal was always to the parsimonious, and by the end of the 1970s most Reliants were being driven very slowly by elderly retired gentlemen in flat caps, and in the 1980s a yellow Reliant Regal Supervan III driven by a middle aged man in a flat cap became the single most famous Reliant of all. The car featured in many episodes of the long-running BBC comedy programme *Only Fools and Horses* starring Ronnie Barker's protégé David Jason.

At one time Reliant employed around two thousand workers at its three main sites, and had developed a somewhat complex and confusing corporate structure. My long-suffering bank manager RT Fishall would vouch for the fact that I am no accountant, but one might suppose that the string of companies involved might explain why Reliant is now no more. Wiggin was a splendid and amiable fellow, but who really pulled the financial strings in the background?

Still, let us not forget that in the mid 1970s while BL was falling apart and costing the taxpayer billions, Reliant was busy turning out 250 Robins, 80 Kittens and 50 Scimitars every week, and distributing them through a network of 230 dealers. These figures are impressive, especially considering that all the firm's models were essentially hand-made and inevitably sold for more than their mass-produced competition. Consider that when a Kitten cost £1,900 a basic 850cc Mini was less than £1,700, and when a Scimitar was listed at £5,500, a Capri with the same V6 engine was £2,000 cheaper.

On the face of it there was little incentive to spend more on a Reliant, but there were plenty of home market customers wedded to the idea of buying British, particularly when the product had a personal recommendation from HRH Princess Anne. Moreover, the Scimitar had no direct competition initially (more so later, and when the GTC convertible arrived in 1980). To borrow some present-day PR mumbo-jumbo, the Kitten's 'USP' was a justifiable claim of being the most economical car available, while the Robin still had a captive audience of ex-motorcyclists who could drive a three-wheeler of restricted weight without a full car licence. According to lore, a large slice of production ended up in the hands of Yorkshire and Lancashire miners, who seemed to have an allergy to vehicles contacting the ground in more than three places!

Reliant was bought by Beans Engineering in 1992, then fell into the hands of Jonathan Heynes, son of illustrious Jaguar engine guru, William. Interestingly, my old chum Lofty England, another key figure in the history of Jaguars, of course, was also connected with Reliant. Having taken early retirement in 1974, the tall fellow moved to Austria, of all places, and became Reliant's European technical consultant, and that, of course, was where my Froggie pals and I were bound in a two-tone Scimitar in 1978.

VEHICULAR METAMORPHOSIS

Flicking through my diary, I have been reminded of a tale told to me by a now very famous motoring journalist concerning psilocybin fungi, perhaps better known as magic mushrooms. As a teenage undergraduate in the hedonistic 1970s, it seems he bunged a dozen or so of the little blighters in a potful of PG Tips which he imbibed just before setting off home from university in his Fiat 126 at the end of the Michaelmas term. All went well to start with but he was rather alarmed after an hour or so when his car quite inexplicably turned into a flying saucer, right before his very eyes, and under his floating bottom. Somewhat frightened to say the least, he coasted into a convenient lay-by to consider his next move. 'It was all rather disturbing,' the chap recounted to me some twenty years or more later, 'but then I came to realise that all the ship's controls were, in point of fact, laid out in exactly the same manner as the Fiat, so I pulled myself together and hovered happily home.'

PORSCHE 911 TURBO

Doctor Ferdinand Porsche was born in Bohemia in 1875. A precocious genius as a child, he became an engineer, rising to occupy senior positions at Daimler, and doing important work for Mercedes, before setting up his own mechanical and technical design studio in Stuttgart in 1930. The rear-engined Auto Union Grand Prix car was a successful government commission, and helped by his son of the same name (although known as Ferry), he also gave his attention to Hitler's Volkswagen project. Although the Beetle design was not finalised until 1938, and none were sold to the public until 1939 (and none again thereafter until 1945 for obvious reasons!), he had got its basics pretty much sorted by 1935 and had turned his attention to yet another big job for Hitler's Reich Chancellory; designing and constructing the factory where the people's car was going to be built.

After War Two, in which Herr Doctor (an honorary title, as was his professorship) had a hand in building Tiger tanks and V1 flying bombs, Ferry and his pater set up in the barn by the family home in Stuttgart making aluminium-bodied sports cars. The first Porsche 356 appeared in 1948, a rear-engined job using Volkswagen components, and as hand-built production got under way, Ferry's modest aim was to build just 50, but by 1951 a factory had been acquired, and annual production had got into the thousands.

I tested quite a number of 356 Porsches for *The Auto* in the 1950s and early 1960s, and while I appreciated their looks, and acknowledged various improvements through the years until production ended in 1965, I found them all awkward to get into and out of, as noisy as old threshing machines, and, performance and handling-wise, hardly the greatest thing since bottled beer in any event, (although commendably low weight saved them from being a lot worse!). Altogether, I'm afraid, they were not my glass of pilsner!

The first drawings for 356's replacements were the product of yet another Ferdinand Porsche – Herr Doctor's grandson (the family patriarch had by then popped his clogs, so Ferdinand II was running the show), who was known as 'Butzi' (he of Porsche Design: watches, sunglasses and much else). Similarities in appearance between the new car and the 356 were deliberate, likewise its layout. The old boy had always insisted on rear engine designs, believing them superior, a view no doubt influenced by his pre-war successes in European grands prix. Although to be fair to him, I'm sure he appreciated more than anyone that a central position was the most ideal (and that's actually where the gigantic engines were located in those pre-war propaganda-fuelled monsters of the tracks), but in a road car that space had to be taken up by the occupants, and a rear location was the next best thing. Even overhanging the lump at the rear was acceptable in Porsche's book, as long as light metals were used.

The Porsche 911 of 1964 was lower and narrower than its predecessor, and also longer, although it did not look it (integrated bumpers were a clever touch, saving a few inches at each end). Its cabin was much more roomy, and there was considerably more glass. The 911's chassis was of monocoque construction, of course, and MacPherson struts played a part in its compact front suspension. The car had disc brakes, and a five speed gearbox, and was powered by a new air-cooled, overhead-camshaft six-cylinder 'boxer' engine of two litres capacity, producing 130bhp. Subsequent versions of the 911 would get bigger and more powerful incarnations of the flat six engine over the years, and a turbocharger arrived on production cars in 1974.

The plan was to build 400 special three litre turbo cars to homologate a new crop of racers, but well over a thousand ended up being manufactured within two years, and revised versions followed. The all alloy flat six was fuel injected by Bosch, and fitted with a KKK Kompressor (Kuhle, Kopp and Kausch!), and to cope with the car's power and torque, its four-speed gearbox and clutch were mightily beefed up. A stiffened body featured flared arches to accommodate ultra-wide wheels and huge tyres, and a distinctive 'tea tray' rear spoiler projected at the rear. Also at the back end, big banana-type cast aluminium trailing arms did their best to help the torsion bar rear suspension keep everything tied down.

The Porsche 930 Turbo as it was officially called (everybody ignored that including Porsche's marketing people) was a 150mph sports car, and most probably the fastest accelerating production car in the world, but it was also a luxury carriage with quality carpets, leather seats, air conditioning, and electric windows. The showroom price, unsurprisingly, was as huge as its performance.

Back in 1974, all the bright young things in the office were scrambling over one another in their efforts to secure the keys for a test drive in Porsche's muscular world-beater, so I let them get on with it and my time for a proper blast in a Turbo didn't come until four years later, but I did have a spin as a passenger in an early car (I have chosen my words carefully!). It was a drizzly autumnal day and one of the aforementioned BYTs (now a moderately well-known classic magazine scribe and automotive author), was at the wheel as we approached the roundabout on which was situated the Old Cock, a Coventry pub aka the midlands office of *The Auto*.

The rain that had been heavily on, was now easing off, and the windscreen wipers scraped back and forth painfully while the blower struggled to demist the fug on the inside of the Porsche's windscreen. Traffic had been heavy, and as a test of the car's performance our ten minute jolly had been a complete waste of time. I expect my young colleague had become frustrated, and doubtless he was conscious that many critical pairs of eyes would be observing our arrival from within the hostelry ahead, and I offer further mitigation and not condemnation when I mention we had not long earlier been inside the mock-tudorised Cock ourselves, and that we were glowing from a not immoderate intake of golden ale.

We were travelling at about 20mph on the overrun as we breasted a slight rise and entered the roundabout. With perfect timing and good fortune, a generous gap had appeared, and then, as so rarely happens any longer, the whole gyratory junction miraculously opened up empty ahead of us and BYT decided it was showtime. Planning to complete a full circuit for the benefit of our watching audience (and no doubt the old stager in the passenger seat), he floored it in second gear. You can guess the rest. We rocketed forward, sliding the rear slightly, but then the turbo kicked in, flicking us through 180 degrees in the blink of an eye. As we fell back to rest in our seats, we found ourselves stationary, sideways across the road, facing the bay window of the Cock that only a moment before had been at our backs. On the warm side of its bulls-eyed panes, half a dozen pint glasses were raised simultaneously in mocking salute, and a faint ironic cheer could be heard filtering through the gaps atop the Porsche's steamy side windows.

In 1978 I drove an uprated 3.3 litre version of Porsche's Turbo on a test day at the Nürburgring, and my experience was also not an entirely happy one. Perhaps I was not on the very best form, I had driven up from Italy late the previous evening (a joy in a new BMW Funfer, after a delightful and relaxing week on holiday in Lambrusco con la mia amante), and the German weather was not kind either, but in my opinion such a potent car with its engine in the wrong place and its drivetrain behind its rear wheels can never be a completely reliable and trustworthy companion.

The Nürburgring is a purpose-built race track situated in Eiffel, a densely forested, formerly volcanic region on the west side of the old West Germany. Built in the mid 1920s with government backing as a dedicated test facility for the German motor industry, it originally comprised two sections which could be linked to form a circuit as long as 17.6 miles, but most major races took place on the 13 mile northern section (Nordschleife). The southern part (or Sudschleife) has now been subsumed into the modern grand prix circuit which opened in the 1980s.

The Nordschleife has been tamed a little in recent years, but it survives pretty much intact to this day, and the public can pay to hare around it in and on all manner of unsuitable machinery. It still features 1,000ft elevation changes, more than 70 corners, and lots of dull grey Armco running alongside the black stuff.

Jackie Stewart called it green hell, although he was a prolific winner there. It is still a treacherous place, and when I tested the second generation Porsche 911 Turbo in 1978, it was even more dangerous still. It was just two years since Niki Lauda's terrible accident at Bergwerk, and everybody knew the F1 circus would not be returning.

I left the hotel at 8.15am after a chilled ham and cheese breakfast, and made my way to the circuit through five kilometres or so of light drizzle and softly enveloping low-lying clouds. Having signed in at race control, I found the paddock was abuzz. Race and performance cars from several factories were taking advantage of the test day. Men in overalls attended to exotic and expensive machinery and the whoop and rasp of performance engines being brought to life, and up to temperature, rent the air.

The Porsche pit was a particularly busy place. Several exotic race cars were being prepared, and I acknowledged Belgian ace Jackie Ickx while slipping unseen past the tiresome German scribe Otto von Schoffl, who had clearly bagged a lap or two in a 911 development racer of some sort, and was busy telling the technicians exactly how he wanted it setting up. No doubt Otto had arranged a spezielle exklusive for his rag, *Deutsch Weg und Strecke*, and I would be unlikely to avoid hearing a long and tedious preview of it later over dinner.

It occurred to me that although the silver Porsche 911 Turbo that was to be the subject of my attentions was strikingly muscular and squat, it was also small, and even unpretentious as is often the German way. But there would be nothing small about its performance. The beefed up 3299cc car allegedly made 300bhp, and was much faster and torquier than the three litre model it replaced, although discreet modifications had been made to calm the turbo down a little, essentially obliging it to make its entrance a little less dramatically than in the past.

But in increasing the engine's capacity, Porsche's engineers had replaced almost every component. This made the lump physically larger, and an intercooler had been added to the package. Worryingly, all this meant the engine, which was already a very long way back behind the rear axle, had been shifted another inch or more rearwards. Recommended psi for the back tyres had been increased considerably, a grinning mechanic shouted in my ear, in an effort to compensate for the shift this change had brought about in the car's front-rear balance.

The engine fired explosively and settled into a deep drone while I fastened my safety belts, and the cooling fan, activated right from the start, contributed an urgent whirr. The pedals felt awkward, strangely high, and the steering wheel oddly low, but the seat was supportive, and I guessed the Porsche ergonomics people knew what they are doing. The clutch was heavy and the gearbox initially a tad resistant, but it was easy enough to drive at low speeds as I made my way through the paddock and pit-lane and straight onto the circuit, merging into a second gear cavalcade of exotica being held behind some sort of pace car. Flags were waving. There had been an accident up ahead, it seemed. Sure enough, in the Hatzenbach section we passed German policemen in those funny caps waving their bats and blowing their whistles, while a coterie of marshals swarmed around an expensive-looking shunt involving a BMW 635 and a new Alfetta.

Then I gunned it. The needles snapped clockwise as the car surged forward like a bull terrier bitch straining on her leash. There was an exhilarating rush at 2,000rpm or so as boost pressure rose, and massive torque began shoving me in the back with no sign of letting up. I saw 60mph in a couple of seconds, but it was what happened after that that was truly mind-altering. The thing just kept right on pulling, and 100mph was left behind at an astonishingly early stage of the game. Deep green pine forest and galvanised steel Armco flashed past, and corners came and went with astonishing rapidity under the increasingly opalescent German sky. I left would-be followers behind, straining dots in my mirror, and, having anticipated their erratic lines, zapped the creepers ahead like a 21st century adolescent acing an X-Box game. Even at 130 or 140 there was much more in hand.

But while the 911 was an outstanding goer right enough, and its suspension tied it to the road admirably, enabling curves to be rounded at speeds which would represent the maxima of many so-called sporting machines on the straight, I could not but sense that as we plunged into hills and dips, streaked over crests, and scorched around blind bends with aplomb, the wonderful feeling of complete control, so calming and vital when driving at full chat like this, was somehow, naggingly, disturbingly, just fractionally lacking.

Powering out of low-speed corners, brought about wild snaking as the little dragster's wide tyres gripped aggressively (I could barely get them to spin), and the turbo was virtually lag-free when operating in its zone. To scrub off speed, the brakes needed a firm boot despite the assistance of the servo. That was of no consequence, but a sudden flick and tremolo through the structure when shutting off was a little unnerving. The Flugplatz was a thrill as ever, and I pressed on, ready for a white knuckle ride through the relentlessly fast roller-coaster sections of the track.

Aha! Not the Scandinavian pop combo, but a light bulb coming on in the de Forte noggin. A speck up ahead was confirmed not as a fly on the windscreen, but as the aforementioned overweening bore, Herr Von Schoffl, a man immoderately fond of bragging about his knowledge of the Nordschleife. He looked to be held up behind a slowcoach or two, so I set off in pursuit, planning to grab a tow and learn a thing or three, and if I could show him a nose and put him off his line, so much the better! Darker through the trees on this part of the circuit, the misty drizzle turned to penny-sized spots of rain, and after a couple of failed attempts, I found the lights and wipers.

The Porsche manifests consistent understeer, but when pushing on in the wet its tail will whiplash into power oversteer, snapping back again as one lifts off. Hairy stuff, and one imagines fishtailing or a lurid spin will result if a pilot is less than fully adept at the art of opposite lock. Reeling the German in now, I seemed to have the measure of my little silver brute. All going to plan, in fact. But then... Yikes! A missed braking point and rapid retardation is required for a medium-fast left. Yikes again! Too hard on the anchors and I'm ploughing straight on, careering deep, deep into the bend, way off the racing line towards the steely Armco. Heart in the mouth and down to first gear, but we recover and make it through.

Why the mistake? Clearly, I was beginning to find the experience as fatiguing as it was exciting. The steering was light enough, but rough surfaces were shaking the beast, making the wheel twitchy in my hands, and in bends it was ever eager to self-centre. Point and squirt driving is always dashed hard work, I grant you, but I was having to work overtime to remain the Porsche's master, and it wasn't helping that however cool and breezy it was outside, the inside of the 911's cabin was becoming ever more unbearably hot and humid. Sweat trickled down the de Forte phizzog, and the dratted screen kept misting up. Lightning dabs at the demister controls brought no improvement to either situation, and when every setting combination had been tried, I finally found slight relief by opening the driver's window just a crack. Noise will have been another factor, of course. Although raspy and raucous, the 3.3 Turbo was actually quieter than other 911s I had tried, and until the side window was set ajar I could just about hear the turbo whistling its siren song, but the tyres made such a damn racket! Much to do with the extraordinarily high pressures we were running, I should imagine.

I pressed on, and got nicely back into the groove, but hurtling around a 100mph bend on a blind crest (I know not which one, there are so many), I came upon a racing Porsche facing backwards, slap-bang in the middle of the road. The dratted von Schoffl had spun the blasted factory race car! Instinct took over and we jinked around it somehow, but alas my Little Silver just clipped the Schoffl-mobile, and the bump provoked her rear end a tad too much. A full 360 ensued, but in the surreal moment of silence and calm that often occurs in these dreadful situations I fortuitously recalled observing the mercurial Niki Lauda recovering from just such a predicament a few weeks before in his Brabham at Clearways, on a practice day at Brands Hatch. I depressed the clutch pedal and, as I watched the revolving horizon, pinioned in the still point at the centre of the vortex, I selected second gear and waited (it was as if I could have gone away and made a pot of tea) as in perfect clarity Armco and trees swept past the windscreen, then the stricken scribe, then more Armco and trees, and then, finally, as the corner's exit appeared in full view, I dropped the clutch and booted the loud pedal. Little Silver punched out, snaking sinuously up the track, barking her head off and wagging her fat tail. A check in my mirrors saw the German reaching the relative safety of the dewy greensward before anyone else piled through. Then came the palpitations.

Further on, the Karussel set me tingling, as ever, and I saw 160mph on the clock on the Dottinger straight, but generally I completed the lap at a relatively modest pace while other braver souls thundered past me in the spray. Wham! A Renault Le Mans car howled by into a bend 50mph faster than I would ever dare, and then the extraordinarily talented Jackie Ickx found time to raise a gloved hand while slithering underneath me in his ultra-lightweight 935 at the Eiskurve. My word! Masters at their work. I would never match those men, of course, no matter what car I drove, but I built a rhythm, after a fashion, and found myself at peace with my chunky little 911. Driven at sub-racing speeds, the Porsche Turbo's effortlessness and good manners are deceptive, you see. It seems utterly trustworthy, and predictable. But it is not. Drive it foolishly, or oafishly, or push it right up to its limits and it is the opposite of those things. It is capricious, and a very difficult car to drive indeed. It will bite you hard.

When I returned to the paddock, news of the incident had already reached the crew and they waved away my apologies for bashing Little Silver's tinware. When von Schoffl returned, did I want to try the racing version of their new car? The sun had begun flashing through gaps in the clouds, but I knew the track was drenched with rain, and my back was slick with sweat. I spotted Jackie making for the paddock cafeteria with a pal. Who was it? Ah yes, Derek Bell. An interview with those two luminaries, and a stiff espresso seemed a much better idea. I peeled off my stringbacks and declined. It was not yet lunchtime, but a man can have too much excitement in one day.

Chapter Ten

For my part I travel not to go anywhere, but to go. I travel for travel's sake. The great affair is to move.

Robert Louis Stevenson

OLD BILL

THE 1980S WAS THE beginning of the end. By that I mean it was the decade when I noticed significant figures in my life who were not much older than me had started dying off with disturbing frequency, and not least of those was Jaguars' illustrious chief, Sir William Lyons, who popped his clogs in February 1985.

Bill Lyons left a motoring scene very different to that which he began influencing back in the 1920s. The 1980s was the decade of the brutish Audi Quattro; the ubiquitous Ford Fiesta XR2 and Escort XR3, the super-fast Cosworth Cortina; the brash GTi, or GTI (dependent on whether a Peugeot 205 or Volkswagen Golf), and the purposeful Renault 5 Turbo. But for performance and prestige from the mid 1930s to the 1970s, no factory did it better than Jaguar, latterly of Browns Lane, Coventry, and the man responsible for every successful model right up to the XJ6 saloon was its founder.

Lyons was a master stylist, but also an astute businessman who costed every component carefully, making sure he bought shrewdly, and that in-house items were very long-lived, recovering their tooling costs many times over. Famously he had an eye, style, flair, call it what you will, and there was a touch of genius about all he did, but he was also a hard-working autocrat, spending long hours at his desk, and his being a dictator, having a hand in, and maintaining control of absolutely everything (even a switch had to be approved) caused problems.

I first came across him as a child when he attended a summer beano at Hornbeam Hall in the late 1920s. Tall, aloof, and I'm sure an arch-Tory even then, I recall him talking to Pater about the beach races on Blackpool Sands. He wore Plus Fours and arrived on a Brough Superior SS80. In 1922, at just 20 years of age, he had started in business by founding his Swallow sidecar manufacturing company in that north-west seaside town. It became the country's leading brand (appropriate here, I think, but how dreadfully overworked that word has become). Then he manufactured Swallow Sevens on Austin Seven rolling chassis before moving on to develop his own larger, more elegant and prestigious models, and in 1928 he moved the firm to Coventry. Rakish motor cars followed under the registered name of SS Cars Ltd (Swallow Sports, Standard Swallow, Swallow Special? Who knows? Lyons always said the name was inspired by the Brough Superiors he once rode).

The SS models of the 1930s were motors with panache sold at the lowest possible price, and that would be Lyons' philosophy for decades to come. As well as being far cheaper than any comparable opposition (an Alvis, perhaps, or even a Bentley), an SS was also intoxicatingly symbolic of freedom and virility, and not at all hard to drive. The chassis were by Standard, and they were propelled by asthmatic old Standard side-valves (albeit aided in their breathing by the attentions of the curmudgeonly Harry Weslake), but they reflected Lyons' styling and price philosophy, had a deal of panache, and exuded an air of quality. It was said Jaguars always spent their money where it would be noticed, and in some circles an SS was considered a little vulgar. Perhaps the Standard Avon was a better car. Whatever. The public went for the SS, and by 1939 Lyons was selling 5,000 cars a year.

In what would be my last job for *The Auto* before war was declared, I was detailed to deliver a 3.5 litre SS Jaguar convertible to Lyons at his golf club just outside Coventry, where he was waiting with my boss, features editor, Murdo Graves. Its exciting combination of looks, performance and price (just £445), was quite incredible. When asked, most people thought it would be double. That was the day I first experienced driving a Lyons Jaguar, and, feeling one of fortune's favourites. I revelled in being surrounded by plenty of wood and leather, sitting behind a powerful engine that I knew would not let me down. It was a 90mph car that would cruise comfortably at 80, and I was probably travelling at that velocity when I missed the turning to the golf club, carrying on for some 20 miles before realising my mistake. Where on earth have you been de Forte? he railed as he skipped briskly down the clubhouse steps and strode purposefully towards the car when I eventually arrived. Everybody else has gone home. Now shove over old man and let me drive. I suppose I'll have to run you to the station, he added, stowing his clubs behind the seats, or should I drop you at the Cock? I had inconvenienced him and he was brusque and direct, but also considerate and kindly. Typical Lyons, and I later learned that apart from one or two old lags at the works, he called absolutely everybody by their surnames. Checking my notebook I see the Jaguar returned only 15mpg, and there were further negatives. Its cruciform chassis was not light, and consequently acceleration was poor; its rod brakes were unremarkable; and acrid fumes permeating the firewall had been a slight concern, although I was rather pushing on!

The model reappeared in 1945, and ran until the Mark V appeared in 1948, itself a stopgap, of course before the big saloons of the 1950s which were supplanted by the even more massive, America-orientated Mark X. But from February 1945 the SS name was dropped, its unfortunate connotations not helped by smart badging which bore marked similarities to nazi insignia. Grace, Space and Pace became Jaguars' advertising motto. Of course, MG had used the phrase first, albeit with the attributes listed in a different order.

The world-beating XK sports cars of the 1950s and the wonderful E-Type and Mark II compact saloons of the 1960s were all fabulous Lyons-made motor cars about which I have waxed lyrical elsewhere in these pages. They had their faults. That inept gearbox made by Moss Gears blighted far too many cars; the Mark II suffered from too much weight over the front wheels and low-geared steering, E-Types would go all feathery at the front and wriggly at the back at very high speeds, the V12 E was essentially unbalanced, and never a favourite of mine, and they also suffered terribly from water ingress, steaming up, ruining shoes and greatly upsetting females of the species. Also, as Bill himself famously said, the raised roof of the 2+2 E-Type made the cabin look like a conning tower!

But the XJ6… now what a car that was. My favourite Jaguar of all, and Bill's too, as it turns out. The next time I rode with the Jaguar chief was in early 1979 in a 4.2 litre XJ6 Series III, a newly announced model released on exclusive test to *The Auto*. Yes, your man can have one today, said the Jaguar press department to my bibulous boss Murdo Graves, but perhaps he could use it to take Sir William out for the day. His regular driver phoned in sick this morning, and he wants very much to try the new car.

Sir William had observed my arrival between the giant stone gateposts of Wappenbury Hall, and as I turned the damson red car around on its broad asphalt drive, he emerged from his magnificent ivy-clad, country house and locked his front door firmly behind him. He walked with a stick by this time, having suffered at least one stroke, but he nonetheless strode briskly and purposefully across to join me, and having placed the stick in the back, seated himself alongside me looking straight ahead. I had met and indeed interviewed Sir William on many occasions so I was completely unprepared for his opening remark. I thought it would be you, he said. You thrashed that SS you brought to the club that afternoon, and I had to talk to Sir Harold about it (*The Auto*'s ultimate big cheese). My spies saw you tearing back to the club like a madman. I don't want any sort of repeat of that sort of thing while I am in this car, do you understand? Where shall we go? I said, after digesting this astonishing instruction. Just drive, he said.

The 1968 XJ6 was a much better proportioned car than the Mark X, or 420G as it had become, and far more modern than the Mark II. A quite fabulous and luxurious large saloon, in fact, that was improved by the Series II version of late 1973, and now, five and a half years later, had come the Series III at a total cost of more than £7 million. With Sir William in retirement, the third generation XJ had been styled by the Pininfarina studio in Turin. The car had been modernised by a new bodyshell and doors (with flush handles), together with subtle changes to wings and valances et cetera. But the Lyons look had been successfully retained, surviving even the introduction of the obligatory (it seemed in those days) rubber-clad bumpers.

The new car had more glass and a taller cabin, but it was the same overall height as the Series II, and, if anything, it looked lower. Definitely not a conning tower! A triumph, I had thought when I picked it up from Browns Lane half an hour earlier, much as the new Mark II compact saloon had been ten years before. The car had been successfully revitalised, and indeed, it still looks elegant to this day. The 'fully loaded' (as chaps now say) XJ6 in which we were by now bowling along that March morning looked particularly admirable in Damson Red, I had thought, which was why I had chosen it ahead of a Cotswold Yellow example parked alongside, and inside it right now we were cosseted in typical Jaguar wood and leather luxury. The comfortable seats, trimmed in biscuit hide, seemed improved over those of the Series II, the dashboard, while unaltered in layout, had been successfully refreshed, the carpets were rich and thick (like some people I have known!), and on the move it was just so quiet. At 40mph I could hear the minute whirrings of the little electric motor that angled the door mirror as I operated its tiny joystick! Altogether the car was a delight to be in. I revelled in its smoothness, and delighted in driving it on my very fingertips. Had it not been for my intimidating passenger I'm sure I would have found the whole experience most relaxing.

What do you think of it? I asked Sir William. Mercedes, BMW, I have driven them all, he said, even Rolls-Royce, but I have to say I have always preferred our own car. Of course, it was partly my personal creation, and that may sway my judgment, but ultimately I have always found an XJ to be a better driving car. What do you think? I said while its German rivals were perhaps a little cheaper to buy and run (it depended on the model), they somehow lacked the specialness of the Jaguar, which generally came much better equipped. I said a Silver Shadow had to be perfectly set up to match an XJ for ride quality, and that even an ill-maintained, ten-year-old XJ6 in dire need of attention to its steering and suspension would give a superbly smooth ride. He raised an eyebrow at this, but I pressed on. While the XJ12 had famously been called the best car in the world, I continued, less was sometimes more and I still preferred the XJ6 and its

4.2 litre straight six. I don't necessarily disagree with you there, he said, looking me over properly for the first time.

Sir William had retired in the spring of 1972, and since then the Jaguar board had been disbanded and the firm he had founded had been further subsumed into British Leyland. Beset by strikes and problems caused by careless and shoddy workmanship, Jaguar production was now at its lowest ebb since the 1950s. Was he sad about that? I asked. There's a them and us culture that was never there before. It's irksome but no, I can't say I'm sad. His face told another story. We drove along in silence for a while. An estate version of this car would be good for a family, he said finally, especially one with dogs. Hard thing to get right, though. What did I think? I said it was a capital idea.

I know, I said impulsively, shall we call in here. There's motorcycle testing on today I believe. It was a Wednesday and we were passing Mallory Park racing circuit. A good plan, he said. Are you a motorcycling man? Oh yes of course, you're Basil's boy, and there was a de Forte who raced a Douglas on dope on Blackpool Sands (he was referring to my Uncle Bof, I presume). I had the beating of him of course, on my Harley-Davidson.

We arrived during the lunch-break, and after driving on the circuit to get to the infield, we parked next to the paddock cafe and went inside for a warming mug of tea. Barry Sheene, whom I knew from Holborn days, was there, fresh from victory in the Venezuelan Grand Prix the previous weekend. Do you drive a Jaguar young man? Nah, I've got a Roller. Sir William didn't seem to mind. The pinnied battle-axe pouring out mugs of char, a line at a time from a two-handled gallon-sized aluminium teapot asked if there would be anything else. Do you know, I fancy sausage, egg and chips, said Sir William, and the same for my friend here. As we sat wolfing our grub, the steamy cafe filled up with racers and hangers-on, and a marshal parked a new Honda CBX1000 outside our window before coming in for a brew. My word, said Sir William, what a machine. As a regular visitor, I knew the chap, and following introductions he proceeded to explain the technicalities of the Honda six to Sir William before going on to describe riding it. In fact, he said after a while, would you like to try it. You could do a lap or two with some of the senior marshals before we re-open the circuit. That's very kind but I couldn't possibly, or could I?

A helmet and riding kit were found in a jiffy, and soon the Jaguar man was suited and booted and ready to go in the pit-lane. The five bar gate allowing access to the circuit was swung open and my hand on his shoulder signalled it was time to go. Then the half a dozen or so experienced riders set off with their elderly charge for two safe, but brisk laps of the Leicestershire circuit. Sir William returned glowing. Did you realise, he said, we were hitting it up to 100 and more on the straight. Following a word in the right ear (that of top motorcycle racing journalist Christopher James Carter) we then spent two happy hours in the press office, enjoying a birds-eye view of action as motorcycles of many types and sizes hared round the track. Several works teams were in attendance, prior to travelling to Austria for the first European grand prix of the year, as well as some top class privateers.

I'll drive back if you don't mind, said Sir William when we got back to the car after the session ended. Alert, sharp, he drove well despite the gathering dusk, and we made excellent time until coming up behind a slow-moving caravan (aren't they all?) towed by a wheezing Ford Cortina. I expected restricted progress from then on, but very soon, and completely without warning Sir William pulled smartly onto the opposite carriageway and floored the (not very) loud pedal. After taking half a second to gather its skirts, the big car sat down a little at the rear and then verily scorched past the snail-like combo. Lofty England hates caravans, said Sir William as we pulled in neatly ahead of it, the timing having been perfectly judged to avoid alarming or inconveniencing the oncoming traffic. Thinks they should all be banned! Now then de Forte, we had better get a serious move on, because we eat early at the Hall, and my wife will become worried about me if I'm late.

I shouldn't have been surprised he was a fast driver. Back in the early 1950s Lyons had bought a derelict cafe on a clifftop near Salcombe in Devon with panoramic sea views and gun emplacements in the grounds. He had it restored, employed a man to keep the gardens immaculate, and added an outdoor swimming pool. It was called the Bolt, and it became his holiday bolt-hole, where he invited family friends, and 'tame' members of the press. Murdo was invited there once, and said Bill would take everybody out for day trips in a Mark VII. Apparently he cornered it on the door handles.

We chatted about this and that. The XJS V12 of 1975 was not really a sports car, we agreed. More of a GT. It was based on the XJ12, of course, although stiffened up, and after all, it was the product of a mature company whose designers were getting on a bit. What did people expect? Did he still believe in race on Sunday, sell on Monday. Oh yes, Jaguars would be back at Le Mans. What about Le Mans in 1954, I reminded him, when Jaguar was beaten into second place by Ferrari. Hadn't they clearly broken the rules by having too many mechanics on the job? Yes, said Sir William, but he had not wanted to make a fuss. Did he have any regrets at all? What I said went, he admitted, and that slowed things down a bit, and people said I should have borrowed from the bank to expand the business. But better to keep things under my own control, make modest profits and reinvest, than getting into debt, lose my grip and put the company at risk. No de Forte, no real regrets.

Back at the Hall at precisely 6pm, he shook me by the hand and thanked me for a most enjoyable day. I look forward to seeing you again soon, he said as he turned to walk to his front porch, and as he did so I noticed an extra sprightliness about his bearing. For the next few years I took to calling in on Sir William when I had an interesting machine on test, but never without telephoning first. He was quite formal like that. The last time I saw him was a glorious summer day in 1984. I took Martha to buy some flowers for the garden from the nursery business he encouraged his gardener to operate on the Wappenbury Hall estate. He was terribly frail but he took the time to chat. It was almost as if he were saying goodbye. I had admired and respected William Lyons since I was a boy. I'm glad we became friends in the end.

FAREWELL TINA: THE END OF AN ERA
(First published *The Auto* – October 1982)
So, RIP Cortina. The king of the rep-mobiles is dead. Long live the Sierra! Astonishingly, it's over twenty years since we were all agog at the new Ford, named, for apparently no good reason, after the venue of the 1956 Winter Olympics. My goodness, 1962 seems a lifetime ago in some ways, an insignificant scintilla in others, but history records that the model was a roaring success. Despite or because of the slightly lukewarm reception it received from some of my press colleagues, Ford hit their production targets and over a million Mark Is were made in just four years, a figure that speaks for itself. As does the fact that ten times more Cortinas were made than the preceding Ford Consul Classic (how strange it is that even the most mundane cars are being feted as 'classics' nowadays!).

While we're crunching numbers, consider also that the Corsair, first seen in October 1963 and sold alongside the Cortina as a replacement for the Consul, amassed total sales of only around a third of a million, and that in a production period of seven years. One might have forecast that the longer-wheelbase Corsair, with its upmarket interior, later wobble-knocker V4 engine, and unique sharky style would have taken sales from the rather basic and unadventurous 'Tina', but the reverse seems to have been the case. It is to some extent unavoidable, but one of the biggest mistakes a car manufacturer can make is produce models that compete with each other for the same customer. Just ask an observer of the farce that is British Leyland!

That is another story for another time, but to return to Dagenham, Essex in 1962, Ford really needed to churn out at least a thousand Cortinas a week to meet demand, but production capacities were more modest in those pre-robotic days, and Ford couldn't simply transfer production to another country with cheaper, less bolshie workers.

At that time Henry's global spin-offs were all very independent, explaining why Germans were presented with a 'futuristic' Taunus that dragged itself along, rather than shoved, as did the rear-wheel-drive Cortina. Who had the better deal? One mustn't mention the war, but the Taunus 12M (aka P4) was a relative failure. Certainly, few British buyers were tempted, not least because of a UK price some 30 percent up of the Dagenham division's 'big car with small car costs', to quote from the Cortina's advertising spiel. It was also not much to look at, and altogether lacking in style.

By 1966 Tina was showing her age, so Ford pulled off a clever trick. By installing a capacious new body on the same floorpan, the Mark II, as it was christened (a dimbo would search in vain for a Cortina with Mark I badges!), was presented to the populace. It was well received, and the company's accounts were set fair for another four years. The Mark II looked squarer, wider and plainer, but no less handsome. Indeed, many preferred it. It also boasted improved performance, having received reworked versions of Ford's ohv engines. In the Autumn of the following year the Kent crossflow arrived with a five bearing crankshaft. In its day it was a smooth, sweet motor and thoroughly up to its work. The 1200 became a 1300, while the 1500 was boosted to 1600, these changes more than offsetting any extra weight or drag. Indeed, the 'cooking' 1600 could just about clock 100mph in favourable conditions, and was almost indecently sporty for a conveyance of workhorse status.

Just scraping in under the £1,000 barrier, the 1600E (for Executive) was particularly attractive, and it remains so to this day. The 1600E made 88bhp and its lowered suspension was of the same specification as the car's Lotus cousin. Inside, it had leather look seats, thick carpets, and an eyeable wooden fascia, replete with many dials, set off by a smart aluminium spoked steering wheel. Outside, paintwork came in several special colours (knockout in purple!), and its Rostyle wheels, unique to the model at the time, looked splendid too. The stylish 1600E went well, handled well, conferred Kudos upon its owner, and was just as cheap to run and maintain as a standard car. For all the fuss about Lotus Cortinas, the E was a far cheaper and more practical proposition for everyday driving. Dashed clever really.

Unfortunately, my final memory of the Mark II Executive includes an incident I wish could be forgotten. One cold autumnal night in 1980, I was a passenger in a rather battered high mileage example tooling up Motorway Six to sweaty-sock-land. The old girl's transmission had been making some odd noises over the last seventy miles, but according to its owner and driver, an impoverished young journalist called Rod, it had sounded sick for months, so no cause for alarm. But then somewhere near Tebay services, doing about 70mph in the outside lane, from under the floor there came an almighty metallic scrunch. The rear wheels immediately locked and with a shriek of burning tyres the car lurched sideways, then fishtailed wildly along the road in a cloud of smoke, its pop-eyed, panicked pilot frantically doing his best to control the sinuous oscillations. What felt like ten minutes and several miles later, we came to rest, somehow crossing three lanes to the hard standing without contacting either the central barrier or another vehicle. Traffic was a lot less dense in those days, but it was close to a miracle that we were able to emerge from the Ford unscathed, if a little shaky, choking on the acrid stench of smouldering rubber. The two long wavy black lines created by our skid were visible for months to come! Not the car's fault, of course, but hopefully that little digression was less dull than some of this history, which, as Henry Ford allegedly said, is bunk in any case!

The Mark II also sold a million, and in 1970, a new decade brought another new Cortina. The Mark III shared the outgoing model's Kent pushrod engines, but was completely new in all other respects. A wider, longer machine with wishbone front suspension and better secured rear axle, it had a definite American look both inside and out, with what came to be known as 'Coke bottle' sides and sunken dashboard accoutrements. It was the best-handling and steering Cortina yet, but I am afraid I never really liked the Mark III. I forget the exact figure, but, as with the Capri, by juggling with the options list, one had a choice of several thousand, if not a million variations. Alas, they were all horrid, no matter how many sets of headlamps or inorganic wood appendages. Naturally, they still sold like proverbial hot cakes to fleets and private buyers alike, but the impression was that Ford had developed ideas above its station.

In 1974 Betjeman summed it up perfectly in a few lines:

> I am a young executive. No cuffs than mine are cleaner;
> I have a Slimline brief-case and I use the firm's Cortina.
> In every roadside hostelry from here to Burgess Hill
> The maitres d'hotel all know me well and let me sign the bill.
> You ask me what it is I do. Well, actually, you know,
> I'm partly a liaison man, and partly PRO.
> Essentially, I integrate the current export drive
> And basically I'm viable from ten o'clock till five.*

Sons of Uncle Sam were responsible for the new overhead-camshaft Pinto engine, available initially as a 1600 alongside the familiar Kent crossflow, but also as a two litre lump developing close to 100bhp. This gave a top speed of well over 100mph and a 0-60mph sprint in ten and a bit seconds, despite creeping middle age spread. Plenty of speed for Cortina-driving 'executives' to reach their destinations on time (and clean-cuffed, one might suppose). Yes, but the poke came at a price: the Pinto was generally coarse and unpleasant in use –

* 'Executive' from Collected Poems, by John Betjeman © 1955, 1958, 1962, 1964, 1968, 1970, 1979, 1981, 1982, 2001. Reproduced by permission of John Murray, an imprint of Hodder and Stoughton Ltd.

and that was before the camshaft ground itself to oblivion due to oil starvation, which happened to any poor schmuck who took a relaxed attitude to servicing schedules. In fact, it happened sooner or later to even the most mollycoddled examples. The urban 'street' sound of the 1970s was a all too often a clacking chorus of Pinto camshafts.

The Mark III lasted until 1976, when the boxy Mark IV took over. Once again, Ford had cleverly re-bodied an existing platform, but Tina was much more of a global car now, with a good deal of European input. There were strong Taunus links once more, and a 'Cologne' option featured a new 2.3 litre V6, which was a much more refined motor than its raucous smaller cousins. Finally, the 'Mark V' was introduced in August, 1979. Or was it? Although officially called the Cortina 80, many industry bods preferred to continue the sequential chronology. At first glance, the Four and Five looked very similar, but in fact the car was much changed with more glass and subtle changes to virtually all bodywork.

Although 'Ford gives You More' had been a believable claim, selling what looked like the same car a decade after the Mark III launch, while constantly hiking prices, began stretching goodwill, not to mention credibility. The last Cortinas were far from cheap and cheerful, and twenty years after the first 1200cc Cortina rolled out of Dagenham, it was possible to pay £10,000 for the ultimate Mark V. A far cry from the days when one could even buy a special Fleet model, which was so pared down it didn't even have a passenger seat!

Now in late 1982, after a total production run of 4.3 million, its replacement has arrived, and there will be no Mark VI (whatever would the chaps at Bentley have said anyway!). Instead we have the new 'aero' Sierra, which actually isn't really very new mechanically beneath that jelly-mould body. The worst of both worlds, perhaps? Interestingly, the wishbone front end has reverted to struts. No doubt Earle MacPherson would have approved. What do I think of the Sierra? A brave leap forward in some respects, a safe step sideways in others. With the genuinely new front-wheel-drive Mark II Vauxhall Cavalier already established and attracting plenty of orders, I wonder if Ford will have difficulty persuading customers their wacky looking pseudo-Cortina is a better choice. Reckon so. Nevertheless, I will have to clock up some decent mileages in both of them to come to a firm opinion.

ANYONE FOR GOLF?
(First published *The Auto* – April 1984)
The noise made by an errant car colliding with roadside furniture is not pleasant. Inevitably in a long career at the wheel, I have had my fair share of what the racing fraternity call 'offs'. Sometimes I only had myself to blame, but on this

most recent occasion the fault was that of an utter bounder in a Golf GTI – the other Golf GTI, that is, because we both happened to be driving the same type of vehicle, VW's celebrated 'hot hatch'.

The Golf, or Rabbit to US customers, might be compact, but two definitely won't fit through a gap of less than ten feet, particularly when the surface is bumpy and their relative velocity is 100mph. Cue the aforementioned sickening series of sounds, followed by a deafening silence. On a positive note, neither of us was injured, but our motors had fared less well. One was in a muddy ditch, one was in a hawthorn hedge. Both engines still ran, but didn't provide propulsion, so further movement had to be by means of a cable and winch attached to a low loader. The nearside was the battered half in both cases, which reminded me that after launching the GTI for continental markets in 1975, UK customers could only buy LHD cars until 1979, when the steering wheel finally migrated to the right, thanks to a rather Heath-Robinson crossover brake linkage. Had I been in one of these left hookers I would likely have been in hospital, not reporting in *The Auto* on the new Mark II GTI.

For the past few years the roads (and sometimes hedges), have thronged with 'Mark I' GTIs, usually driven at entirely inappropriate speeds by people with large grins and small petrol bills. The example I was driving had to be written off, for which I was truly sorry, although possibly less so than the owner, who understandably might be less enthusiastic about lending me cars in the future.

Post accident, the distinctly under par state of this pair of Golfs suggested that these weren't the strongest of bodyshells. So, although I would heartily recommend a 'Mark I' to almost anyone with a pulse, it seemed that they aren't the most crashworthy cars. In that respect at least, the new Mark II is likely to be significantly better.

But what about the rest? Sadly, on admittedly brief acquaintance, I am not convinced that VW has made much progress. Firstly, the new version lacks the crisp lines of the original, which was styled by an Italian, not an in-house slumberparty. Secondly, the increase in size and weight has sapped away its spirit, no matter the extra horsepower and valves hidden by the humpy dumpy contours. Above all, I grinned a lot less in the Mark II, particularly when I saw the price list. Perhaps if I drove one into a ditch and emerged with a functional car I would appreciate the new solidity, but I'm inclined to think that the Golf has gone off course.

ROVER RETROSPECTIVE
(First published *The Auto* – October 1987)
What's in a name? Quite a lot, so we are to believe. For instance, it has been announced this week that BL, formerly British Leyland, itself the product of

a merger between Leyland-Triumph and British Motor Holdings, is now to be renamed the Rover Group. This, of course, is because Rover is the only remaining marque of the so very many accumulated and recycled by BL over the last 20 years (all once representing proud and independent motor car manufacturers) that now remains largely unsullied. And this is primarily because of the success of the Land Rover and the Range Rover.

My ingenious friend Spen King popped in to see me this morning, and we repaired immediately to the newly opened Taj Mahal in Beedle for a long luncheon. What did he make of it all? Enjoying retirement and glad I'm out of it, was his brusque response. I'm not sure I believed him entirely, but the production line travails of his SD1 executive car have seemingly knocked a lot of the stuffing out of the once brilliant young engineer, and nephew of the sainted Wilks brothers, who joined Rover from Rolls-Royce, aged just 20, in 1945. He worked on the Land Rover and went on to design the Range Rover from scratch, but Spen described building the SD1 as an absurd and surrealistic exercise in turning expensive materials into rubbish. Sadly, British cars simply do not have the inbuilt quality of those of the Japs, he said (prophetic indeed given the events that would unfold in the 1990s!).

Coincidentally, production of the SD1 has recently ceased. It was built at first in a huge extension to Rover's Solihull plant, but the bodies were made badly in Castle Bromwich, and paintwork was the source of terrible problems, frequently cracking during assembly. Later the car was built at Cowley by Austin Morris wallahs, and it became a Leyland product, and not a Rover one at all. Over the years BL succumbed to a progressive loss of vitality and self esteem, and the nationalised behemoth became a national joke. That's what's killing us, said Spen splenetically over the onion bhajis, forgetting for a moment he was no longer on board the sinking ship. Disrespect for the customer. The cars are unreliable and lack quality, but Stokes (Lord Stokes, BL chairman from 1977 – ed) thinks the public are idiots who'll buy anything (clear parallels with the British motorcycle industry here, particularly AMC!). But I tell you he is wrong: people need to feel good about their cars. Rover, on the other hand, did listen to its customers, he insisted, and we were always very keen to design and build our motor cars to the best of our abilities. Then Edwardes (Michael Edwardes, Stokes' successor, who lasted until 1982 – ed) spent all his time focusing on pacifying the troops, and he too ignored the product itself. Another terrible mistake. Another Kingfisher?

I first came across Charles Spencer King at Rover's former shadow factory in Solihull back in 1945, when I was still in uniform. Aero components of many kinds had been made there, and Spen was part of a small team working on a gas turbine project which resulted in the JET1 car, and engines for more than one aircraft. Rover, of course, had made a fully functioning jet turbine aircraft engine way back in 1941, which I had glimpsed propelling a prototype aeroplane to a then quite incredible 466mph during secret trials over the Lincolnshire flatlands (even TE Lawrence and Boanerges would not have kept up!). What would have happened, I often wonder, if Frank Whittle, such a difficult character, and so reluctant to give others credit, hadn't gone behind Rover's back to ensure Rolls-Royce were given the contract to continue its development. No matter. As you might expect, the heads of the two distinguished British companies conducted themselves with impeccable decorum. Rolls-Royce's Ernest Hives gave Spencer Wilks his Nottingham tank engine factory in return for taking over one of Rover's two jet engine facilities (secreted in a former textile mill in Barnoldswick in deepest Lancashire), and the arrangement was sealed by the two men with a simple handshake in a pub. Interesting that it was Rover's designs, not Whittle's that were developed by Rolls-Royce for the Gloster Meteor, and laid the foundations for all that followed.

The first post-war Rover motor cars were essentially the same as the company's pre-war ones, both mechanically and bodily, but the 1948 P3, featured numerous mechanical improvements, and the Studebaker-inspired P4 range announced in late 1949, which replaced the retrospectively-named P3 after just two years, was altogether new and rather radical in appearance. But naturally, as a driving machine, the P4 remained the epitome of automotive good manners. It was still a time when cars said more about their owners than their jobs. A 1950s Rover still spoke of understatement, discreet comfort, silence, and safety; not speed, and most definitely not flamboyance. It was the car of the professional man, and its reputation was hard-earned, not shaped by slick publicity. The P4's American look drew a cool response at first, but this was soon toned down by the removal of its central 'Cyclops' passing light, and further ameliorated by the addition of chromium headlamp bezels and other adornments. It became a sales success, and remained in production until 1963, although it must be remembered that in the middle-late 1950s Ford and BMC made half the cars sold in Britain, with Rover selling just 12,000 units a year, not counting Land-Rovers.

The larger, Rover P5 – at first known as the Three Litre – had a similarly long and remarkable production life, spanning the years 1959 to 1973, with a total of 70,000 cars manufactured. The P4's inlet over exhaust engine was beefed up and bored out to 2995cc for deployment in the early cars, raising its power output to 115bhp @ 4,250rpm. Then in 1963 a Weslake head boosted performance a little further, but Solihull still didn't have a Jaguar beater in its stable. The P5 was a big luxury saloon aimed at buyers who did not want to stoop to get in and out of a car. It was cheaper than a big Jag Mark IX or X, but it ran out of puff at 90, while the Jags would pull an easy ton. A solution was required, and when in-house experiments came to naught, a happy accident of my making would see Rover turn to Detroit and adopt V8 power. Funny old world!

A likeable young designer called David Bache, the son of a famous footballer, and formerly a student apprentice at Austin, had joined Rover in the early 1950s, specifically to mollify Rover's more conservative customers by modifying the appearance of the P4, but without huge cost. Having succeeded well in this, he was then given the job of styling the P5, both inside and out. Inside, the driver sat behind a large, thin steering wheel typical of the era, through which the instruments could be observed, sited neatly in a large and chunky black binnacle. Across the entire bulkhead, he specified a wide walnut dash panel, which ran atop a capacious under-shelf. The seats were of deeply pleated leather, the carpets of deep pile, and the result was altogether pleasing and classical in style. I liked it.

On the move, however… Most P5s were built with Borg-Warner automatics, ubiquitous in the industry, of course, but my first test victim was fitted with Rover's glacially-slow manual box, an appalling mid-1930s design with no synchromesh on its first two ratios. It got worse. Axle tramp restricted fast getaways, and long-wave bumps set the confounded thing hopping wildly; steering was heavy (power steering fitted from 1961 onwards was lifeless and peculiarly weighted), and tyre squeals were an embarrassment in town. On the open road it would pitch alarmingly, understeer like a battleship, and body roll was a limiting factor when really pressing on. The P5 was a monocoque, but Rover built a mini chassis for the engine, transmission, and front suspension, determined to keep the car quiet at all costs. But despite this, and close attention to tyre design, sound damping, and engine silencing, the dratted thing was still noticeably noisier than an Auntie Rover.

The P6 was an innovative and novel medium-sized car for which Peter Wilks, Spen King and David Bache can all claim a degree of credit. The model was decided upon in 1958, and arrived in late 1963, by which time Spencer Wilks had retired, and dear Maurice had died, although he had had a hand in the car's early development, and tested a P4-bodied mule that was running around in the mid 1950s (I tried it too, apparently, but that memory is lost!). I do recall a strange-looking test car badged up as a Talago with headlamps in pods and no visible grille. The name was intended to gull the curious into thinking it was some sort of utterly unobtainable Italian thing, said Spen, and various patents were filed under a Polish name to keep snoopers off the scent.

Monocoque construction was the future, but noise suppression and a level ride were always Rover's core values and this posed Spen and co a problem. Built up tubs are noisy sounding boards, so chief chassis man Gordon Bashford designed a pressed steel skeleton, to which the car's mechanical components and body panels were attached. As with the P5's sub-frame, this base body idea was a good compromise, but it added a good deal of weight. The skeleton was intended to be rust resistant and long-lasting so the bolt-on body panels could be replaced in the event of corrosion, but sadly the deadly tin worm attacked from the inside as well as from without. At least crash repairs were simplified, and future styling changes could be accommodated without great fuss or difficulty. In production, the outer body would be added last, and it was amusing to see cars test driven around the works without wings, outer sills, doors, bonnets and boots, let alone grilles lights, and bumpers.

Rover's old six was finally jettisoned, and replaced by an all-new engine and gearbox combination. The two-litre, four-cylinder, overhead-camshaft, heron-type motor with a five bearing crank and aluminium head was as advanced as anything around, but it was a bit clattery from cold, disappointingly harsh altogether, and sadly lacking in urge. It took an absolute age to drag the new car up to the ton. To please a government becoming concerned about unemployment in the valleys (such different times!), Rover tooled up and built their new gearbox in a new factory on a disused airfield and former speed testing facility near Cardiff in South Wales. Like the arrangement, the unit was far from perfect, but it was positive, at least, and all-synchro at last. The P6 was well-made and clever engineering touches abounded. Indeed, it was the first ever car of the year, and it got my vote despite *The Auto*'s editor suggesting we should all back Rootes' Hillman Imp.

The Rover P6 was comfortable and well mannered, with handling, roadholding, braking and stability all top drawer. The front suspension was designed so stresses were fed back into the car's base body, and together with the wheel location and steering arrangement, it allowed for a big, clear engine bay. The idea was to accommodate larger engines in the future (a good thing as we shall see), and even a gas turbine version was envisaged. At the rear, a beautifully engineered de Dion axle featured a sliding joint to accommodate wheel movement, and inboard brakes. The car was tastefully furnished inside, with wood and leather to please traditionalists, yet thoroughly modern and appealing to the young executive, for whom it was specifically intended. It had a strip speedo (later deemed unfashionable and changed, but I rather liked it), a height-adjustable steering column (rare then), a centre console (so terribly modern) and voluminous storage compartments or 'shin bins' under the dashboard. Ergonomics was a new discipline and David Bache embraced it. Switches were shaped according to usage, and multi-purpose stalks projected from behind the steering wheel. The upholstery was handsome and supportive, and shaped rear seats sent the message: four in comfort, five's a squeeze!

It looked sharp, and drove like no other Rover, but the new box was a bit whiny, as were its new radial tyres, and its engine was gruff and coarse. Again, the P4 was quieter. A twin carburettor version was made ready for the 1966 Geneva Show that was a tad faster, but it made the car more raucous and thirsty still. Pater would definitely not have approved, just as he would have struggled to come to terms with the lamb madras and chicken bangladesh that had us glowing slightly at this point in proceedings. Two more Kingfishers if you please.

By that time industry unrest and upheaval had resulted in Rover being sucked helplessly into BL where, by 1971, the year dear old Spencer Wilks popped his clogs, its engineering department would be combined with that of arch-rival Triumph, and Spen was made its chief. He would have an input on the Triumph TR7, but there was no Rover P7, and Jaguar joining the combine in 1968 killed the P8 at an early stage. Just as well, said Spen, it was just a bloated, vainglorious attempt to acquire prestige. If you try to make something grandiose rather than good, you're barking up the wrong tree entirely.

So it was a good job that partly thanks to me, Spen and his men had an aluminium V8 ready to rumble by then, a fine engine that with relatively minor alterations fitted perfectly under the P6's bonnet, and kept it in production until 1977. Spen also designed a sports car powered by the V8, but that fell foul of Jaguar too. Bill Lyons objected.

Back in 1962, at my suggestion, Rover's William Martin-Hurst visited Carl Kiekhaefer's Mercury Marine concern at Fond du Lac, Wisconsin. He was looking for a partner to develop his gas turbine engines for marine applications, and I thought Kiekhaefer might fit the bill. The rest is well known. While in the Mercury works, Bill spotted an aluminium V8 languishing in a corner of the experimental department that had been tried in a racing boat. It was a Buick, no longer being made by General Motors, but which had been used to propel three-quarters of a million cars including many Pontiacs and Oldsmobiles. Back home, a cast iron straight six was in development for the P6, but it was long and extremely heavy, and early road tests were not especially encouraging. The Buick was compact, less than an inch wider than Rover's new four, and it would likely drop into the engine bay of the P5 as well as the forthcoming P6. Furthermore, it was only 12lb heavier than Rover's four. Aha! thought Bill, the aluminium V8 could be a solution to a lot of problems.

After picking up a bit of handy business supplying Land-Rover diesel engines to Mercury for adaptation for use in Chinese fishing junks, Bill beetled off to the New York Motor Show to meet up with GM bigwigs and try to strike a deal. Meanwhile, Kiekhaefer agreed to ship the Buick engine to Solihull. Bill learned the aluminium V8 was surplus to requirements at GM because the giant had developed iron V8 blocks that were almost as light, and much cheaper to produce. A 200bhp version of the aluminium engine had been developed, but it was expensive, suffered problems with oil and coolant sealing, and it clogged radiators when owners used incompatible antifreeze. The iron block version went on until 1980, but the aluminium engine had just gone out of production. At that time V8s were not a popular choice among European motor manufacturers. The 90 degree 6.2 litre V8 in the Rolls-Royce Cloud II built from 1959 onward had an aluminium block, but only because they lacked the expertise to make it out of iron, and then there was Edward Turner's surprisingly sporty Daimler 2.5, which used Triumph motorcycle pistons.

It took two years for Rover to come to an agreement with GM, with a manufacturing licence finally being granted in 1965, but while negotiations continued, Rover set about modifying the design for their purposes, adding press-fit cast iron liners, sand-diecast heads, twin SU carburettors, and a Lucas distributor. The engine's designer, Joe Turlay came over to help with this. An old hand, with around 40 years' experience, his input was priceless. Not many people realise a version of the same engine developed by Jack Brabham won the world F1 championship in 1966 and 1967, but the Rover variant was detuned to just 160bhp on the bench. Consequently it was hugely understressed, but nonetheless made terrific torque. Machining processes were carried out at the former Alvis factory which Rover had taken over in 1965, while assembly took place at Acocks Green, the former shadow factory where the Meteor tank version of the Rolls-Royce Merlin engine had been made, and where I had spent many happy days in the 1950s working with Rover's technical film unit.

At last! A post-war Rover that was not underpowered. The V8 transformed the performance of the P6, and David Bache added tweaks to keep the car fresh and acknowledge its change of character. In the P5 too, as a replacement for the three litre, it was just wonderful. Around 200lb lighter, it solved the car's chronic understeer problems at a stroke. Moreover, the P5B (for Buick) was 10mph quicker than the six and got there in barely more than half the time. Borg-Warner automatic transmissions were used in both cars, with manual boxes not being mated to the V8 until 1971.

As a colleague of mine once wisely opined, a Land-Rover's suspension is designed for the longevity of the vehicle, not the comfort of its passengers. In fact, Rover once suggested washing one's smalls on safari by putting them in a sealed drum with water and washing powder, and placing the container over the rear axle. After 100 miles of off-road travel, the contents would be sufficiently agitated for the clothes to have been thoroughly cleaned! But the Range Rover, which was launched in 1970, was an altogether different kettle of Y-fronts: a luxury Land-Rover that would be as good on the road as off it; a tough, dual-purpose machine capable of 90mph motorway cruising and decorous town driving, as much as horse box hauling and serious off-roading. Spen styled the aluminium body – reputedly drawing it up on a sheet of notepaper in five minutes flat – as well as being responsible for its overall engineering; while Gordon Bashford designed its separate chassis; and David Bache found time to add a few deft external touches, while laying out its smart, yet practical, saloon car appointments. Under the bonnet, of course, was Rover's ex-Buick V8.

King and the gang got it right first time. The Range Rover was something altogether new, and quite simply brilliant. It remained largely unchanged for ten years, and it is still sold today (a remarkable enough fact when this was written in 1987, more astonishing still that it is still sold to this day! – ed). The Range Rover had a lovely simple shape, not at all pretentious in any way, and while it was a comfortable performance saloon car, it was also a highly practical one for the discerning farmer or estate owner. It was a masterful cross country machine, all-conquering and able to keep itself on the level on its long-travel coil spring suspension; it could come with winches and other accessories; its rubber covered floor could be hosed out; its big door handles could be opened by gloved hands; the trim was extremely hard-wearing; and while the seats looked like leather, they were, in fact, tough, washable plastic. All it lacked was quietness: its dual-purpose Michelins were quite marvellous on-road and off, but one can't have everything: they hummed more than a little at high speeds. Despite this, I am sure Pater would have heartily approved of what was perhaps Spen's most marvellous creation.

As we drove home through the lanes, Spen fell into deep thought. The Range Rover did suffer from some quality control problems, but it was so good it transcended them, he said finally, and with characteristic frankness as we arrived back at the farm. I always considered it very much a product of the old Rover company, rather than BL. Perhaps I shouldn't be so hard on myself about the SD1. It sold well in the early days, and given the labour relations problems we had, it was a minor miracle it was as good as it was. Indeed. While I suppose I have always been something of a champagne socialist, there is no doubt the obtuse belligerence and short-sighted bloody-mindedness of the BL workforce contributed greatly to the poor quality of its products, and the company being held in such low esteem among the car-buying general public.

SPEN

It was fully dark when I waved Spen off to his magnificent restored manor house in Cubbington, near Leamington Spa, after coffee at the farm that evening. Tell him to come again, I told his wife, Moyra a few minutes later when I telephoned ahead on his behalf to tell her he was on his way (of course, I knew her well from decades past when she had been Peter Wilks' secretary). I will Wilby, she said. He's thinking of buying a motorcycle. I'm sure he will be round to see you when he does.

Well, it was 2000 before Spen finally got round to buying a motorcycle, but call round again he did, and we went on several long rides together after that. He would din my ear during coffee breaks about poor visibility in modern cars due to huge window and door pillars, and he would be ruthlessly scathing about the idiocy of Chelsea Tractor drivers who bought the now quite vulgarian, high fashion Range Rover as a status symbol (he was right on both counts, of course). He died a year after Moyra, following a fall from his bicycle in 2010. More good folk gone.

ALFA ROMEO ALFASUD
(First published *The Auto* – December 1992)
The Hillman Imp and the Alfa Romeo Alfasud have a good deal in common. Now before devotees of both cars blow a fuse and rush off in search of Parker Duofolds and Basildon Bond, hell-bent on writing to *The Auto*'s letters page regarding this absurd and ridiculous assertion, let me endeavour to explain. Of course, even the most clueless motorist can appreciate the difference between a rear-engined, rear-wheel-drive British car, and a front-engined, front-wheel-drive Italian one, but that is not the point I am making. My contention concerns the fact that both cars had broadly similar beginnings, in that they had much to do with politics.

When, in 1960, good old Rootes decided to take on the Mini with the Imp, they already had five plants in the south and midlands, but a new government-backed factory was built up in Bonnie Scotland to provide much needed gainful employment for the veritable army of Jocks displaced from the rapidly sinking Clydeside shipbuilding industry. And in the later 1960s, when Alfa Romeo of Milan decided they needed a new, modern car, they too were aided by a national government to build a new factory at the other end of the country in an attempt to revive a depressed area. The other end of the country in this case was Naples, which is in the south of Italy, and the Italian word for south is, incredibly enough, 'sud'!

Traditional Alfas featured longitudinally-mounted twin-cam engines with lots of carburettors, driving the rear wheels. The coming of front-wheel-drive cars in all shapes and sizes during the '60s made these devices look distinctly old-fashioned. The packaging and space utilisation advantages of front-wheel-drive could easily be ascertained by anyone who tried to swing a cat in an Austin 1800 after attempting the same sadistic feat in a Cambridge made by the same company. Aerodynamics was another consideration (although the deceptively boxy Alfa saloons were actually very slippery customers), the way forward being in the fastback-with-chopped-tail style, it was generally accepted.

Then what about an engine? The faithful old twin-cam four could probably have been adapted and shoe-horned in somehow, but the Alfasud was designed as a whole, and a flat-four was the only type of power unit that fitted in perfectly with the overall concept. Engines with horizontal cylinders have their disadvantages, of course, generally costing more to make and being wider (assuming they're mounted across the car). The first of these apparent drawbacks bothers the bean-counters, but the second is of no great consequence when weighed against the various benefits of flatness. Although wide across its cylinders, a horizontally opposed engine will likely be shorter and lower than an in-line one. This helps to lower the centre of gravity of the car receiving it, reducing frontal area, and aiding air penetration into the bargain. It also means it can be mounted further forward, which increases cabin space for the occupants.

Alfa made their decision, and ex-Porsche man, Rudolf Hruska, did the designing. Belt-driven cams sat atop each pair of cylinders, which were fed by a single carburettor situated at the head of long inlet tracts – hardly ideal, but a logical twin-carb arrangement did arrive eventually. Very much over-square at 80 x 59mm bore and stroke, the first 1.2 litre Sud developed a claimed 63bhp. Alfa's engineers made intelligent use of the engine's shortness by incorporating two bulkheads in the scuttle, a clever feature which stiffened the structure, isolated mechanical noise and gave the battery and other ancillaries a clean and cool environment in which to spend their days. A four-speed gearbox was used originally, but five cogs came on later models, starting with the 5M in the mid 1970s. Bolted right next to the transmission were the front discs, a move that reduced unsprung weight compared with their more usual location at the wheels, although making routine maintenance work more of a palaver.

Front suspension duties were taken care of by MacPherson struts, set with a fair degree of macho negative camber to increase roadholding and impress informed onlookers. At the rear end things were pretty simple too, with nothing more high-tech than a dead axle to be found underneath the floorpan, although an extremely positive location, courtesy of Panhard rods and Watts linkage, ensured the wheels were kept pointing in the right direction at least as well as with any independent alternatives. Disc brakes were used at the back, a feature of mixed benefit in the long term, because they tended to be so underworked that they gradually seized up.

Despite appearances, it wasn't a hatchback... yet. The bodyshell was a natty little number from Giorgetto Giugiaro that was quite aerodynamically efficient for the time, even if it did make the car look disturbingly like an Austin Allegro from certain angles. Interior space was impressive, accommodating five adults quite adequately, but the first cars were rather plasticky inside, lacking even carpets.

Production started in mid-1972, but right-hand-drive cars didn't reach Britain until the following summer. My views at the time and those of my contemporaries all concur. The handling was incredible, the finish was lousy and although the engines were smooth and balanced, more power would bring about improvement. After a year, some of these prayers were answered by the Ti model, a mildly tuned and slightly more luxurious version with five gears, distinguished externally by twin headlights and only two quick-to-droop doors. Along with bigger engines in the later 1970s came the option of the pretty Sprint bodyshell, another stylish Giugiaro creation, which disappointed by offering cramped accommodation, and much the same performance as the relatively dumpy saloons.

The logical appearance of a carburettor on each bank of cylinders made the Sprint Veloce the fastest Sud yet, and this engine later featured in the ultimate Green Cloverleaf saloons of 1983. This was the end for the standard Sud, supplanted by the 33 (basically a rebodied version of the same thing), but the Sprint carried on for another five years, finally gaining a 1712cc engine for its final incarnation.

Around 900,000 Suds were made altogether, in an eleven year production run. In the UK, total sales were around 37,000 – a small number, and of these only a microscopically tiny proportion still exist. Let's get one thing straight: the Alfasud, however inspired and wonderful its handling and performance, was an absolute disgrace for the way it rusted. Some Suds were already flaking by the time they left the showrooms, and there were various reasons for this. First, the quality of the steel (apparently of Russian origin, and presumably discarded by the Russkies as not even good enough to make Moskviches) was appalling, and secondly, corrosion-prevention measures were either non-existent or so ineffective as to actually accelerate the rotting process where water-retaining foam was injected into box-sections. This sodden foam also hampered future attempts at rectification, incidentally, sending hapless welders fleeing because, believe it or not, it was inflammable, even in a saturated state!

If any would-be restorer reading this wants to know where an Alfasud rusts, I can tell them the answer is 'everywhere', with the possible exception of the tyres and seat cushions. The only original '70s example likely to be still un-rusted is one that has been stored in a giant bag of silica gel all its life. This is not an overstatement of the severity of a problem, which makes a car like the Austin 1100 seem like a paragon of structural integrity. Things improved a little from about 1981 onwards, when the Alfasud III arrived, a mildly facelifted hatchback version, made out of better metal and benefiting from a few dabs of wax and underseal.

As for joy of ownership, mechanical problems were usually relatively minor.

The engine was basically strong and reliable, though when things did go wrong it tended to cost a fair bit of time and money to fix. Generally, the bigger the engine, the more strained and short-lived was it existence. The gearbox was not the slickest nor the quietest, but kept working well enough, though the synchro was inclined to vanish, and a rattle at idle was normal.

Inside, the trim and fittings became increasingly lavish as time went by, the early air of wall-to-wall plastic going in favour of cloth and carpets, although none of it was of fine quality, and most things warped, fell off, split or turned to dust in a depressingly short space of time. Some of the electrics could be troublesome, too. Well, what else would you expect of a car with its heater fan operated by what the rest of the world thinks should be an indicator stalk?

ALGY'S ALFASUD
When it comes to Alfasuds I can speak from experience, although thankfully, once removed. It was late September 1979 and my perennially potless pal Algy needed new wheels, his latest hair-shirt heap having been towed off to the scrappers following a prognosis by Colin Haynes (diagnosed with much head shaking while it underwent pre-inspection on his ramp at the garage in Bales) of acute and unavoidable MoT failure due to chronic chassis corrosion.

Having purchased that day's editions of *Exchange & Mart* and the *Shrops Auto Trader* following a morning walk across the fields to Maynard's in Beedle, Algy returned to the village with an optimistic spring in his step, arriving for lunchtime opening at the Rose & Crown. Settling himself down by the fireside, he laid open a packet of Golden Wonder on the table, took a first sip of his pint, and, red pen in hand, began surveying his very limited options. At 3pm, two very slow pints later, he finally found the bargain he was looking for: a practical, five-year-old saloon that drove and sounded like a sports car for just £800. How could one resist? It was, of course, an Alfasud. After returning home and carrying out his usual careful inspection routine over the telephone, he bought it. And so keen was the seller for someone else to start enjoying his Italian stallion straight away, he came up from Shrewsbury that evening with a pal, and by 10pm the car was Algy's.

Naturally, it was the colour that all thoroughbred Italian sports cars should be, the lurid hue that stirs the soul of the tifosi. Um... beige. Oh well, at least it didn't look too rusty, I thought, as I surveyed it for the first time, covered in a million tiny beads of moisture, the following dewy autumn morning. In fact, it positively gleamed, a low mileage example of the original four-speeder with a slightly musty interior featuring swathes of sweating plastic. What's more, it had an MoT. But sadly one that would soon expire. It ran out at Halloween, I recall. With an involuntary shiver, I hoped its visit to Haynes for a replacement wouldn't be the stuff of nightmares.

A run up the road was encouraging. Good cling and an all of a piece feeling, despite the dampness and front tyres that had clearly seen better days, coupled with responsiveness, eagerness, and that indefinable readiness to rev which distinguishes a happy engine. But the brakes pulled a bit, and wasn't it a bit noisy? Back at the farm I peeled back the mats fore and aft to views of gravel and grass underneath. Further inspection showed the suspension mounts were perilously close to further holes, and general crumbliness abounded in the inner wings. Algy emerged from the house carrying steaming cups of char. Bad news old chap, I'm afraid.

It got worse. An attempt to secure 13 months' MoT (a nice trick if you are about to sell) saw us beetle straight round to Haynes' Garage. 'Brake pipes, mate... rustier than the *Titanic*,' said Colin, wiping a nasty cut on his hand. Alfasuds hide their brake pipes in rather inaccessible places somewhere behind the fuel tank. Inboard discs brakes are marvellous from an engineering point of view, but do tend to be tricky blighters in real life. Ask a Citroën mechanic! For one thing, it's difficult to get at brakes when they're surrounded by other bits, and in the second place the gearbox or axle living nearby tends to spray its oil onto them, which is not really ideal.

Where was I? Oh yes. Sadly new pipery and vigorous bleeding (hydraulics and Colin's hands) failed to cure the Alfa's tendency to dive for the scenery upon application of its anchors (question: why is that brake imbalances don't seem to show up on the rollers that replaced the supposedly unscientific Tapley road test meter of yore?), but this pipework, two new tyres and a day and a half's welding allowed our venerable village mechanic to deem Algy's beautiful Italian thoroughbred fit for ministry approval. Incidentally, as my poor pal was totally boracic and struggling even to pay the rent, I footed the bill for this remedial work. That's what friends are for, don't you know. Besides, it meant I could borrow it from time to time between test victims.

With new rubber at the front end, I expected superb handling to be manifest, but the Alfasud's standard tyres were quite avant garde, low-profile jobs for their time, so naturally enough the local tyre suppliers didn't have the correct size. Unwisely, I authorised fitment of some slightly larger boots instead, and I remember testing the car at Colin's behest, thinking what a dreadful mistake I'd made. Those things gripped about as well as a greasy sausage in a polytetrafluoroethylene frying pan, or vice versa. But within fifty miles, the waxiness had rubbed off, and they began sticking to the road with impressive tenacity, possibly even improving the handling balance of a car with a large share of its weight over its front wheels.

It has been whispered that Italian cars don't like the rain, and this was perfectly correct in the case of Algy's Sud, which showed a distinct reluctance to fire up of a morning after a cold, damp winter's night on the drive. Fitting a set of new plugs and points turned out to be a more involved business than usual, and Algy requested my assistance. Removing the commendably accessible sparkers uncovered some decidedly odd-looking devices featuring multiple electrodes, and a subsequent phone call to our friendly local(ish) Alfa dealer confirmed that Gold Lodges were the only things to put in a Sud engine, and that to do otherwise risked holed pistons and a ruinous repair bill. So I took his advice and bought Algy a new set of apparently 24-carat sparking plugs. Starting was transformed – it now fired up on the fifty-fifth attempt instead of the seventy-fifth on moist and chilly mornings.

With all this under its bonnet, I could at least console myself with the thought that I had played my part in preserving one of the few non-rusty Alfas in captivity. As winter turned to spring, the engine even began starting reliably from cold, and I would regularly see Algy and Myrtle happily pootling off doing whatever it was they did of a morning, giving me a cheery wave as they passed the farm.

Ah, the sun, the warmth, the budding of nature... and the budding of front wings? As the days were stretching towards the end of June, I was walking back from the Rose & Crown early one evening in pale golden sunlight, having deposited my column for next month's *Auto* in the postbox opposite, when I paused to consider the Alfa, and its true and rightful place in the great and wonderful scheme of things. That was when I first noticed little bubbles were appearing on its previously pristine front wings. And as the summer days became ever warmer and the sun got hotter, I observed the bubbles getting bigger, and joining together into ominous-looking pustules. Then, one August Sunday afternoon of about 80 degrees Fahrenheit, these misshapen boils could contain themselves no longer, and, one by one, they burst, crying streams of rusty red water down the car's pale flanks. Underneath these multiple eruptions there was revealed some peculiar mixture of filler and ferrous oxide, and only minimal traces of real and unblemished metal. The car was a rust bomb waiting to explode.

By this time other causes of grief were visiting themselves upon us. Any synchromesh that had ever existed on the two lower gears had mysteriously vanished, so much cog crunching ensued if you weren't a dab foot at double de-clutching (Algy wasn't). There was also a constant buzz from the linkage below the lever, which I found out was endemic, but easily curable by replacing a bush (presumably a burning one lit with a handful of my five pound notes). Failing window winders were another constant joy of early Alfasuds. The mechanism was simply not up to the job. The choice lay between a new winder or a soggy seat and a tanned right elbow, because once the window had dropped into its den it was difficult to retrieve. As was common, Algy eventually broke the glass trying.

So, plenty of pain. What about the gain? Well, the legendary handling was fact, not fiction, as I have already alluded, and the car could corner as fast as one dared without any more drama than a faint squeal from the front tyres. It seemed to oversteer rather than understeer, like most front-drivers, the rear end drifting controllably while the pilot treated himself to that characteristic musicality of the exhaust. Enjoyable too was a delicious and distinctive pop-poppety-popping on the overrun. Also worthy of praise was the ride comfort. Despite a fairly basic set of suspenders, the smoothness and freedom from thumps and bumps was impressive. It wasn't very fast on paper, being the single-carb 1186cc version, but it managed to get us to places fairly quickly, nevertheless.

Sadly, the place most Suds got to very quickly indeed was the scrapyard, and by the look of the front wings and some other parts of its anatomy, Algy's looked destined to be joining its friends in the queue for the crusher sooner rather than later. I persuaded him to get rid of it while its MoT ticket still had a month or two to run, and then to be sure to invite me along with him to the Rose & Crown the next time he sat down there to choose a new set of wheels.

A MINI MUSTANG FOR THE MASSES
(First published *Classic Auto* – January 2002)

The motoring world was a simple place back in the '60s, full of simple people buying simple cars for simple reasons. Fords had always been built on the principle that there was no point in designing something complicated if it cost more to make, and in any case wouldn't be appreciated by a rep en route to his next commission. Essentially, all the average Joe Soap and his fleet manager cared about was whether he got there, and that if anything did break, it would be easy and cheap to fix. Style, or advanced engineering features like independent rear suspension, didn't mean much to a committed Ford man.

Then along came the original Classic-Capri of 1962. As if to prove the theory that Ford were messing with things they didn't understand, this car was rather short-lived, and failed to inspire hearts, minds or wallets. However, over in America a sporty number called the Mustang, released in 1964, did a whole lot better.

So, the stage was set for a European version on the same theme, a half-decent looking compact coupe that would persuade drooling marketing victims to part with more to buy a car that gave them less. Enter, stage left, the new Ford Capri, 'The Car You Always Promised Yourself.' Long bonnet, fastback style, and those hockey stick curves! For a mere £860, a Capri owner could make the ladies go weak at the knees and be the envy of the chap next door.

The new star was to be built in Germany and Britain, with differing engines and suspension settings to suit national tastes, and the production lines began rolling in 1968 so a reasonable supply of cars would be in showrooms for launch the following year. Although squat styling, and a mean and macho image was a new departure for a European Ford, under the skin the Capri was still basically an iron-age device, and those who cared to peer under the long and bulging bonnet expecting to uncover a throbbing V8 were ever so dreadfully disappointed as there was enough unused space in the engine bay to park a Fiat 500.

The bottom of the range model was in fact an altogether rather silly car, its weedy 1300cc 'Kent' engine developing about as much power as an American Mustang's windscreen wiper. Slower than a scissor-grinder's handcart, a vehicular mastodon it most definitely was not. Next up came the 1300GT, with Weber carburation, but only the two litre V4 variant (as seen in Corsairs, Transits and roadside clouds of steam throughout the land) could crack the ton, and then only by a few miserable mph. Those expecting tyre-smoking performance to match the Capri's aggressive mien were in for a disappointment.

The famed 3000 V6, which finally delivered the power to match the appearance, came later in 1969. This 'Essex' motor had already been seen in big Fords, but in Capri guise it was beefed up to cope with expected boy-racer use. At the same time, the bodyshell was stiffened, and the springs, brakes and retail price were all uprated accordingly. Run against a stopwatch the three-litre's figures were hardly shattering (0-60 in just over ten seconds, and a top speed of maybe 115mph) but it sounded quick, looked fine, and had young road testers dribbling down their kipper ties with excitement. For about £1,340 you could be the proud owner of a car that belched and burbled like a mini-Mustang should.

There were detail changes in 1972 and a roll bar replaced the rear suspension's upper locating links, although without improving the rear end's capriciousness (sorry!). The 3000 was by then credited with 138bhp and its gearbox had been updated to the German type with simplified change mechanism and better action. A top speed of 122mph was now available to the lawless. The only major change made to the Capri during its seventeen year life came in the middle of a fuel crisis in February 1974, when the hatchback version was launched. The car's profile remained similar, but the bodyshell was altered extensively in the course of gaining another door, increasing in width, height and weight. Middle-age flab was creeping up on our once lean hero. The car's distinctive hockey stick mouldings and air vents disappeared, and the waistline now dipped around the doors. At least the low-slung occupants could see where they were going! Ford claimed their new hatchback held three times as much luggage, boasted 14 per cent more glass area, and used two thousand new parts. How could we not believe them, but it wasn't a beautiful car.

Ford had acquired the Ghia coach-building firm of Turin in 1970, and were keen to stick this distinguished badge on tarted up versions of all their cars as part of the corporate strategy to move 'the brand' (is it only me who thinks this word needs to be rested for at least a decade?) upmarket. Ghia Capri came with sunroofs, deep-pile carpets, and cloth trim, these items still clearly being classed as luxuries.

By 1975, the true meaning of 'GT' had been lost in the mists of time and some new designation had to be dreamed up to get fleet buyers salivating. It was decided 'S' was the thing to have written on one's boot, but by 1977 the Capri had begun to slide down the sales charts and early the following year the third incarnation was released in an attempt to get a few more years out of the old bus. Although Ford talked of lowered drag coefficients and longer service intervals, they could not disguise the car's basic antiquity in the face of new-generation front-wheel-drive competitors like VW's exciting new Scirocco. Ford prices had been escalating rapidly for some years, and the only way a Capri could look good value, mph-per-pound, was in comparison with a Reliant Robin. Rumours were rife of the model's demise, but the old stager made it into the '80s in surprisingly good health.

Modifications continued to be made, with all sorts of important performance aids such as matt black bumpers and checked seats adding exponentially to its appeal. However, the most significant (and final) evolutionary step was in 1981, when the 2.8 Injection hit the streets. It was ten years before that a team from Ford's Advanced Vehicle Operations department had produced the high performance, limited edition RS2600 and RS3100 Capris, versions which had dominated saloon car racing in the early 1970s, and the 2.8i was developed by the very same engineers, led by that seafaring mastermind, Rod Mansfield. The Ford Germany 2.8 unit, which spun up to over 6,000rpm and produced 150bhp, proved potent enough to urge the fairly aerodynamic Capri to the naughty side of 130mph. This startling speed might have been a dangerous liability, but some changes to the suspension and footwear improved the car's handling immensely.

Coincidentally, Alfa Romeo had recently launched their own V6-engined coupe, the GTV6, and road test comparisons between the sophisticated Italian and basic Brit were inevitable. On the face of it, the overhead cam, de Dion rear suspension Alfa should have walked all over the primitive Ford with its single-leaf live axle and thrashing pushrod engine, but somehow, it didn't quite happen like that. Enthusiasts everywhere had to admit that the Capri went faster, handled better, cost far less to buy and run, and was likely to hang in one piece for a lot longer, even if the GTV6 did look and sound rather marvellous. The 2.8i gave the whole range an image and credibility boost, and the Capri struggled on in Britain until 1987, when it finally died in a profusion of special editions.

Thinking of buying one? Like most of the world's motor cars, Capris only became relatively rust-proof in the 1980s, so any survivors are likely to be well perforated by now. Suspension mountings were particularly prone to attack, and rust also ate its way into the sills, floorpan and wings. Mechanical parts, however, are reasonably easy to find and fit, and cheap to buy, although V4 engines might pose a few problems. The early Pinto engine is well known for its camshaft troubles, but as this is generally not too calamitous for the bank balance it would not necessarily be a reason for rejecting an otherwise sound car. Kent and Essex fours and the V6s all soldier on for many a mile without complaining too much, and the under-stressed three litre in particular goes for ever.

Incidentally, when test driving a Capri, don't be surprised by the jerky ride, harsh, raucous engine and lousy brakes. They're all like that, Sir, with the exception of the 2.8i, which is rather more civilised in manner.

Chapter Eleven

It is always tiresome to read an article by a private owner about some interesting car in his possession and to find that it consists entirely of praise and loud boasting.

Alan Clark, 1951

A LOST DECADE

AFTER A BRIGHT ENOUGH start, the 1990s was something of a lost decade for me, at least professionally. I had reached the national retirement age in 1985, and five years or so after that the powers that be (or should I say were) at *The Auto* obviously decided the old boy was approaching his use-by date, and that it would soon be time for de Forte to pack up his portable Olivetti and depart the scene. Certainly, as the century's ninth decade wore on, the bright young chaps in the editorial office (moved out from historic High Holborn to a featureless brutalist block in Milton Keynes in 1992) began to take my telephone calls with a discernible lack of enthusiasm (when they weren't conveniently 'unavailable', ensconced in interminably protracted meetings of doubtful validity). Gradually, inexorably, *The Auto*'s editorial department stopped commissioning new de Forte material; and increasingly my unsolicited efforts and suggestions were confined to the new editor's waste bin, or else, in a lamentable dereliction of decency and all good manners, they would appear in revised form under others' or spurious bylines.

I could see that I did not fit easily into the brash new world of hot hatch shoot-outs and big Bavarian saloon burn-ups, but I was upset at my rude exclusion nonetheless. I was sad too that *Motorcycle Review* went into receivership before re-emerging under another name, and with an altogether new ethos and revised target market: Britain's non-existent biking yoof. *'Quick Bikes'* primary aim was seemingly the irresponsible encouragement of wheelie popping, so-called stoppies, roundabout knee-down contests, and lurid riding in general. No wonder the government sought to legislate two-wheelers off the road! The *Review*'s owner and founding editor, my good friend and contemporary Carlton Flaxton-Penge, was sent on what would today be called gardening leave, before being put out to grass on a permanent basis.

I also had a sense that cars and motorcycles were becoming less interesting than heretofore, or perhaps it was just sour grapes on my part. Whatever, I was finding it harder to get excited about new machinery, whether new 90s curvy or old-hat 80s boxlike (it appeared to be a time of transition from the latter to the former). Or perhaps my mood was affected by the loss of my best pal.

In December 1995 I wrote in my diary: 'Algy is dead. Whenever he appeared, life became brighter immediately, and there was never a dull moment. There are plenty now he's gone.' All his life Algy had in copious quantity that uplifting quality which perhaps most clearly characterises the young and young at heart – namely a blithe, unquestioning belief that all the most wonderful and exciting things in life must, by some inescapable natural law, come to him. He had a sense of wealthiness, despite being as poor as a church mouse throughout all but the earliest years of his life. Above all else, he was a reasonable and decent man, and proof that real wealth comes from being a good human being. I feel strangely enfeebled by this loss.

By that time I was not working much at all. A submission sent back to me in error, was stamped 'do not use' and annotated with sarcastic margin notes to the effect its style was hopelessly dated. Someone else had written across the top: Who is this? A door had shut – the secret door to another dimension which I had sought and so fortuitously found before the war – a door through which, as with flying and riding motorcycles, I could find myself metaphysically transported to another place. Few find these magical entryways at all, or else cannot open them, but before the age of 20, I had discovered three such, and in due course I made two of them central to my life. I had been a lucky fellow indeed. If it was over, I had had a good innings. But then came a telephone call from a young man called Ker who professed himself an admirer. The quietly spoken Mr Ker was setting up an independent magazine called *Jalopy*, would I contribute? I penned a few words. Then as the decade reached its end, an extraordinary series of events would open up unexpected new opportunities.

MAZDA MX-5: PART ONE
(Diary extract – 14 May 1990)
Ambling along Kensington High Street on a beautiful sunny spring afternoon, en route to the underground railway station after attending an altogether forgettable trade bash at Olympia, my attention was diverted by a pretty young thing emerging from a bright red open-topped sports car. Probably sensing my eyes were upon her, she in turn glanced rather coyly up at me, no doubt wondering why such an elderly, if still spritely cove should be gawping at her rather than toddling along to his nursing home for further medication and a teatime nap.

To say anything would only have made matters worse, particularly if 'W de(crepit) Forte' had tried to convince her of the sad truth, that he was really only interested in the car. Her seated chauffeur beau, meanwhile, nodded in tacit acknowledgement of my honourable intentions, and proceeded to raise the canvas hood with a flourish. That this operation took only seconds and gave no cause for swearing or grunting was enough to confirm to me that this was indeed a new Mazda MX-5, the first I've seen on UK roads. Thousands are already swarming around the US of A wearing Miata badges, and the home market Eunos version is proving a huge hit, but as usual the British are right at the end of the queue. Not only that, we will be paying dearly for the privilege – more in 1990 pounds than our American cousins are stumping up in dollars, i.e. twice as much wonga in real terms.

Still, global marketing has always been a mystery to me, more so than ever, I find, as I enter my dotage. If motor noters were presented with badgeless cars and had no access to price lists they would often come to very different conclusions, I am sure. Is the MX-5 really 'worth' more than £14,000, considerably more cash than a 100% practical Ford saloon? Of course it is! If you disagree, I'd suggest checking *The Times* obits to see if you're actually still alive.

It is strange but nevertheless true that the new Mazda owes its existence to a motoring journalist, possibly the only time one of our number has done anything useful or worthwhile, as someone close to home is apt remind me at every opportunity! The scribe in question is one Bob Hall, a Los Angeles native and auto magazine editor of my acquaintance. Just over a decade ago, when BL, Britain's imploding giant, was in the throes of axing all its traditional ragtops for reasons unfathomable, Bob and I were lamenting the situation together over drinks in an airport lounge somewhere, and perhaps as a result of our liquid luncheon, he was later moved to suggest to sympathetic ears at Mazda that Japan should fill the void and build a small, sporty roadster very much in the MGB/Spitfire/Elan mould, a car that in essence would draw on the genetic pool that began with the pre-war T-series Midget, but with all the bad traits of that lineage carefully filtered out.

Mazda listened, then acted, and after a not entirely smooth gestation the fruits of their labours gave us the M(azda) X(perimental) 5. While Californian Bob had maintained that a front engine and rear wheel drive were essential ingredients, the Hiroshima bean counters had demurred. insisting that in a world almost exclusively filled with front-wheel-drive, transverse engine cars, what was the point in going to the trouble of doing things differently in the creation of a niche product? Fortunately for my cool young friends in Kensington and many other likeminded souls far and wide, the voice of the enthusiast prevailed, and so the easy option was rejected, pronto.

I would add that although the Nipponese firm's '70s generation hatchback did feature RWD (unusually, as even backward companies like Ford had embraced front-wheel-drive), by the time the MX-5 was taking shape an entirely new range of 323s had appeared, powered by revvy twin cam fours. History (or at least my fading memory of it) doesn't record whether using this engine longitudinally had ever been planned, but in the event a tuned version rotated through 90 degrees was employed in the new ragtop.

A suitable gearbox might have been a problem for some factories, but Mazda's lumbering 929 saloon willingly donated its five-speed transmission, thus taking care of the basic mechanicals. Were this a simple 'new body, same platform' fudge, no doubt the suspension would also have been inherited from elsewhere in the ranks, but the engineers demanded double-wishbones at each corner, promising good things in terms of wheel control and dynamic geometry.

Of course, the perennial problem with roofless cars is that they have a tendency to twist. The traditional British roadster used a separate chassis, but unitary construction could work too, as MG's B first demonstrated some thirty years ago. Abingdon's monocoque crew gained the necessary rigidity by means of multiple sill box sections (an aspect lost on many restorers, who only replace the visible parts!), while Mazda's design team had the luxury of computers to aid them in their work. Still, I suspect most of the real maths was done by enthusiastic humans.

It is generally true that losing a few pounds of roof steel will necessitate adding a far greater amount of tinware to restore a bodyshell's strength, and apparently the somewhat bendy tubs of the first MX-5 prototypes were woefully weak for this very reason. This problem made a maximum target weight of just 1000kg seem impossible to achieve, but much midnight oil combustion followed, and a suitable lightweight structure was eventually developed, although it's worth noting that bracing struts between the front suspension turrets and across the rear deck are a welcome addition for both show and go, as they say.

Adding lightness, as Colin Chapman put it in one of his lucid moments, preoccupied Mazda's hard-working team. This can be seen in the rather flimsy interior accoutrements, and the use of a small, motorcycle-type battery stowed in the boot, along with a fairly ridiculous space-saver spare wheel. In countries requiring a full-size spare, the MX-5 simply isn't being sold. Their loss, as Mazda is already struggling to meet demand.

At the sharp end, the iron-blocked engine with its Alfa-like twin cam head, but hopefully Mazda-like dependability, must account for a significant chunk of the 1000kg total. Yet because it's set well back in the wheelbase, mass is distributed evenly between axles, so this is no arrowhead machine likely to send one straight forwards through a hedge. Indeed, less adept customers accustomed to idiot-proof hatchback handling will probably exit facing in the other direction!

Despite wasting space and adding weight, this scribe approves wholeheartedly of the inclusion of pop-up headlights on this little motor car. Lotus may have blazed the fashion trail here, but we can expect the MX-5's eyes to open on command, not stick up, down, or even halfway in-between depending on the soporific qualities of the weather, as was the habit of the hapless Elan. I was delighted to hear that some electronically minded owners have contrived to operate each headlight separately, allowing them to give a mischievous clin d'oeil to other road users!

I also approve of the 'retro', to coin a phrase, interior: simple, clear instruments, not too much clutter, and a good helping of chromium plate and aluminium, real or otherwise. It was intriguing to hear that during development Mazda put great effort into the relationship between seating and windscreen angle, the intention being to make the hoodless cabin breezy but not so turbulent that it would imperil caps and toupees or blur forward vision. Contrast this with the attitude of most other convertible manufacturers, whose designers try to exclude from the driver's senses each and every indication that one is even moving. Do these dolts not realise that not everyone wishes to be cosseted in an artificially air-conditioned environment? We want 93 million miles of headroom, to borrow the Triumph TR7 droptop's clever advertising slogan!

Possibly the most important yet misunderstood part of the MX is its 'Power Pack Frame'; essentially an aluminium spar bolted to both the engine and the differential. The idea here is to lessen torque reaction effects in both components. It is not structural, in the sense that it doesn't form part of the bodyshell, and it seems the confusion here is caused by assumptions that Mazda copied the Elan's backbone chassis. In fact, an early prototype MX made for the Japanese by IAD in Worthing on England's south coast and coded V705, did have a backbone chassis, but that was soon abandoned.

There is much more to tell about development, but once more the wee small hours are upon us, so all of that will have to wait until another day. To summarise, despite the enormous handicap of being inspired by a journalist of all people, Mazda's lightweight sports car thoroughly deserves its rapturous reception. Seemingly no-one has a bad word to say about it. Indeed, the only negative comment that has reached me from those fortunate enough to attend last year's Chicago launch was that the car needed more power, which seems to be an example of someone missing the point entirely.

Although a committed internationalist, I am also, deep down, something of a patriot, and it dismays me considerably that this splendid little two-seater doesn't wear a Triumph or MG badge, but nonetheless Mazda should be congratulated heartily for creating something really special for us all to enjoy.

Ironically, the MX-5's impending British Motor Show debut will see it sharing a room with the all-new Lotus Elan, which features a transverse engine driving the front wheels! Being of necessity a low-volume model with a premium price, the Lotus isn't a direct competitor. Forgive me for saying it, but I hazard a guess that only one of this duo will live long and prosper in the showrooms.

At present I have only sampled pre-production Mazda MX-5s, but I am confident that the first UK imports will be as good or better, whether used for flitting around London town or threading through twisty country lanes. When my promised loan car arrives I expect to be smiling from ear to ear, and I defy anyone who buys one not to do the same.

CITROËN 2CV
(First published – *Classic Auto* August 1990)
It would be fair to say that after Great Aunt Margot perished on *Titanic*, clan WdF was generally less keen to venture long-distances overseas. Fortunately, however, few icebergs were to be found in the English Channel, so back in the '20s and '30s the family still travelled regularly to Europe, particularly France, which was at that time a quite sparsely populated land sprinkled with vinous peasant farmers who lived as they had for several centuries. Outside the main conurbations, it was a largely parochial world, generally unaffected by mechanisation and the internal combustion engine.

The precise year escapes me now, but very likely in 1931, we loaded up the faithful Jennings shooting brake with famille WdF and every imaginable piece of detachable Shropshire, then headed down to Dover, destination Paris, which was indeed gay in those days. After the lurching ferry trip had ensured all our stomachs were entirely empty by the time we hit terra firma once again, off we set along quiet and largely straight tree-lined highways. In an era when most continental journeys took days rather than hours, the trip to the capital seemed relatively brisk, for which we could probably thank Napoleon and the Romans.

Approaching at dusk, the outskirts seemed gloomy and devoid of artificial light, but as we neared the city centre, the streets were bustling with life and colour. Pater had considerable difficulty driving on the wrong side of the road (unusually for him, we joked!) and he was befuddled by these 'priorite a droite' signs that seemed designed to cause near misses at every junction. London traffic was always a great deal more ordered and civilised, I must say. We later realised that providing these foreign types knew we were British they would usually move out of one's way, PDQ.

Suddenly, gesticulating east, Nanny shrieked: 'Look at that!' There on the horizon was an immense, dazzling edifice rising into the skies. We must have been twenty miles distant, but it was still incredibly bright – unlike poor Nanny, who wasn't particularly educated and must have thought Jacob's Ladder started in Paris. We de Fortes, of course, knew we were gazing at the Eiffel Tower, a shameless copy of the magnificent construction in Blackpool. Only much later did Pater acknowledge that this French chap had actually started work first, and the good burghers of Blackpool had, in fact, built a half-scale replica.

In 1930, Eiffel's Parisian erection was usurped as the tallest man-made structure by the Chrysler Building in New York (in 1957 the tables were turned, as an additional aerial had been added to the tower), but it was still spectacular, standing in splendid isolation, its base clearly visible. As our faithful woodie homed in on its goal near the Seine, we could see a quarter of a million lightbulbs spelling 'CITROEN', rising 1,000 feet into the sky. We stopped the car near one of the huge legs and looked ever upwards, agog with awe. Some sixty years later, I can remember the moment as if it were yesterday. What is Citroën?, Nanny asked Father. A very clever man who makes motor cars, he told her, in that slightly begrudging tone he reserved for those rare instances when British might not have been absolutely best.

Alas, in 1934, after a decade as the world's largest advertisement hoarding, this very clever man's lights went out, literally and figuratively, but a takeover by Michelin ensured that the company he founded continued to blaze a technological trail. The Traction Avant was one highlight, the 1955 DS another. Sandwiched in between those came the 2CV 'Toute Petite Voiture', which was in gestation for more than a decade before finally being unveiled at the 1948 Paris Salon.

Students of history will know that this early October event was staged a few weeks before the more important London show at Earls Court, where Morris first displayed the Minor and Jaguar launched the XK120 sports car. Leaving aside the Jaguar, the ownership of which can only ever have been a distant dream for the vast majority of motorists, the Minor and 2CV could conceivably be considered Anglo-French interpretations of the vehicular requirements of Mr et Madame Average.

The capitals of both Britain and France had emerged from the Second War in some desolation, perhaps the biggest difference being that Haussmann's elegant Paris architecture was relatively unscathed, while parts of London had been bombed to oblivion. But the residents of these great cities were not the automotive industry's target customers. In those straitened days, as indeed pre-war, it was recognised that the man on the Clapham omnibus and his European confreres already had their means of transport, and that the bods in the most urgent of mobilisation, were provincial types without access to reliable bus services, and whose travel requirements exceeded the bicycle's comfortable daily range.

Thus, back in the 1930s, Citroën had come up with its 'umbrella on wheels' concept, essentially a lightweight car that would cope with delivering a clutch of eggs and a pig to market, irrespective of whether there was a ploughed field or river to impede progress; and in a brave move, driving the device had to be within the capabilities of the farmer's wife, as well as her agrarian spouse.

Mimicking the horse and cart it was intended to replace, the device had to be quick steering, front-wheel-drive, and with its means of propulsion ahead of its front wheels. Speed and performance were considered of no consequence, so the initial proposal included a feeble two-cylinder water-cooled engine of just 375cc, developing less than 10bhp. That meagre string of internally combusted chevaux eventually became the production reality, but the completed 2CV that emerged postwar was very different to the batch of 250 prototypes that had been assembled back in 1939. Intended to be shown the very day after war erupted, most were destroyed in anticipation of the Germans' occupation of France, although a few were secreted away and happily re-discovered several decades later.

A post-war redesign ditched the prototype's complicated torsion bar suspension in favour of interconnected coil springs hidden in tubes running fore and aft, and attached to leading arms at the front, and trailing arms at the rear. With nothing except Citroën's 'batteurs' (inertia dampers) to control movement, the 'Tin Snail' rolled mightily in corners, but it nonetheless remained incredibly stable and provided a magically smooth, if bouncy ride that arguably still hasn't been bettered.

While the engine remained a flat twin, Citroën's new engine man, Walter Becchia, wisely changed to air cooling (as with VW's People's Car and the BMW motorcycle engine used in prototypes) in the interests of simplicity and reliability. But while it was simple in that it had few moving parts, the 2CV's mechanicals were actually very advanced. The crankshaft was pressed together and used sleeve bearings rather than split shells, and like the aluminium block it was made to incredibly tight tolerances. The engine needed no gaskets, and proved virtually unburstable, as demonstrated by tests in which they were run for a hundred hours at full throttle. Less happily, if the crankshaft did fail the only way of fixing it involved very much more than a tractor toolkit and some DIY nous.

Despite Becchia's best efforts, the TPV (Toute Petite Voiture!) on display at the Paris show in 1948 shared a guilty secret with the slinky Coventry cat that was launched at virtually the same time. Neither car had a functioning engine until some time later! It took another year for Citroën to finalise the power source, and an electric starter only appeared at the very last minute, when it was realised that most farmer's wives wouldn't be able to fire the engine up by hand. Fortunately, Becchia guessed this was going to happen and had incorporated the necessary mountings. So, at the next Paris show in 1949, visitors were finally allowed to open the 2CV's corrugated bonnet and see what marvels lurked within.

As in Britain, new cars were largely unobtainable in France. Only a few hundred dark grey 2CVs were made in the first year and prospective buyers were tightly vetted by the authorities. Farmers and other rural types were prioritised, and not even the most rich and influential string-puller could circumvent the process! However, by 1953 the supply and demand equation became less critical, thanks in part to Citroën's satellite factories, one of which was in Slough (set up in 1926), where a right-hand-drive 2CV was assembled next to the Traction Avant. Whether or not we agree with Betjeman's cruel damnation of the place ('Come, friendly bombs and fall on Slough, it isn't fit for humans now.') at least UK motorists were being given a wider choice of workaday motor car. No longer did one necessarily have to buy a humdrum Morris Minor, baby Austin A30 or John Black's Standard 8. True, the Citroën was about ten percent more expensive than proper British cars, but it had a unique gallic charm.

Further developments saw a slightly more powerful 425cc engine installed, and in 1959 the 'any colour you want as long as it's grey' dictum finally passed into history for UK consumption. Incidentally, although some classic scribes insist that all 2CVs worldwide were various shades of grey for the first ten years, I vividly remember seeing pale blue ones in their homeland in the mid 1950s.

There were various offshoots, the most bizarre being the 4WD Sahara, a 2CV with an engine at each end. It was a very effective off-road device, but sales were slow and only a few hundred were ever made. Meanwhile, the British factory struggled to find customers and took the brave step of supplanting the standard tin snail with the Bijou, a car based on the same platform but clothed in curvaceous fibreglass. Again, a bold machine, this one designed by the same chap as the Lotus Elite! It had many keen admirers but sadly very few buyers, despite its DS elements and impressive aerodynamics, as you might expect. Only 211 were made before the Liverpool Road plant began being used for the manufacture of chocolate biscuits (we will all pause to say 'crumbs!' in unison). While the British determination to buy truly home grown products was a factor in Citroën Cars Ltd's despondent demise, the final straw was the decline in exports due to increasing self-sufficiency by the colonials.

My first experience of everyman motoring, continental-style, was a trip to northern Italy in 1957. A top speed of just 50mph would seem to be a severe handicap, but in practice I found it made little difference to my journey times.

In a hectic week I drove two press colleagues from Paris to Monza, combining a road test for *The Auto* with attending an historic Nations Motorcycle Grand Prix (a meeting which marked the end of an era, as the leading Italian manufacturers would withdraw from top level racing after the event). Throughout a two-way adventure of over 1,000 miles, I relished the direct steering and the way the little car could be thrown into corners with gay gallic abandon. Amusingly, my passengers were alarmed by the roll angles and squealing tyres, but, once acclimatised, they too warmed to the game little voiture, especially on learning that fuel consumption figures were over 50mpg.

Around 1960 I did consider buying one myself, but the disappearance of right-hand-drive models made me think again. Alas, while I pondered and prevaricated, the world moved on, and eventually I would buy one of the first E-Types instead! Not an obvious substitute, you may say, but in their separate ways both cars were, above all other considerations, très agréable to drive.

By the mid 1960s a lot of our Froggie friends had begun to fall out of love with the 2CV, many of them buying Renault people cars instead (a trend that began when 'La Régie' finally saw sense and put their engines and transmissions in the front rather than the rear!). But while the French became slightly less interested, the Germans and British in particular had come to appreciate Citroën's minimalist concept, so production continued unabated, peaking in 1966. The following year the Dyane arrived, complete with a mighty 28bhp, 602cc engine. This unit duly appeared in the standard 2CV-6 for 1970. After a long gap, British sales recommenced in the wake of the 1970s oil crises, and clever marketing and a plethora of special editions ensured that the model thrived on this side of the Channel, but right-hand-drive 2CVs now came from Belgium or France rather than Slough.

Although the snail's back-to-basics approach was a large part of its appeal, and its appearance changed little over the years, development continued underneath its tinware. In 1976 the quaint friction dampers were finally displaced by something more conventional (and effective), and in 1981 the inaccessible inboard front drum brakes were supplanted by equally inaccessible discs. At the same time the 2CV was enjoying the limelight, thanks to a starring role in the James Bond film, *For Your Eyes Only*. The car used was fitted with a GS flat-four, an already tried and tested idea adopted by in-house genius Flaminio Bertoni's deliciously peculiar Ami, another model based on the same platform, and one targeted primarily at liberated French females. In 1988 the ancient Paris-Levallois factory, a 1920s facility based in the heart of the capital, closed for good, having produced nearly 3.5m umbrellas on wheels. For two years the 2CV was manufactured in Portugal, but now that facility has closed too. Notionally replaced by the new Visa, the 2CV has passed into history, although it's safe to assume that we will continue to see them on our roads for decades to come as the nascent 'classic' movement gathers pace.

A recent refresher course in an anything but grey 'Charleston', which I gather was the top-seller of many multi-coloured special editions, convinced me that the escargot d'etain still makes a lot of sense. With three times at much power as the one I careered through the French countryside in back in August 1957, it is relatively fast and can hold its own on most motorways. More than ever, my rickety frame appreciated its sublimely smooth ride. Where had all the potholes gone, I wondered. My nearest dealer still has stock. Perhaps it's time to consider buying a 2CV again, while I still have the opportunity.

MAZDA MX-5: PART TWO
(Diary extract – 7 September 1995)

You may be aware that I am rarely moved to buy a new car. Cynics suggest that this is because for many years I have been loaned a stream of road test victims, fuelled, insured and FOC, so why would I bother to spend my hardly-earned on something that would likely be used only infrequently? They have a point. Looking back, my 1963 acquisition of a new Jaguar E-Type was probably the wisest purchase I ever made. Much as it hurt to write a cheque for £2,000, I consoled myself that a comparable motor made by any other than my esteemed friends at Browns Lane would cost twice as much.

Some 28 years on, I wrote another cheque for another two-seater roadster. Had I paid the full price, the bottom line, as young ripstitches now refer to it, would have been circa £15,000 this time. I had no reason to suppose this car should cost £30,000, although I fancy that it might be priced at £50,000 if wearing a Ferrari badge! However, money is a sordid subject, particularly when considering the little MX-5, an absolute jewel of a motor which I believe deserves to be feted and is much more than the sum of its Japanese parts.

I have now been my Mazda's official keeper, as the Swansea DeVil's Licensing Authority insists on referring to us, for four years, since purchasing it from *The Auto* after a year's testing, to keep it out of others' hands and make it my own. My annual mileage is modest, but I have certainly travelled far and fast enough to confirm my beloved Little Red Roadster represented wise use of Captain Mainwaring's money (read on gentle reader, and see below).

Long-term tests traditionally detail faults and breakdowns. In days of yore, it was accepted that cars needed regular servicing yet still broke down with depressing regularity. Returning to my beloved E, although I considered it undiplomatic to make much fuss at the time, it suffered some serious engine problems within months of taking delivery. Lyons and his spanner-wielding minions did all they could, but eventually virtually an entire new engine had been installed. Even so, it was still considerably slower than the original 150mph road test cars, as we all know!

In contrast, the Mazda has been faultless. If all cars were this dependable, mechanics throughout the world would have to take early retirement. Once the manufacturer's warranty had expired I had no further occasion to visit the Mazda agent in Wassail Bridge. Truthfully, that was a relief, because the sparse dealer network had a confused attitude to the MX-5 in general, and how the sporty interloper fitted in with the other essentially dull products with which it shared showroom space.

In turn, they were likely relieved that a rotary engined 'MRX-5' didn't appear, as once rumoured (and since built by enthusiastic Wankelers). I can still remember the head scratching and consternation when Britain's workshops were faced with the RX models of the 1970s. Many of these rapid machines suffered premature death solely through the blunders of ignorance, inflicted by oafs who knew everything about Morris Marinas but who wouldn't recognise an epitrochoid if it hit them in the face. Still, I'll admit that generally speaking a knowledge of 16th Century mathematics isn't a prerequisite for joining the ranks of the bleeding-knuckled.

I digress! Freed of the need to pay main dealer prices for oil and sundries, the car was entrusted to Ron 'Rusty' Nutt, who by then had taken up temporary residence at Haynes' in the village. He reported that it was a delightful machine to work on, with almost everything presented in an orderly and logical manner. Always a realist, Rusty gave short shrift to the notion that the MX was in any way like an MGB or Midget. 'Give me one of these Japanese jobs every time,' he told me, before launching into a familiar diatribe on imperial nuts, bolts and thread varieties. 'You only need about six sizes of spanner for the Mazda. More like sixty for the MG... it's – bleep – ludicrous! Why didn't those – bleeping – bleeps – sort it out fifty years ago?' he opined, in typically ripe argot.

De Forte admits to being one of the world's worst grease monkeys, but even he found the MX easy to fettle when he braved an oil change. The filter was tiny and tricky to unscrew, but beyond that the only difficulty was common to all sports cars, including the E-Type; that is, the lack of space betwixt sump plug and terra firma, which meant the drain receptacle had to be decidedly flatter than a very flat thing. No matter, as a Mazda owner-mechanic I wager I could have been entirely self-sufficient had I not been so terminally paresseux (negative traits seem so much more forgivable when translated into a foreign language).

Naturally, I have driven the MX hard at times. While the 1.6 engine is quite tame in terms of ultimate power, it delights in spinning up to 6,000rpm or more, facilitated by a creamy-smooth gear change action. As with past British ragtops, one can enjoy a feeling of great speed while going, essentially, quite slowly, but several visits to racing tracks have confirmed the chassis' excellence when the car is pushed to extremes. The tail can be snappy, so it's not idiot-immune like a front-wheel-drive 'euroboite', but sliding soon becomes second nature. Unleash the latent Fangio, I say!

Some of my fellow motor noters demanded more power, so it was inevitable that Mazda granted their wishes and expanded the twin-cam engine to 1.8 litres in 1993. With around twenty-five more horses in harness and a nicely swollen torque curve, the result is a significant increase in performance. On the debit side, the engine is a tad more gruff and has lost some of its smoothness and zest. To put things into perspective, however, the iron-blocked four is still greatly more refined than the coarse B-series lump used by MG between 1962 and 1980.

Another option was a turbocharger. Soon after the British launch, Mazda officially sanctioned one such beast put together by Brodie Brittain Racing. Using a Garret turbo, 150bhp and considerably more speed was available, without over-stressing the engine (forced induction actually tends to reduce mechanical strain, of course).

But as I've said far too often already, the power-crazed rabble of young journalists completely miss the point. To be enjoyable and entertaining to drive, a car or motorcycle must have balance – in all things. Why should the ability to reach 60mph or some other arbitrary velocity be important when one isn't on a drag strip or wasting the planet's natural resources by going round in expensive circles at Brands Hatch, or enduring that ridiculously featureless racetrack built on top of Corby steelworks?

The same applies to tyres and wheels. Mazda deliberately fitted a set of narrow 185/60x14 boots to its rather cheeky faux Minilite alloys. The same dolts who lust for bhp immediately throw these away and squeeze larger diameter wheels and wider, flatter rubber under the arches. Result: a car that darts around in search of smooth tar Macadam (rarely found near Bales, I must say, and nonexistent in some northern parts), steers less precisely and sacrifices much of its ride quality. In case there is any doubt, the WdF MX-5 will be staying in standard trim until the day I hang up my stringbacks!

The former National Provincial bank in Beedle (later NatWest) was managed for thirty years by a Mr Roland T Fishall, someone in later life bearing a striking resemblance to the rotund martinet played by Arthur Lowe in the TV series, *Dad's Army*. Having started there as a teenage 'stupid boy', all and sundry eventually came to refer to him as Captain Mainwaring, which he loathed to the point that he would go crimson with blustering rage and flap his ears. After decades of devoted service (not to mention some generous loan terms for loyal customers buying motor cars on a whim!), RTF suddenly vanished in 1991 and was never seen again. His handsome house on Riverbank Lane remained empty for many years, prey to vandals, its once beautifully manicured lawns and gardens growing wild.

The accepted explanation was that RTF had suffered a sudden major illness, but the truth that eventually emerged was rather more titillating. It seems he had been siphoning off the bank's cash since first being put in charge, and by the time of the eventual detection of his crime in the early 1990s, a near seven-figure sum had been successfully diverted into obscure offshore interests. Alas, or not, it appears he realised he had been rumbled (allegedly a tip-off from 'sympathetic' friends in the force) and he fled the country, accompanied by Miss Kendall, his comely young assistant.

The happy couple were last heard of settled in South America. I see my diary records a mysterious Christmas card received shortly after the revelations became public: 'Who's the stupid boy now, then, Wilby? Regards, Mainwaring.'

While criminality cannot be condoned, I admit I still chuckle to myself about it all. Joan, RTF's wife of thirty years, certainly did not receive an invitation to South America, but she may or may not have been a victim. Apparently a sizeable amount had been invested in an investment portfolio in her name. So, courtesy of her husband, she enjoyed a comfortable existence in Harrogate, where she became something of a celebrity for her topless appearances in WI charity calendars.

JAGUAR XK120
(Submitted to *The Auto* September 1999)
Another of de Forte's motoring acquaintances has departed this earth. Alan Clark, Member of Parliament and bon vivant of my acquaintance, recently shuffled off this mortal coil, aged just 71. A very bright fellow indeed with a razor wit, and an expert on most subjects except humility, Right Hon Al was also, of course, a great car enthusiast, and his magazine and newspaper columns were essential reading. To call him the 'Samuel Pepys of the 20th Century' would perhaps be taking it too far, but he was a gifted writer, an engaging diarist, and no mean driver of motor cars. As a young man he competed in hillclimbs, and won, but unfortunately for others, in more recent years he tended to hone his skills by proceeding as fast as possible on public roads.

Rather in the manner of Mr Toad, Alan treated motoring law, the Highway Code and suchlike with sneering disdain. Whether he was in his Citroën 2CV, Porsche-engined Beetle or Bentley Continental S, 'Big Red', one got in his way at one's peril. Parp, Parp, indeed! Saltwood Castle, the family seat, was chock full of cars, stashed away in its outbuildings. Perhaps most prized of all was the Jaguar XK120 he bought new in 1950 when up at Oxford. Few of his fellow undergraduates would have been able to walk into City Motors and buy a model that was in any case in far greater demand than supply, but Clark came from a privileged background and no doubt could take advantage of strings pulled in high places.

Whatever, the sad news gives us an excuse to time travel back to 1948, when the first post-war Motor Show at Earls Court witnessed the XK's public debut. In reality, the model on display was not much more than a mock-up, brought along to draw attention to Jaguars' new twin camshaft six cylinder engine which, as every skoolboy once knew, had been developed by Bill Lyons and his chums during lulls between bombing raids while firebomb watching during the Coventry blitz. Work continued in peacetime with both four and six cylinder versions, but after setting speed records the four was effectively put out to grass, despite its confusing appearances in publicity material for some years! With the tremendous benefit of hindsight, we can see that a cheaper 'XK100' or indeed a two-litre Mark VII saloon would not have had the same sort of allure as anything fitted with the powerhouse six, so it turned out nice again, as per George Formby's contemporary catchphrase (incidentally, and parenthetically(!), George was another man mad about infernal combustion machines, although he preferred two-wheelers, particularly Nortons).

Jaguar's modest expectation that the XK120 would attract a few hundred advance orders proved absurdly pessimistic, leaving them with a problem the opposition envied! How could their 'Open Two-Seater Super Sports', to use its full title, be put into production when it was a car that didn't really exist, even in prototype form? Initially, the solution was to adopt old-fangled coach-building techniques whereby, starting with a shortened saloon chassis, the aluminium body panels were attached to a traditional ash frame. But for a car that would come to be sold in tens of thousands this could only be a temporary solution, and only around 240 of these 'lightweight' (about 110lb less than the later steel version) Roadsters were made before true volume manufacture began.

Apart from young Alan, another famous early XK owner was a Clark – a certain Mr Gable of Hollywood fame, and he was to be seen in widely distributed factory publicity shots looking mighty pleased with his new wheels. Incidentally, its such a shame most restored Jaguars from the '40s, '50s and '60s are equipped with chromed wire wheels, when in fact most cars were supplied new with their wires painted in body colour, or else sported disc wheels and chromed hubcaps. A disappointing lack of discernment. Surviving photos of Clark's handsome machine show it with discs in Blighty and painted wires in the USA, but perhaps he really didn't give a damn, because what the British publicity pictures didn't reveal was that his car didn't even have a functioning engine. This was another unfinished element of the 120.

Nevertheless, just looking at the model's sweeping lines was a treat to the senses. William Lyons had a natural knack for proportion and styling, which defined Jaguar right up until the 1970s and the XJ Coupe, the last car from Browns Lane produced under his full control. With the maestro in retirement, the XJS that followed certainly didn't attract universal praise, to coin an understatement. Cats led by donkeys, as it were! (A tortuous allusion to Alan Clark's military history book, *Led by Donkeys* – ed.) Pertaining to Lyons' Jaguars, 'styling' always included what was under the bonnet. To whit, that magnificent double-knocker six, with two, or three, SU carburettors, topped by delicious polished aluminium camshaft covers and neatly ordered ignition leads. Although chief engineer William Heynes and his team were by no means breaking new ground, the XK engine, upped in capacity from three litres in prototype form to 3442cc in the interests of torque, was a mechanical masterpiece as well as an aesthetic one. Aside from its superlative performance and refinement, the engine was also brilliantly simple in most respects. Even valve lash adjustment, by means of shims lurking under bucket tappets, was an easy enough proposition for backstreet mechanics – provided they didn't try to do the job without the special tool for positioning the camshafts, which could result in bent valves. Please don't ask how I found that out, dear reader. I cringe at the memory, even now!

In other areas the XK120 was a mixture of new and old. Separate chassis weren't entirely obsolescent at the time, even if contemporaries like the Morris Minor, also launched at the 1948 Motor Show, had demonstrated that unitary construction was the thing of the future. A live rear axle was also forgivable, but it did contrast somewhat with the advanced front suspension, a double-wishbone affair sprung by torsion bars and controlled by telescopic dampers. The world was undoubtedly a better place once lever-arms had been displaced (although that didn't stop Triumph from bringing them back from the dead in 1968 for the Mark II Vitesse!).

With such a substantial chassis, even the early 'lightweight' XKs were relatively hefty so, even with a claimed 160bhp on tap, performance wasn't at all spectacular by today's standards. Fifty years ago, however, in an era when half the traffic on British highways was composed of smoky pre-war relics barely able to break the urban speed limit, it was quite exceptional. Relaxed cruising at 100mph was regarded as a miracle, and Jaguar tester Ron 'Soapy' Sutton created a sensation when he clocked over 130mph on a Belgian motorway in a slightly modified car. Soon afterwards, it became possible for any Joe Soap to tune the XK using factory parts which added about 20 horsepower without losing any of the big six's easy tractability. The abysmal pool limited further progress on British shores, but high-octane petroleum would later release more power still.

Naturally, the XK120 soon took to the tracks, winning its debut race at Silverstone and purring to victory at the Dundrod TT with a youthful Stirling Moss at the wheel. More kudos came from a win by Herefordshire farmer Peter 'Skid' Walker at the 1951 Le Mans 24 Hours in a streamlined XK120C ('C' stood for Competition, of course). Although its other basics were the same as the road car, by using different rear suspension the C-Type was moving away from standard specification in more ways than its appearance. The days of driving a machine to a circuit and winning races in it were fading. As were the brakes, because drums just couldn't cope with all that mass and speed. The solution soon arrived, in the form of Dunlop discs, a spin-off from the aero industry. Jaguar and the denizens of Fort Dunlop first developed the 'bacon slicers' for an assault on the 1953 Le Mans. Duncan Hamilton and Tony Rolt won at record speed. A clear case of racing improving the breed, and inevitably, it wouldn't be long before discs were turning up everywhere, notably on the 1955 Citroën DS and Triumph TRs from '56.

So it was therefore a shame that the new XK140 available from 1954 was still lumbered with drums, even though it needed better brakes more than ever, as it weighed more than the 120 and came as standard with what had been the 'Special Equipment' engine, which developed 190bhp at 5,500rpm. The other major change was an enlarged cabin, achieved by moving the bulkhead forward, along with the engine and gearbox. This made the car more comfortable, but upset the weight distribution somewhat.

Three years later the final variation on the theme was announced. The XK150 was an altogether fatter cat, and one that offered far more creature comforts than the original, which didn't even have a heater as standard. Goodness gracious! The 150 even had the option of a Borg-Warner automatic transmission. I ask you, what kind of a sports car has a slushbox! One that sells like hotcakes in America, is the answer. Yet, in many other respects the last of the line had moved on considerably, and the final S version came with the 265bhp, triple carb 3.8 engine that would power its E-Type successor. A top speed of around 135mph was the result, but even in this fire-breathing form, perhaps the enlarged XK had become more of a grand tourer than a sports car.

While I pause to wash my mouth out by gargling Castrol R, let me say that the XK has stood the test of time better than most cars… better in a way than the E-Type, as the latter's complex structure and propensity to rust always made it a rather risky buy. Not so the XK and its bridge-like chassis, which could tolerate decades of neglect. As proof, consider that around half the sports cars that left

Browns Lane in the 1950s are still with us, a good many still in enthusiastic use. I also endorse the XK crowd's open-minded attitude to improvements. In some old car circles any departure from standard is treated as an unforgivable crime, but among the XK fraternity, functional changes, such as uprating a 140's brakes to discs or replacing the diabolical Moss gearbox with a modern five-speed, are seen for what they are: intelligent improvements. And apart from being built like a proverbial battleship, XK longevity has also been assisted by the fact that the styling never really went out of fashion. What looked right in 1948 still looked right in the '60s, '70s, '80s, etc, and things are unlikely to change as we head into the 21st century.

Thirty and more years ago I owned and/or drove plenty of XKs, including the 120 FHC that I bought from Rowley Birkin in, I think, 1960, before selling it back to him to finance my purchase of an E-Type. Some ten years after that, Rowley B's health was ailing (or so he claimed, the blighter!), and he asked me if I wished to buy her back. Prices were probably at their lowest ebb then, so I needed little persuasion. What I hadn't realised was the way the car had deteriorated. The chassis could still have served as a makeshift Bailey bridge, of course, but some on the bodywork was perforated, and decidedly frilly around its edges. It had also suffered from various drunken excursions into the scenery and modifications required for motorsport purposes. Still, its much-modified 'special equipment' engine was capable of pushing out over 200 gee-gees (of the British rather than 'gross' variety), thanks to Rowley's factory contacts. Although running on triple SUs by this stage, under the bonnet one could still see vestiges of an early Lucas fuel injection system, as used by the Jaguar works racers in the mid 1950s, before resurfacing in the Triumph TR5 and 2.5PI many moons later. I gathered that it might have been worth 40bhp on the 3.8 six, but one really needed a Lucas technician riding shotgun to cope with its foibles.

I doubt my irascible chum Alan would have been amused, explaining why he stuck with tried and tested tuning parts on his Saltwood specials. Launched early 1951, the FHC provided a saloon car-type environment for its low-seated pilot, cosy under a padded roof lining, and behind an attractively figured walnut veneer dashboard (the OTS featured a leather-covered instrumentation board – simpler, but no less pleasing). Like the open versions of the car, the closed model was simple and elegant, sporting art deco curves that, although not highly modern even when new, were nonetheless undeniably beautiful and redolent of speed.

Running both my 3.8 E and the XK at the same time proved an interesting experience. Obviously, the 120 was cruder in many ways and attracted far less attention. In those days as much as today, anyone at the wheel of an E-Type was always given much more than a second glance. Some of the attention was welcome, but the police would pull one over for a roadside chat with disturbing regularity, either because they wanted to reel off the old line, 'Who do you think you are, Stirling Moss?', or simply to admire the car. Even when I had been spotted travelling at a rather elevated velocity, I was usually let off with a stern warning. It was a time when officers used their discretion and had a sense of fair play. Do something completely asinine, of course, and they would 'nick' one in a shot, but high speed travel in appropriate circumstances was treated with enlightened lenience. In contrast, the XK tended to fade into the background, its elegant shape having been around for so long, even then. Mostly this was an advantage, if not for one's ego…

Which must surely bring us back to our Rt Hon friend, someone who would admit to possessing an ego fit to fill the Albert Hall. His beloved 1950 Jaguar OTS often featured in his writings, either because he had diced heroically in it with some other car, or a motorcycle (although decidedly a car man, he once astutely opined that motorcycles were better for experiencing the thrill of motion, describing them as being as sensitive and responsive as a Stradivarius violin, agile, obedient, and possessing more power than necessary in every gear), or because it had a battery problem (together with a lack of covered space for his collection, flat batteries were the automotive bête noire of Saltwood Castle).

Of course, all his cars were comprehensively thrashed on public roads, but his Jaguar XK120 had a special place in his heart. The only XK120 bought new whose original owner-driver still had his own teeth and hair, he would boast in recent times! Clark's preferred epitaph was, 'He always went for the third lane', and his last ever words were also about motor cars. Something rather more prosaic, however, but no less poignant: a thoughtful dictated message about the location of some gearbox parts that would be required by a future owner of the fleet. When or if this will happen we do not know at present.

Chapter Twelve

Life is not a journey to the grave with the intention of arriving safely in one pretty and well preserved piece, but to skid across the line broadside, thoroughly used up, worn out, leaking oil, shouting Geronimo!

Unknown

TODAY'S AUTOMOBILES ARE PRODUCED in huge numbers and are stuffed full of fiendishly complex electronics that cannot be fixed by a backstreet mechanic. Devoid of character and without a discernible soul, the few that survive will mostly just become old cars. But real joy in motoring can still be captured by the ownership and in the driving of classic, vintage and veteran motor cars. Stepping inside them is the closest thing to entering a time machine: with every creak and beat and mesh of gears we can share the experiences of our forefathers and by the evocative aroma of oil, wood and leather we are returned to the days of our youth. They take us to another world where things were very different, and dare I say it, generally rather more agreeable.

A NEW BEGINNING

I wrote the above to introduce my arrival as a contributor to the then newly-founded magazine, *Classic Auto*, which had risen phoenix-like from the ashes of the burnt-out wreck of that once great organ, *The Auto*. It had been driven perilously close to total ruin by its past careless owners, but now, joyfully reinvented under new stewardship, it was ready to play a part of the burgeoning 21st century classic car scene. As was I.

As I picked it up from the mat that day in January 2000 I noted straight away it was one of those envelopes that was far more intriguing than most. For a start, it lacked a window (do those types exist at all any more?), so it probably wasn't a bill, and there was no 'return to' information to give its sender's identity away. It promised to be something interesting, and indeed it was... *The Classic Auto* magazine. An offer of work. A regular column, and as many road tests of 'classics' as I felt able. Perhaps I could give the editor a call to discuss. One Jeremy 'Jez' Richardson.

A new millennium and a new start. With Haynes Garage in the village being readied for a grand reopening as a classic car emporium by an enterprising new owner, it seemed I would have a ready source of interesting test victims on my doorstep. Things were definitely looking up.

There have been phases in my post-war working life. The 1950s and 1960s were times of glorious abundance, expansion and full bloom. The 1970s brought a period of steadiness and maturity, which continued well into the 1980s before fading just a little by that decade's end. The 1990s was an increasingly cold, cutting, and barren period, but now, incredibly, the new century seemed to have brought opportunities for new beginnings. I might be able to put out a late flower or two, after all.

MAZDA MX-5: PART THREE
(Diary extract – 5 May 2005)

Goodness, hasn't time done its proverbial flying! A decade has passed since last I gathered thoughts on my little 1990 Mazda, which I would have gladly purchased straight away that summer for exactly the same undiscounted price as any other member of the public, had I not first taken delivery of it on long-term test for *The Auto*. And whatever I paid for it a year later to prevent it falling into other hands, let me assure my readers past and present there was not a special deal from Mazda, ensuring that only nice things would appear in print. As it happens, there is no need for diplomacy or suspect bulges in the de Forte carpeting. Generally, the little red MX, now approaching 100,000 miles, has been absolutely faultless.

Yes, dear reader, 'generally'... Inevitably, the hood went the way of all plastic and began to split and fray. Some have said it was my fault for not unzipping the yellowing rear window before lowering to the roof, as urged by the manufacturer, but I accept only part of the blame. Providing the temperature is over about 50 degrees (yes, metric enthusiasts, I'm talking Fahrenheit), the fabric is pliable enough to stow away without putting up too much resistance.

In my impecunious youth I would have patched the hood, or even persuaded Martha to make me a new one on her dear mother's faithful Singer sewing machine, but idleness and slightly increased wealth have got the better of me in 2005. A firm in Birmingham (anywhere in Staffs, Warks, and Worcs counts as Brummagem to me now) fitted a new one at a keen price, and I was in business again within hours. I doubt very much if the aftermarket version matches Mazda's original in terms of materials and longevity, but paupers can't be choosers, what, and there have been no more embarrassing soggy bottom incidents.

The splendid group of lads doing the work allowed me to watch the process.
⸱ made it look easy, but I am sure it would have proved far more difficult had

I attempted a head transplant in the top barn at Bales. From my position as an observer, the way the hood met the rear deck had fascinated me since I saw the first prototype. Instead of overlapping, Mazda's ruse involved an underlap, which on the face of it was a very silly idea almost guaranteed to cause a diluvian disaster long before Noah considered weighing the Ark's anchor. I needn't have worried. The small amount of water making it past the joint was ducted through channels just inside the B pillars, whence it emerged from the rear sills. Dashed clever, but only up to a point, Lord Copper, because I have it on good authority that the first MX-5s are already suffering from corrosion near the sluices. Touch a Morgan chassis, my car is thus far unafflicted.

The other blot on the horizon concerns the tappets. These are hydraulic devices, so no adjustment is required, or indeed, possible, which is rather good. Rather less good, as the engine ages, the oil supply that 'pumps up' the tappets and controls lash becomes tardy. As a result, leave the car for more than a few days and there's an unholy rattle before normal service is resumed on start up. Unless the clatter becomes permanent, my trusted spannerman, Ron 'Rusty' Nutt, assures me there's nothing to worry about, as 'They're all like that, Sir.' He is reluctant to meddle as apparently some owners have been moved to strip the entire cylinder head, replace everything that moves, and afterwards find their engines rattling as much as ever they did before.

My only other gripe is the battery, a special small-scale device more usually employed on motorcycles where weight is particularly crucial and space is at a premium. Special translates as 'expensive' when replacement is necessary, as you might guess. Luckily, it is possible to install a more normal battery with minor adaptations to the securing bracketry in the offside boot (trunk, as our US readers would have it). However, there are those who give dire warnings about this course of action, the theory being that one might suffer an explosion from within one's rear end due to a build up of gases. Is there any real evidence to support the claims of the doom-mongers? None that I have seen, but if you hear reports of fiery reports in rural Shropshire you'll know why.

CLASSIC SCENE
(First published *Classic Auto* – February 2007)
I had a chinwag with a classic motorcycle dealer yesterday; a most interesting chap. David was his name. Thing is, he said, I don't want to sell this bike to someone who doesn't realise how rare and important it is. I need to find someone who'll look after it. If only more car and motorcycle dealers shared his attitude. The bike was a Honda 400/4, absolutely as new with fewer than 2,000 miles on its odometer, and completely unspoilt in every way. It had original paint, all its surface finishes were as it left the factory, and it was mechanically perfect.

David also had a Triumph that had only covered a couple of hundred miles. Once it is ridden it will no longer be unique, he said. I want these bikes to go to people who will really appreciate them and understand what they represent. I find myself telling customers a bike will not be suitable for them and talking them into buying something else. I'm happy to keep bikes here. At least I know they will be looked after. A Kawasaki H2 750 David keeps in an inflatable cocoon remains in his showroom, despite having been sold three years ago. It's owned by a wealthy man who flies around the world doing deals for his boss, said David. He has bought a few machines from us over the years and we are keeping the Kawasaki until he judges the time is right to tell his wife he's bought yet another bike. We made another of our customers buy a new garage. Should I be bothered about what happens to to the bikes we sell? Increasingly, I am. Does he have a typical customer? I asked. My customers are becoming richer, more and more strange and eccentric, and increasingly old, David said. Increasingly they don't even see their bikes. They have them stored somewhere.

I still believe that the classic car and motorcycle scene is mainly driven by people who find themselves having sentimental associations with vehicles they owned or aspired to owning in their youth, or the cars their parents drove. But I find it amazing how many classic collectors now neither drive (or ride) any distance, or even clean their machines. Both these activities are essential for understanding them. I have long lamented the fact so many classics are trailered to shows, and how vanity drives men to arrange their acquisitions in rows and polish them. But increasingly they are being locked away, hidden from view. They are purely investments. Dear reader, I despair. For a while yet, these motorbikes and motor cars are for driving, not hiding, or showing. I have never been an advocate of the concours movement. More vanity. As long as there are a few perfect examples in museums, complete to the last nut and washer, and with every tool in the toolkit present and correct, that's enough.

If not purely an investment, what else do we want classic cars for? Showing off? There's nothing at all wrong with that, but real fun is to be had by driving them, especially over distance. It is a romantic experience which can never be matched in a modern vehicle. It is an adventure! As that great parliamentarian motorist Alan Clark has said: Classic cars are like horses. They will always be faithful but do not ride them too far without rest or water! He has also compared a classic car to a rescue dog which, having been beaten, abused and revved to ʾeath, now knows it has come home and is loved. Yes, I say in agreement with esteemed former friend, look after your classic car or motorcycle, but unless it ᵗ rare unblemished example with a minuscule mileage and factory lacquer ʾant on its engine cases, keep it regularly exercised and take it out for occasional long runs. Treated well, a classic can be a faithful, reliable and most endearing companion. Even man's best friend.

Classic cars are steeped in nostalgia, and while driving along memories arise at random from the subconscious, prompted by odour, colour, sounds, and responses. A classic car really is the nearest thing to a time machine, but only for going backwards!

INDUSTRY TYPES

Arthur Daley once said: 'You make contact with your customer, understand their needs, and then flog them something they could well do without.'

I am not a natural businessman, and although I feel I have a good eye for quality, I have occasionally failed to buy or sell a motor car at the right price. It's a cruel world, but my bad deals are my own fault. Caveat Emptor and all that! But although there are some good, kind men among them, second-hand car dealers are generally a strange and somewhat dubious lot, and indeed so are many unscrupulous garage owners, bodyshop desponds and other such motor trade types. This is regrettable.

Sadly, the classic scene is not a safe haven from such rogues and blackguards, and a few names come to mind immediately. The awful man at Chapel Lane Garage in Wales and his grubby sidekick; the junior spiv at RL Classics (formerly RL Motors) in rural Derbyshire; the newest big shark in the water, one Nick Shakespeare in leafy Surrey; those purveyors of tarted up garbage that operate as Top Classics in the Lincolnshire wolds; and the bungling sycophant who, until relatively recently, operated what he called his classic car emporium here in the Shropshire village of Bales, one Wilf Kettle.

Of course, amateur wheeler-dealers can be even worse. Only this week it came to my attention that an internationally renowned marque expert has been buying up and stripping down fully functional classic motorcycles of his specialist type, in order to sell their component parts at very high prices to collectors and builders (forgers?) of the most valuable models of the period by the same manufacturer. As a result of this greed, wonderful 50-year-old classic machines are being destroyed, and bogus classics are being created.

The widow of a friend of mine recently asked me to help dispose of her late husband's splendid Bentley R Type, a model of which I have a good deal of knowledge and familiarity. After making an appointment by telephone, I took it along to Gerald Lodestone at Chapel Lane Garage, as its deceased owner had requested. Lodestone's cars tend to be expensive, so it followed his buy-in valuations might also be a tad on the generous side. This assumption would be proved incorrect. Having pontificated pompously about how he only sold proper cars to proper people (whatever in the world that means), Lodestone looked over the Bentley in cursory fashion. Then the odious man made a brief signal, and from the open workshop nearby emerged Gollum, or if not Tolkien's creation, some remarkably similar creature in whom craftiness and gormlessness were clearly equally compounded. Lodestone's oleaginous hireling then proceeded to slither all over and under the car, poking it painfully with a screwdriver and leaving fingerprints on its body panels while following what was clearly a practised routine. After perhaps two minutes of this charade, he then turned to his employer with a malignant glint in his gimlet-eyes (master will be pleased), shook his head balefully and bustled back to his pit. His paymaster then curled his lip and spoke. To me, it's 12 grand's worth. I was astounded. But you'll sell it for at least 22. Yeah, well, I'd have to spend that on it.

My friend Elmley Greenidge in Shrewsbury sold it a month later for £24,000, having spent nothing on it. He charged us ten percent commission. Elmley is that rare type of motor dealer who realises that deceiving people is not the road to success. He understands that would put him in the gutter, rather than on the highway, and that life is about more than survival or getting one over on the next man. Expertise and honesty are what he has to offer. His prices are fair, and his customers come back.

Lodestone, I later discovered, often works in cahoots with that other unscrupulous scoundrel Nick Shakespeare, in as much as they pass stock around. I've had a good go with this one, it's beginning to look bad on my website. You have a try. A pal of mine recently told me about a friend who had bought a Jaguar Mark IX from Shakespeare. It looked a million dollars and came with a bulging folder of paperwork, but it turned out to be a terminally rusty car that had been skilfully tarted up for sale. The buyer had asked about corrosion and recent bodywork repairs, and was told there had been none, but a bodyshop bill inadvertently left in what was laughingly referred to as the history file told another story. It turned out the car had been the victim of a flood and had spent several weeks standing up to its wheel tops in river water. Lodestone bought it cheap, and having dried it out, instructed a bodyshop to sort it out superficially. New carpets and interior trim finished the job and the Jag went into his showroom.

But it was not there long. In a complicated swap deal involving a hugely expensive Derby Bentley, Shakespeare acquired it from Lodestone, and passed it on to a private buyer. Within weeks, as might well have been expected, the car's floor, door bottoms and other panels began rusting profusely. The new owner became alarmed, and after discovering the truth about the scabby Coventry cat's partial drowning, having spoken to its original keeper at a Jaguar Drivers' Club bash, he set about trying to obtain a partial refund. This was eventually agreed only after he parked the crumbling saloon outside Shakespeare's premises and announced through a loud-hailer to all the browsing visitors there, that the proprietor was a dishonourable spiv who lied and sold substandard goods.

Incidentally, it is often the fact that so-called history folders are far from comprehensive. Invoices for mechanical work are usually present, but bodywork bills not so. This is because they tell a story of temporary and superficial work the seller would rather not be told. Instead, the car's file will usually be bulked out with tyre bills, old MOTs, an assortment of recent tax discs, Waxoyl receipts (undersealing, of course, is good way of hiding all manner of rusty horrors), and lots of Halfords till receipts for batteries, oil filters, and other consumables. All references to paint and bodywork are generally carefully removed.

Wilf Kettle took over Haynes Garage in Bales in January 2000, offering storage, workshop services, and sales. His seemingly propitious arrival coincided with my journalistic rebirth as chief tester for *Classic Auto*. We struck a deal. In return for his providing a ready source of classic vehicles for review, I would supply editorial publicity and contacts, and send storage, restoration and service customers his way. This mutually beneficial arrangement appeared to work well at first, but as time went on I became nettled by his negativity, dismayed by his incompetence, disillusioned by his duplicity, and peeved by his arrogance. Sadly, I came to greatly dislike him.

Kettle was a professional northerner. Small and portly, he wore thick glasses under a flat cap, on a chubby, pink and shiny face adorned with large red pustules. One of which, central on the front of his chin, he had a habit of rubbing between his thumb and forefinger, in order to appear for all the world deep in thought. Forever adjusting tick-overs to pointless effect, a small screwdriver was kept permanently in the back pocket of his overalls for this specific purpose.

Poor Wilf was obsessed by status, and a quite dreadful snob. Never happier than when hobnobbing with the wealthy or well known, he showed obsequious deference to those he perceived to be his social betters. Upon spotting such characters (which, to my great discomfort, included myself) he would immediately abandon customers of his own social class with whom he might have been in mid-conversation, before scuttling around his emporium at their heels, bobbing at the knee, and secreting sebaceous ooze from every pore.

Sadly, over a prolonged period the man caused me a good deal of inconvenience and no little embarrassment. He was a blusterer. A master of obfuscation who never admitted blame or accepted responsibility for mistakes. They all do that, show me one that doesn't. Leave it with us was another catchphrase, but this actually meant, I have little or no idea what to do and you will be paying for me to find out. Booking a car into Wilf's workshop was rather like taking a dog to an inexperienced vet – one generally had to pay for two or three false diagnoses before any malady was properly identified and remedied!

Often, in fact, he was quite hopelessly out of his depth and unable to diagnose and rectify faults at all.

A less intelligent type of professional man, Kettle was clearly ignorant as well as a rogue. A study of any series of bills revealed a pattern involving a good deal of repetition – utterly futile work which was nonetheless keenly invoiced. He often gave the impression he was doing something as a favour, then charged for it. On his invoices he generally charged for more hours than actually spent, always added a sum for 'consumables' (a handy way of giving himself a tip), and he also overcharged for parts supplied. He would tell blatant lies too: yes, we've had a look at it, or yes, we have tried that, when, in fact, neither was the case.

Then there was the incessant moaning (ironic! – ed). In Wilf's world, business was always bad, he would criticise others in the trade at every opportunity, no job was ever straightforward, large cars took up valuable space in his storage area, and he charged such low prices he could not make a profit. Forgive the rancour gentle reader, but I felt personally let down by this odious individual.

So what happened to Wilf Kettle? You will have noticed I have written about him in the past tense. Divine intervention perhaps. Soon after I stopped dealing with him back in 2009, I was gratified to hear that one of my test cars, a pre-war Rover, exacted violent revenge on motoring's behalf by breaking his arm while he was attempting to start it using the hand crank. But what happened next perhaps took things scarily too far. No sooner had he returned to work when a well-to-do customer's aristocratic 1950s Maserati, which he had frequently treated disrespectfully, impatiently, even cruelly, and absolutely without any sensitivity of feeling at all, coolly killed him on a test run while inflicting minimal damage upon itself. The end was brutal, but swift, I understand. Mrs Wilf, whom I have since been led to believe was the brains of the outfit (someone had to be) soon sold up, and as far as I am aware, is now running a Harry Potter themed hotel and tea room in her native North Yorkshire.

GOOD DRIVING
(First published *Classic Auto* – September 2010)
You know you are getting old when everybody who drives faster than you is an idiot, and everybody who drives slower than you is an idiot! As I prepare to journey through my ninth motoring decade, I increasingly find myself subscribing to the view that most other drivers are incompetent. Quite ridiculous, of course, and an indication of my great age and decrepitude rather than an accurate reflection of reality. But it is the absence of good manners and the lack of human courtesy prevalent among drivers today that is often more disturbing to me than the rate, rapid or otherwise, at which these dimwits go about their business.

A former editor of mine volunteered the amusing suggestion that a credit system should be built into all modern cars. 'Every time you let someone through, slow down to allow someone to overtake, etc, you get a credit point that flashes up on your roof. Then other drivers know that you have been driving considerately and react to you accordingly,' he wittily opined. But the problem with this otherwise estimable idea is most motoring miscreants are not really drivers, merely getters-about from place to place, and, sadly, driving is now rarely considered a demonstrable art, or roadcraft an improvable skill. Motorists today need to make greater efforts to develop their abilities. They must practise good roadmanship in order to truly earn the freedom of the road. A man should be taught to drive a car as his ancestors drove horse drawn vehicles, so that the bonds of tradition and good manners can be maintained.

Here are some suggestions for chaps keen to raise their sights:

1) Set a high standard of behaviour and maintain one's temper at all times. Avoid deliberate actions aimed at making life awkward for the other fellow, and other unseemly displays of ill humour.

2) Do not drive scandalously when trying to make up time, and lighthearted driving to prove dash and verve is also to be discouraged.

3) Raise a hand to acknowledge other drivers who have put themselves out to allow your discretionary progress.

4) Exercise forgiveness when someone makes a mistake, and resist using the horn by way of reprimand.

5) In situations of impasse, it is sometimes easier to assume incompetence on the part of the other party, concede gracefully and reverse rather than insist on one's right of way.

6) Pottering along annoys other motorists. Keep your speed up and do not let the car wander!

7) Practise delicacy in the fine art of throttle control. Avoid sudden swerves, and never cause the car to lunge backwards or forwards under acceleration or braking. Change gear early and gently. Use the brakes progressively.

8) Handle the car so that passengers are not aware what you are doing except that the car goes faster or slower without obvious effort, noise or fuss. Speed should vary in accordance with the quality of the road surface, and occupants should never be sure whether the surface is good or bad. An increasingly difficult trick to achieve on roads now clearly inferior to those of many third world countries!

9) Let people into the space in front of you because only very rarely will it affect your overall journey time.

10) For the benefit of one's neighbours, avoid racing the engine on arrival or departure, and close doors quietly at night.

11) Make sure to use the turn signals, then return the switch or indicator arm to the off position. Make use of the repeater light on the fascia board!

12) Avoid dazzling oncoming traffic at night by dipping one's headlights in good time.

13) While fog lights are often left on erroneously, indicators sometimes barely get used at all, particularly in town. Quite apart from the bamboozlement it causes other road users, how on earth are pedestrians supposed to gauge when it is safe to cross the road if drivers do not signal their intentions?

14) We have all heard the tales about mindless dimwits obeying their navigation aids and changing direction without even looking outside the car, and this is indeed a worry, but programming these devices judiciously whilst on the move is surely just a matter of common sense. There have always been distractions in the cabin – tuning the wireless, winding door windows up and down, reaching to extend the aerial mast, adjusting heater controls, filling one's pipe, reading maps, and so on ad infinitum. An intelligent driver will pick his moment to tune his radio and the like. But whenever I am on a motorcycle and I come up behind a car being driven erratically, hugging the kerb or proceeding too slowly, or see a driver failing to take advantage of opportunities afforded by gaps in traffic, or struggling to make a perfectly simple manoeuvre at a junction, the blighter is almost always talking on a dratted mobile telephone! People seem to find it impossible to control their vehicles adequately while using these attention-sapping devices.

15) The proper procedure for turning right at rotary junctions is not to drive around the outside of them, trapping people on the inside. Nor is it acceptable to drive directly across roundabouts by travelling in a straight line from inner entry kerb to centre circle to nearside exit kerb. It's all in the highway code!

16) While most of the so-called vanity plates which are corrupting the vehicle registration system are depressingly second-rate, I must also say I really can't see the point of illegal number plates. That is to say, wrong script, wrong spacing, wrong size. Wrong in the noggin, more like! I am baffled as to why the vain types who display these on their vehicles seem to be immune from prosecution by the police.

Having said that, I greatly admire the ingenuity of a veteran motorcyclist, and no doubt inveterate speeder I occasionally come across in the High Peak, who has taken careful measures to protect himself from detection via speed cameras. This crusty middle-aged outlaw has made the registration plate of his Yamaha sporting motorcycle illegible by clever application of brown paint to give the appearance of splashed mud, and he has cunningly attached a Suzuki mud flap underneath it to further throw the authorities off the scent. Lastly, he wears a plain black crash hat and a drab brown anorak over his leather racing suit.

MAZDA MX-5: PART FOUR
(Diary extract – 15 May 2015)

Twenty-five years. A quarter of a century. Or more depressing still, seven thousand sunsets. It is with a sense of wonder tinged with melancholy that I again apply rheumatic digit to keyboard on the subject of my sweet little Mazda MX-5. Ten years ago, somewhat more sound in wind and limb than I am now, I was still using the Little Red Roadster a great deal. I never tired of its character and pure, unalloyed joie de vivre, so I would fire it up and motor off into the landscape at the least excuse, often overlooking some exotic, expensive and impossibly glamorous classic road test vehicles, awaiting my reappraisal, complete with free fuel and insurance.

And I can assure you that an ostensibly superior modern sports car such as an oversized Ferrari, Lamborghini or modern bloated Porsche (the old ones were pleasantly petite, even if they did make a racket like Martha's old Singer) is nothing more than a liability for threading between the hedges along Shropshire's leafy lanes. Having come close to creating a combine harvester that really lived up to its name some years ago as a result of a contretemps with a loaned F40, I have no wish to do the same again, particularly as I have realised the new tenant at Shriglow Bank Farm obviously fancies himself as the next Hamilton (I nearly wrote Moss there, but only senior readers would have known what I meant!) and rarely lets others hinder his lap times around the blue-remembered hills.

Leaving the thought of a Massey-Ferguson sponsored F1 team aside for now, it is with regret that my mileage aboard LRR has steadily dwindled. My motorbicycling accident has left me with what dear Mr Frackett, orthopaedic surgeon extraordinaire, describes as 'legs like ninety-five year-old Twiglets'. Alas, I am finding entry and egress increasingly difficult.

This week I braved an afternoon trip to Beedle Market to visit what few shops are left in that once-thriving town and found myself completely unable to extricate ancient bones from the driver's seat. A few passers-by wished me good morning, probably assuming I wished to listen to the Archers before hobbling off to the chemist to collect my batch of potions, but in truth I simply lacked the strength and agility to clamber out. A cruel testament to age. I seems only yesterday that I would wake up with boundless energy (funny name for a girl, as dear old Eric Morecambe would swiftly rejoinder!) and run through a fitness regime that included a hundred press-ups, half being of the one-handed variety.

Yet, when ensconced behind the wooden-rimmed wheel I am transported in all senses, back to my carefree days when to be young was very heaven, as Mr Wordsworth put it.

Thank you, Mazda.

An afternoon trip to Beedle Market.

FINAL THOUGHTS

It's now five full years since my accident in Belgium in March, 2011, and it's still all I can do to lower myself into the Mazda to drive to the chemist for my medication, or indeed to the Pee-off (presumably Post Office – ed). As for motorcycling, I toddle down to the middle shed to look wistfully at Apollo, my faithful BMW bahnstormer, standing ready to go. I touch its twist grip fondly, but even sitting on it is out of the question now, and I look across to where, just a few short years ago, my other two-wheeled machines were once housed. The Velo that broke Algy's leg, the sweet Duggie that proved to be Pater's last bike, the Laverda 3C on which I rode non-stop to Breganze with Dave Minton. They're all gone now. Trailered away by middle-aged and elderly collectors, not ridden to their new homes by vibrant young men. Beattie was trailered off too, of course, and then shipped to America. For the foreseeable future she will spend her days in an air-conditioned, subterranean garage in Florida, where her stupendously wealthy owner, the peerlessly avaricious Waverley Scrunge Junior, whose father was a friend and contemporary of mine at Cambridge, no doubt sits in her from time to time, but never so much as starts her engine. What was the alternative? To dismantle her? I suppose she will re-emerge one day, although I will not be around to see it.

The classic car scene has changed greatly in the last 15 years. I wrote about the popularity of car shows ten years ago, but already they're dying out. I criticised owners who hauled their cars to them, rather than drive, but values have now risen to levels beyond even the reasonably well off, let alone the ordinary man; and more and more rare and important cars and motorcycles are being shut away by investors who never even clap eyes on them, or, if they do, like Waverley, they never think to share them with the world.

Motor car journalism has changed, too. Motoring's past, as I have often said, has more to look forward to than its present. Classic magazines go round and round in ever decreasing circles, repeating themselves (and perpetuating errors) again and again, whereas the modern scene is all about immediacy, and not at all reflective. A young motoring scribe of my acquaintance told me recently about attending a new model launch at a minor racing circuit in Spain. He wrote the main piece from press releases on the aeroplane going over, uploaded his first driving impressions after just one lap of the track, then added further sage thoughts after only three or four more. From handouts, he wrote a technical piece in the hotel room that evening, uploading it to his magazine's website before supper, and then the following afternoon he filed a full 'road test' while on the plane home, having being taken, with 20 of his fellows on a two-hour guided excursion before lunch.

Additionally, throughout his 24 hours in Spain, and for the whole of the next week, he tooted and blogged and goodness knows what else about the car pretty much incessantly. All that from a total of less than three hours actually sitting behind the wheel! In my day one would generally keep the car for a fortnight, or certainly a week. I would endeavour to write about what it was like to live with, to own, and to use on an everyday basis. After all, for all but a fortunate few, the purchase of a new motor car is a serious and practical matter involving considerable expenditure. Surely that is still the case today, although I understand most people now rent their cars.

So much for the present; what of the future? My young friend filled me in. Driverless cars will soon be with us, and in the not-too-distant future, too, and we've already got traction control, cars that play engine sounds through the hi-fi system (I kid you not!), electronic rev matching, ABS, and so-called infotainment. All this is not for me. Character should be engineered into a car, not falsified, and added digitally.

Believe me, dear reader, I am not complaining. I have enjoyed my wonderful life and career, and I'm jolly glad I had my time when I did. I thank my stars I have never been obliged to catch a daily train to my work alongside those poor wrecks in human shape who populate the moving miasma, creeping day after day into some ghastly office where everybody hates everybody else. And I have now been absolved from the itch to travel, and finally freed from the urge to own things. I may even have reached that level of self knowledge which is perhaps the beginning of wisdom. A little late, I hear you cry! Yes, the light is fading, and sometimes now the thoughts won't go down as they once did, rather as if there is grease under the pen. I nod off and later awake to discover I have written very little. But the next day I might manage a few pages, and as long as blood continues to trickle through my veins I will continue to sit at my desk and write, and to make occasional sorties in my little red Mazda. Better by far to die while still alive than to live on though long dead, if that makes any sense at all!

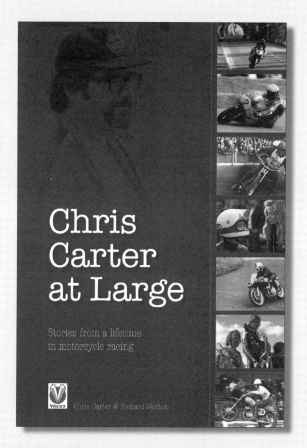

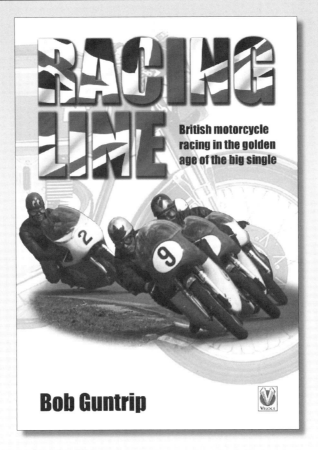

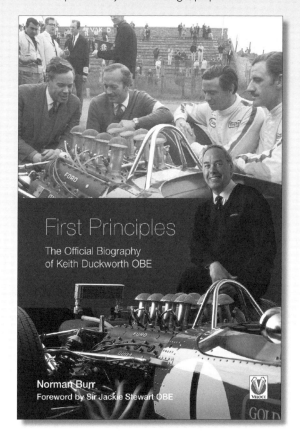

Index

Index